SOPHIE MCCALLUM

Sophie started her artistic career at Camberwell College of Arts in the early 1990s. She went on to study Maths and Philosophy at Durham University, leading to a very enjoyable 20-year spate in horticulture and conservation. She completed a degree in Environmental Studies and Creative Writing at the Open University in 2015 and has subsequently published five books on the environment and other matters.

She has been lucky enough to build a shed in her back garden, and is now enjoying her first love – of making art.

First published in the UK in 2022 by Supernova Books
67 Grove Avenue, Twickenham, TW1 4HX

Supernova Books is an imprint of Aurora Metro Publications Ltd.
www.aurorametro.com Twitter: @aurorametro FB/AuroraMetroBooks

Instagram @aurora_metro

The Contemporary Artists' Guide to Art Galleries by Sophie McCallum © copyright 2022 Sophie McCallum

Editor: Cheryl Robson

Production: Saranki Sriranganathan

Cover design Aurora Metro © copyright 2022 Aurora Metro Publications Ltd.

Images are included by permission of the artist who retains copyright. No rights to reproduce..

All rights are strictly reserved. For rights enquiries contact the publisher:
rights@aurorametro.com

We have made every effort to trace all copyright holders of material included in this publication. If you have any information relating to this, or would like to add or change a listing, please contact: editor@aurorametro.com

Printed in the UK by 4edge, Essex, on sustainably resourced paper.

ISBN 978-1-913641-20-7 print

ISBN 978-1-913641-21-4 ebook

THE CONTEMPORARY ARTISTS' GUIDE TO ART GALLERIES

by

Sophie McCallum

SUPERNOVA BOOKS

With thanks to my father, Tony.

FOREWORD

Sophie McCallum

An art dealer in London once told me that to get your artwork exhibited you had to email up to ten images of your work, or a link to your website, with a few paragraphs detailing your resumé and a similar amount of information describing your art.

With this advice, I used the information in this book to gain an exhibition at the Birmingham Contemporary Art Gallery, although I had to go to a fabric house in Spain to get intellectual copyright for the use of their fabric in my work. They willingly gave me this, in exchange for photos of the artwork. I was also successful in having two pieces of my work exhibited in the Saatchi Gallery on their video loop in 2019.

The Contemporary Artists' Guide to Art Galleries includes much valuable information including contact details for galleries, including email and website addresses, social media information, location, genres and expertise, and information about what they are looking for.

The book provides a comprehensive list of most of the art galleries in the UK, where I am based, followed by hundreds of international galleries which I have found from my research. The information is listed in alphabetical order, grouped geographically under countries in the world. Within each country, galleries are listed under regions and/or cities for ease of use.

By using this book to aid in your research and approach to galleries, you will be able to stretch far and wide with your applications for exhibitions. It aids you to become more ambitious, and more international in scope. Using the information I gathered for this book I was invited to exhibit my work in a group exhibition in New York.

The purpose of compiling this guide is to make it easier for artists, many of whom may be working in home studios or garden sheds, to reach out to important agents and galleries, and to navigate their way through the complexity of the art world.

There is also a handy list of Art Fairs which is grouped chronologically by month so that you can either visit or approach the art fair with a view to your own calendar, travel plans or diary of events.

Collectors will also find the book useful, as it allows them to source work from around the world in the comfort of their own home. Art students and academics will also find much to explore as it can help to widen their knowledge and access to diverse artists and artwork in geographies previously undiscovered.

My dream when I was a child was to have a large house that was filled with amazing art of all kinds. I imagined filling it with artworks from around the world and having international art students staying in all the bedrooms. Fascinating conversations would take place about favourite artists and art movements. As I grew up and began to take my art more seriously, the rarefied world of art galleries seemed elitist and unwelcoming. It can feel as if it's not possible to break through without the right connections. The mysterious business of buying and selling art seemed to go on behind closed doors.

However, the internet has given artists huge opportunities to connect directly with collectors, galleries and art fairs. As galleries and museums seek to decolonise their collections, opportunities have arisen. Curators seeking to be more inclusive of a wider range of artists, are interested in knowing the nationality, race, class and gender of an artist as a way of providing context for their work.

There are now wonderful art galleries with stylish websites operating in cyberspace, which can be visited by anyone with a smartphone. This has led some larger, more well-known galleries to become inundated with unsolicited submissions so it is wise to check if they have windows when debut artists can submit their work and be considered for inclusion. Those galleries which say 'No unsolicted submissions' really do prefer to discover new artists in their own way, so just move on. Thankfully, these seemed few and far between.

Since exhibiting your artwork virtually is now commonplace with many galleries, shipping costs of the original will only be incurred once a sale has been made. For traditional exhibitions, I suggest you start with art galleries in your city or region, to reduce the transport costs of your artwork if it is large or bulky.

For those of you who are creators, I hope that you will find this book useful in not only finding new places to show your work but also to develop your ability to market your work as most artists today need business skills as well as artistic skills in order to make a living from their art. I know how rewarding it can be to find new audiences for your artwork and I wish you the best of luck with your creative endeavours.

Do let us know how you get on.

Notes: If you know of a gallery which would like to be included in future editions, please contact the editor on editor@aurorametro.com

My work can be viewed at **sophiemccallum.org**

CONTENTS

TIPS TO GET YOU STARTED

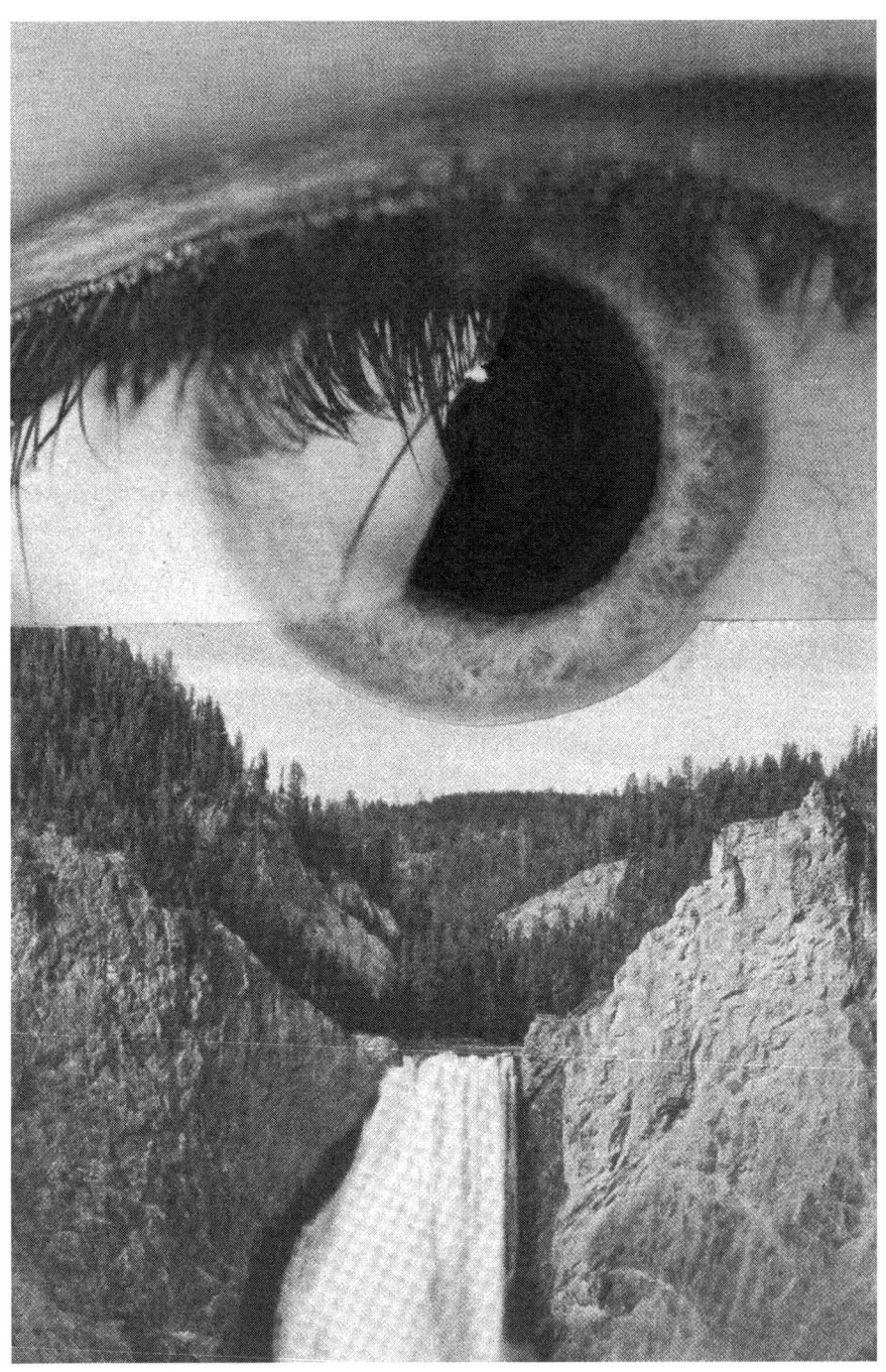

Cry Me A River by Joe Webb

Get your work out there!

Create a platform where you can feature your work. Whether it is on a website or on social media such as twitter, Instagram, Facebook, Pinterest, Etsy, etc. You can choose to feature your work across some or all of these platforms, but we would recommend you have at least one strong platform on which you present your work well. From our research, galleries sometimes seek out artists themselves and can follow your posts and online work for a year before approaching you.

Artist Submissions

When looking through this art guide, make sure to look at the other works which the art gallery have already featured and only reach out to them if you think your artwork would be a good fit. Finding a gallery which has an interest in the type of work you make is key to finding the right gallery for your artwork. The gallery may typically ask you to send five or six images by email which best represent your work, as well as an up-to-date CV, detailing any awards, shows or exhibitions to date.

Submissions are reviewed periodically, and due to the volume of work being submitted, it can take a few months before hearing back from an art gallery. Some galleries will provide an exact time period by which you may or may not hear back from them. If you do not hear back, assume that the gallery does not want to include your work at that time. If a gallery says 'No Unsolicited Submissions' please take note.

Open Art Call Outs

When using this art guide, you will come across galleries that you think would be best suited for your work. Sign up for alerts and newsletters from them as there are often call outs to artists with opportunities to feature your work in upcoming exhibitions.

If successful, they may ask for your work to be only exclusively available for sale at that Gallery for a limited period of time.

Make sure to read the requirements carefully for the artwork size, how to send it to them whether by post or email, including the labelling of your image files according to their specification. This could affect your chances of being selected.

Your Data

During the promotion of an exhibition featuring your artwork, your name, the name of your artwork and any social media links and handles associated would be shared publicly. If you are an emerging artist, think carefully about the information you share online and whether you want your artwork made available in this way.

See more: Interview with Gallerists www.contemporaryartgalleries.net
Information compiled from Cameron Contemporary Art, Nude Tin Can Galleries and others.

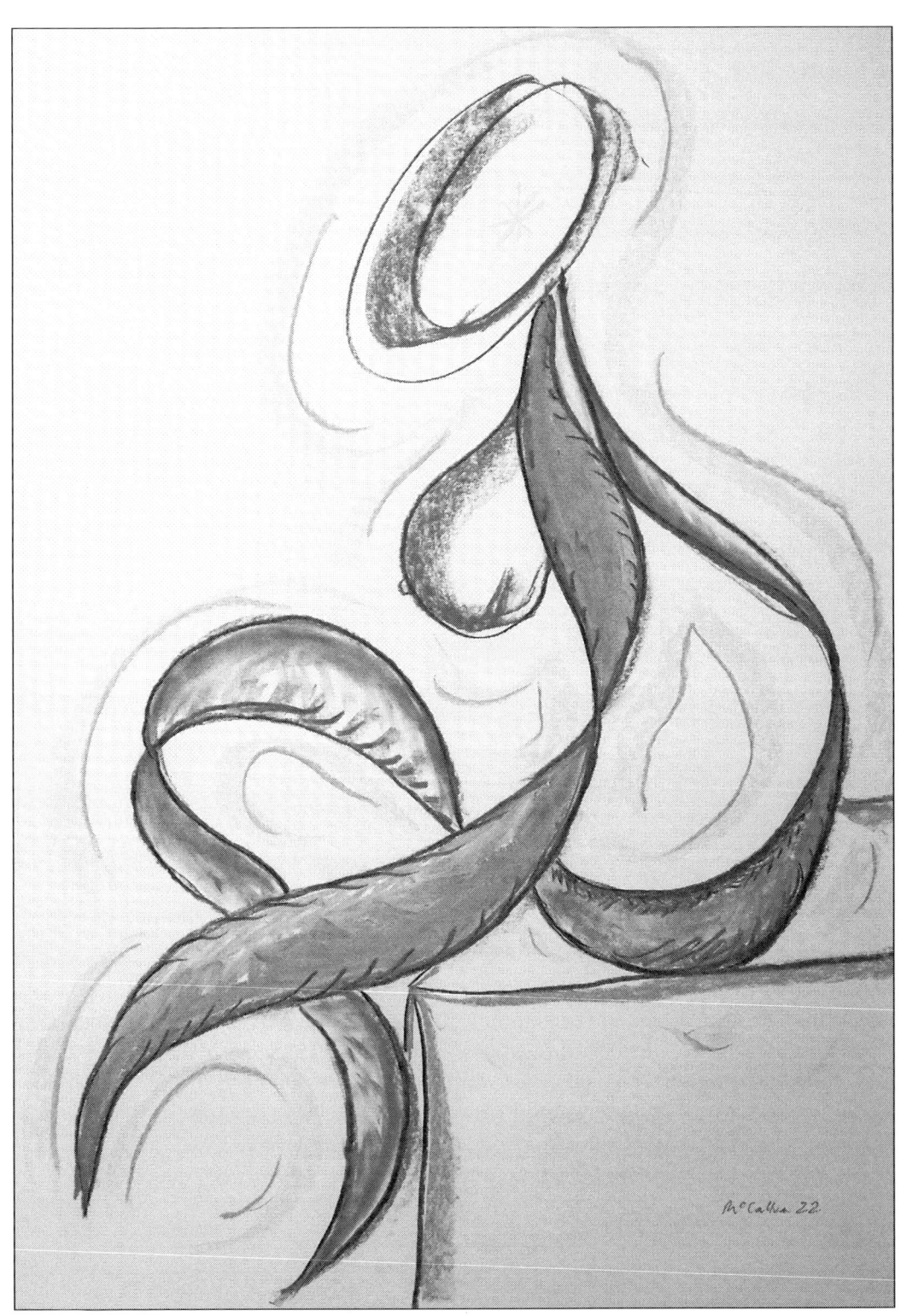

Abstract Nude 8 by Sophie McCallum

ART GALLERIES

UNITED KINGDOM
ENGLAND
Berkshire
Modern Artists Gallery

The gallery is in Whitchurch on Thames.
Address: High Street, Reading RG8 7EX
Phone: 0118 984 5893
Website: modernartistsgallery.com
Email: info@modernartistsgallery.com
Twitter.com/modernartists
Facebook.com/modernartistsgallery
Instagram.com/modernartistsgallery/

Contemporary Fine Art Gallery

Specialising in contemporary sculptures and
paintings. Established 30 years ago.
Address: 51 Peascod Street, Windsor,
Berkshire SL4 1DE
Phone: 01753 854315
Website: cfag.co.uk
Email: mail@cfag.co.uk
Twitter.com/CFAGALLERYETON
Facebook.com/CfagEton

T G ART Gallery

Contemporary art, glass and sculpture.
Established over 30 years ago. Also offering
a framing service
Address: 47B Peach Street, Wokingham
RG40 1XJ
Phone: 0118 979 2707
Website: tgartgallery.co.uk
Email: emma@tgartgallery.co.uk
Facebook.com/TGArtGallery
Instagram.com/tgartgallerywokingham

Bristol
Arnolfini

Established in 1961, Arnolfini is the
International Centre for Contemporary Arts
in Bristol. Showing visual art, performance,
dance, music and film.
Address: 16 Narrow Quay, Bristol BS1 4QA
Phone: 0117 917 2300
Website: arnolfini.org.uk
Twitter.com/ArnolfiniArts
Facebook.com/arnolfiniarts
Instagram.com/arnolfiniarts

Courtyard Gallery

Exhibits new and emerging artists as well as
those more established.
Address: Unit 4.22 Paintworks, Bristol BS4
3EH
Phone: 07977 219037
Website: courtyardgallery.org
Email: info@courtyardgallery.org
Twitter.com/CourtydGallery
Facebook.com/CourtyardGalleryBristol

Lime Tree Gallery

Fine art and glass, especially work from
contemporary Scottish artists.
Address: 84 Hotwell Road, Bristol BS8 4UB
Phone: 0117 929 2527
Website: limetreegallery.com

Clifton Fine Art

Contemporary art, especially from London,
Cornwall and the South West. Shows work
by several members of the Royal Academy.
Address: 12 Perry Road, Bristol BS1 5BG
Phone: 0117 239 7684
Website: cliftonfineart.com
Email: info@cliftonfineart.com
Twitter: @FineArtClifton
Facebook.com/cliftonfineart
Instagram: clifton_fine_art

View Art Gallery

Exhibits new and emerging artists.
Address: 159-161 Hotwell Road, Bristol BS8 4RY
Phone: 056 0311 6753
Website: viewartgallery.co.uk
Email: contact@viewartgallery.co.uk
Facebook.com/ViewArtGallery
Instagram.com/view_art_gallery
LinkedIn.com/company/view-art-gallery

Clifton Contemporary Art

Contemporary paintings, prints, ceramics and sculpture, especially from the West Country Cornwall to the Cotswolds.
Address: 25 Portland Street Clifton, Bristol BS8 4JB
Phone: 0117 317 9713
Website: cliftoncontemporaryart.co.uk
Email: info@cliftoncontemporaryart.co.uk
Facebook.com/cliftoncontemporaryart
Instagram.com/cliftoncontemporaryart

That Art Gallery

Contemporary art gallery in Bristol.
Address: 17 Christmas Steps, Bristol BS1 5BS
Phone: 0117 329 2522
Website: thatartgallery.com
Twitter.com/thatartgallery
Facebook.com/thatartgallery
Instagram.com/thatartgallery

See No Evil

A huge open air gallery in the middle of Bristol, hosting diverse art and events with permanent street art projects and musical accompaniment.
Address: Nelson Street, Bristol BS1 2HF
Phone: 0117 953 0320
Email: studio@inkie.co.uk
Facebook.com/seenoevilbristol

Here Gallery

Local and international artists with particular emphasis on printmaking and illustration. Showing six exhibitions a year.
Address: 108B Stokes Croft, Bristol BS1 3RU
Phone: 0117 942 2222
Website: heregallery.co.uk
Email: here_shop@yahoo.co.uk

Room 212

Interesting and original art and gifts.
Address: 212 Gloucester Road, Bristol BS7 8NU
Phone: 07702 598090
Website: room212.co.uk
Email: newtwist@mail.com
Twitter.com/room212gallery
Facebook.com/room212art
Instagram.com/room212gallery

Spike Island

Exhibits new and emerging artists, giving support and space for their first solo exhibition, as well as those more established.
Address: Spike Island
133 Cumberland Road
Bristol BS1 6UX
Phone: +44 (0)117 929 2266
Website: spikeisland.org.uk
Email admin@spikeisland.org.uk
Twitter.com/_spikeisland
Instagram.com/spikeisland/
Facebook.com/spikeisland

Buckinghamshire

MK Gallery

An iconic building shows international art in five large gallery spaces, with contemporary art alongside Old Masters. Also on offer are contemporary films, lectures and concerts and an artist-designed play area for children.
Address: 900 Midsummer Boulevard, Milton

Keynes MK9 3QA
Phone: 01908 676900
Website: mkgallery.cloudvenue.co.uk
Email: info@mkgallery.org
Twitter.com/MK_Gallery
Facebook.com/MiltonKeynesGallery
Instagram.com/mk_gallery

Kraftinwood

Contemporary art, woodturning and crafts.
Address: Kraft Village, Grafton Street, High
Wycombe HP12 3AJ
Phone: 01494 533302
Website: kraftinwood.com
Email: robert@kraftinwood.com

Emerald Bespoke Picture Framing

Contemporary art gallery, picture framing.
Address: 1 Blays House Churchfield Road,
Chalfont St Peter SL9 9EW
Phone: 07507 774017
Website: emeraldframes.com
Email: cath@emeraldframes.com
Facebook.com/Emeraldframes
Instagram.com/emeraldframes

Stanley Spencer Gallery

Dedicated to the work of Sir Stanley Spencer
(1891-1959).
Address: High Street, Maidenhead SL6 9SJ
Phone: 01628 531092
Website: stanleyspencer.org.uk
Email: info@stanleyspencer.org.uk
Twitter.com/SpencerCookham

Cambridgeshire

Cambridge

Cambridge Contemporary Art

With an exhibition every month, over 100
UK artists are shown, specialising in prints,
paintings, crafts and sculpture.
Address: 6 Trinity Street, Cambridge CB2 1SU
Phone: 01223 324222

Website: cambridgegallery.co.uk
Email: info@cambridgegallery.co.uk
Twitter.com/CCAandCCC
Facebook.com/
CambridgeContemporaryArt
Instagram.com/cca_gallery

Byard Art

Both 2D and 3D work in a range of mediums.
Will oversee international commissions.
Address: 14 King S Parade, Cambridge CB2
1SJ
Phone: 01223 464646
Website: byardart.co.uk
Email: info@byardart.co.uk
Twitter.com/ByardArt
Facebook.com/byardart
Instagram.com/byard_art
Pinterest.co.uk/byardart

Tyrrell Art Gallery

International contemporary art.
Address: 3 Nuttings Road, Cambridge CB1
3HU
Phone: 07762 537188
Website: tyrrellartgallery.com
Email: info@tyrrellartgallery.com

Lynne Strover Gallery

A leading British contemporary art gallery.
Address: 23 High Street Fen Ditton,
Cambridge CB5 8ST
Phone: 01223 295264
Website: strovergallery.co.uk
Email: Lynne@lynnestrover.co.uk
Instagram.com/Lynnestroversilver

Primavera

British arts, craft, including jewellery, textiles,
ceramics, sculptures, silverware and glass.
Address: 10 Kings Parade, Cambridge CB2 1SJ
Phone: 01223 357708
Website: primaverauk.com
Twitter.com/Primavera1945

Cambridge Art Salon

An arts organisation that provides exhibitions, workshops, talks and networking with events.
Address: 29 Cromwell Road, Cambridge CB1 3
Phone: 01223 244391
Website: cambridgeartsalon.org.uk
Email: info@cambridgeartsalon.org.uk

Ely

Angela Mellor Gallery

Contemporary bone china ceramics.
Address: 38A St Mary S Street, Ely CB7 4ES
Phone: 01353 666675
Website: angelamellor.com
Email: angela@angelamellor.com

Peterborough

Peterborough Art House

Contemporary fine art gallery.
Address: 26 Fitzwilliam Street, Peterborough PE1 2RX
Phone: 01733 319581
Website: peterborougharthouse.com
Email: helen.mould@btinternet.com

Peterborough Museum and Art Gallery

Housing the art work of Peterborough.
Address: Priestgate, Peterborough PE1 1LF
Phone: 01733 864663
Website: vivacity-peterborough.com
Twtter.com/VivacityPboro
Facebook.com/vivacitypeterborough

Cheshire

Vermilion Art Gallery

A large collection of art, both national and international with sculpture and bespoke furniture.
Address: 10A Princess Street, Knutsford WA16 6DD
Phone: 01565 633330
Website: vermiliongallery.co.uk
Email: info@vermiliongallery.co.uk
Twitter.com/Vermilion_Art
Facebook.com/vermiliongallery
Instagram.com/vermilion.galleries/

Whitewall Galleries

Whitewall Galleries have over 40 galleries in the UK showing paintings and sculptures from internationally acclaimed artists as well as the best of emerging talent.
Address: 8 Regent St, Knutsford WA16 6GR
Phone: 01565 631196
Website: whitewallgalleries.com
Email: newartist@demontfortfineart.co.uk
Twitter.com/wwgalleries
Facebook.com/whitewallgalleries
Instagram.com/whitewallgalleriesofficial
YouTube.com/user/WhitewallGalleries

Cheshire Art Gallery

Contemporary art gallery.
Address: 13 Ack Lane East, Bramhall, Stockport SK7 2BE
Phone: 0161 217 0625
Website: cheshireartgallery.co.uk
Email: info@cheshireartgallery.co.uk

Marburae Gallery

An artist led gallery showing contemporary visual art.
Address: Marburae House Athey Street, Macclesfield SK11 6QU
Phone: 0800 032 9919
Email: marburaegallery@gmail.com

Attitude

Showing emerging and established artists especially that which causes a reaction.
Address: 6 Bridge Street, Congleton CW12 1AH
Phone: 01260 299143
Website: attitudegallery.co.uk
Twitter.com/attitudegallery
Facebook.com/AttitudeArt

Chester

Watergate Street Gallery

Local, national and international work. Paintings, etchings, screenprints and signed limited editions
Address: 60 Watergate Street, Chester CH1 2LA
Phone: 01244 345698
Website: watergatestreetgallery.co.uk
Email: alex@watergatestreetgallery.co.uk

Castle Galleries

Exciting art from around the world. With galleries across the UK, Castle Fine Art are open to discovering new and talented contemporary fine artists suggesting they email directly artreview@washingtongreen.co.uk for an appraisal. Or use the online form at: castlefineart.com/submit-your-art.
Address: 18 St, Chester CH1 1EF
Phone: 01244 345800
Website: castlefineart.com
Email: artreview@washingtongreen.co.uk
Twitter.com/castlegalleries
Facebook.com/castlegalleries
Instagram.com/castlegalleries
Pinterest.co.uk/castlegalleries
YouTube.com/castlegalleries

Cloud Gallery

Collectable art from the UK.
Address: 47 Lower Bridge Street, Chester CH1 1RS
Phone: 01244 324638
Website: cloudgalleryfineart.co.uk
Twitter.com/cloudgallery1
Facebook.com/Cloud-Gallery-167716153314661/
Instagram.com/cloudgalleryfineart

The Arc

Best of British craft and design including ceramics, glass, textiles, jewellery, wood, leather, metalwork and limited edition prints.
Address: 4 Commonhall St, Chester CH1 2BJ
Phone: 01244 348379
Website: thearcgallery.co.uk
Email: enquiries@thearcgallery.co.uk
Twitter.com/TheArcGallery
Facebook.com/TheArcGallery
Instagram.com/The_Arc_Gallery
Pinterest.co.uk/Thearcgallery

Whitewall Galleries

Whitewall Galleries have over 40 galleries in the UK showing paintings and sculptures from internationally acclaimed artists as well as the best of emerging talent.
Address: Unit 5-7St Michaebs Row, Chester CH1 1EL
Phone: 01244 400401
Website: whitewallgalleries.com
Email: clientservices@demontfortfineart.co.uk

Chester Visual Arts

A charity dedicated to showing art to the region including 4 successful international exhibitions in 18 months. Currently working with the Grosvenor Estate, Chester Cathedral, Marketing Cheshire Cultural Destinations, The University of Chester and the V&A Museum, London.
Address: The Old Library, Northgate Street, Chester CH1 2EF
Website: chestervisualarts.org.uk
Email: info@chestervisualarts.com
Twitter.com/chestervisarts
Facebook.com/chestervisualarts
Instagram.com/chestervisualarts
Instagram.com/learningcva
YouTube.com/channel/UCmGGPtwVgZDxuZawusG06kA

Cornwall

Falmouth Art Gallery

A publicly funded art gallery with an art collection that features work by old masters, major Victorian artists, Impressionists, leading surrealists and maritime artists, children's book illustrators, automata, contemporary painters and printmakers.
Address: Municipal Buildings, The Moor, Falmouth TR11 2RT
Phone: 01326 313863
Website: falmouthartgallery.com

Mid Cornwall Galleries

One of the biggest galleries showing contemporary art and craft in the West Country, showing paintings, etchings, ceramics, blown and formed glass, jewellery, woodwork, prints and metalwork.
Address: St Austell Rd, Par PL24 2EF
Phone: 01726 812131
Website: midcornwallgalleries.com
Twitter.com/MidCornwallGall
Facebook.com/MidCornwallGalleries
Instagram.com/midcornwallgalleries

Cornwall Contemporary

Showing national and international work, as well as emerging talent, with a recent emphasis on Cornish sculpture and painting.
Address: 1 Parade Street, Penzance TR18 4BU
Phone: 01736 874749
Website: cornwallcontemporary.com
Email: sarah@cornwallcontemporary.com
Twitter.com/sarah_cornwall
Facebook.com/cornwallcontemporary
Instagram.com/cornwallcontemporary
Pinterest.co.uk/cornwallcontemp

The Drang Gallery

Contemporary and modern art with galleries in Padstow, Rock, Salcombe and Marlborough.

Address: Rock Road, Rock, Cornwall. PL27 6NW
Phone: 01208 863954
Email: rock@thedranggallery.com
Address: 8-9 Drang, Padstow, Cornwall. PL28 8BL
Phone: +44 (0)1841 533 114
Email: padstow@thedranggallery.com
Website: thedranggallery.com
Instagram.com/the_drang_gallery

Tate St Ives

Intending to show the best of British Art from the 16th century to the present day, including modern and contemporary works.
Address: Porthmeor, St Ives TR26 1TG
Phone: +44 (0)1736 796 226
Website: tate.org.uk
Email visiting.stives@tate.org.uk
Email: hello@tate.org.uk
Facebook.com/tategallery
Instagram.com/tate
Pinterest.co.uk/tategallery
YouTube.com/user/tate

Cornwall Galleries

Established in 1960 to promote unknown artists, this gallery has seen them going from strength to strength, many becoming internationally renowned. Now showing both new and established artists.
Address: 4 Bank St, Newquay TR7 1JF
Phone: 01637 873678
Website: cornwallgalleries.co.uk
Facebook.com/CornwallGalleries

Driftwood Gallery

Located in Padstow, between St Ives and Ilfracombe on the north Devon coast, specialising in art, bronzes and glass.
Address: 26 Fore Street, St Ives TR26 1HE
Phone: 07757 409045
Email: stives@driftwoodcontemporary.co.uk
Address: 4 The Strand, Padstow PL28 8AJ

Phone: 07787 409045
Email: padstow@driftwoodcontemporary.co.uk
Address: 19 St James Place, Ilfracombe,
North Devon EX34 9BJ
Phone: 07787 409045
Email: ilfracombe@driftwoodcontemporary.
co.uk
Website: driftwoodcontemporaryart.co.uk
Twitter.com/DriftwoodArts
Facebook.com/driftwoodcontemporary
Instagram.com/driftwoodcontemporary

Veryan Galleries

Exhibits a small group of established artists
as well as ceramics, jewellery and prints.
Address: Veryan Green, The Roseland TR2
5QQ
Phone: 01872 501469
Website: veryangalleries.co.uk
Email: info@veryangalleries.co.uk
Twitter.com/veryangalleries
Facebook.com/Veryan-
Galleries-169594623221788
Instagram.com/veryan_galleries

Beyond The Sea

Leading Cornish contemporary artists.
Address: 22 Middle Street, Padstow PL28
8AP
Phone: 01841 533588
Website: beyondthesea.co.uk
Email: contact@beyondthesea.co.uk
Twitter.com/beyond_the_sea
Facebook.com/BeyondTheSeaPadstow
Instagram.com/beyondtheseagallery

The Harbour Gallery

Contemporary art.
Address: 8A The Quay, Portscatho, Truro
TR2 5HF
Phone: 01872 580807
Website: theharbourgallery.co.uk
Twitter.com/HarbourGallery

Facebook.com/TheHarbourGalleryPortscatho
Instagram.com/theharbourgallery.co.uk

Truro
Lemon St. Gallery

A leading UK gallery situated in the heart
of Truro, exhibiting both emerging and
established artists, with solo and group
exhibitions. Also tours exhibitions at national
and international art institutions.
Address: 13 Lemon Street, Truro TR1 2LS
Phone: 01872 275757
Website: lemonstreetgallery.co.uk
Email: info@lemonstreetgallery.co.uk
Twitter.com/LemonStGallery
Facebook.com/TheLemonStGallery
Pinterest.co.uk/LemonStGallery

Lander Gallery

Exhibiting contemporary art as well as art
from the last four centuries with an emphasis
on work inspired by Cornwall.
Address: 6- 8 Lemon Street, Truro TR1 2LS
Phone: 07966 673173
Website: landergallery.co.uk
Email: info@landergallery.co.uk

Tregony Gallery

National and international art, as well as
emerging British talent.
Address: 58 Fore Street Tregony, Truro TR2
5RW
Phone: 01872 530505
Website: tregonygallery.co.uk
Email: info@tregonygallery.com
Twitter.com/TregonyGallery
Facebook.com/tregonygallery
Instagram.com/tregonygallery

County Durham
Baltic Centre for Contemporary Art

Showing a range of exhibitions and events
throughout the year

Shore Road, Gateshead NE8 3BA
Phone: 0191 478 1810
Website: balticmill.com
Twitter.com/balticgateshead
Facebook.com/balticgateshead
Instagram.com/balticgateshead

Shipley Art Gallery

In the five gallery spaces there are a series of exhibitions throughout the year, as well as artist and curator talks, concerts, vintage and craft fairs. Five bursaries, funded by the Henry Rothschild Bursary and Northumbria University are available each year to emerging ceramists.
Address: Prince Consort Road, Gateshead NE8 4JB
Phone: 0191 477 1495
Website: shipleyartgallery.org.uk
Email: info@shipleyartgallery.org.uk
Twitter.com/theshipley
Facebook.com/shipleyartgallery
YouTube.com/user/TWMuseums

Gallerina

Local, national and international contemporary art.
Address: 1 Victoria Road, Darlington DL1 5SJ
Phone: 01325 363635
Website: gallerina.co.uk
Facebook.com/GallerinaHQ
Instagram.com/gallerina_hq
YouTube.com/user/gallerinadarlington

Durham
The Kemble Gallery

Fine art, prints, gifts and art supplies with a bespoke framing service
Address: 62 Saddler Street, Durham DH1 3NU
Phone: 0191 386 4034
Website: kemblegallery.com
Email: info@kemblegallery.com
Twitter.com/kemblegallery

Facebook.com/KembleGallery
Instagram.com/kemblegallery

Sunderland
Northern Gallery for Contemporary Art

An Arts Council England National Portfolio Organisation.
Address: City Library and Arts Centre Fawcett St, Sunderland SR1 1RE
Phone: 0191 515 5555
Website: ngca.co.uk

CIRCA Screen

Exhibitions, as well as independent publishing and commissioning of new works. Events and performances.
Address: Athenaeum Street, City Of Sunderland SR1 1QX
Phone: 07973 538876
Website: circaprojects.org

Cumbria
Carlisle Contemporary Arts

An artist's partnership, with Carlisle connections, especially in the visual arts. Guest artists invited.
Address: Old Fire Station, Carlisle CA3 8QP
Phone: 07856 820680
Email: ccartcarlisle@gmail.com
Facebook.com/CCArtists10

Derbyshire
The Old Lock Up Art Gallery

Fine and contemporary art, ceramics and sculpture, life drawing and art workshops.
Address: The Old Lock Up Gallery, 19 The Hill, Swifts Hollow, Cromford DE4 3RF
Phone: 07960 097605
Website: theoldlockupgallery.org
Email: theoldlockupgallery@gmail.com
Twitter.com/oldlockupstudio
Instagram.com/theoldlockupgallery

Chesterfield Museum

Telling the story of Chesterfield from Roman origins. The small art gallery shows temporary exhibitions and events.
Address: St Marys Gate, Chesterfield S41 7TD
Phone: 01246 345727
Website: chesterfieldmuseum.co.uk
Twitter.com/chfldmuse
Facebook.com/chesterfieldmuseum

St. John Street Gallery

Exhibiting local and national paintings, sculpture, ceramics and craft with an award winning café.
Address: 50 St John Street, Ashbourne DE6 1GH
Phone: 01335 347425
Website: stjohngalleryandcafé.co.uk
Email:enquiries@stjohngalleryandcafé.co.uk
Twitter.com/StJohnGallery
Facebook.com/gallery50

Peak District Photography Gallery

The gallery has been funded with a grant from the Peak District National Park Authority's Sustainable Development Fund to capture the beauty of the Park whilst also helping landscape and wildlife photographers show and sell their work.
Address: Bridge Street, Bakewell DE45 1DS
Phone: 01629 813227
Website: peakgallery.co.uk
Email: info@peakgallery.co.uk
Twitter.com/PeakGalleryFive
Facebook.com/PeakGallery

Derby
Tarpey Gallery

Painting, printmaking, photography and sculpture in a historic converted barn with four main exhibition spaces.
Address: 77 High Street, Derby DE74 2PQ
Phone: 07772 404293
Website: tarpeygallery.com
Email: info@tarpeygallery.com
Twitter.com/TarpeyGallery
Facebook.com/TarpeyGallery
Instagram.com/tarpeygallery

Castle Fine Art

Exciting art from around the world. With galleries across the UK, Castle Fine Art is open to discovering new and talented contemporary fine artists.
Contact: artreview@washingtongreen.co.uk
Or: castlefineart.com/submit-your-art
Address: Unit 249 Level 2 East Mall, Westfield Centre, Derby DE1 2PQ
Phone: 01332 209333
Website: castlegalleries.com
Email: hello@castlefineart.com
Twitter.com/castlegalleries
Facebook.com/castlegalleries
Instagram.com/castlegalleries

Whitewall Galleries

Whitewall Galleries have over 40 galleries in the UK showing paintings and sculptures from internationally acclaimed artists as well as the best of emerging talent.
Address: Unit 213, Level 2 East Mall, Derby DE1 2PQ
Phone: 01332 342656
Website: whitewallgalleries.com
Email: derby@whitewallgalleries.com

Museum and Art Gallery

Run by and for the residents of Derby, exhibiting artwork that will delight and inspire.
Address: The Strand, Derby DE1 1BS
Phone: 01332 641901
Website: derbymuseums.org
Email: info@derbymuseums.org
Twitter.com/derbymuseums
Facebook.com/derbymuseums
Instagram.com/derbymuseums

Matlock

Gallerytop

Painting, limited edition prints, sculpture, ceramics, glass and jewellery with several exhibitions a year.
Address: Chatsworth Road, Rowsley, Matlock DE4 2EH
Phone: 01629 735580
Website: gallerytop.co.uk
Email: info@gallerytop.co.uk
Twitter.com/galleryview
Facebook.com/gallerytopDerbyshire

Cromford Studio & Gallery

Fine art, prints, jewellery, glass, ceramics and cards. Watercolour lessons.
Address: Unit 4 Market Place, Matlock DE4 3RE
Phone: 01629 826434
Website: cromfordstudioandgallery.weebly.com
Facebook.com/CromfordStudioandGallery

Devon

The Brownston Gallery

One of the leading contemporary fine art galleries in the SW of England. Representing both established and emerging artists in a range of styles.
Address: 36 Church Street, Bury PL21 0QR
Phone: 01548 831338
Website: thebrownstongallery.co.uk
Email: art@brownstonart.com
Facebook.com/thebrownstongallery
Instagram.com/brownston_gallery

Hope Cove Gallery

Exhibiting around 40 Devon-based artists and craft workers in a large range of mediums.
Address: Hope Cove, Kingsbridge TQ7 3HE
Phone: 01548 561981
Website: hopecovegallery.com
Email: hopecovegallery@hotmail.com
Facebook.com/HopeCoveGallery

The Drang Gallery

Contemporary and modern art with galleries in Padstow, Rock, Salcombe and Marlborough.
Address: 5 Fore St, Salcombe Regis TQ8 8BY
Phone: 01548 844004
Website: thedranggallery.com
Email: Salcombe@thedranggallery.com
Instagram.com/the_drang_gallery

Devon Guild Of Craftsmen

Contemporary craft and design in a large gallery situated on the edge of Dartmoor. Events and exhibitions as well as craft making lessons.
Address: Riverside Mill Fore Street, Newton Abbot TQ13 9AF
Phone: 01626 832223
Website: crafts.org.uk
Twitter.com/devonguild
Facebook.com/DevonGuildofCraftsmen
Instagram.com/devonguildcrafts

Cockington Court

A leading visitor attraction in the SW, with a blacksmith, glass blower and chocolatier as well as over 20 other skilled artisans.
Address: Cockington Lane, Torquay TQ2 6XA
Phone: 01803 607230
Website: cockingtoncourt.org
Email: marissa.wakefield@tedcltd.com
Twitter.com/CockingtonC
Facebook.com/cockingtoncourt

Strand Art Gallery

Situated by the beautiful Brixham harbour the gallery specialises in fine art paintings by internationally renowned local painters, particularly marine and landscape art.
Address: 2 The Strand, Brixham TQ5 8EH
Phone: 01803 854762
Website: strandartgallery.com

Burton at Bideford

A community venue that hosts art galleries, shops, a café and museum.
Address: Kingsley Road, Bideford EX39 2QQ
Phone: 01237 471455
Website: burtonartgallery.co.uk
Email: info@theburton.org

Thelma Hulbert Gallery

A cultural hub, with events, exhibitions and workshops strengthening rural arts through partnership and collaboration.
Address: Elmfield House, Dowell Street, Honiton EX14 1LX
Phone: 01404 45006
Website: thelmahulbert.com
Email: info@thelmahulbert.com
Twitter.com/ThelmaHulbert
Facebook.com/ThelmaHulbertGallery

Brook Gallery

Starting with original prints in 1997, the gallery has expanded to show paintings, sculpture and ceramics with quality and value at its heart.
Address: 30 Fore St, Budleigh Salterton EX9 6NH
Phone: 01395 443003
Website: brookgallery.co.uk
Email: info@brookgallery.co.uk
Twitter.com/BrookGallery
Facebook.com/BrookGallery
Instagram.com/brookgallery
Pinterest.co.uk/brookartdevon

The Art Room Topsham

Now a web-based art gallery, showing modern and contemporary painting, sculpture and ceramics by established artists with a connection to the SW of England.
Address: 76 Fore St, Topsham
Phone: 07808 148586

Website: theartroomtopsham.co.uk
Email: deborah@theartroomtopsham.co.uk

Mayne Gallery

Local and international art featuring paintings, sculpture, jewellery, ceramics and glass.
Address: 14 Fore St, Kingsbridge TQ7 1NY
Phone: 01548 853848/07801 248210
Website: maynegallery.com
Email: info@maynegallery.co.uk
Twitter.com/infomayne
Facebook.com/maynegallery
Instagram.com/mayne.gallery
Dartmouth

Ainscough Contemporary Art

Originated in 1995 with 10 shows a year of British contemporary art in Chelsea. The gallery opened in 2005, showing contemporary paintings, ceramics and sculpture.
Address: 14 Foss Street, Dartmouth TQ6 9DR
Phone: 01548 855732
Website: acag.co.uk
Email: art@acag.co.uk

Baxters

Exhibiting contemporary art, prints, craft and jewellery including themes of the Devon and Cornish coast as well as animals.
Address: 12 Foss Street, Dartmouth TQ6 9DR
Phone: 01803 839000
Website: baxtersgallery.co.uk
Twitter.com/BaxtersGallery
Facebook.com/BaxtersGallery
Instagram.com/baxtersgallerydartmouth

Dart Gallery

Showing a large selection of work from established, British contemporary artists, with several solo and group exhibitions a year.
Address: 4 Lower Street, Dartmouth TQ6 9AJ
Phone: 01803 834923

Website: dart-gallery.com
Email: info@dart-gallery.com
Twitter.com/lovedartgallery
Facebook.com/dartgallerydartmouth
Instagram.com/dartgallerydevon

Exeter
Centre for Contemporary Art & the Natural World

Founder Clive Adams now acts as a consultant curator in Art, Ecology, and Environment.
Email: hello@cliveadams.art,
Phone: +44(0)145 376 2103
Website: cliveadams.art
Email: hello@cliveadams.art

Surridge Gallery

International art from award winning artists
Address: 11-15 Bedford Street, Exeter EX1 1GG
Phone: 01392 477722
Website: surridgegallery.co.uk
Email: exeter@surridgegallery.co.uk
Twitter.com/surridgegallery
Facebook.com/surridgegallery

South Gate Gallery

Gallery and picture framers
Address: 64 South St, Exeter EX1 1EE
Phone: 01392 435800
Website: southgategallery.co.uk
Email: admin@southgategallery.co.uk
Facebook.com/southgategalleryandframers
Instagram.com/south_gate_gallery

Royal Albert Memorial Museum & Art Gallery

The largest museum and art gallery in Exeter
Address: Royal Albert Memorial Museum & Art Gallery, Queen Street, Exeter EX4 3RX
Phone: 01392 265858
Website: rammuseum.org.uk

Castle Galleries

Exciting art from around the world. With galleries across the UK, Castle Fine Art is open to discovering new contemporary fine artists. Email artreview@washingtongreen.co.uk for an appraisal. Or use the online form at: castlefineart.com/submit-your-art
Address: 7 Roman Walk, Exeter EX1 1GN
Phone: 01392 425242
Website: castlefineart.com
Email: artreview@washingtongreen.co.uk
Twitter.com/castlegalleries
Facebook.com/castlegalleries
Instagram.com/castlegalleries
Pinterest.co.uk/castlegalleries
YouTube.com/castlegalleries

Polka Dot Gallery

Contemporary jewellery from gold and platinum rings to wood, titanium and textile pieces pushing the boundary of convention.
Address: 12 Martins Lane, Exeter EX1 1EY
Phone: 01392 276500
Website: polkadotgallery.com
Email: jewellery@polkadotgallery.com
Facebook.com/polkadotjewellerygallery
Instagram.com/polkadotgallery

Ilfracombe
Driftwood Gallery

Art from around the world
Address: 19 St James Place, Ilfracombe EX34 9BJ
Phone: 01271 862590
Website: driftwoodgallery.co.uk
Email: ilfracombe@driftwoodcontemporary.co.uk
Twitter.com/DriftwoodArts
Facebook.com/driftwoodcontemporary
Instagram.com/driftwoodcontemporary
YouTube.com/user/viewarttv

Fleek Gallery

Online and in the gallery, the Fleek Gallery shows contemporary fine art by emerging and established artists across the globe. Ilfracombe is becoming well-known for its progressive art scene.
Address: 21 St. James Place, Ilfracombe EX34 9BJ
Phone: 07711 803811
Website: fleekgallery.com
Twitter.com/fleekgallery
Facebook.com/fleekgallery
Instagram.com/fleek_gallery
Pinterest.co.uk/fleekgallery

Ilfracombe Arts & Craft Society

Exhibiting a wide selection of paintings, from seascapes and harbour views to the landscapes of North Devon. Glass sculptures and jewellery, pottery, ironwork and textiles are available, also hand-carved walking sticks and violins.
Address: The Emmanuel Church Wilder Rd, Ilfracombe EX34 9AW
Phone: 01271 864864
Website: ilfracombeartandcraftsociety.co.uk
Email: ilfracombeartsociety@hotmail.co.uk
Facebook.com/IlfracombeArtCraftSociety
Instagram.com/ilfracombeartandcraftsociety

Plymouth
Host Galleries

With a new exhibition every month, the gallery shows original contemporary art from some of the bestselling artists of today.
Address: 12 Whimple Street, Plymouth PL1 2DH
Phone: 01752 241234
Website: hostgalleries.co.uk
Email: art@hostgalleries.co.uk
Twitter.com/hostgalleries
Facebook.com/hostgalleries
Instagram.com/hostgalleries

Totnes
White Space Art

Established in 2003, the gallery shows emerging and established British artists, mainly from the SW of England.
Address: 72 Fore St, Totnes TQ9 5RU
Phone: 07412 450776
Website: whitespaceart.com
Email: info@whitespaceart.com
Twitter.com/WhiteSpaceArt
Facebook.com/WhiteSpaceArt
Instagram.com/WhiteSpaceArt

Dorset
Westover Gallery

Exhibiting local, national and international artists.
Address: 4 Westover Road, Bournemouth BH1 2BY
Phone: 01202 297682
Website: westovergallery.co.uk

Hatch Gallery

Hatch exhibits British contemporary art, ceramics, handmade jewellery as well as driftwood furniture and sculpture, with a wide range of styles particular along a sea theme.
Address: 7A Church Street, Christchurch BH23 1BW
Phone: 07787 517958
Website: hatchgallery.co.uk
Email: jodyton@hatchgallery.co.uk
Twitter.com/hatchgallery
Facebook.com/hatchgalleryuk
Instagram.com/hatchgallery
Linkedin.com/in/jo-dyton-240a7035

The Art Stable

Contemporary and 20th century British paintings, prints and ceramics with 8 exhibitions a year for established and emerging artists. Situated in the courtyard of an organic farm, café and farm shop with

views to the iron age fort at Hambledon Hill.
Address: Gold Hill Organic Farm Ridgeway
Lane, Child Okeford, Blandford Forum
DT11 8HB
Phone: 01258 863866
Website: theartstable.co.uk
Email: kellyross@theartstable.co.uk
Facebook.com/theartstable

The Gallery at 41

Set in a restored 17th century building
in the ancient village of Corfe Castle,
surrounded by the Purbeck Hills and World
Heritage coastline. The gallery specialises in
contemporary Dorset painters and sculptors,
with, with invited artists from the wider
region. Also showing ceramics and jewellery.
Address: 41 East Street Corfe Castle,
Wareham BH20 5EE
Phone: 01929 480095
Website: galleryat41.com
Email: contact@galleryat41.com
Facebook.com/TheGalleryAt41

Essex

Hayletts Gallery

Wide range of local artists. Modern British
original prints and contemporary fine art
limited editions by leading UK artists.
European modern masters, such as Verve
cut-out lithographs by Henri Matisse.
Address: Oakwood House 2 High Street,
Maldon CM9 5PJ
Phone: 01621 851669
Website: haylettsgallery.com
Email: sally@haylettsgallery.com
Twitter.com/haylettsgallery
Facebook.com/Hayletts-Gallery-
Instagram.com/haylettsgallery

Sculpt Gallery

One of only a handful of UK galleries
specialising in contemporary British
sculpture and studio ceramics. Showing
established and emerging talent. Permanent
collection of sculpture by gallery's lead artist,
Maurice Blik.
Address: Priory Mews Braxted Park Road,
Colchester CO5 0QB
Phone: 07980 768616
Website: sculptgallery.com
Email: info@sculptgallery.com
Twitter.com/sculptgalleryuk
Instagram.com/sculptgallery

Turner Barnes Gallery

International artists, both emerging and
established. Realism, abstract, pop and urban
with pictures, photography, sculpture and
installations.
Address: 21 Hutton Road Shenfield,
Brentwood CM15 8JU
Phone: 01277 500554
Website: interiorangle.co.uk
Email: info@turnerbarnesgallery.com
Address: 37a Little, Boyton Hall Ln,
Chelmsford CM1 4LN
Phone: 01245 248662
Website: interiorangle.co.uk
Email: info@interiorangle.co.uk
Twitter.com/turner_barnes
Facebook.com/turnerbarnesgallery
Instagram.com/turnerbarnesgallery

Chappel Galleries

Set in the beautiful Colne Valley, adjacent to
the River Colne, overlooking the Romanesque
32 arch viaduct. Selling 20th and 21st century
art, from around the country and those with
regional connections.
Address: 15 Colchester Road, Colchester
CO6 2DE
Phone: 01206 240326
Website: chappelgalleries.co.uk
Email: info@chappelgalleries.co.uk

The Minories Galleries

With an in-house gallery run by Colchester School of Art, the site also sells the best regional arts and crafts. The gallery is next door to Firstsite, Colchester's contemporary art space.
Address: 74 High Street, Colchester CO1 1UE
Phone: 01206 712437
Website: theminoriesgalleries.co.uk
Email: the.minories@colchester.ac.uk
Twitter.com/MinoriesArt
Facebook.com/TheMinoriesGalleries
Instagram.com/the_minories

Chelmsford

Gallery43

Paintings, limited edition prints, jewellery, crafts and gifts by contemporary British artists, with a series of exhibitions throughout the year.
Address: 43 Moulsham Street, Chelmsford CM2 0HY
Phone: 01245 353825
Website: gallery43.co.uk
Email: art@gallery43.co.uk
Twitter.com/Gallery43
Facebook.com/artgallery43

Chelmer Fine Art

Founded in 1999 to find the best contemporary fine art.
Address: 6 New London Road, High Chelmer, Chelmsford CM2 0SW
Phone: 01245 456677
Website: chelmerfineart.com
Email: sales@chelmerfineart.com
Twitter.com/Chelmerfineart
Facebook.com/Chelmer-Fine-Art-Chelmsford

Whitewall Galleries

Whitewall Galleries have over 40 galleries in the UK showing paintings and sculptures from internationally acclaimed artists as well as the best of emerging talent.
Address: 15-16, Bond Street, Chelmsford CM1 1GD
Phone: 01245 330427
Website: whitewallgalleries.com
Email: clientservices@demontfortfineart.co.uk

Gloucestershire

The Art Gallery

Both internationally established artists and emerging talent. An online presence of over 4,000 artists.
Address: 34 Long Street, Tetbury GL8 8AQ
Phone: 01666 505152
Website: artgallery.co.uk
Twitter.com/art_gallery_uk
Facebook.com/ArtGallerycouk-107535012616718
Instagram.com/artgallery.co.uk

Gallery Pangolin

Contemporary and modern work, specialising in sculpture and related drawings and prints.
Address: Unit 9, Chalford Industrial Estate, Chalford GL6 8NT
Phone: 01453 889765
Website: gallery-pangolin.com
Email: gallery@pangolin-editions.com
Twitter.com/GalleryPangolin
Facebook.com/Gallery-Pangolin-295993655057

Campden Gallery

Established painters, sculptors and printmakers from across the UK as well as emerging artists. Group and solo shows.
Address: High Street, Chipping Campden GL55 6AG
Phone: 01386 841555
Website: campdengallery.co.uk
Email: info@campdengallery.co.uk
Instagram.com/campdengallery

Gloucester
Nature in Art

The only museum in the world dedicated solely to art inspired by nature.
Address: Main A38 Twigworth, Gloucester GL2 9PA. SatNav Postcode: GL2 9PG
Phone: 01452 731 422
Website: natureinart.org.uk
Email: enquiries@natureinart.org.uk
Twitter.com/Nature_in_Art
Facebook.com/natureinartofficial

Sabre Art

An online art gallery.
Address: Unit 32, Sabre Close Green Farm Business Park, Gloucester GL2 4NZ
Phone: 01452 397479
Website: sabreart.co.uk
Email: mail@sabreart.co.uk

Stow-on-the-Wold
Fosse Gallery Fine Art

Since 1980, the Fosse Gallery has shown important British and international art.
Address: The Square, Stow-on-the-Wold GL54 1AF
Phone: 01451 831319
Website: fossegallery.com
Email: mail@fossegallery.com
Twitter.com/fosse_gallery
Facebook.com/FosseGallery
Instagram.com/fossegallery

Cotswold Galleries

Since 1961, the gallery has shown traditional landscape oil and watercolour paintings of the Cotswolds and the UK in a building dating back to the early 16th century.
Address: The Square, Stow-on-the-Wold, Cheltenham GL54 1AB
Phone: 01451 870567
Website: cotswoldgalleries.co.uk

Artysan

Contemporary art gallery in the heart of the Cotswolds.
Address: Howman House, Stow-on-the-Wold GL54 1BQ
Phone: 01451 831399
Website: artysancotswolds.co.uk
Email: art@artysancotswolds.co.uk
Instagram.com/artysancotswolds

Wychwood Art

Representing over 350 contemporary artists in the gallery and online, as well as the annual Affordable Art Fair in Battersea.
Address: The Town Hall, Market Place, Deddington, Oxfordshire OX15 0SE
Phone: 01869 338155 / 07799 535 765
Website: wychwoodart.com
Email: deborah@wychwoodart.com

Red Rag Gallery

British contemporary art and sculpture with a worldwide customer base.
Address: 5-7 Church Street, Stow-On-The-Wold GL54 1BB
Phone: 01451 832563
Website: redraggallery.co.uk
Twitter.com/redraggallery
Facebook.com/RedRagGallery
Instagram.com/redraggallery

Hampshire
Isle of Wight
Yarmouth Gallery

Contemporary art from the Island and around the UK.
Address: High St, Yarmouth PO41 0PL
Phone: 01983 761424
Website: yarmouthgallery.com
Email: yarmouthgallery@gmail.com

Kendalls Fine Art

A large gallery in Cowes that specialises

in marine art, including contemporary and traditional paintings and sculptures.
Address: Bath Rd, Cowes PO31 7QN
Phone: 01983 281414
Website: kendallsfineart.co.uk
Twitter.com/KendallsFineArt
Facebook.com/kendallsfineart
Instagram.com/kendalls_fine_art

Portsmouth
Artists Harbour

Contemporary art and prints. Framing and reproduction services using the latest technology in image copying, giclee printmaking and greeting cards.
Address: 8 Whitwell Road, Southsea PO4 0QR
Phone: 023 9273 2003
Website: artistsharbour.com
Email: info@artistsharbour.com

Art2arts

A leading online gallery.
Address: 30 Lower Derby Road, Portsmouth PO2 8EX
Phone: 023 9269 9990
Website: art2arts.co.uk
Email: sales@art2arts.co.uk
Twitter.com/art2arts
Facebook.com/art2artsgallery
Instagram.com/art2arts_gallery
Pinterest.co.uk/art2arts/_created
LinkedIn.com/company/art2arts
YouTube.com/user/Art2Arts/videos

Aspex Art Gallery

For 40 years this gallery has been exhibiting emerging artists, with off-site projects and participation events, striving to make the creative art process more inclusive.
Address: Gunwharf Quays, City Centre, Portsmouth PO1 3TW
Phone: 023 9277 8080
Website: aspex.org.uk

Email: info@aspex.org.uk
Twitter.com/aspexportsmouth
Facebook.com/aspexgallery
Vimeo.com/aspex

Sticks Contemporary

Aiming to increase engagement and participation in the arts. Part of Live Art Local CIC, which is an artist-led not for profit program. Supports emerging artists.
Address: The Precinct South St, Gosport PO12 1HA
Phone: 023 9250 1744 / 07910832850
Website: sticksgallery.co.uk
Email: admin@sticksgallery.co.uk
Twitter.com/Live_Art_Local
Instagram.com/liveartlocal

Salisbury
Fisherton Mill

Set in a Victorian grain mill dating from 1880, providing a venue for viewing art, shopping and dining.
Address: 108 Fisherton St, Salisbury SP2 7QY
Phone: 01722 500200
Website: fishertonmill.co.uk
Email: thegallery@fishertonmill.co.uk
Twitter.com/FishertonMill
Facebook.com/FishertonMill
Instagram.com/fisherton.mill

Southampton
Southampton City Art Gallery

Both contemporary and historic exhibitions, collaborating with artists and art institutions.
Address: Commercial Road, Southampton SO14 7LP
Phone: 023 8083 4536
Website: southamptoncityartgallery.com
Email: museums@southampton.gov.uk
Twitter.com/ArtGallerySoton
Facebook.com/SouthamptonCityArtGallery

John Hansard Gallery

Part of the University of Southampton, this gallery exhibits contemporary visual art.
Address: University Of Southampton, University Road, Southampton SO17 1BJ
Phone: 023 8059 2158
Website: hansardgallery.org.uk

Solent Showcase

Contemporary art at Solent University.
Address: Sir James Matthew Building 157-187 Above Bar Street, Southampton SO14 7NN
Phone: 023 8201 2621
Website: solent.ac.uk

Stockbridge
The Wykeham Gallery

Since 1985, the gallery has been showing contemporary paintings of all media, as well as sculpture and ceramics by both established and emerging artists.
Address: High Street, The Wykeham Gallery, Stockbridge SO20 6HE
Phone: 01264 810364
Website: wykehamgallery.co.uk
Email: enquiries@wykehamgallery.co.uk
Facebook.com/TheWykehamGallery
Instagram.com/wykeham_gallery
www.Artsy.net/wykeham-gallery

The Garden Gallery

Art and furniture for the home, office or garden, including contemporary sculpture (stone, bronze, glass, steel and copper), ceramics, stone or slate lettering, glass, wood engraving, works on paper such as original prints. Also large scale work for public places. Commissions can be arranged.
Address: Rookery Lane, Stockbridge SO20 8AZ
Phone: 01794 301144
Website: gardengallery.uk.com
Email: rachel@gardengallery.uk.com

Twitter.com/gardengalleryuk
Facebook.com/TheGardenGalleryHampshire
Instagram.com/rachelbebbgardengallery
LinkedIn.com/in/rachel-bebb-15a33314

Courcoux & Courcoux Contemporary Art

Representing established painters, sculptors and ceramicists, such as Elizabeth Frink. Stages exhibitions in unusual and interesting venues in the South, and London. Acts as consultants to private and corporate clients.
Address: Sunnyside House, High Street, Nether Wallop, Stockbridge SO20 8EZ
Phone: 01264 781528 / 07711 874902
Website: courcoux.co.uk
Email: ian@courcoux.co.uk
Facebook.com/Courcoux-Contemporary-103281496683216

The New Forest
Stephen Lees Original Contemporary Art

Contemporary seascapes, landscapes and abstract paintings.
Address: Gallery on the Cobbles, 2 Quay Street, Lymington SO41 3AS
Phone: 01590 670668
Website: stephenleescontemporaryart.com
Email: Galleryonthecobbles@icloud.com

Ytene Gallery

Named after the ancient name of the New Forest, the gallery shows contemporary art.
Address: 47 Brookley Road, Brockenhurst SO42 7RB
Phone: 01590 623566 / 07940 562462
Website: ytenegallery.co.uk
Email: info@ytenegallery.co.uk

Winchester
The Minster Gallery

Located opposite the cathedral, the gallery exhibits figurative and abstract paintings

and sculpture by contemporary British and international artists.
Address: 3A Great Minster Street, Winchester SO23 9HA
Phone: 01962 877601
Website: minstergallery.com
Email: info@minstergallery.com

Bell Fine Art

Contemporary and period paintings, as well as prints, posters and limited editions and a framing service. Working with local and international artists for over 30 years.
Address: 67B Parchment Street SO23 8AT
Phone: 01962 860439
Website: bellfineart.co.uk
Email: bellfineart@btconnect.com
Twitter.com/bellfineart
Facebook.com/bellfineartuk
Instagram.com/bellfineart_winchester

Whitewall Galleries

Whitewall Galleries have over 40 galleries in the UK showing paintings and sculptures from internationally acclaimed artists as well as the best of emerging talent.
Address: Unit 2 4-8 Market Street, Winchester SO23 9EP
Phone: 01962 867790
Website: whitewallgalleries.com
Email: winchester@whitewallgalleries.com

Herefordshire

Greenstage Gallery

Painting and sculpture from the abstract to still life. A large gallery allowing a significant amount of work to be shown at one time with regular exhibitions.
Address: The Hop Pocket, Worcester WR6 5BT
Phone: 01885 490839
Website: greenstagegallery.co.uk
Email: info@greenstagegallery.co.uk

Twitter.com/GreenstageG
Facebook.com/GreenStageGallery
Instagram.com/greenstagegallery

Hereford
Apple Store Gallery

Monthly exhibitions of local artists' work from Herefordshire, the Royal Forest of Dean and the Welsh Borders, including painting, drawings, prints, photography, ceramics, textiles and sculpture.
Address: Unit 1, Rockfield Road Industrial Estate Rockfield Road, Hereford HR1 2UA
Phone: 01432 263937
Website: applestoregallery.com
Email: applestoregallery@btinternet.com
Twitter.com/applestoregall
Facebook.com/applestoregallery
Instagram.com/applestoregall
LinkedIn.com/in/apple-store-gallery-b1589433

Canwood Gallery

All profits go to Bart's Charity. The gallery aims to allow the public to see stimulating art for free.
Address: Canwood Farm, Hereford HR1 4NF
Phone: 07776 138668
Website: canwoodgallery.com
Twitter.com/CanwoodGallery
Facebook.com/canwoodgallery
Instagram.com/canwoodgallery

Timothy Hawkins Gallery

Situated near Hereford Cathedral, the gallery shows contemporary multi-media work from dozens of skilled artisans in the UK who are able to take commissions.
Address: 14 Church Street, Hereford HR1 2LR
Phone: 01432 507007
Website: timothyhawkinsgallery.co.uk
Email: info@timothyhawkinsgallery.co.uk

Old Mayor's Parlour

2D and 3D work shown in a gallery in a 14th century building.
Address: 23 Church Street, Hereford HR1 2LR
Phone: 07790 367497
Website: oldmayorparlour.com

Hereford Museum and Art Gallery

Art gallery and museum in a Victorian Gothic establishment, opened in 1874, showing fine and decorative art and local artefacts.
Address: Broad Street, Hereford HR4 9AU
Phone: 01432 260692
Website: herefordshire.gov.uk

Leominster
Old Chapel Gallery

The best of British contemporary fine art and crafts, by both established and emerging creators.
Address: The Old Chapel East Street, Pembridge, Leominster HR6 9HBPhone: 01544 388842
Website: oldchapelgallery.co.uk

Lion Gallery

Over 300 artists and makers are exhibited, including printmakers, painters, ceramicists, sculptors, jewellers, woodworkers, glass makers and textile artists from Herefordshire and around the UK. Regular exhibitions.
Address: 15B Broad Street, Leominster HR6 8BT
Phone: 01568 611898
Website: liongallery.co.uk
Email: info@liongallery.co.uk
Twitter.com/wordpress
Instagram.com/explore/tags/wordcamp

Hertfordshire
Icas Vilas Fine Art

Art gallery, art restoration and picture framing. Founded in 1984. Leading national and international dealer in contemporary art and sculpture, with recent additions of photography.
Phone: 01462 677455
Website: vilasart.co.uk
Email: info@vilasart.co.uk

Walkern Gallery

Originating with an artist with a love of landscape, the gallery has now shown the work of over 60 artists with exciting and varied forms of creativity.
Address: 56 High Street, Hertford SG2 7PG
Phone: 01438 860363
Website: walkerngallery.com
Email: sales@walkerngallery.com
Twitter.com/WalkernGallery
Facebook.com/Walkern-Gallery-352185138255126

Art Nrshinga

Contemporary British artist, Paresh Nrshinga creates abstract and figurative paintings for corporate and private collections across the world.
Address: 7 Willow Way, Radlett WD7 8DU
Phone: 07970 531675
Website: artnrshinga.com
Email: info@artnrshinga.com
Facebook.com/pareshnrshingaart
Instagram.com/pareshnrshingaart
Pinterest.co.uk/pareshnrshinga

Gallery Rouge

Contemporary art shown in two studios in Hertfordshire. Regular exhibitions showing colourist and abstract, to figurative and photorealistic. Nurtures new talent as well as working with globally established artists, representing them in Europe and the UK.
Address: 78 High Street, Harpenden AL5 2SP
Phone: 01582 760332
Website: galleryrouge.co.uk

Email: harpenden@galleryrouge.co.uk
Twitter.com/galleryrouge
Facebook.com/GalleryRougeArt
Insagram.com/galleryrouge

Montague's Gallery

Traditional and contemporary paintings and sculpture, including the world renowned Frogman bronze collection.
Address: 40 High St, Kings Langley WD4 9HT
Phone: 01923 263311
Website: montaguesgallery.com
Email: info@montaguesgallery.com
Twitter.com/montaguesart
Facebook.com/montaguesgallery
Instagram.com/montaguesgallery/
Montaguesgallery.wordpress.com

John Brown – Sculptor

Contemporary garden sculptures, abstracted figurative. Clients purchase for the garden, interior, corporate, large public spaces and hospitals.
Address: 35 Wood Street, Barnet EN5 4BE
Phone: 020 8441 5841
Website: johnbrown-sculptor.co.uk
Email: info@johnbrown-sculptor.co.uk

Berkhamsted

Berkeley Gallery

Leading contemporary art gallery in Hertfordshire, offering range of services including free home consultancy, bespoke picture framing, delivery and installation.
Address: 41-43 Lower Kings Road, Berkhamsted HP4 2AB
Phone: 01442 878300
Website: berkeley-galleries.com
Email: paul@berkeley-galleries.com
Twitter.com/BerkeleyBerko

Upstairs Gallery

Contemporary art gallery.

Address: 268 High St, Berkhamsted HP4 1BL
Phone: 07341 907853
Website: upstairsgalleryberkhamsted.co.uk

St Albans
Gallery Rouge

A leading UK contemporary art gallery based in Norfolk and Hertfordshire, showing work from colourist and abstract, to figurative and photorealistic.
Address: 27 Chequer Street, St Albans AL13YJ
Phone: 01727 860401
Website: galleryrouge.co.uk
Email: harpenden@galleryrouge.co.uk
Twitter.com/galleryrouge
Facebook.com/GalleryRougeArt
Instagram.com/galleryrouge
Pinterest.co.uk/galleryrouge
YouTube.com/user/GalleryRouge

Gallery 105

Art restoration and picture framing. Prints by the late Beryl Cook, Snoopy limited editions and black and white photographs of pop and sporting heroes.
Address: 105 Victoria Street, St Albans AL1 3TJ
Phone: 01727 833557
Website: gallery105.co.uk
Email: jean@gallery105.co.uk
Facebook.com/gallery105StAlbans

Whitewall Galleries

Whitewall Galleries have over 40 galleries in the UK showing paintings and sculptures from internationally acclaimed artists as well as the best of emerging talent.
Address: Christopher Place, St Albans AL3 5DQ
Phone: 01727 844466
Website: whitewallgalleries.com
Email: stalbans@whitewallgalleries.com

Nude Tin Can

Contemporary art gallery exhibiting original artwork by professional and emerging artists..
Address: 125 Hatfield Road, St Albans AL1 4JS
Phone: 01727 569291
Website: nudetincan.com
Email: info@nudetincan.com
Twitter.com/NudeTinCan
Facebook.com/nudetincan
Instagram.com/nudetincan
YouTube.com/watch?v=pCWlrzgrsno

Victoria Fine Art

Established in 1965, specialising in 19th and 20th century oils with a global client base from kings to corporations.
Address: Long Spring 3 Porters Wood, St. Albans AL3 6NQ
Phone: 01727 861669
Website: victoria-fine-art.com
Email: info@victoria-fine-art.com
Facebook.com/VictoriaFineArt
LinkedIn.com/company/victoria-fine-art/about

Island Of Art

An online art gallery established in 2003 to promote artwork to private and corporate buyers.
Address: 9, St Albans Enterprise Centre, Long Spring, St Albans AL3 6EN
Phone: 01727 751446
Website: island-of-art.com
Email: info@island-of-art.com

Kent

Lilford Gallery

Contemporary art galleries.
Address: 8 The Old High Street, Folkestone CT20 1RL
Phone: 01303 487294
Address: Palace Street Gallery
3 Palace Street, Canterbury, Kent, CT1 2DY
Phone: 01227 639086
Address: Castle Street Gallery
76A Castle Street, Canterbury, Kent, CT1 2QD
Phone: 01227 766616
Website: lilfordgallery.com

Linden Hall Studio

An open space for contemporary art exhibitions. 11 shows annually in a building dating from 1775, first used as a chapel.
Address: 32 St Georges Road, Deal CT14 6BA
Phone: 01304 360411
Website: lindenhallstudio.co.uk
Email: info@lindenhallstudio.co.uk
Twitter.com/Studio_Linden
Facebook.com/lindenhallstudio
Instagram.com/linden_hall_studio
YouTube.com/channel/UCfs4rBwqUZGxEoQK8mEZwaQ

Liberty Gallery

Affordable original art and limited editions prints for the home or office.
Address: 7 Queen St, Kings Hill ME19 4AU
Phone: 01732 522311 / 07881 830709
Website: liberty-gallery.com
Email: info@liberty-gallery.com
Twitter.com/libertygallery
Facebook.com/libertygallerylimited

Turner Contemporary

Named after JMW Turner, who stayed at the same site on his visits to Margate. Situated on the seafront. Exhibitions, events and education. A key destination for art lovers.
Address: Rendezvous, Margate CT9 1HG
Phone: 01843 233000
Website: turnercontemporary.org
Email: info@turnercontemporary.org
Twitter.com/TCMargate
Facebook.com/turnercontemporary
Instagram.com/turnercontemporary

Canterbury
Stark Gallery

Exhibiting art and contemporary craft from across the UK, including paintings, photography, lino prints, screen prints and etchings, glass, ceramics, wood and jewellery.
Address: 68 Castle Street, Canterbury CT1 2PY
Phone: 01227 767128
Website: starkgallery.com
Email: starkgallery@btconnect.com

Beaney House Of Art & Knowledge

Address: 18 High Street, Canterbury CT1 2RA
Phone: 01227 862162
Website: canterburymuseums.co.uk
Email: beaney@canterbury.gov.uk
Twitter.com/The_Beaney
Facebook.com/TheBeaney
Instagram.com/the_beaney

Tunbridge Wells
Fairfax Gallery

Contemporary paintings and sculpture, including landscapes, portrait, abstract and the unexpected. Featuring both emerging and established artists. Founded in 1995.
Address: 23 The Pantiles, Tunbridge Wells TN2 5TD
Phone: 01892 525525
Website: fairfaxgallery.com
Email: andrew@fairfaxgallery.com
Twitter.com/fairfaxgallery
Facebook.com/FairfaxGalleryThePantiles

Beumee Contemporary Fine Art

Investment art from established UK and international artists. Collectors from across the world.
Address: 50 The Upper Pantiles, Tunbridge Wells TN2 5TN
Phone: 01892 512365
Website: beumee.com
Email: art@beumee.com
Facebook.com/BeumeeContemporary FineArt
Instagram.com/beumeefineart

Redleaf

Watercolours from the 19th and 20th century, oil paintings and Modern British art on paper, with a special emphasis on drawing.
Address: 1 Castle Street, Tunbridge Wells TN1 1XJ
Phone: 01892 526695
Website: redleafgallery.com
Email: info@redleafgallery.com

Iaysha Art Advisory

Private art consultant, Iaysha Salih has worked for 25 years, establishing and expanding private and corporate art collections.
Address: Camden Road, Tunbridge Wells TN1 2PT
Phone: 07876 253324
Website: iaysha.com
Email: iaysha@iaysha.com
Twitter.com/iaysha_art
Facebook.com/iaysha.salih
Instagram.com/iayshas

Whitstable
Chappell Contemporary

Emerging and established artists, with particular focus on limited edition prints.
Address: 30 Oxford Street, Whitstable CT5 1DD
Phone: 01227 637329
Website: chappellcontemporary.com
Email: mail@chappellcontemporary.com
Facebook.com/chappellcontemporary
Instagram.com/chappell_contemporary

Lancashire
Art Decor Gallery

Modern British artists, in particular art from the north. Regular exhibitions

to promote emerging artists, as well as showing internationally successful art, with contemporary sculpture in bronze, aluminium, steel, Murano glass, ceramic and clay. Bespoke framing and restoration, in-situ home trials and sourcing of particular artists on request.
Address: 6 The Arches, Whalley, Clitheroe BB7 9SG
Phone: 01254 824840 / +44 (0) 7976 258 999
Website: artdecorgallery.co.uk
Email: chris@artdecorgallery.co.uk

Centurion Gallery

Displaying art in all mediums, particularly limited editions.
Address: 1 Turpin Green Lane, Leyland, Preston, Lancashire. PR25 3HA
Phone: 01772 424131 / 07742155570
Website: centuriongallery.co.uk
Email: info@centuriongallery.co.uk

Water Street Gallery

Exhibits leading and up and coming artists, with solo and group exhibitions. Also crafts and gifts.
Address: 25 Water Street, Todmorden OL14 5AB
Phone: 01706 839714
Website: waterstreetgallery.co.uk
Email: info @ waterstreetgallery.co.uk
Twitter.com/wsg_uk
Facebook.com/WSG.UK
Instagram.com/wsg.uk
Pinterest.co.uk/waterstreetgallery

Gallery Oldham

Public art gallery with changing exhibitions of art, natural and social history.
Address: Oldham Cultural Quarter, Greaves Street, Oldham OL1 1AL
Phone: 0161 770 4653
Website: galleryoldham.org.uk
Email: galleryoldham@oldham.gov.uk

Twitter.com/galleryoldham
Facebook.com/galleryoldham
Instagram.com/galleryoldham

Hebden Bridge
Heart Gallery

In the heart of beautiful Hebden Bridge, this independent contemporary art gallery sells affordable art, crafts and timeless jewellery.
Address: 4 Market Street, Hebden Bridge HX7 6AA
Phone: 01422 845845
Website: heartgallery.co.uk
Email: heartgallery@btinternet.com
Twitter.com/HeartGallery
Facebook.com/HeartGalleryHebden
Instagram.com/heartgallery
Pinterest.co.uk/heartgallery

Snug Gallery

Showing ceramics and contemporary craft from leading makers.
Address: 58 Market Street, Hebden Bridge HX7 6AA
Phone: 01422 847435
Website: snug-gallery.com
Twitter.com/snug_gallery
Facebook.com/Snug-Gallery-186190621427522
Instagram.com/snug_gallery
Pinterest.co.uk/snuggallery

Lancaster
The Elles Gallery

Artist's studio and gallery. Paintings of modern townscapes and music icons.
Address: 4 Gage Street, st. Nicholas Arcades, Lancaster LA1 1UH
Phone: 07930 941694
Website: elles.gallery

King Street Studios

Modern and contemporary art, with 12 exhibitions a year, working with artists groups

in the northwest and wider UK. Also offering classes, workshops and art related events.
Address: 5A King St, Lancaster LA1 1JN
Phone: 01524 849311
Website: kingstreetstudios.art
Email: info@kingstreetstudios.art
Twitter.com/kingststudios5a
Facebook.com/KingStStudios5a
Instagram.com/kingststudios5a

Live at LICA

Comprising of the Nuffield Theatre, Great Hall and the Peter Scott Gallery, developing and presenting cutting edge contemporary art. Part of the Arts Council of England.
Address: Lancaster University, Lancaster LA1 4YW
Phone: 01524 594151
Website: lancasterarts.org
Email: boxoffice@lancasterarts.org
Twitter.com/lancasterarts
Facebook.com/lancasterartsuk
Instagram.com/lancasterartsuk

Arteria

Interior and lifestyle arts and crafts. Commissioned pieces.
Address: 23 Brock Street, Lancaster LA1 1UR
Phone: 01524 61111
Website: arteriashop.co.uk
Email: info@arteriashop.co.uk
Twitter.com/arteriashop
Facebook.com/arteriashop
Instagram.com/arteriawithgallery23

Liverpool
Bluecoat

The oldest centre for contemporary art in the UK. Annual program of exhibitions, music, dance, literature, live and heritage events. Receiving 700,000 visits per year, the venue is also a base for 30 or so artists and craftspeople.

Address: School Lane, Liverpool L1 3BX
Phone: 0151 702 5324
Website: thebluecoat.org.uk
Email: info@thebluecoat.org.uk Twitter.com/theBluecoat

Open Eye Gallery

Exhibitions, long-term collaborative projects, publications, festivals and university courses. Over 200,000 visitors to projects and 85,000 visitors to the gallery each year. Taking risks and pushing for change, particularly in socially orientated photography.
Address: 19 Mann Island, Liverpool L3 1BP
Phone: 0151 236 6768
Website: openeye.org.uk
Email: info@openeye.org.uk
Twitter.com/OpenEyeGallery
Facebook.com/OpenEyeGallery
Instagram.com/openeyegallery

The Walker Art Gallery

Contemporary art and art going back to the 13th century. The Pre-Raphaelite collection is thought to be the best in the world.
Address: William Brown St, Liverpool L3 8EL
Phone: 0151 478 4199
Website: liverpoolmuseums.org.uk/collections/walker-art-gallery-collections
Twitter.com/NML_Muse
YouTube.com/user/NMLWebTeam

Corke Art Gallery

Free entry to exhibitions, which feature paintings by acclaimed local, national and international contemporary and fine artists.
Address: 296-298 Aigburth Rd Sefton Park, Liverpool L17 9PW
Phone: 07773 287827
Website: corkeartgallery.co.uk
Email: nic@corke.net

dot-art

Working with over 100 artists to provide affordable original art and limited edition prints to homes and businesses.
Address: 14 Queen Avenue, Castle Street, Liverpool L2 4TX
Phone: 0345 017 6660
Website: dot-art.co.uk
Email: info@dot-art.com
Email: artists@dot-art.com Twitter.com/dotart
Facebook.com/dotart
Instagram.com/dotartliverpool
LinkedIn.com/company/dot-art-ltd
YouTube.com/user/DotArtLiverpool
Flickr.com/photos/dot-art

Tate Liverpool

Working to increase the enjoyment and understanding of British art from the 16th century to today, with international modern and contemporary art.
Address: Albert Dock, Liverpool L3 4BB
Phone: +44 (0)15 1702 7400
Website: tate.org.uk
Email visiting.liverpool@tate.org.uk
Email: hello@tate.org.uk
Facebook.com/tategallery
Instagram.com/tate/
Pinterest.co.uk/tategallery
YouTube.com/user/tate

Wall to Wall Art Gallery

Original and limited edition art and sculpture, mainly from the UK fine art publisher, Washington Green, but also building on local and independent artists.
Address: 35 Whitechapel, Liverpool L1 6DA
Phone: 0151 227 4844

Editions

Exhibitions of contemporary painting and prints. Virtual galleries showing all artists work including acclaimed regional artists in the northwest.
Address: 16 Cook Street, Liverpool L2 9RF
Phone: 0151 236 4236
Website: editionsltd.net

Manchester

Philips Art Gallery

Showing 20th century British and European masters with contemporary painting and photography.
Address: 10A, Little Lever St, Manchester M1 1HR
Phone: 0161 941 4197
Website: philipsartgallery.com
Email: info@philipsartgallery.com
Instagram.com/philipsartgallery

Manchester Art Gallery

The building dates to 1823, when it was constructed for a learned society. Following a major renovation, it reopened in 2002 as one of the country's leading art museums. International contemporary work is shown alongside historic collections, seen by more than ½ million yearly visitors.
Address: Mosley Street, Manchester M2 3JL
Phone: 0161 235 8888
Website: manchesterartgallery.org
Email: manchesterartgallery@manchester.gov.uk
twitter.com/mcrartgallery
facebook.com/ManchesterArtGallery
instagram.com/mcrartgallery
YouTube.com/user/ManchesterArtGallery/videos

Artzu Gallery

Leading contemporary art gallery showing national and international work.
Address: Gallery, Old Granada Studios, Quay Street, Manchester M3 4PR
Phone: 0161 827 1717
Website: artzu.co.uk

Twitter.com/Artzu
Facebook.com/Artzu
Instagram.com/artzu_gallery
LinkedIn.com/company/artzu-gallery

Mather Gallery

Original artwork from an online gallery.
Address: Mather Gallery, The Sharp
Project, Thorp Road, Manchester. M3
1NQ (by appointment only)
Phone: 0161 40 85 123
Website: mathergallery.co.uk
Email: info@mathergallery.co.uk
Twitter.com/mathergallery
Facebook.com/mathergallery
Instagram.com/mathergallery
Pinterest.co.uk/mathergallery

Richard Goodall Gallery

Contemporary fine art, photography and
rock posters shipping worldwide daily.
Address: Thomas Street, Manchester M4
1NA
Phone: 0161 832 3435
Website: richardgoodallgallery.com
Twitter.com/rgoodallgallery
Facebook.com/richardgoodallgallery
Instagram.com/richardgoodallgallery

Manchester Art Gallery

18th and 20th century art in a large municipal
gallery.
Address: Mosley Street, Manchester M2 3JL
Phone: 0161 235 8888
Website: manchesterartgallery.org
Twitter.com/mcrartgallery
Facebook.com/ManchesterArtGallery
Instagram.com/mcrartgallery
YouTube.com/user/ManchesterArtGallery/
videos

Chinese Arts Centre

Promoting and developing contemporary
Chinese artists. Socially engaged exhibitions,
events and artist residences exploring
global issues from different international
perspectives.
Address: Unit 1, Market Buildings 13
Thomas Street Northern Quarters,
Manchester M4 1EU
Phone: 0161 832 7271
Website: chinese-arts-centre.org
Email: hello@cfcca.org.uk
Twitter.com/CFCCA_UK
Facebook.com/cfccauk
Instagram.com/cfcca_uk
YouTube.com/user/cfcca1986

Whitworth Art Gallery

With a £15 million development in 2015, this
gallery has doubled in size. With indoor and
outdoor events showing historic exhibitions
to contemporary commissions.
Address: Oxford Road, Longsight,
Manchester M13 9RN
Phone: 0161 275 7450
Website: whitworth.manchester.ac.uk
Email: whitworth@manchester.ac.uk

Castlefield Gallery

Established by artists in 1984, this gallery was
Manchester's first public contemporary visual
art gallery. Delivering exhibitions and events
around the year showing early and mid-career
artists' work with over 100,000 national and
international visitors in 2018/19.
Address: 2 Hewitt Street, Manchester M15
4GB
Phone: 0161 832 8034
Website: castlefieldgallery.co.uk
Email: info@castlefieldgallery.co.uk
Twitter.com/castlefieldGall
Facebook.com/castlefieldgallery
Flickr.com/photos/castlefieldgallery
Vimeo.com/user7815357

Saul Hay Gallery

One of Manchester's foremost independent galleries selling a wide range of original artwork.
Address: Railway Cottage, Behind Bass Warehouse, Castle Street, Manchester M3 4LZ
Phone: 0161 222 4800
Website: saulhayfineart.co.uk
Email: info@saulhayfineart.co.uk
Twitter.com/SaulHayFineArt
Facebook.com/SaulHayFineArt
Instagram.com/saulhayfineart

Generation Gallery

Located in the heart of Manchester's city centre, this gallery exhibits UK emerging artists as well as selling fine art collections from major Hollywood Studios, such as Disney, Marvel and Lucas Films.
Address: E3 New York Street, City Tower, Manchester M1 4BD
Phone: 0161 247 7870
Website: toonsart.com
Email: info@generationgallery.com
Twitter.com/generation_art
Facebook.com/GenerationPOP
Instagram.com/generationgallery

Contemporary Six - The Gallery

Situated opposite the town hall in Manchester, this gallery sells work by emerging and internationally acclaimed artists. Exhibiting original paintings, prints, sculptures and ceramics.
Address: Unit 6, The Royal Exchange Arcade, Manchester M2 7EA
Phone: 0161 835 2666
Website: contemporarysix.co.uk
Email: info@contemporarysix.co.uk
Twitter.com/contemporarysix
Facebook.com/contemporarysix
Instagram.com/contemporarysix

Paper Gallery

An artist-led, commercial gallery showing emerging and mid-career artists mainly working on paper. Drawing, painting and printmaking as well as artists' books, video and performance with funding from Arts Council England.
Address: 14-20 Mirabel Street, Manchester M3 1PJ
Phone: 07799 813062
Website: paper-gallery.co.uk
Email: papergallerymanchester@gmail.com

Philips Art Gallery

Opened in 1996, with an exhibition of a small group of art graduates. Now showing 20th century British and European art alongside contemporary painting and photography.
Address: 14A Tib Lane, Manchester M2 4JA
Phone: 0161 941 4197 / 07968 047 224
Address: 10A, Little Lever St, Manchester M1 1HR
Website: philipsartgallery.com
Email: philipsartgallery@btinternet.com
Instagram.com/philipsartgallery

Wendy J Levy Contemporary Art

Online Gallery
Phone: 01565 650563 / 07773 121574
Website: wendyjlevy.com
Email: info@wendyjlevy.com
Twitter.com/wendyjlevy
Facebook.com/wendyjlevy

De Lacey Fine Art

Bringing the very best of Modern British Art to the North of England.
Address: 9 South King Street, Manchester M2 6DG
Phone: 0161 839 8660
Website: delaceyfineart.com
Email: info@delaceyfineart.com
Twitter.com/delaceyfineart
Facebook.com/Delaceyfineart
Instagram.com/delaceyfineart

Mooch Art

Beautiful, inspirational and affordable art prints.
Address: Unit 19, The Triangle, 37, Hanging Ditch, Manchester M3 1
Phone: 0161 819 2199
Website: mooch-art.co.uk

Preston
Gallery D52

Paintings, sculpture, photography and performance art. Workshops, community events. Gallery space to rent.
Address: 234 Ribbleton Lane, Preston PR1 5LD
Phone: 07749 707314
Website: galleryd52.co.uk

Longridge Gallery

Fine art and picture framing. Original artwork, signed limited edition prints, bronze and porcelain sculpture from the UK's most collectable artists.
Address: 78 Berry Lane Longridge, Preston PR3 3WH
Phone: 01772 782006
Website: longridgegallery.co.uk
Email: info@longridgegallery.co.uk
Twitter.com/longridgegall
Facebook.com/Longridge-Gallery-637335386445992
Instagram.com/longridgegallery

Centurion Gallery

With a purpose-built exhibition space for art in all mediums, specialises in signed limited editions and framing for corporate clients, and more recently, original art for a worldwide market.
Address: 1 Turpin Green Lane Leyland, Preston PR25 3HA
Phone: 01772 424131 / 07742155570
Website: centuriongallery.co.uk
Email: info@centuriongallery.co.uk

Ascot Studios

Founded in 2005, with a worldwide client base. Representing leading contemporary artists. Corporate and private commissions are welcomed. Offering home trials and bespoke in-house framing. Mainly open by appointment. 2,500 sq. ft. Bee Mill in the heart of the Ribble Valley.
Address: Unit H Bee Mill Preston Road, Preston PR3 3XJ
Phone: 01254 820081
Website: ascotstudios.com
Email: info@ascotstudios.com
Twitter.com/ascotstudios
Facebook.com/ascotstudios
Instagram.com/ascotstudios

Salford
Salford Museum And Art Gallery

Open since 1850, this museum and art gallery offers exhibitions and activities.
Address: Peel Park, The Crescent, Salford M5 4WU
Phone: 0161 778 0800
Website: salfordmuseum.com
Email: dan.stribling@scll.co.uk
twitter.com/SalfordMuseum
facebook.com/salfordmuseum
instagram.com/salford_museum
YouTube.com/user/salfordcommleisure

The International 3

Emerging and established artists and independent curators showing solo and group shows and events on and off-site. Work at national and international art fairs with brokering of exhibitions and private commissions.
Address: 142 Chapel Street, Salford M3 6AF
Phone: 07960 038063
Website: international3.com
Email: ll@international3.com
Email: ptb@international3.com

Leicestershire

Leicester

West End Gallery

Picture framing services, fine art printing and scanning.
Address: White Gables, Mill Hill Road, Arnesby, LE8 5WG
Phone: 0116 251 3558
Website: westend-gallery.co.uk
Twitter.com/westendgallery1

Whitewall Galleries

Whitewall Galleries have over 40 galleries in the UK showing paintings and sculptures from internationally acclaimed artists as well as the best of emerging talent.
Address: Unit R2, 9 Bath House Lane, Leicester LE1 4SA
Phone: 0116 251 0711
Website: whitewallgalleries.com
Email: leicester@whitewallgalleries.com

Cank Street Gallery

The largest independent contemporary art gallery in Leicester, situated in the Old Town. Emerging and established local and national artists, showing paintings, handmade prints and sculpture.
Address: 44-46 Cank Street, Leicester LE1 5GW
Phone: 0116 253 0313
Website: cankstreetgallery.co.uk
Email: art@cankstreetgallery.co.uk

New Walk Museum And Art Gallery

The oldest museum in Leicester, exhibiting wide ranging collections from the natural and cultural world.
Address: 53 New Walk, Leicester LE1 7EA
Phone: 0116 225 4900
Website: leicester.gov.uk
Twitter.com/Leicester_News
Facebook.com/leicestercitycouncil
Instagram.com/leicestercitycouncil

Lincolnshire

Lincoln

Trent Galleries

A diverse portfolio of award winning artists.
Address: 28 Sincil Street, Lincoln, Lincolnshire. LN5 7ET
Tel: 01522 522000
Website: trentgalleries.co.uk
Email: sales@trentgalleries.co.uk
Email: Lincoln@trentgalleries.co.uk
Twitter.com/TrentGalleries
Facebook.com/trentgallerynewark
Instagram.com/trent_galleries

Bluestone Art

Exciting contemporary art in numerous styles and media featuring national and international artists to suit all tastes and budgets.
Address: 139-140 High Street, Lincoln LN5 7PJ
Phone: 01522 531177
Website: bluestoneart.co.uk
Email: sales@bluestoneart.co.uk
Twitter.com/BluestoneArt
Facebook.com/Bluestone-Art-481795091885477
Pinterest.co.uk/bluestoneart

The Little Red Gallery

Situated between Lincoln's cathedral and castle, showing international and emerging artists.
Address: 8 Bailgate, Lincoln LN1 3AE
Phone: 01522 589134
Website: thelittleredgallery.co.uk
Email: art@thelittleredgallery.co.uk
Twitter.com/TheRedGallery
Facebook.com/TheLittleRedGallery

Spencer Coleman Fine Art

Located in the Castle Square adjacent to the Cathedral and Magna Carta, showing art from nationally and internationally recognised artists across a wide range of subjects such as landscape, figurative, equestrian, marine and still-life.

Address: 2 Exchequergate, Bailgate, Lincoln LN2 1PZ

Phone: 01522 521794

Website: spencercolemanfineart.co.uk

Email: lincoln@spencercolemanfineart.co.uk

Twitter.com/LincsFineArt

Facebook.com/spencercolemanfineart

Gallery at St. Martin's

Situated in the cultural quarter of Lincoln, hosting an exciting program of exhibitions from emerging and established artists.

Address: 37B Hungate, Lincoln LN1 1ET

Phone: 07720 810468

Website: galleryatstmartins.co.uk

Email: phil@galleryatstmartins.co.uk

The Collection

Bringing together an award-winning archaeology museum and the foremost art gallery in the historic region of Lincoln – the Usher Gallery.

Address: Danes Terrace, Lincoln LN2 1LP

Phone: 01522 782040

Website: thecollectionmuseum.com

Email: thecollection@lincolnshire.gov.uk

Twitter.com/collectionusher

Facebook.com/collectionusher

Instagram.com/collectionusher

Harding House Gallery

Located in a timber 16th-century building near the cathedral. Set up in 1994 by a team of local contemporary artists, now one of the most successful co-operatives in the UK.

Address: Harding House 50 Steep Hill, Lincoln LN2 1LT

Phone: 01522 523537

Website: hardinghousegallery.co.uk

Email: info@hardinghousegallery.co.uk

Twitter.com/HardingHGallery

Facebook.com/HardingHouseGallery

Sam Scorer Gallery

Run by an artists' trust passionate about facilitating the exhibition of innovative contemporary local artists. Offering two week exhibitions.

Address: 5 Drury Lane, Lincoln LN1 3BN

Phone: 01522 589899

Website: samscorergallery.co.uk

Email: samscorergallery@gmail.com

Twitter.com/scorer_sam

Facebook.com/SamScorerGalleryLincoln

Instagram.com/samscorergallery

Midas Arts

Local, national and international jewellery, glassware, ceramics and gifts.

Address: 26 Bailgate, Lincoln LN1 3AP

Phone: 01522 532299

Website: midasarts.com

Email: midasartslincoln@gmail.com

Facebook.com/midasarts

London
Saatchi Gallery

The gallery opened in the King's Road location in Chelsea in 2008, showing new work from China, the Middle East, India, America and the UK, providing an innovative forum for contemporary art for unknown young artists as well as international artists, whose work is new to the UK.

Address: Duke of York's HQ, King's Road, Sloane Square, London SW3 4RY

Phone: 020 7811 3085

Website: saatchigallery.com

enquiries: admin@saatchigallery.com

membership enquiries: membership@saatchigallery.com

Twitter.com/saatchi_gallery

Facebook.com/saatchigalleryofficial

Instagram.com/saatchi_gallery

Institute Of Contemporary Arts

An artistic and cultural centre on The Mall in London, just off Trafalgar Square. It contains galleries, a theatre, two cinemas, a bookshop and a bar. It is an ideas-led institute, examining world issues and challenging the status quo.
Address: The Mall, London SW1Y 5AH
Phone: 020 7930 3647
Website: ica.art

Tate Modern

Aiming to increase the public's enjoyment and understanding of British art from the 16th century to the present day and of international modern and contemporary art.
Address: 53 Bankside, Bankside SE1 9TG
Phone: 020 7887 8888
Website: tate.org.uk
Email: hello@tate.org.uk
Twitter.com/tate
Facebook.com/tategallery
Instagram.com/tate
Pinterest.co.uk/tategallery

Serpentine Galleries

Since 1970 the gallery has been championing innovative ideas in contemporary art, with pioneering exhibitions from the leading international artists of the day.
Address: Kensington Gardens, London W2 3XA
Phone: 020 7402 6075
Website: serpentinegalleries.org
Email: information@serpentinegalleries.org
Twitter.com/SerpentineUK
Facebook.com/SerpentineGalleries
Instagram.com/serpentineuk
YouTube.com/channel/
UCW657nmvH2XddytwZRnFqcg

Barbican Centre

Europe's biggest multi-arts centre, pushing the boundaries of performance, film, music, learning and art.

Address: Silk Street, London EC2Y 8DS
Phone: 020 7638 8891
Website: barbican.org.uk
Email: tickets@barbican.org.uk
Art Gallery enquiries: Lily Booth
Acting Senior Communications Manager –
Visual Arts 020 7382 6162
lily.booth@barbican.org.uk
Visual Arts 020 7638 4141 ext. 8280
jemima.yong@barbican.org.uk
Twitter.com/BarbicanCentre
Facebook.com/BarbicanCentre
Instagram.com/barbicancentre

Opera Gallery

A leading international dealer in modern and contemporary art with galleries worldwide, such as New York, Miami, Aspen, London, Paris, Monaco, Geneva, Singapore, Hong Kong, Seoul, Beirut and Dubai. Notable exhibitions and international collaborations with museums, art centres and foundations
Address: 134 Bond Street, London. W1S 2TF
Phone: 020 7491 2999
Website: operagallery.com
Email New York: nyc@operagallery.com
Email Miami: miami@operagallery.com
Email Bal Harbour: balharbour@operagallery.com
Email Aspen: aspen@operagallery.com
Email London: london@operagallery.com
Email Paris: paris@operagallery.com
Email Monaco: monaco@operagallery.com
Email Geneva: geneve@operagallery.com
Email Dubai: dubai@operagallery.com
Email Beirut: beirut@operagallery.com
Email Hong Kong: hkg@operagallery.com
Email Singapore: spore@operagallery.com
Email Seoul: seoul@operagallery.com
Twitter.com/operagallery
Facebook.com/OperaGalleryOfficial
Instagram.com/operagallery
Pinterest.ch/operagalleryPinterest
Weibo.com/operagallery

Beaux Arts London

Beaux Arts opened their Maddox Street Gallery in 2014 after 20 years in Cork Street, exhibiting contemporary painters and sculptors. Focusing on promoting the next generation of emerging artists, whilst also showing those who are established. Representing the estates of Terry Frost and Elizabeth Frink.
Address: 48 Maddox Street, W1S 1AY (off Bond Street)
Phone: +44 (0)207 493 1155
Email: info@beauxartslondon.uk
Twitter.com/beauxartslondon
Instagram.com/beauxartsgallery

Battersea Arts Centre

A creative hub since 1974, supporting local, national and international change, seeing projects start from seed and go on to tour the world.
Address: Battersea Arts Centre Battersea Old Town Hall Lavender Hill, Battersea, London SW11 5TN
Phone: 0870 286 0066
Website: bac.org.uk
Email: boxoffice@bac.org.uk
Twitter.com/battersea_arts
Facebook.com/batterseaartscentre
Instagram.com/batterseaartscentre

Riflemaker

Set in a former gunmaker's workshop off Regent Street in a building dating back to 1712, making it one of the oldest in the West End. Shows emerging artists as well as publishing books, poetry readings, music and film events, discussions , talks and performances.
Address: 79 Beak Street, Regent Street, London W1F 9SU
Phone: 020 7439 0000
Website: riflemaker.org
Email: info@riflemaker.org

Twitter.com/Riflemaker_Soho
Facebook.com/riflemaker79

The Colomb Art Gallery

Contemporary and traditional fine art from some of the best practitioners today.
Address: 52A George Street, London W1U 7EA
Phone: 020 7487 5118
Website: colombart.co.uk
Email: info@colombart.co.uk Facebook.com/colombartgallery

ArtsHouse

Online gallery of contemporary British art with figurative, Indian and African influences. Regular group exhibitions in Asia House and The Royal Geographic Society.
Website: artshouse.co.uk
Email: enquiries@artshouse.co.uk

Halcyon Gallery

Exhibits world-class modern and contemporary art and sculpture in 3 galleries in London, featuring a wide range of living practitioners from around the globe including the UK, US, Colombia, Spain, Italy and Russia.
Address: 144-146 New Bond Street, London W1S 2PF
Phone: 020 7100 7144
Email: info@halcyongallery.com
29 New Bond Street, London. W1S 2RL
Email: info@halcyongallery.com
Phone: +44(0)20 7499 4508
3rd Floor, Harrods, 87-135 Brompton Road, London. SW1X 7XL
Email: Artatharrods@halcyongallery.com
Phone: +44(0) 2075817980
Website: halcyongallery.com
Twitter.com/HalcyonGallery
Facebook.com/HalcyonGalleryLondon
Instagram.com/halcyongallery
Pinterest.co.uk/halcyongallery

Gallery Different

In the heart of Fitzrovia, exhibiting contemporary painting, sculpture, drawing, print, photography and mixed media from the UK and internationally. Collaborating with galleries across the world to promote and curate exhibitions for their artists.

Address: 14 Percy Street Fitrovia, London W1T 1DR

Phone: 020 7637 3775

Website: gallerydifferent.co.uk

Email: info@gallerydifferent.co.uk

Zari Gallery

A cultural and artistic hub in London's Fitzrovia. With the aim of showing art that transcends borders, the gallery works with artists from around the world, who have a mixed heritage. Using paintings and sculpture, photography and video to produce inclusive and inspirational work with talks and educational events.

Address: 73 Newman Street, London W1T 3EJ

Phone: 020 7580 7759

Website: zarigallery.co.uk

Email: info@zarigallery.co.uk

Jill George Gallery

Paintings, drawings, watercolour, monoprints and limited edition prints by contemporary artists in the UK.

Address: 38 Lexington Street, Soho, London W1F 0LL

Phone: 020 7439 7319

Website: jillgeorgegallery.co.uk

Email: info@jillgeorgegallery.co.uk

Ed Cross Fine Art

Working from the Exchange office space at Somerset House in Central London. Work can be viewed by appointment

Address: Exchange, West Service Yard , Somerset House, Strand, London WC2R 1LA

Phone: 07507 067567

Website: edcrossfineart.com

Email: ed@edcrossfineart.com

Twitter.com/edcrossfineart

Facebook.com/edcrossfineart

Instagram.com/edcrossfineart

Beaconsfield Gallery

Exhibits sculptures, paintings and 3D work, based in the former Lambeth Ragged School. Talks and interdisciplinary events. A long history of collaboration with artists, helping them develop, as well as working with national and international art institutions.

Address: 22 Newport Street Vauxhall, London SE11 6AY

Phone: 020 7582 6465

Website: beaconsfield.ltd.uk

Email: admin@beaconsfield.ltd.uk

Twitter.com/BeaconsfieldArt

Facebook.com/BeaconsfieldGallery

Instagram.com/beaconsfield_gallery_vauxhall

Flow Contemporary Art Gallery

Situated in Nottinghill, the gallery curates contemporary craft makers creating hand making and unusual pieces.

Address: 1-5 Needham Road, London W11 2RP

Phone: 020 7243 0782

Website: flowgallery.co.uk

Email: info@flowgallery.co.uk

Instagram.com/flowgallery

MMX Gallery

Based in SE London, the gallery shows work by new and established contemporary photographers ranging from the abstract to the documentary, as well as vintage prints.

Address: 448 New Cross Road, London SE14 6TY

Phone: 020 8692 6728

Website: mmxgallery.com

Email: info@mmxgallery.com
Twitter.com/mmxgallery
Facebook.com/MMXgallery
Instagram.com/mmxgallery
Artsy.net/mmx-gallery

Bearspace

The gallery exhibits UK emerging artists, with painting, print editions, sculpture and drawing especially those with a strong technical element and fresh twist on traditional techniques.
Address: 152 Deptford High Street, London SE8 3PQ
Phone: 020 8694 8097
Website: bearspace.co.uk
Email: info@bearspace.co.uk

Lewisham Arthouse

An artist-run co-operative, with 45 studios and a busy gallery, classes, workshops and community activities and events.
Address: 140 Lewisham Way, London SE14 6PD
Phone: 020 8691 9113
Website: lewishamarthouse.org.uk
Email: info@lewishamarthouse.org.uk
Twitter.com/arthousenews
Facebook.com/thelewishamarthouse
Instagram.com/lewishamarthouse

Agency Gallery

Established in 1996 focusing on global and socially relevant art strategies working with artists of all genres and collaborating with a wide range of institutions. No unsolicited material.
Address: 66 Evelyn Street, London SE8 5DD
Phone: 07908 910277
Website: theagencygallery.co.uk
Email: info@theagencygallery.co.uk
Facebook.com/agencygallery
Instagram.com/agencygallery

Jealous Gallery and Print Studio

Dealers and publishers of limited edition prints from both emerging and established artists.
Address: 53 Curtain Road, London EC2A 3PT
Phone: 020 7739 4107
Address: 27 Park Road, Crouch End, London, N8 8TE
Phone: 020 8347 7688
Website: jealousgallery.com
Email: info@jealousgallery.com
Twitter.com/jealous_gallery
Facebook.com/jealous.london
Instagram.com/jealous_london

Iconic Images Gallery

Situated in Chelsea, representing the leading photographers of the world. In collaboration with top museums and art galleries globally. Chronicling our cultural heritage from vintage fashion to the birth of rock 'n' roll, with recent fine art photographs that have surged in value of the last decade.
Address: 13a Park Walk, Chelsea London SW10 0AJ
Phone: +44 207 349 9332
Website: iconicimagesgallery.net
Email: sales@iconicimages.net

Bartha Contemporary

Founded in 2000, it relocated to St James' in 2019 with a strong focus on non-figurative and conceptual contemporary art.
Address: 25 Margaret Street, London W1W 8RX
Phone: 020 7985 0015
Website: barthacontemporary.com
Email: info@barthacontemporary.com
Pinterest.co.uk/bclondon

Gagliardi Gallery

Specialising in contemporary art from emerging, mid-career and established artists.

Address: 509 King's Road Chelsea, London SW10 0TX
Phone: 020 7352 3663
Website: gagliardigallery.org
Instagram.com/gagliardigallery

Cadogan Contemporary

An English gallery with international appeal. From 1980, trading in photorealism to pure abstraction, with an eclectic range of work by established and critically acclaimed artists as well as looking out for new talent.
Address: 87 Old Brompton Road, London SW7 3LD
Phone: 020 7581 5451
Website: cadogancontemporary.com
Email: info@cadogancontemporary.com
Facebook.com/cadogancontemporary
Instagram.com/cadogan_contemporary

Transition Gallery

Exhibiting work by emerging and established artists. Produces publications and periodicals.
Address: Unit 25A, Regent Studios, 8 Andrews Rd, London E8 4QN
Phone: 020 7254 4202
Website: transitiongallery.co.uk
Email: info@transitiongallery.co.uk
Twitter.com/Transitionart
Facebook.com/transitionart

Danielle Arnaud Contemporary Art

Established in 1995, encouraging artists to develop without the constraints of the market through curated exhibitions, solo shows and projects, within the gallery and in the public realm.
Address: 123 Kennington Road, London SE11 6SF
Phone: 020 7736 8292
Website: daniellearnaud.co.uk

Contemporary Applied Arts

CAA has championed the very best of British craft for 70 years fostering quality and innovation. A registered charity with over 300 British-based craftsmakers working in ceramics, furniture, glass, jewellery, metal, paper, textiles and wood.
Address: 89 Southwark Street, London SE1 0HX
Phone: 020 7436 2344
Website: caa.org.uk
Email: shop@caa.org.uk
Twitter.com/CAAGallery
Facebook.com/ContemporaryAppliedArtsGallery
Instagram.com/caagallery
Pinterest.co.uk/caagallery

Paul Stolper

Contemporary art and publisher of contemporary editions of prints and sculptures. Established in 1998. Exhibitions throughout the year. Work shown has been included in collections of the Tate Britain, British Council, MoMA New York, the Arts Council and the Government Art Collection.
Address: The Studio 31, Museum Street, London WC1A 1LH
Phone: 020 7580 7001
Website: paulstolper.com
Email: info@paulstolper.com
Twitter.com/paulstolper
Facebook.com/Paul-Stolper-Gallery-219811954699905
Instagram.com/paulstolpergallery

October Gallery

Exhibits a wide range of contemporary art from around the world, including sculptures, paintings and multimedia. Instrumental in the career of many of the world's leading artists. Cultural hub in central London for writers, poets, intellectuals and artists with talks, performances and seminars. The education department works with all ages from pre-school up. Work shown in the gallery has

been collected by the British Museum, Metropolitan Museum of Art in NY, Centre Pompidou in Paris and others.
Address: 24 Old Gloucester Street, London WC1N 3AL
Phone: 020 7242 7367
Twitter.com/octoberlondon
Facebook.com/octobergalleryholborn
Instagram.com/octobergallery

London Contemporary Art

LCA works with artists from around the world, also supplying art for exhibition and interior design companies, private members clubs, hospitals and businesses in London.
Address: 32 Store Street, London WC1E 7BS
Phone: 020 7580 2118
Website: londoncontemporaryart.co.uk
Email: info@londoncontemporaryart.co.uk
Twitter.com/LCAgallery
Facebook.com/londoncontemporary

Flowers Gallery

The gallery represents over 50 internationally acclaimed artists, and artists' estates. With 50 years of experience, and more than 900 exhibitions around the world, as well as supporting artists' publication and work in fairs, public galleries, museums and institutions globally. Also promoting emerging artists.
Address: 21 Cork Street, London W1S 3LZ
Phone: 020 7439 7766
Website: flowersgallery.com
Email: info@flowersgallery.com
Twitter.com/flowersgallery
Facebook.com/FlowersGalleries
Instagram.com/flowersgallery
Artsy.net/flowers
www.flowersgallery.com/wechat

Redfern Gallery

Founded in 1923 as a small artists' cooperative, now a leading modern British and contemporary art gallery representing over 30 artists. An extensive stock of paintings, drawings, watercolours, sculpture and original prints.
Address: 20 Cork Street, London W1S 3HL
Phone: 020 7734 1732
Website: redfern-gallery.com
Email: art@redfern-gallery.com
Twitter.com/redferngallery
Facebook.com/RedfernGallery
Instagram.com/theredferngallery

Helly Nahmad Gallery

Specialising in classic modern and post-war art.
Address: 8 St. James's Square, London SW1Y 4JU
Phone: 020 7494 3200
Website: hellynahmad.com
Email: mail@hellynahmad.com

Walton Fine Arts

Modern, contemporary, pop and street art. Original paintings, lithographs, prints and sculptures by international artists such as Banksy, Chagall, Picasso and Warhol. Launching breaking new talent. See website for submission guidelines.
Address: 121 Walton Street, London SW3 2JJ
Phone: 020 7581 2332
Website: waltonfinearts.com

Bankside Gallery

Home of the Royal Watercolour Society and Royal Society of Painter Printmakers. Exhibits contemporary water-based media and original prints from both emerging and established artists.
Address: 48 Hopton Street, London SE1 9JH
Phone: 020 7928 7521
Website: banksidegallery.com
Email: info@banksidegallery.com

Twitter.com/BanksideGallery
Facebook.com/banksidegallery
Instagram.com/banksidegallery

South London Gallery

Founded in 1891, showing the best of international contemporary art + events program. New work by British and international emerging and established artists + a residency program. Thousands of children and adults take part in wide-ranging activities
Address: 65-67 Peckham Road, London SE5 8UH
Phone: 020 7703 6120
Website: southlondongallery.org
Twitter.com/SLG_artupdates
Facebook.com/southlondongallery
Instagram.com/southlondongallery
SoundCloud.com/south-london-gallery
YouTube.com/user/SouthLondonGallery

Parasol Unit

A not-for-profit institution showing contemporary art.
Address: 14 Wharf Road, London N1 7RW
Phone: 020 7490 7373
Website: parasol-unit.org
Email: info@parasol-unit.org
Twitter.com/parasolunit
Facebook.com/Parasolunitfoundationforcontemporaryart
Instagram.com/parasolunit
YouTube.com/channel/UCMwg2K9jNs_vUQR8fZ5vAkQ

Camden Arts Centre

Contemporary art, café, with a bookshop and educational classes. Free entry.
Address: 50, Arkwright Road, Hampstead, London NW3 6DG
Phone: 020 7472 5500
Website: camdenartscentre.org
Email: info@camdenartscentre.org

Twitter.com/camdenartcentre
Facebook.com/camdenartcentre
Instagram.com/camdenartcentre
YouTube.com/channel/UC78G3w-dYhh3_PERqopfb5g?view_as=subscriber

Modern Art

Contemporary art gallery.
Address: 4-8 Helmet Row, London EC1V 3QJ
Phone: 020 7299 7950
Website: modernart.net
Email: info@modernart.net
Instagram.com/stuartshavemodernart

Exhibit at Golden Lane Estate

Situated in a highly regarded modernist housing estate in the City of London, adjacent to Hoxton, Shoreditch and Clerkenwell, the gallery is a hub of new ideas. Promoting emerging talent producing unique pieces.
Address: 20 Goswell Road, London EC1M 7AA
Phone: 020 7253 6668
Website: exhibit-goldenlane.com
Email: info@exhibit-goldenlane.com

Whitechapel Gallery

For over a century the gallery has premiered world-class artists such as Picasso, Pollock and Rothko. A gallery with a vibrant local and international presence.
Address: 77-82 Whitechapel High Street, London E1 7QX
Phone: 020 7522 7888
Website: whitechapelgallery.org
Email: info@whitechapelgallery.org
Twitter.com/_TheWhitechapel
Facebook.com/WhitechapelGallery
Instagram.com/whitechapelgallery

Sway Gallery

Introducing Japanese art to Europe and the wider world, with branches Paris and

Sweden. Emerging and established Japanese artists and craftmakers, as well as those who find inspiration in Japanese culture.
Address: 70-72 Old Street, London EC1V 9AJ
Phone: 020 7637 1700
Website: sway-gallery.com
Twitter.com/swaygallery
Facebook.com/swaygallerylondon
Instagram.com/swaygallerylondon

Guildhall Art Gallery

Permanent display of 250 artworks with smaller, temporary exhibitions.
Address: Guildhall Yard, London EC2V 5AE
Phone: 020 7332 3700
Website: cityoflondon.gov.uk
Twitter.com/cityoflondon
Facebook.com/CityofLondonCorp

Contemporary Art Society

Donates modern and contemporary art to 72 member museums and public galleries in the UK. Over 12,000 works have been donated since their foundation in 1910, appreciated by 21 million visitors each year. Artists include Bacon, Freud, Hepworth and Moore.
Address: 59 Central Street, London EC1V 3AF
Phone: 020 7017 8400
Website: contemporaryartsociety.org
Email: info@contemporaryartsociety.org
Twitter.com/ContempArtSoc
Facebook.com/thecontemporaryartsociety
Instagram.com/contemporaryartsociety

Beers Contemporary Art

Cutting-edge contemporary art, from emerging and mid-career artists. Progressive and thought-provoking art. Primarily painting, but also sculpture, photography, textiles and ceramics. Summer Exhibition offers emerging artists a solo exhibition.

Address: 1 Baldwin Street, London EC1V 9NU
51 Little Britain
London EC1A 7BH
Phone: 020 7502 9078
Website: beerslondon.com
Email: info@beerslondon.com
Twitter.com/beerslondon
Facebook.com/BeersLondon
Instagram.com/beerslondon

100 Sculptors of Tomorrow

Website: 100sculptorsoftomorrow.com
Twitter.com/100sculptors
Instagram.com/100sculptors

Frameless Gallery

Promoting the best emerging and established contemporary artists with cutting-edge projects and exhibitions.
Address: 20 Clerkenwell Green, London EC1R 0DP
Phone: 07546 817937
Website: framelessgallery.com
Email: info@framelessgroup.com
Email: us@framelessgallery.com

Norfolk

Bircham Gallery

With over 200 artists and craftworkers represented, the gallery shows paintings, sculpture, original prints, glass, ceramics and jewellery.
Address: 14 Market Place, Holt NR25 6BW
Phone: 01263 713312
Website: birchamgallery.co.uk
Email: info@birchamgallery.co.uk
Twitter.com/BirchamGallery
Facebook.com/birchamgallery
Instagram.com/birchamgallery14
Pinterest.co.uk/birchamgallery

Gallery Plus

Paintings, original prints, sculpture, ceramics and jewellery by British artists on the beautiful north Norfolk coast.
Address: Warham Road, Wells next the Sea NR23 1QA
Phone: 01328 711609
Website: gallery-plus.co.uk
Facebook.com/galleryplus.wells
Instagram.com/galleryplus.wells
Email: info@gallery-plus.co.uk

Norwich

Mandells Gallery

Located in the historic Elm Hill, the gallery opened in the 1960s showing the Norwich School of Painters. Now exhibiting a diverse range of traditional and contemporary art.
Address: Elm Hill, Norwich NR3 1HN
Phone: 01603 626892
Website: mandellsgallery.co.uk
Email: info@mandellsgallery.co.uk
Twitter.com/Mandellsgallery
Facebook.com/mandellsgallerynorwich
Instagram.com/mandellsgallery

Moosey Art

Contemporary art gallery.
Address: Unit 16 Capitol House, Norwich NR2 4TE
Phone: 07792 011541
Website: mooseyart.co.uk

East Gallery at Norwich University of the Arts

Dating back to 1845, the gallery has a forward-looking focus. With cutting-edge facilities, it has developed a reputation as an innovative and creative community.
Address: Saint Andrews St, Norwich
Phone: 01603 610561
Website: nua.ac.uk
Email: info@nua.ac.uk
Twitter.com/NorwichUniArts
Facebook.com/NUAnews
Instagram.com/norwichuniarts

Norwich Castle Museum & Art Gallery

One of Norwich's most famous landmarks, the castle exhibits archaeology, natural history and fine art.
Address: Norfolk Museums Service, Shirehall, Market Avenue, Norwich NR1 3JQ
Phone: 01603 493625
Website: museums.norfolk.gov.uk
Facebook.com/NorfolkMuseums

Sainsbury Centre

An inspirational gallery designed by Norman Foster exhibiting outstanding contemporary art, and objects in the sculpture park.
Address: University of East Anglia, Norfolk Road, Norwich NR4 7TJ
Phone: 01603 593199
Website: sainsburycentre.ac.uk
Twitter.com/sainsburycentre
Facebook.com/sainsburycentre
Instagram.com/sainsburycentre

Outpost

An artist-run charity presenting contemporary art, with 5 exhibitions a year. Off-site projects and events. Studio space for over 80 artists.
Address: 10B Wensum Street, Norwich NR3 1HR
Phone: 01603 612428
Website: norwichoutpost.org
Email: questions@norwichoutpost.org
Twitter.com/outpostgallery
Facebook.com/OUTPOSTGallery
Instagram.com/outpost.gallery

Riverside Art & Glass

The sole gallery in Norfolk to specialise in glass from the top UK and European glass artists. Also showing contemporary paintings, prints, ceramics, sculpture and jewellery from local and British makers, alongside furniture, outdoor lamps and sculpture.

Address: 24 Norwich Road, Norwich NR12 8RX
Phone: 01603 784000
Website: riversideartandglass.co.uk
Email: info@riversideartandglass.co.uk
Twitter.com/riverside_art
Facebook.com/RiversideArtGlass

The Jade Tree

Art and craft shop run co-operatively in the heart of Norwich. Artists' studios on the premises, with over 60 makers represented. In the historic quarter of Norwich.
Address: 15 Elm Hill, Norwich NR3 1HN
Phone: 01603 664615
Website: thejadetree.co.uk
Email: info@thejadetree.co.uk
Twitter.com/jadetreenorwich
Facebook.com/thejadetreenorwich

Northumberland

The Wallington Gallery

An eclectic collection of mainly oils and watercolour paintings from Victorian times to the present day.
Address: Bishops Yard, Corbridge NE45 5LA
Phone: 01434 633663
Website: thewallingtongallery.co.uk
enquiries@thewallingtongallery.co.uk
Facebook.com/thewallingtongallery

Newcastle upon Tyne

The Biscuit Factory

A contemporary art gallery exhibiting emerging and established artists, showing over 250 artists at any one time. Also selling prints, glass, ceramics, textiles, photography, furniture and jewellery. Welcomes more than 50,000 visitors each year. Collaborates with national agencies and art organisations.
Address: 16 Stoddart St, Shieldfield, Newcastle Upon Tyne NE2 1AN
Phone: 0191 261 1103

Website: thebiscuitfactory.com
Email: art@thebiscuitfactory.com
Twitter.com/biscuit_factory
Facebook.com/thebiscuitfactorynewcastle
Instagram.com/thebiscuitfactorygallery
Pinterest.co.uk/biscuitfactory

Hatton Gallery

Their collection includes over 3,000 works from the 14th – 20th century including paintings, sculpture, prints, drawings and textiles.
Exhibitions of modern and contemporary art, with artist and curator talks and family activities. Annual exhibitions from students at Newcastle University.
Address: Kings Road, Newcastle University, Newcastle Upon Tyne NE1 7RU
Phone: 0191 208 6059
Website: hattongallery.org.uk
Email: info@hattongallery.org.uk
Twitter.com/hattongallery
Facebook.com/thehatton

Laing Art Gallery

An internationally important collection of art, with a special focus on British oil paintings, watercolours, ceramics, silver and glassware. Regular exhibitions of historic, modern and contemporary art, with talks and activities.
Address: New Bridge Street, Newcastle Upon Tyne NE1 8AG
Phone: 0191 278 1611
Website: laingartgallery.org.uk
Email: info@laingartgallery.org.uk
Twitter.com/laingartgallery
Facebook.com/laingartgallery

North East Art Collective

Many display rooms in the heart of Eldon Garden shopping centre, with a range of media from watercolour, acrylic, oil and pastel pictures alongside photography, glass, ceramics, woodwork and jewellery, with new pieces coming in every week.

Address: 45 Eldon Gardens, Newcastle Upon Tyne NE1 7RA

Phone: 0191 231 2483

Website: northeastartcollective.co.uk

Email: info@northeastartcollective.co.uk

Twitter.com/northeastartcol

Facebook.com/northeastartcollective

Instagram.com/north_east_art_collective

Pinterest.co.uk/neac1234

LinkedIn.com/company/north-east-art-collective

The Glamorous Owl

Featuring work from over 40 artists, showing paintings, jewellery and leatherwork. The workshop of the silversmith and owner is above the shop, where you can participate in jewellery courses creating a bespoke wedding ring or longer 12-week silversmithing courses.

Address: 2 Old George Yard Cloth Market High Bridge, Newcastle Upon Tyne NE1 1EZ

Phone: 0191 261 7283

Website: theglamorousowl.com

Email: theglamorousowl@gmail.com

Facebook.com/theglamorousowl2

Instagram.com/theglamorousowl

Vane

Based within the Orbis building; a creative community within Newcastle city centre. Representing artists from the north east, the UK, Europe and the USA. Works in partnership with others, exhibiting artists at all stages of their career, with talks, performances, workshops and other events.

Address: Commercial Union House 39 Pilgrim Street, Newcastle Upon Tyne NE1 6QE

Phone: 0191 261 8281

Website: vane.org.uk

Email: info@vane.org.uk

Twitter.com/VaneGallery

Facebook.com/vanegallery

Instagram.com/vanegallery

Gallagher & Turner

Modern and contemporary art with specialist picture framing. Exhibits well-known international artists as well as local emerging talent. Paintings, drawings and craftwork.

Address: 30 Saint Mary›s Place, Newcastle Upon Tyne NE1 7PQ

Phone: 0191 261 4465

Website: gallagherandturner.co.uk

Facebook.com/gallagherandturner

Instagram.com/gallagherandturner

The Globe Gallery

Emerging and established artists. Volunteer program and emerging artist support system that increases confidence and improve skills.

Address: 45-47 Pilgrim Street, Newcastle-Upon-Tyne NE1 6QE

Phone: 0191 597 9278

Website: globegallery.org

Email: rashida@globegallery.org

Twitter.com/globegallery

Facebook.com/theglobegallery

Instagram.com/theglobegallery

Northamptonshire

Northampton Museum and Art Gallery

A public museum owned by Northampton Borough Council. Houses a collection of over 12,000 shoes – the largest in the world. Established in 1865.

Address: 4-6 Guildhall Road, Northampton NN1 1DP

Phone: 01604 838111

Website: northampton.gov.uk

NN Contemporary Art

A contemporary art gallery in the centre of Northampton. Works with artists at all stages

of their career, with an international program.
Address: 9 Guildhall Road, Northampton NN1 1DP
Phone: 01604 638944
Website: nncontemporaryart.org
Email: info@nncontemporaryart.org
Facebook.com/nncontemporaryart

Primrose Gallery

Original paintings, fine art prints, ceramics, sculpture and glass.
Address: 6-8 Harborough Road, Northampton NN2 7AZ
Phone: 01604 792871
Address: 26 High Street, Thrapston NN14 4JH
Phone: 01832 730022
Website: primrosegallery.co.uk
Email: art@primrosegallery.co.uk
Twitter.com/PrimroseGallery
Facebook.com/primrosefineart

Nottinghamshire
Trent Galleries

A diverse portfolio of award-winning artists.
Address: 3 Chain Lane, Newark On Trent NG24 1AU
Phone: 01636 646426
Website: trentgalleries.co.uk
Email: sales@trentgalleries.co.uk
Twitter.com/TrentGalleries
Facebook.com/trentgallerynewark
Instagram.com/trent_galleries

Nottingham
Nottingham Contemporary

A contemporary art centre in the Lace Market area on the site of a Saxon fort.
Address: Weekday Cross, Nottingham NG1 2GB
Phone: 0115 948 9750
Website: nottinghamcontemporary.org
Email: info@nottinghamcontemporary.org

Surface Gallery

An artist-run contemporary art gallery operating as a social enterprise, engaging with the immediate community, broadening participation in the arts. Run by early-career artists, supporting each other in learning how to run a successful, independent art gallery.
Address: 16 Southwell Road, Nottingham NG1 1DL
Phone: 0115 947 0793
Website: surfacegallery.org
Email: info@surfacegallery.org
Facebook.com/surfacegallery
Instagram.com/surfacegallery

The Fletcher Gate Art Gallery

Contemporary fine art in the heart of historic Nottingham.
Address: 18 Fletcher Gate, Nottingham NG1 2FZ
Phone: 0115 950 9966
Website: fletchergateartgallery.com
Email: info@fletchergateartgallery.com
Twitter.com/FletcherGate
Facebook.com/fletchergategallery
Instagram.com/thefletchergateartgallery
Pinterest.co.uk/claire0566/the-fletcher-gate-art-gallery/

P Spowage Art Gallery

Contemporary and original art by painter Pete Spowage.
Address: 2 Byard Lane, Nottingham NG1 2GJ
Phone: 07935 945677
Website: pspowageartgallery.com
Email: pspowage@googlemail.com
Twitter.com/Pspowageartist
Facebook.com/pspowageartgallery
Instagram.com/pete_spowage
Linkedin.com/in/pete-spowage-2158a651

Lauren Paige Fine Art Gallery

Original paintings by fine artist, poet, writer, researcher, curator and painting tutor Lauren Paige, who was a semi-finalist on the BBC's *Show Me the Monet*. Lauren paints on site.
Address: 211 Mansfield Road, Nottingham NG1 3FS
Phone: 07773 982464
Website: laurenpaigefineartgallery.com

Oxfordshire

Sarah Wiseman Gallery

The largest independent gallery space in Oxford. Exhibits contemporary art by emerging and established artists, focusing primarily on British painters, with both solo and group exhibitions.
Address: 40/41 South Parade, Summertown, Oxford OX2 7JL
Phone: 01865 515123
Website: wisegal.com
Email: info@wisegal.com
Twitter.com/Sarah_WiseGal
Facebook.com/sarahwisemangallery
Instagram.com/sarahwisemangallery
Pinterest.co.uk/sarahwisemangal

Bohun Gallery

Contemporary British fine art, including paintings, drawings, watercolour, sculpture, original prints and ceramics from both established and emerging talent. Up to 9 exhibitions a year, with a sculpture garden.
Address: 15 Reading Rd, Henley On Thames RG9 1AB
Phone: 01491 576228
Website: bohungallery.co.uk
Twitter.com/bohungallery
Facebook.com/bohungallery
Instagram.com/bohungallery

Hemingway Art

New work from leading emerging and established artists, with paintings, prints, drawings and sculpture. Works closely with selected artists, with 5 solo or group exhibitions a year. and a world-wide client base.
Address: Pennwood House, Pound Lane, Cassington, Oxford OX29 4BN
Phone: 01865 883991
Website: hemingwayart.co.uk
Email: art@hemingwayart.co.uk

Modern Art Oxford

Oxford's only public space dedicated to contemporary art and culture, promoting diversity and internationalism and the importance of contemporary visual culture in today's society.
Address: 30 Pembroke Street, Oxford OX1 1BP
Phone: 01865 722733
Website: modernartoxford.org.uk
Email: info@modernartoxford.org.uk

SOTA Gallery

A contemporary art gallery in the Cotswold town of Witney selling fine art, prints, ceramics, sculpture, glass, jewellery and more.
Address: 11 Langdale Court, Witney OX28 6FG
Phone: 01993 862799
Website: sotagallery.co.uk
Email: sotagallery@gmail.com
Facebook.com/SotaArtGallery

Oxford Ceramics Gallery

World class ceramics with a lifetime of experience.
Address: 29 Walton St, Oxford OX2 6AA
Phone: 01865 512320
Website: oxfordceramics.com
Email: gallery@oxfordceramics.com
Twitter.com/oxfordceramics
Instagram.com/oxfordceramicsgallery
Pinterest.co.uk/oxfordceramics

Dantzig

20th Century Modern and Contemporary Art.
Address: 1 Market Street, Woodstock OX20 1SU
Phone: 01993 812000
Website: dantzig.uk
Email: gallery@dantzig.uk
Twitter.com/dantziggallery
Facebook.com/DantzigGallery
Instagram.com/dantziggallery
LinkedIn.com/company/dantzig-gallery

Ovada

Emerging and established, local, national and international artists. Diverse and inter-disciplinary exhibitions, events and educational programs reaching new audiences.
Address: 14A Osney Lane, Oxford OX1 1NJ
Phone: 01865 200979
Website: ovada.org.uk
Email: info@ovada.org.uk
Twitter.com/OVADA_Gallery
Facebook.com/ovada.gallery
Instagram.com/ovada_gallery
YouTube.com/user/OVADAoxford
Flickr.com/photos/ovada

West Oxfordshire Arts Association

Not-for-profit organisation promoting art in Oxfordshire and the surrounding counties, with a gallery in Bampton. Open to all artists and craftmakers whatever their level of skill or interest.
Address: Market Square, Bampton OX18 2JH
Phone: 01993 850137
Website: westoxarts.com
Email: gallery@westoxarts.com
Facebook.com/WestOxArts
Instagram.com/westoxarts

Surrey

The Watts Gallery

Nestled in the Surrey Hills, the gallery shows Victorian paintings and sculpture, as well as hosting a contemporary exhibition, with gifts, books, homewares and cream teas!
Address: Down Lane, Guildford GU3 1DQ
Phone: 01483 810235
Website: wattsgallery.org.uk
Email: info@wattsgallery.org.uk
Twitter.com/wattsgallery
Facebook.com/wattsgalleryartistsvillage
Instagram.com/wattsgallery
LinkedIn.com/company/watts-gallery

Reem Fine Art

A contemporary art gallery showing emerging British and internationally recognised artists. Also offering bespoke commissions, collection management and bespoke framing.
Address: 52 Obelisk Way, Camberley GU15 3SG
Phone: 01276 65171
Website: reemfineart.com
Email: info@reem.gallery
Facebook.com/reemfineart
Instagram.com/reemfineart

The Fountain Gallery

Exciting and diverse exhibitions showing paintings, prints, ceramics, textiles and jewellery. A new exhibition every fortnight with the exhibiting artist present.
Address: 26 Bridge Road, Hampton Court, East Molesey KT8 9HA
Phone: 020 8941 5865
Website: fountaingallery.co.uk
Email: info@fountaingallery.co.uk
Twitter.com/FountainBonanza
Facebook.com/fountaingallery
Instagram.com/fountaingallerykt8

The Wey Gallery

Original paintings, limited edition prints, sculpture and handmade glass by British artists, including Damien Hirst and Peter Blake as well as new talent.
Address: Bridge Street, Godalming GU7 1HL
Phone: 01483 418013
Website: theweygallery.com
Email: info@theweygallery.com
Twitter.com/theweygallery
Facebook.com/theweygalleryhub
Instagram.com/theweygalleryhub
YouTube.com/channel/
UCSP6Q7i9z3fi2OvQU5tqpsQ

The Art Agency

Original artwork, limited edition prints, sculpture and ceramics. Offering a 'Try Before you Buy' service, as well as framing, hanging and corporate sales and commissions.
Address: 118 - 120 High Street, Esher KT10 9QJ
Phone: 01372 466740
Website: theartagency.co.uk
Email: sales@theartagency.co.uk
Twitter.com/theartagency
Facebook.com/TheArtAgency
Instagram.com/theartagency.esher

Bourneside Gallery

Sought-after ceramics, glass, original limited edition prints and furniture from the mid-20th century, along with contemporary work from British printmakers and Surrey artists.
Address: 1A North Street, Dorking RH4 1DN
Phone: 01306 889988
Website: bournesidegallery.com
Email: studioart@live.co.uk
Facebook.com/Bourneside

Lincoln Joyce Fine Arts Art Gallery

Exhibits representational art, with selected work from the 19th, 20th and 21st centuries.

Address: 40 Church Road, Leatherhead KT23 3PW
Phone: 01372 458481
Website: artgalleries.uk.com
Email: rosemarylincolnjoyce@hotmail.com

McAllister Thomas Fine Art

A leading gallery in the south east. Solo and group exhibitions, with private and corporate clients from around the world.
Address: 117 High Street, Godalming GU7 1AQ
Phone: 01483 860591
Website: mcallisterthomasfineart.co.uk
Email: info@mcallisterthomasfineart.co.uk
Twitter.com/mcthomfineart
Instagram.com/mcthomfineart

Artfulness

Original artwork by Amie Antoniak.
Address: 5 Dunlin Close, Redhill RH1 5HJ
Phone: 07743 317102
Website: artfulness.co.uk
Twitter.com/AmieAntoniak
Facebook.com/artfulness.co.uk

East Sussex

Chalk Gallery

A leading artist-led gallery exhibiting a range of painting, mixed media, sculpture, digital art, photography, ceramics, glass and original prints. Complete exhibition changes every 9 weeks.
Address: 4 North Street, Lewes BN7 2PA
Phone: 01273 474477
Website: chalkgallerylewes.co.uk
Email: chalkgallerylewes@gmail.com

Cameron Contemporary Art

Shows work from established and emerging British artists. Traditional and modern work from figurative to abstract paintings as well as sculpture, ceramics and jewellery with 8 exhibitions a year.

Address: 1 Victoria Grove, Hove BN3 2LJ

Phone: 01273 727234

Website: cameroncontemporaryart.com

Email: info@cameroncontemporary.com

Towner Art Gallery

Founded in 1923, the gallery has 160,000 visitors each year exhibiting historic, modern and contemporary art, with talks, events and creative activities. The gallery has an extensive collection of modern British art and a growing collection of international contemporary art.

Address: Devonshire Park, College Road, Eastbourne BN21 4JJ

Phone: 01323 434670

Website: townereastbourne.org.uk

Email: towner@townereastbourne.org.uk

Twitter.com/Townergallery

Facebook.com/townergallery

Instagram.com/townergallery

Cameron Contemporary Art

Established and emerging work from British artists, ranging from traditional to modern, figurative to abstract as well as sculpture, ceramics and jewellery. With 8 exhibitions a year, talks and theatre.

Address: 1 Victoria Grove, Hove BN3 2LJ

Phone: 01273 727234

Website: cameroncontemporaryart.com

Email: info@cameroncontemporary.com

Twitter.com/Cameronart10

Facebook.com/cameroncontemporary

Instagram.com/cameroncontemporary

Tracey McNee Fine Art

Building an in-depth relationship with their artists, both from the UK and carefully selected international artists from the USA, South Africa and Europe.

Address: Strange Tracey, Restharrow, Moat Lane, Sedlescombe, East Sussex. TN33 0RZ

Phone: 01424 751022 / 07950335737

Website: traceymcnee.com

Email: art@strangetracey.com

Twitter.com/StrangeTracey_

Facebook.com/strangetraceyuk

Instagram.com/strangetracey

Brighton
The ONCA Gallery

Located in Brighton, an arts charity, bridging social and environmental justice issues with creativity.

Address: 14 St Georges Place, Brighton BN1 4GB

Phone: 01273 607101

Website: onca.org.uk

Email: info@onca.org.uk

Twitter.com/ONCA_arts

Facebook.com/ONCAarts

Instagram.com/onca_arts

YouTube.com/channel/UC3bey1_Xwz05eqVmsHSexOw

SoundCloud.com/onca-arts

Tinyletter.com/onca

Kellie Miller Arts Gallery

Located in the historic Brighton Lanes, exhibiting local, national and international work in sculpture, textured paintings, mixed media and ceramics.

Address: 20 Market Street, Brighton BN1 1HH

Phone: 01273 329384/07803 589 059

Website: kelliemillerarts.com

Email: gallery@kelliemillerarts.com

Twitter.com/ArtyKellie

Facebook.com/KellieMillerArts

Instagram.com/kelliemillerarts

Pinterest.co.uk/ArtyKellie

Artrepublic

Online gallery with world-famous names such as Damien Hirst, Tracey Emin and

Banksy as well as up and coming artists, each handpicked by the artrepublic team.
Address: 12A, Bond Street, The Lanes, Brighton BN1 1RD
Phone: 01273 724829
Website: artrepublic.com
Email: hello@artrepublic.com
Twitter.com/artrepublic
Facebook.com/artrepublic.online
Instagram.com/artrepublic
Pinterest.co.uk/artrepublic

Two Kats & A Cow Gallery

The gallery started in 2001, when 3 painters took a studio in the Brighton beach, Victorian seafront arches. Five years later, having successfully exhibited throughout the UK and abroad, they decided to turn this studio into a gallery. Also showing the work of acclaimed silkscreen printers, the best UK jewellers, ceramics and sculptors, becoming a key destination for Brighton's visitors.
Address: 167 Kings Road Arches, Brighton BN1 1NB
Phone: 01273 776746
Website: twokatsandacow.co.uk
Email: info@twokatsandacow.co.uk
Twitter.com/twokatsandacow
Facebook.com/twokatsandacow
Instagram.com/twokatsandacow

Zorian Artworks

Artwork inspired by the natural landscape, human influence on it and worldwide travels. Using vivid colours and detail, with a strong sense of atmosphere.
Address: 246 Kings Road Arches, Brighton BN1 1NB
Phone: 07876 580198
Website: zorianartworks.com
Email: info@zorianartworks.com
Facebook.com/zorianartworks

Fabrica Gallery

A visual arts organisation based in a former Regency church in the heart of Brighton. Commissions contemporary visual art installations specific to the church with a program of educational activities allowing greater access, engagement and understanding.
Address: 40 Duke Street, Brighton BN1 1AG
Phone: 01273 778646
Website: fabrica.org.uk
Email: office@fabrica.org.uk
Twitter.com/fabricagallery
Facebook.com/FabricaGallery
Instagram.com/fabricagallery

Sallis Benney Theatre

Part of the University of Brighton. Hosts a wide range of events in unique spaces designed for visual and performing art.
Address: 58-67 Grand Pde, Brighton BN2 0JY
Phone: 01273 643010
Website: arts.brighton.ac.uk
Email: communityrelations@brighton.ac.uk.
humanresources@brighton.ac.uk
Facebook.com/sallisbenney

Brighton Museum & Art Gallery

Located in the Royal Pavilion garden, bringing together the arts and history, revealing stories about the city and the world.
Address: Royal Pavilion Gardens, Brighton BN1 1EE
Phone: 0300 029 0900
Website: brightonmuseums.org.uk
Email: museums.marketing@brighton-hove.gov.uk
Twitter.com/brightonmuseums
Facebook.com/royalpavilionandbrightonmuseums
YouTube.com/user/BrightonMuseums

Daniel Laurence Home & Garden

Unique, original art with an eclectic mix of accessories, furniture and gifts. Set in the Artists' Quarter of the Kings Road Arches.
Address: 226 Kings Road Arches Lower Seafront Promenade, Brighton BN1 1NB
Phone: 01273 739694
Website: daniellaurence.co.uk
Email: info@daniellaurence.co.uk
Twitter.com/daniel_laurence
Facebook.com/
DanielLaurenceHomeAndGarden
Instagram.com/daniel_laurence_home_garden

Prescription Art

Prescription Art has been sourcing the best Street Art, Graffiti Art and Contemporary Art since 2007.
Address: 83 London Road, Brighton BN1 4JF
Phone: 07941 385715
Website: prescriptionart.com
Email: james@prescriptionart.com
Twitter.com/prescriptionart
Facebook.com/prescriptionart
Instagram.com/prescriptionart

Art5 Gallery

Original painting, ceramics, limited edition prints, architectural art, textiles and recycled ocean glass art.
Address: 5 Bartholomews, Brighton BN1 1HG
Phone: 01273 774222
Website: art5gallery.com
Email: info@art5gallery.com
Twitter.com/artatfive
Facebook.com/artatfive
Instagram.com/art5_gallery
YouTube.com/channel/
UCdLOv2khlRHGL4DmzTmVxRg

Crane Kalman Brighton

Founded in 2005, specialises in contemporary, British photography, showing up and coming young British and some international artists. Solo exhibitions for established photographers, from the UK and abroad. Affiliated to the Crane Kalman gallery in London, which specialises in modern British painters such as Graham Sutherland, Ben Nicholson, L.S. Lowry and Henry Moore.
Address: 38 Kensington Gardens, North Laine, Brighton BN1 4AL
Phone: 01273 697096 / 07775 927143
Website: cranekalmanbrighton.com
Email: enquiries@cranekalmanbrighton.com
Twitter.com/ckbgallery
Facebook.com/Cranekalmanbrighton

Castle Galleries

Showing international art. Open to emerging artists.
Address: 2 Nile Pavilions, Nile Street, The Lanes, Brighton BN1 1HW
Phone: 01273 761495
Website: castlefineart.com
Email: artreview@washingtongreen.co.uk
Twitter.com/castlegalleries
Facebook.com/castlegalleries
Instagram.com/castlegalleries
Pinterest.co.uk/castlegalleries
YouTube.com/castlegalleries

Caia Matheson Visual Artist

The studio of award winning contemporary artist. Oil on canvas and original prints.
Address: 25 Ditchling Rise, Brighton BN1 4QL
Phone: 07961 405351
Website: caiamatheson.com
Email: studio@caiamatheson.com
Twitter.com/CaiaMatheson
Facebook.com/CaiaMathesonArtist
Instagram.com/caiamathesonart

West Sussex

Arundel Contemporary

Promoting contemporary British and international artists. Two exhibition spaces in a historic Grade II listed building, with a blue plaque. Oil and acrylic painting, mixed media, drawings, limited edition prints, etchings, digital art and ceramics. 5-7 annual exhibitions.
Address: 53 High Street, Arundel BN18 9AJ
Phone: 01903 885309
Website: arundelcontemporary.com
Instagram.com/arundelcontemporary

Forest Gallery

Contemporary art from the UK and abroad, representing hundreds of artists over the years, both established and emerging.
Address: Lombard Street, Petworth GU28 0AG
Phone: 01798 368181
Website: forestgallery.com
Email: sales@forestgallery.com
Twitter.com/forestgalleryuk
Facebook.com/ForestGalleryFineArt
Instagram.com/ForestGalleryFineArt
Pinterest.co.uk/forestgalleryuk

Nifty Art Gallery

The working studio of Nigel Emery, who paints the rolling hills of the South Downs and the coastal towns of Sussex, using bright colours and geometric form in acrylic and mixed media on canvas.
Address: 48 High Street, Storrington RH20 4DU
Phone: 01903 745770
Website: niftygallery.com
Facebook.com/niftygallery
Instagram.com/nigel_emery

Zimmer Stewart Gallery

6-8 exhibitions annually, showing contemporary paintings, ceramic and sculpture.
Address: 29 Tarrant Street, Arundel BN18 9DG
Phone: 01903 882063
Website: zimmerstewart.co.uk
Email: james@zimmerstewart.co.uk
Twitter.com/zimmerstewart
Instagram.com/zimmerstewart
Pinterest.co.uk/zimmerstewart

Worthing Museum And Art Gallery

Presenting a year-round program of film, theatre and art, exhibition, dance, music and circus. The 3rd largest annual festival of contemporary circus in Europe.
Address: Chapel Road, Worthing BN11 1HP
Phone: 01903 221448
Website: worthingmuseum.co.uk
Email: museum@wtam.uk

Brett Gallery

A collaborative approach with photographers bringing together unique exhibitions of their work.
Address: 2-3 West Street, Midhurst GU29 9NF
Phone: 01730 601532
Website: brettgallery.com
Email: enquiries@brettgallery.com
Twitter.com/TheBrettGallery
Facebook.com/thebrettgallery
Instagram.com/thebrettgallery

Moncrieff-Bray Gallery

Set in a once derelict farmyard in the South Downs National Park with 3-acre landscaped garden, showing emerging and established artists and sculptors from the UK and abroad. Has successfully nourished the careers of many artists.
Address: Woodruffs Farm, Woodruffs Farm, Egdean, Petworth RH20 1JX
Phone: 07867 978414

Website: moncrieff-bray.com
Email: mail@moncrieff-bray.com
Twitter.com/Moncrieff_Bray
Facebook.com/moncbraygallery
Instagram.com/moncrieffbray

Shoreline Gallery

Showing the work of artist Hettie Pittman, along with beautiful interior design products.
Address: 61 Rowlands Road, Worthing BN11 3JN
Phone: 07527 926179
Website: shorelinegallery.co.uk
Email: shorelinegallery@hotmail.co.uk
Facebook.com/shorelinegallery
Instagram.com/shorelinegallery

Gallery57

Set in a Grade II listed house in Arundel, showing contemporary art and crafts by emerging and established artists.
Address: 57 Tarrant Street, Arundel BN18 9DJ
Phone: 01903 885323
Website: gallery57.co.uk
Email: enquiries@gallery57.co.uk
Twitter.com/gallery57art
Facebook.com/gallery57arundel
Instagram.com/gallery57_arundel

Montague Gallery

Original, affordable work bought directly from talented local artists.
Address: Alexander Terrace, Worthing BN11 1YJ
Phone: 07894 037877
Website: montaguegallery.co.uk
Email: info@montaguegallery.co.uk
Facebook.com/gallerymontague
Instagram.com/gallerymontague

West End Gallery

Contemporary art gallery and studios.
Address: 87 Rowlands Road, Worthing BN11 3JX

Phone: 07734 348569
Website: worthingartstudios.com
Email: info@worthingartstudios.com

Chichester
Candida Stevens Gallery

Exploring important themes through exhibition of work by the best emerging and established artists in the UK.
Address: 12 Northgate, Chichester PO19 1BA
Phone: 0379 087 5744
Website: candidastevens.com
Email: cs@candidastevens.com
Twitter.com/Candida_Stevens
Facebook.com/CandidaStevensGallery
Instagram.com/candida_stevens
Artsy.net/candida-stevens

Whitewall Galleries

Whitewall Galleries have over 40 galleries in the UK showing paintings and sculptures from internationally acclaimed artists as well as the best of emerging talent.
Address: 36A East Street, Chichester PO19 1HS
Phone: 01243 531495
Website: whitewallgalleries.com
Email: chichester@whitewallgalleries.com

Oxmarket Centre Of Arts

A charity promoting art through exhibition, societies and groups, both locally and nationally. With many exhibitions each year and 30,000 visitors. Housed in a Grade II listed, medieval church in the heart of Chichester.
Address: East Street, Chichester PO19 1YH
Phone: 01243 779103
Website: oxmarket.com
Email: info@oxmarket.com
Twitter.com/oxmarketgallery
Facebook.com/oxmarketgallery
Instagram.com/oxmarketgallery

Rutland

Woodbine Contemporary Arts

Established in 1997, showing contemporary original art by emerging and established makers.
Address: 7 Orange Street, Uppingham LE15 9SQ
Phone: 01406 330693
Website: woodbinecontemporaryarts.co.uk
Email: yorath@woodbinecontemporaryarts.co.uk

Samuel Robson Fine Art

Specialising in the sale of modern British art from the 20th and 21st century.
Address: 53 Deans Street, Oakham LE15 6AF
Phone: 07894 086836
Website: samuelrobsonfineart.com
Email: sam@samuelrobsonfineart.com
Instagram.com/samuelrobsonfa

Trent Galleries

Contemporary fine art from a diverse portfolio of award-winning artists.
Address: 11 Mill Street, Oakham LE15 6EA
Phone: 01572 722790
Website: trentgalleries.co.uk
Email: oakham@trentgalleries.co.uk
Twitter.com/TrentGalleries
Facebook.com/trentgallerynewark
Instagram.com/trent_galleries

Shropshire

Shrewsbury Museum and Art Gallery

Owned and run by Shropshire Council, located in a 13th century mansion.
Address: The Square, Shrewsbury, Shropshire SY1 1LH
Phone: 01743 258885
Website: shrewsburymuseum.org.uk
Email: shrewsburymuseum@shropshire.gov.uk
Facebook.com/shrewsburymuseum

Van Gallery

A charity promoting visual art in Shropshire, linking artists, designers, makers, galleries and buyers. Welcoming all artisans.
Address: 45-46 Gallery Stalls, Shrewsbury Market Hall, Claremont Road, Shewsbury SY1 1QG
Phone: 01743 344906
Website: visualArtnetwork.org.uk
Email: admin@visualArtnetwork.org.uk

Twenty Twenty Gallery

Specialising in the best of British art and crafts with regular exhibitions.
Address: 4 Quality Square, Ludlow, Shropshire. UK SY8 1AR.
Phone: 01584 875363
Website: twenty-twenty.co.uk
Twitter.com/2020Gallery
Facebook.com/twentytwentygallery
Instagram.com/twentytwentygallery

Shropshire Sculpture Park

Sculpture park featuring sculpture from across the UK. 2 showrooms with national art and unique products for the home and garden. Resident silversmith.
Address: Aston Way British Ironworks Centre, Oswestry SY11 4JH
Phone: +44 800 688 8386
Website: britishironworkcentre.co.uk
Email: info@britishironworkcentre.co.uk
Twitter.com/BritishIronwork
Facebook.com/TheBritishIronworkCentre
Instagram.com/britishironworkcentre
YouTube.com/user/BritishIronwork

Jerwood Limited

Jerwood is a group of philanthropic organisations which support visual and performing arts in the UK, especially those at an early stage in their career.
Address: PO Box 186, Ludlow SY8 9DX

Phone: 02077921410
Website: jerwood.org
Email: jerwood@jerwood.org

The Willow Gallery

Contemporary art from local and international artists. Workshops, talks, live music, events and exhibitions. Craft shop and café.
Address: 56 Willow Street, Oswestry SY11 1AD England
Phone: +44 1691 657575
Website: willowgalleryoswestry.org
Email: willowgalleryoswestry@gmail.com
Twitter.com/willow_oswestry
Facebook.com/willowgalleryoswestry
Instagram.com/willowgalleryoswestry

The Soden Collection

An eclectic mix of contemporary art and sculpture. Well-established local art with renowned British and international artists, such as Hockney, Miro, Lowry, Picasso and many others. Sculpture garden.
Address: 80 Wyle Cop, Shrewsbury SY1 1UT England
Phone: 01743 341400
Website: sodencollection.com
Email: gallery@sodencollection.com
Twitter.com/sodencollection
Instagram.com/sodencollection

The Angel Gallery

Emerging, mid-career and senior artists, from both home and abroad.
Address: 17 High Street, Broseley, Telford TF12 5HE
Phone: 07808 767972
Website: theangelgallery.co.uk
Email: mikeann@theangelgallery.co.uk
Instagram.com/theangelgallery
Twitter.com/gallery_angel
Facebook.com/AngelGalleryBroseley

Somerset

Churchgate Gallery

Situated in the picturesque village of Porlock, which has been an inspiration for many artists, poets, writers and photographers. Showing a wide selection of work by local and established UK artists, including painting in all mediums, sculpture, jewellery, ceramics, cards and books
Address: High Street Porlock, Minehead TA24 8PT
Phone: 01643 862238
Website: churchgategallery.co.uk
Email: churchgategallery@live.co.uk

West Country Galleries

An online gallery selling beautiful art, contemporary, abstract, seascapes, landscapes, floral work, big art, textiles and photography by talented artists.
Website: westcountrygalleries.co.uk
Email: hilary@westcountrygalleries.co.uk
Facebook.com/wcgalleries
Instagram.com/wcgalleries
Pinterest.co.uk/wcgpin

Tacchi-Morris Art Centre

A multi-purpose community space. State-of-the-art facilities. Theatre, dance and music, with 8 art exhibitions a year:
Address: School Road, Taunton TA2 8PD
Phone: 01823 414144
Website: tacchi-morris.com
Email: info@tacchi-morris.com
Twitter.com/TMAC_Taunton
Facebook.com/TacchiMorrisArtsCentre

Shakespeare Glass Works

Glass-blower, Will Shakespeare, works across the UK and Central and South America. Featured regularly in the press and on TV.
Address: 6 St. James Street, Taunton TA1 1JJ

Phone: 01823 333422
Website: shakspeareglass.co.uk
Email: sales@shakspeareglass.co.uk
Twitter.com/ShakspeareGlass
Facebook.com/shakspeareglass
Instagram.com/shakspeareglass

Bath
Victoria Art Gallery

Bath's public art museum, with a collection of over 1,500 paintings, sculptures and decorative arts in a Grade II Listed building designed in 1897.
Address: Bridge Street, Bath BA2 4AT
Phone: 01225 477233
Website: victoriagal.org.uk
Email: victoria_enquiries@bathnes.gov.uk

Beaux Arts

The longest established commercial gallery in Bath. Sister gallery to Beaux Arts in Maddox Street, London. Specialises in major 20th century painters, sculptors and ceramicists. 8 annual exhibitions, 4 of these are dedicated to emerging artists.
Address: 12-13 York Street, Bath BA1 1NG
Phone: 01225 464850
Email: info@beauxartsbath.co.uk
Twitter.com/Beauxartsbath
Facebook.com/beauxartsbath
Instagram.com/beaux_arts_bath
Pinterest.co.uk/beauxartsbath

David Simon Contemporary

Contemporary art gallery with British painting, original prints, sculpture, ceramics and glass in a historic market town. Emerging and established artists.
Address: 37 High Street, Castle Cary, Somerset, BA7 7AW
Phone: 01963 359102
Website: davidsimoncontemporary.com
Email: gallery@davidsimoncontemporary.com
Instagram.com/visitcastlecary

Rostra Gallery

Contemporary art by emerging and established artists, specialising in limited edition prints, original paintings, sculpture, ceramics, craft, papercut and artisan jewellery with bespoke framing.
Address: 17 Margarets Buildings, Ground Floor, Bath BA1 2LP
Website: rostragallery.co.uk
Phone: 01225 448121
Email: info@rostragallery.co.uk
Twitter.com/rostragallery
Facebook.com/RostraGallery
Instagram.com/rostragallery

Wells
A2 Gallery

Contemporary art for all tastes from artists in the UK, USA and NZ. Diverse media including oil, watercolour, mixed media and acrylic paintings; bronze, resin, ceramic, wood and mixed media sculpture; etching, screen-printing, collagraph, woodcut and linocut printmaking; decorative and functional ceramics to photography, woodturning, glass, jewellery, enamelling, mixed media, craft and greeting cards.
Address: 80 High Street, Wells BA5 2AJ
Phone: 01749 674849
Website: a2gallery.co.uk
Email: info@a2gallery.co.uk
Twitter.com/A2Gallery
Facebook.com/a2gallery.wells
Instagram.com/a2_gallery_wells

Staffordshire
Shire Hall Gallery

Public building completed in 1798. The gallery is located in the Great Hall, with a large temporary exhibition space and a Crafts Council shop. Exhibits local, regional and national works as well as showing the County's Art and Craft Collection.

Address: Market Square, Stafford ST16 2LD
Phone: 01785 278345
Website: staffordshire.gov.uk/shirehall
Email: shirehallgallery@staffordshire.gov.uk

Stoke on Trent
Barewall Art Gallery

British fine art and ceramics. Based in the historic Burslem, the mother town of ceramics. British studio pottery and hand-painted pottery from leading UK potters. Signed limited edition prints. Framing and restoration.
Address: 2-4 Market Place, Burslem, Stoke-On-Trent ST6 4AT
Phone: 01782 258843 / 07932 717 718
Website: barewall.co.uk
Email: shop@barewall.co.uk
Twitter.com/barewall
Facebook.com/barewallltd

Trent Art Gallery

Original paintings and work on paper from a wide range of modern British artists.
Address: 3 Church Lane, Bowers, Stafford ST21 6RW
Phone: 01782 631010
Website: trent-art.co.uk
Email: art@trent-art.co.uk
Twitter.com/trentartgallery
Facebook.com/trentartgallery

Lichfield
Whitewall Galleries

Whitewall Galleries have over 40 galleries in the UK showing paintings and sculptures from internationally acclaimed artists as well as the best of emerging talent.
Address: Demontfort House Europa Way, Lichfield WS14 9NW
Phone: 01543 887336
Website: whitewallgalleries.com
Email: lichfield@whitewallgalleries.com

Wolverhampton
Wolverhampton Art Gallery

300 years of art with exhibitions and permanent galleries. From 18th century masters to thought-provoking contemporary work including painting, sculpture, drawing, photography, multi-media and more. Café and gallery shop.
Address: Lichfield Street, Wolverhampton WV1 1DU
Phone: 01902 552055
Website: wolverhamptonart.org.uk
Email: art.gallery@wolverhampton.gov.uk
Twitter.com/WolvArtGallery
Facebook.com/WolverhamptonArtGallery
Instagram.com/wolvesartandculture

The New Art Gallery Walsall

Modern and contemporary gallery with solo and group shows reflecting the diversity of contemporary practice. Also with a space dedicated to regional artists.
Address: Gallery Square, Walsall WS2 8LG
Phone: 01922 654400
Website: thenewartgallerywalsall.org.uk
Email: info@thenewartgallerywalsall.org.uk
Twitter.com/newartgallery
Facebook.com/newartgallerywalsall
Instagram.com/explore/
locations/344296656
Pinterest.co.uk/NAGEducation
YouTube.com/user/newartgallerywalsall

Fine Art Shopper

Contemporary art online
Address: 85 Worcester Street, Wolverhampton WV2 4LE
Phone: 01902 717775
Website: fineartshopper.co.uk
Email: sales@fineartshopper.co.uk

Suffolk

The Lion House Gallery

Original paintings, ceramics, prints, jewellery and cards from regional and national artists
Address: 12 High Street, Lavenham CO10 9PR
Phone: 01787 249616
Website: lionhousegallery.co.uk
Email: lionhousegallery@btinternet.com
Facebook.com/pages/category/Gift-Shop/The-Lion-House-Gallery-Lavenham
Instagram.com/explore/locations/1015972355/the-lion-house-gallery-lavenham

The Jessica Muir Gallery

Artist-led gallery in Long Melford showing original arts and crafts from across the UK.
Address: Hall Street, Sudbury CO10 9JR
Phone: 01787 310400
Facebook.com/TheJessicaMuirGallery

Gallery East

Established and emerging artists; painters, sculptors and ceramicists from across the UK, with an emphasis on regional and women artists.
Address: 24, Church Street, Woodbridge IP12 1DH
Website: galleryeast.co.uk
Phone: 07836 325497
Email: team@galleryeast.co.uk
Instagram.com/galleryeastwoodbridge

Wildlife Art Gallery

Online gallery specialising in contemporary and 20th century wildlife paintings and prints.
Address: 98-99 High St, Lavenham CO10 9PZ
Phone: 01787 248562
Website: wildlifeartgallery.com
Email: wildlifeartgallery@btinternet.com

Lime Tree Gallery

Specialising in contemporary fine art and glass, with regular exhibitions, each with a web catalogue. Particular emphasis on contemporary Scottish artists. Glass mainly from Britain and Sweden.
Address: Hall Street, Long Melford CO10 9JF
Phone: 01787 319046
Website: limetreegallery.com
Phone: 0178 731 9046

Lavenham Contemporary

Showcasing the work of Paul Evans, landscape painter with 45 years of experience with over 65 solo exhibitions and numerous group shows. Work in watercolours, etchings and linocuts of East Anglia, the Sussex Downs, Kent Weald and Cornish coast with over 500 images used commercially for cards and calendars. Worldwide collectors.
Address: 70-71 High Street, Sudbury CO10 9PT
Phone: 01787 249451
Website: paulevans-artist.co.uk
Phone: 01787 249616
Email: lavenhamgallery@btconnect.com

Woodbridge Art Club Gallery

The club was formed in 1968, with the gallery opening in 1975. Work is shown from its 150 members, many of whom are practising artists.
Address: 15 Tide Mill Way, Woodbridge IP12 1BY
Phone: 07704 078261
Website: woodbridgeartclub.org.uk
Facebook.com/woodbridgeartclub
Instagram.com/woodbridgeartclub

Warwickshire

Montpellier Gallery

Established in 1989, one of the longest established retail craft galleries. Some of the finest studio glass, contemporary jewellery and ceramics, fine art and sculpture from all over the UK.
Address: 8 Chapel St, Stratford Upon Avon CV37 6EP
Phone: 01789 261161
Website: montpelliergallery.com
Email: info@montpelliergallery.com

Reload Gallery

Contemporary and urban art from around the world.
Address: 40 Warwick Street, Leamington Spa CV32 5JS
Phone: 01926 429229
Website: reloadgallery.com
Twitter.com/ReloadGallery
Facebook.com/reloadgallery
Instagram.com/reloadgallery

Warwick Gallery

Online gallery selling work from established and emerging British artists, including paintings, sculpture, ceramics, tableware, greeting cards and mugs.
Address: 116 Regent Street, Leamington Spa CV32 4NR
Phone: 01926 339966
Website: art-is-a-tart.com
Email: sales@art-is-a-tart.com

A E Contemporary Art

Online gallery representing local and international award-winning artists with a collection of modern British artists such as Sir Terry Frost and Mary Fedden. Contemporary art by Damien Hirst, Tracey Emin etc.
Address: Radio House, Swan Street,
Warwick CV34 4BJ
Phone: 01926 495506
Website: aecontemporaryart.co.uk
Email: info@aecontemporaryart.co.uk

Snap Galleries

Celebrating all aspects of popular culture, with a special emphasis on iconic music photography.
Address: 50 Warwick Street, Leamington Spa CV32 5JS
Phone: 020 7493 1152
Website: snapgalleries.com
Email: info@snapgalleries.com
Facebook.com/SnapGalleriesUK

Nuneaton Museum and Art Gallery

Located in the beautiful grounds of Riversley Park, offering exhibitions, events and activities with permanent shows of local history, fine art and local writer George Eliot.
Address: Riversley Park, Nuneaton CV11 5TU
Phone: 024 7637 6158
Website: nuneatonandbedworth.gov.uk

Coventry

Herbert Art Gallery & Museum

Celebrating the city's culture, history and arts.
Address: Jordan Well, Coventry CV1 5QP
Phone: 024 7623 7521
Website: theherbert.org
Email: info@culturecoventry.com
Twitter.com/The_Herbert
Facebook.com/theherbert
Instagram.com/the_herbert_cov
YouTube.com/user/HerbertArtMus

Mead Gallery

One of the largest multi-artform venues in the UK, with an engaging and diverse program of performing and visual arts in world-class venues in the University of

Warwick campus acting on a national and international level.
Address: University Of Warwick, Coventry CV4 7AL
Phone: 024 7652 4524
Website: meadgallery.co.uk
Email: arts.centre@warwick.ac.uk
Twitter.com/warwickarts
Facebook.com/WarwickArtsCentre
Instagram.com/warwickarts

West Midlands

Birmingham

Artifex Gallery

A stunning gallery selling the best in contemporary British art and craft with a UK -wide client base.
Address: The Mitchell Centre, The Royal Town Of Sutton Coldfield B75 6NA
Phone: 0121 323 3776
Website: artifex-gallery.blogspot.co.uk
Email: sales@artifex.co.uk
Facebook.com/artandcraftartifex

Ikon Gallery

Internationally acclaimed art gallery set in a neo-gothic school building, working as an educational charity to encourage public engagement with contemporary art. Featuring artists from around the world in a variety of media including sounds, film, mixed media, photography, painting, sculpture and installation. Developing challenging projects outside the gallery as well as educational talks, tours, workshops and seminars.
Address: 1 Oozells Square, Brindleyplace, Birmingham B1 2HS
Phone: 0121 248 0708
Website: ikon-gallery.org
Twitter.com/ikongallery
Facebook.com/ikongallery
Instagram.com/ikongallery
YouTube.com/user/IkonGallery

Birmingham Museums & Art Gallery

Opening in 1885, situated in a Grade II listed building in the city centre, with over 40 galleries showing art, applied art, social history, archaeology and ethnography, with major work from modern British artists. In addition to these permanent galleries, there is also a diverse exhibition program changing throughout the year.
Address: Chamberlain Square, Birmingham B3 3DH
Phone: 0121 348 8000
www.birminghammuseums.org.uk
Email: enquiries@birminghammuseums.org.uk
Facebook.com/ birminghammuseums.org.uk

Barber Institute Of Fine Arts

Monet, Manet, Magritte; Renoir, Rubens, Rossetti, Rodin; Degas, Delacroix, Van Dyck. The list goes on. Free entry with talks, workshops and family activities.
Address: University Of Birmingham, Edgbaston, Birmingham B15 2TS
Phone: 0121 414 7333
Website: barber.org.uk

RBSA Gallery

The Royal Birmingham Society of Artists is an artist-led charity promoting visual arts through exhibitions, events and workshops. Set in the historic Jewellery Quarter of Birmingham, the shop sells contemporary craft by regional and national makers.
Address: 4 Brook Street, Birmingham B3 1SA
Phone: 0121 236 4353
Website: rbsa.org.uk
Email: rbsagallery@rbsa.org.uk
Twitter.com/rbsagallery
Facebook.com/rbsagallery
Instagram.com/rbsagallery
Flickr.com/photos/rbsa-gallery
Vimeo.com/user52891443

MAC

Founded in 1962, Midlands Arts Centre is a pioneering arts complex for everyone, aiming to make art an important part of people's lives. 1 million visitors a year, from the UK and abroad. Specialising in contemporary work, such as theatre, dance, independent cinema, exhibition and events, classes and workshops. Recognised nationally for their work with children, families and young people from all backgrounds. Also supporting emerging and mid-career artists.
Address: Cannon Hill Park, Birmingham B12 9QH
Phone: 0121 446 3232
Website: macbirmingham.co.uk
Twitter.com/mac_birmingham
Facebook.com/macbirmingham
Instagram.com/mac_birmingham

Sara Preisler Gallery

With many years in business, Sara Preisler is a multi-award winning jewellery and product designer. Her gallery sells her own work as well as the very best of British contemporary jewellery.
Address: The Custard Factory, 7 Gibb Street, Birmingham B9 4BF
Phone: 0121 794 0205
Website: sarapreislergallery.co.uk
Email: admin@sarapreislergallery.co.uk
Twitter.com/SaraPreisler
Facebook.com/sara.preislergallery
Instagram.com/sarapreisler
LinkedIn.com/in/sara-preisler

St. Pauls Gallery

The world's leading retailer of signed limited edition album cover fine art. With more than 100 signed prints on permanent show as well as signed portrait photographs. Rare fine art prints and originals by world renowned artists, such as Andy Warhol, Picasso, Bridget Riley and Salvador Dali.
Address: 94-108 Northwood Street Jewellery Quarters, Birmingham B3 1TH
Phone: 0121 236 5800
Website: stpaulsgallery.com
Email: info@stpaulsgallery.com
Facebook.com/stpaulsgallery
Instagram.com/stpaulsgallery

The Birmingham Contemporary Art Gallery

Allowing creativity to surface and realising the potential in those who have barriers to getting their work seen. A diverse range of emerging and established artists, especially those underrepresented. Grassroots approach with art and music wellbeing programs.
Address: Unit 5 Arena King Edwards Road, Birmingham B1 2AA
Phone: 0121 769 0966
Website: birmingham-cag.uk
Email: info@birmingham-cag.uk
Twitter.com/thebcag
Facebook.com/The-Birmingham-Contemporary-Art-Gallery
Instagram.com/thebcag
LinkedIn.com/company/the-birmingham-contemporary-art-gallery

Wiltshire

Bradford Gallery

Paintings and watercolours, with limited edition sculptures in the historic town of Bradford on Avon.
Address: 15 Station Approach, Bradford on Avon, Wiltshire BA15 1FQ
Phone: 01225 309 335
Website: bradfordgallery.co.uk
Email: art@bradfordgallery.co.uk

Katharine House Gallery

An eclectic mix of affordable paintings, prints, constructions, sculptures and ceramics by Modern British artists.
Address: Katharine House, The Parade,

Marlborough SN8 1NE
Phone: 01672 514040
Website: katharinehousegallery.co.uk
Email: chrisgange.khg@gmail.com

Bluestone Gallery

Established in 2000. One off the leading Galleries in the southwest.
Address: Old Swan Yard 8 High Street, Devizes SN10 1AT
Phone: 01380 729589
Website: bluestonegallery.com
Email: info@bluestonegallery.com

Rabley Drawing Centre

A contemporary art gallery specialising in original prints and work on paper. Established in 2005, incorporating a gallery, printmaking studio and educational rooms in 2 converted Victorian barns with a bespoke viewing room in London. Showing internationally established artists and emerging talent.
Address: Rabley Barn, Mildenhall, Marlborough. SN8 2LW
Phone: 01672 511999
Website: rableydrawingcentre.com
Email: info@rableygallery.com

The Drang Gallery

Contemporary and modern art with galleries in Padstow, Rock, Salcombe and Marlborough
Address: 124 High Street, Marlborough SN8 1LZ
Phone: 01672 513011
Website: thedranggallery.com
Email: Marlborough@thedranggallery.com
Instagram.com/the_drang_gallery

Worcestershire

John Noott Galleries

John Noott has a lifetime's experience in dealing 19th and 20th century paintings including on the major art fairs and working closely with the premier auction houses. By appointment only. The gallery specialises in art, sculpture, ceramics, furniture and glass from internationally regarded British makers as well as talented graduates. Set in a 17th century building with a garden for contemporary sculpture in stone, glass and metal.
Address: 20 High St, Broadway WR12 7AA
Phone: 01386 858969
Website: john-noott.com
Email: gallery@john-noott.com
Twitter.com/JNoott_Gallery
Facebook.com/NoottGalleries

Little Buckland Gallery

Situated in a listed barn, the gallery shows Cotswold, national and international work, with paintings, sculpture, prints, ceramics, jewellery, enamel, glass, photographs and film.
Address: Little Buckland, Broadway WR12 7JH
Phone: 01386 853739
Website: littlebucklandgallery.co.uk
Email: info@littlebucklandgallery.co.uk
Twitter.com/littlebuckland
Facebook.com/artinabarn
Instagram.com/little_buckland_gallery
Pinterest.co.uk/ajkiszely
LinkedIn.com/in/arabella-kiszely-baa12625

Richard Hagen

The gallery, in the beautiful village of Broadway, specialises in original, contemporary British art. By appointment only.
Address: 55/57 High St, Broadway WR12 7DP
Phone: 01386 853624
Website: richardhagen.com
Email: fineart@richardhagen.com

Priory Gallery Broadway

Liz James has worked with 19th-21st century art for over 25 years. She opened the gallery

in 1998 and runs it with her daughter. Several exhibitions a year showing contemporary art and sculpture from established artists who have a large following.
Address: 34 High Street, Broadway WR12 7DT
Phone: 01386 853783
Website: priorybroadway.com
Email: info@priorybroadway.com
Facebook.com/Priory-Gallery-Broadway-185017621634161
Instagram.com/priorygallerybroadway

Callaghan Fine Paintings

Specialising in European 19th and 20th century oils and watercolours as well as contemporary paintings by exciting British and European artists. Bronze sculptures by leading names, and period fine furniture, silver, Italian glass, ceramics and interiors. The gallery exhibits nationally and internationally.
Address: 22 St Mary's Street, Shrewsbury SY1 1ED
Phone: 01743 343452
Website: callaghan-finepaintings.com
Email: art@callaghan-finepaintings.com
Facebook.com/callaghansart

Worcester
The Gallery at Bevere

With 12 years' experience in the gallery, representing over 100 leading ceramicists, encouraging and promoting high level skills and supporting range and diversity in new and emerging talent. Realising the importance of contemporary studio ceramics has on cultural life.
Address: Bevere Lane, Worcester WR3 7RQ
Phone: 01905 754484
Website: beveregallery.com
Twitter.com/Bevereart
Facebook.com/Bevereart
Instagram.com/beveregallery

Greenstage Gallery

Opening in 2005, the gallery showcases local, national and international artists with a flair for originality and colour. With a range of styles of painting and sculpture, and a large exhibition space showing significant bodies of work. Located at a former hop farm, with other independent shops and cafés.
Address: The Hop Pocket, Worcester WR6 5BT
Phone: 01885 490839
Website: greenstagegallery.co.uk
Email: info@greenstagegallery.co.uk
Twitter.com/GreenstageG
Facebook.com/GreenStageGallery
Instagram.com/greenstagegallery

The Kestrel Gallery

Selling a range of original art and craft. Commissions undertaken, bespoke framing.
Address: 103 Sidbury, Worcester WR1 2HU
Phone: 01905 767007
Website: kestrelgalleryandstudio.com
Email: info@kestrelgalleryandstudio.com

Worcester City Art Gallery and Museum

Gallery and online exhibitions of contemporary art. Arts Council funding.
Address: Foregate Street, Worcester WR1 1DT
Phone: 01905 25371
Email: gallerymuseum@ museumsworcestershire.org.uk
Twitter.com/worcestermuseum
Facebook.com/ worcestercityartgalleryandmuseum
Instagram.com/museumsworcestershire

Yorkshire
Zillah Bell Gallery

Leading contemporary art gallery, established in 1988, selling local, national and international artwork. Monthly exhibitions

of emerging and established artists in a wide range of media, from printmaking to painting, ceramics and jewellery including work by Royal Academicians. The largest collection of Norman Ackroyd's etchings in the north of England, which can be purchased from the gallery if still in edition.
Address: 15 Kirkgate, Thirsk YO7 1PQ
Phone: 01845 522479
Website: zillahbellgallery.co.uk
Email: info@zillahbellgallery.co.uk
Twitter.com/ZillahBell
Facebook.com/TheZillahBellGallery
Instagram.com/zillahbellgallery

Art In The Mill

Opened in Knaresborough in 2007. Working with over 250 talented artists. Paintings, prints, cards, sculptures and ceramics by acclaimed local artists.
Address: Green Dragon Yard, Knaresborough HG5 8AU
Phone: 01423 862963
Website: artinthemill.co.uk
Email: mail@artinmill.co.uk
Twitter.com/artinthemill
Facebook.com/artinthemill
Instagram.com/artinthemill

Browns Gallery

Showing well-known UK artists as well as popular local artists. Bespoke picture framing and gifts.
Address: Wesley Street, Otley LS21 1AZ
Phone: 01943 464656
Website: brownsgallery.co.uk
Email: brownsgallery@hotmail.co.uk

Cupola Gallery

Established in 1991, the gallery is known for selling fine art and craft. Showing over 300 works at any given time.
Address: 178-178A Middlewood Road, Sheffield S6 1TD

Phone: 0114 285 2665
Website: cupolagallery.com
Email; info@cupolagallery.com
Instagram.com/cupolacontemporaryart
Pinterest.co.uk/cupolagallery

Wildgoose Gallery

Fine art and gifts in the picturesque village of Fairburn, overlooking the R.S.P.B Fairburn Ings Nature Reserve.
Address: Silver Street, Knottingley WF11 9JA
Phone: 01977 675089
Website: wildgoosegallery.co.uk
Email: enquirieswildgoosegallery@gmail.com
Facebook.com/www.wildgoosegallery.co.uk

The Barefoot Gallery

Online gallery established in 2008, showing carefully selected British and European artists with the aim of discovering exceptional new artists in all medium.
Address: 144 High Street 49 Nook Road, Wetherby LS23 6BW
Phone: 01937 845135
Website: thebarefootgallery.com
Email: info@thebarefootgallery.com
Twitter.com/BarefootGallery
Facebook.com/thebarefootgallery
Instagram.com/the_barefoot_gallery

Post Fine Art

Situated in the old post office, specialising in modern British artists as well as new and emerging artists.
Address: 19 Westgate, Tadcaster LS24 9JB
Phone: 01937 831062
Website: postfineart.co.uk
Twitter.com/postfineart
Facebook.com/postfineart

Rural Arts

Charity running programs and performances enriching lives and connecting communities in North Yorkshire. Based in an arts centre in Thirsk.

Address: 4 Westgate, Thirsk YO7 1QS

Phone: 01845 526536

Website: ruralarts.org

Email: max@ruralarts.org

Twitter.com/ruralarts

Facebook.com/ruralartsnorthyorkshire

Instagram.com/ruralartsthirsk

Pinterest.co.uk/ruralartsthirsk

Trent Galleries

Contemporary fine art from a diverse portfolio of award-winning artists.

Address: 9 Butcher Row, Beverley HU17 0AA

Phone: 01482 874621

Website: trentgalleries.co.uk

Email: beverley@trentgalleries.co.uk

Twitter.com/TrentGalleries

Facebook.com/trentgallerynewark

Instagram.com/trent_galleries

Yorkshire Artspace Society

Established in 1977, providing good, affordable studio space for more than 160 artists and makers. Creating opportunities for the public to connect with the artists and their work.

Address: Persistence Works, 21 Brown Street, Sheffield S1 2BS

Phone: 0114 276 1769

Website: artspace.org.uk

Email: info@artspace.org.uk

Twitter.com/YArtspace

Facebook.com/YorkshireArtspace

Instagram.com/yartspace

Bradford

Impressions Gallery Of Photography

A charity helping people understand the world through photography since 1972. Presenting world-class exhibitions that explore issues such as identity, race, gender and politics as well as historical avant-garde photography. 50,000 visitors each year and 100,000 more seeing the gallery on tour.

Address: Centenary Square, Bradford, BD1 1SD

Phone: 01904 654724

Website: impressions-gallery.com

Email: hello@impressions-gallery.com

Twitter.com/ImpGalleryPhoto

Facebook.com/impressionsgallery

Instagram.com/ImpGalleryPhoto

YouTube.com/user/ImpressionsGallery

Fuse Art Space

Gallery, art space, performance venue and shop with exhibitions, artist talks, film screenings, workshops and performances and concerts featuring international music.

Address: 5-7 Rawson Pl, Bradford BD1 3QQ

Phone: 01274 730926

Website: wearefuse.co

Email: hello@wearefuse.co

Cartwright Hall Art Gallery

A leading regional art gallery in the UK in the picturesque Lister Park with a permanent collection and curated exhibitions, working with partners such as the National Portrait Gallery, V&A, Museum of Childhood and other national and international venues. Workshops and events.

Address: N Park Road, Bradford BD9 4NS

Phone: 01274 431212

Website: bradfordmuseums.org/venues/ cartwright-hall-art-gallery

Facebook.com/bradfordmuseums

Instagram.com/bradfordmuseums

Flickr.com/groups/bradfordmuseums

South Square Centre

Situated in 19th century cottages in the village of Thornton, renowned for the Bronte sisters and its 20-arch viaduct, it now hosts studios for ten artists as well as a gallery, community

spaces, archive, fine art framers, bar and café with events and workshops.
Address: South Square Centre South Square, Bradford BD13 3LD
Phone: 01274 834747
Website: southsquarecentre.co.uk
Email: info@southsquarecentre.co.uk

Rogue Gallery

Online gallery showcasing collectable urban contemporary art.
Address: 907 Harrogate Rd, Bradford BD10 0QY
Phone: 07917 773989
Website: vandalart.co.uk
Email: info@vandalart.co.uk
Twitter.com/rourkevandal
Facebook.com/rourke.vandal

Harrogate
Silson Contemporary

Exciting, independent art gallery, opened in 2016. Emerging and established artists from Yorkshire and the rest of the UK with contemporary painting, illustration, ceramics and sculpture.
Address: 17 Harlow Oval, Harrogate HG2 0DS
Phone: 07940 742029
Website: silsoncontemporaryart.co.uk
Email: sarah@silsoncontemporaryart.co.uk
Facebook.com/silsoncontemporary
Instagram.com/silsoncontemporary

Walker Galleries

19th and 20th century English and European paintings and watercolours. Ceramics and sculpture. Monthly exhibitions.
Address: 13 Montpellier Parade, Harrogate HG1 2TJ
Phone: 01423 526366
Website: walkergalleries.co.uk
Email: walkergalleries@gmail.com
Twitter.com/walkergalleries

Sutcliffe Galleries

19th and 20th century paintings as well as contemporary work; paintings, signed limited edition prints, sculpture and studio glass.
Address: 6 Montpellier Street, Harrogate HG1 2TQ
Phone: 01423 562976
Website: sutcliffegalleries.co.uk
Email: info@sutcliffegalleries.com

Watermark Gallery

Specialising in works on paper and paper conservation. Also ceramics, jewellery, sculpture and textiles, modern British prints and original illustration from children's books from artists across the UK.
Address: Burnside Wormald Green, Harrogate HG3 3PS
Phone: 01765 570038
Website: watermarkgallery.co.uk
Email: info@watermarkgallery.co.uk
Twitter.com/art_watermark
Facebook.com/gallerywatermark
Instagram.com/watermarkgallery

Whitewall Galleries Harrogate

Whitewall Galleries have over 40 galleries in the UK showing paintings and sculptures from internationally acclaimed artists as well as the best of emerging talent.
Address: 1A James Street, Harrogate Yorkshire HG1 1QS
Phone: 01423 740042
Website: whitewallgalleries.com
Email: clientservices@demontfortfineart.co.uk

Kingston upon Hull
Ferens Art Gallery

After a £5.1 million refurbishment, the gallery reopened in 2017, when Hull was UK City of Culture. Internationally renowned permanent collections and vibrant temporary exhibitions, from the medieval period to the

present day. Education and events program.
Address: Hull Culture & Leisure, Queen
Victoria Square, Hull HU1 3RA
Phone: 01482 300300
Website: hullcc.gov.uk
Email: museums@hcandl.co.uk

Modern & Contemporary Art

Framed modern and contemporary art by
20th century artists such as Sir Terry Frost,
Sandra Blow, Sir Howard Hodgkin and
Victor Pasmore.
Address: 26 Farlington Close, Bilton Grange,
Hull HU9 4AT
Phone: 07870 896625
Website: gallery17.co.uk
Email: lamb@gallery17.co.uk

Kingston Art Group

An artistic community providing studio
space for a variety of fine artists.
Address: 1st & 2nd Floors, 91 Barmston St,
Hull HU2 0PJ
Phone: 01482 215177
Website: kingstonartgroup.co.uk
Email: kingstonartgroup@gmail.com
Twitter.com/kingstonart
Facebook.com/KingstonArtGallery
Instagram.com/kingstonartgroup

The Ropewalk

Regionally acclaimed centre for the arts, with
galleries, a sculpture garden, coffee shop and
Ropery Hall, which hosts live music, theatre
and cinema in the former rope factory.
Address: Ropewalk, Maltkiln Road, Barton-
Upon-Humber DN18 5JT
Phone: 01652 660380
Website: the-ropewalk.co.uk
Email: info@the-ropewalk.co.uk
Twitter.com/Ropewalkbarton
Facebook.com/RopewalkBarton

Leeds

Leeds Art Gallery

Dynamic exhibition program with a
significant collection of modern and
contemporary British art.
Address: The Headrow, Leeds LS1 3AA
Phone: 0113 378 5350
Website: museumsandgalleries.leeds.gov.uk
Email: museumsandgalleries@leeds.gov.uk
Twitter.com/LeedsArtGallery
Facebook.com/LeedsArtGallery
Instagram.com/LeedsArtGallery
YouTube.com/user/LeedsArtGallery

The Stanley & Audrey Burton Gallery

Innovative art exhibitions from the
University Art Collection with paintings and
prints from the 17th century to present day,
as well as sculpture, ceramics, miniatures and
photographs. Events program.
Address: Woodhouse Lane, Leeds LS2 9JT
Phone: 0113 343 2778
Website: library.leeds.ac.uk
Email: gallery@library.leeds.ac.uk
Twitter.com/LuLGalleries
Facebook.com/LULGalleries
Instagram.com/lulgalleries

The Gallery at 164

Curates exhibitions, working with artists,
the university and other organisations.
Address: Munro House, Duke St, Leeds LS9
8AG
Phone: 0113 243 3266
Website: leedsgallery.com
Email: info@leedsgallery.com
Twitter.com/leedsgallery
Facebook.com/LeedsGallery
Instagram.com/leedsgallery
Pinterest.co.uk/leedsgallery

The Brunswick

Top-floor room available to rent for gallery

launches, pop-ups and other functions.
Address: 82 North Street, Leeds LS2 7PN
Phone: 0113 247 0546
Website: thebrunswick.co.uk
Email: bookings@thebrunswick.co.uk
Twitter.com/brunswickleeds
Facebook.com/thebrunswickleeds

Henry Moore Institute

Established in 1977 by Henry Moore with
the aim of promoting fine art to the public.
Address: 74 The Headrow, Leeds LS1 3AH
Phone: 0113 246 7467
Website: henry-moore.org
Twitter.com/HenryMooreFDN
Facebook.com/henrymoorestudios
Instagram.com/henrymoorestudios
Vimeo.com/henrymoore

Project Space Leeds

Experimental space for exhibitions, perfor-
mances and workshops in the centre of the
School for Fine Art, History of Art and
Cultural Studies. With an annual program
showing installations by internationally
renowned artists.
Address: Whitehall Waterfront, 2 Riverside
Wy, Leeds LS1 4EH
Phone: 07930 236383
Website: ahc.leeds.ac.uk/fine-art-
undergraduate/doc/project-space
Twitter.com/LeedsUniAHC
Facebook.com/universityofleeds
Weibo.com/leedsuniversityuk

The Old Red Bus Station

Space available to hire for exhibition or
events. Capacity for 300 people.
Address: 102-104 Vicar Lane, Leeds LS2
7NL
Phone: 0113 345 1661
Website: theoldredbusstation.com
Email: info@championupnorth.com
Twitter.com/oldredbus
Facebook.com/TheOldRedBusStation

Northern Contemporary Art

The Northern Art Prize is an initiative
profiling contemporary art events and
festivals in the North East, North West and
Yorkshire and Humber regions of the UK.
Address: The Headrow, Leeds LS1 8EQ
Phone: 07516 391430
Website: northernartprize.org.uk
Email: contact@northernartprize.org.uk

Ripon
Hornseys Gallery

Fine, rare and unusual artwork, objects, maps
and books.
Address: 3 Kirkgate, Ripon HG4 1PA
Phone: 01765 602878
Website: hornseys.com
Email: info@hornseys.com
Pinterest.co.uk/hornseys

Masham Gallery

Ever-changing exhibitions throughout the
year from Josie Beszant and Ian Scott Massie
as well as other artists.
Address: 24 Market Place, Ripon HG4 4EB
Phone: 01765 689554
Website: mashamgallery.co.uk
Email: enquiry@mashamgallery.co.uk
Twitter.com/mashamgallery
Facebook.com/MashamGallery

Alans Gallery & Kirkgate Yarns

Original artwork and illustration.
Address: 19 Kirkgate, Ripon HG4 1PA
Phone: 01765 690498

Sheffield
Millennium Gallery

Part of Museums Sheffield, which also
includes Weston Park Museum and Graves
Gallery. Providing inspiration through art,
reflecting on the past, questioning the present

and imagining the future.
Address: Arundel Gate, Sheffield S1 2PP
Phone: 0114 278 2600
Website: museums-sheffield.org.uk
Twitter.com/MuseumSheffield
Facebook.com/Museums.Sheffield
Instagram.com/museumssheffield
YouTube.com/user/MuseumsSheffield

Site Gallery

Collaborating on a local, regional and international level to nurture artistic talent and support the development of contemporary art with exhibitions, talks and events. Promoting emerging and established artists with group and solo shows. Trebled in size after building work, finished in 2018.
Address: 1 Brown Street, Sheffield S1 2BS
Phone: 0114 281 2077
Website: sitegallery.org
Email: reception@sitegallery.org
Twitter.com/site_gallery
Instagram.com/sitegallery

Cupola Gallery

Over 300 artist's work on display, covering the full range of disciplines.
Address: 178-178A Middlewood Road, Sheffield S6 1TD
Phone: 0114 285 2665
Website: cupolagallery.com
Email: info@cupolagallery.com
Instagram.com/cupolacontemporaryart
Pinterest.co.uk/cupolagallery

Smart Art Galleries

Three rooms showing a mix of media from leading artists, including painting, sculpture and photography with regularly changing exhibitions.
Address: Omega Court 368 Cemetery Road, Sheffield S11 8FT
Phone: 0114 235 2429
Website: smartartgalleries.com
Email: info@smartartgalleries.com

Helix Gallery

Leading urban and contemporary art, such as Banksy and Hockney, as well as emerging artists, with an extensive collection selling nationally and internationally.
Address: Sheffield
Phone: 07927 222468
Website: helixgallery.com
Email: craig@helixgallery.com
Twitter.com/HelixGallery
Facebook.com/HelixGallery
Instagram.com/helixgalleryuk
LinkedIn.com/in/craig-mills-6910aa193

The Bessemer II Gallery

Contemporary art and craft with in-house café. Best emerging talent from regional and national sources. Painting, photography, sculpture, jewellery, glassware and ceramics.
Address: 525 Ecclesall Road, Sheffield S11 8PR
Phone: 0114 267 0053
Website: bessemergallery.com
Email: bessemer2@bessemergallery.com
Twitter.com/TheBessemerII
Facebook.com/thebessemerIIgallery

Sheffield Contemporary Art Forum

Learning, enjoying and rediscovering creativity in the Art House.
Address: 3 Persistence Works Brown Street, Sheffield S1 2BS
Phone: 07812 928174
Website: arthousesheffield.co.uk
Email: info@arthousesheffield.co.uk
Twitter.com/arthousesheff
Facebook.com/arthousesheff
Instagram.com/arthousesheff

B & B Gallery

Showing the work of emerging and established contemporary artists, with exhibitions and projects around the world.

Address: 95B Mary Street, Sheffield S1 4Rt, Sheffield S1 4RT
Website: bandbgallery.com

Kelham Island Arts Collective

Bringing art back into the community with an affordable space for artists to meet, create and exhibit.
Address: 40 Ball Street, Sheffield S3 8DB
Phone: 07903 460450
Website: kiac-sheffield.org
Email: KIACsheffield@gmail.com
Twitter.com/KIAC1
Facebook.com/kiacsheffield

Wakefield
The Hepworth Wakefield

Award-winning gallery overlooking the River Calder. Named after Barbara Hepworth who grew up in Wakefield, the gallery shows major exhibitions of the best international modern and contemporary art, with an award-winning learning program. Collection of work from modern and contemporary masters. Large free public garden.
Address: Gallery Walk, Wakefield WF1 5AW
Phone: 01924 247360
Website: hepworthwakefield.org
Email: hello@hepworthwakefield.org
Twitter.com/HepworthGallery
Facebook.com/TheHepworthWakefield
Instagram.com/hepworthwakefield
YouTube.com/user/HepworthWakefield

Lucy Art

Bespoke, original canvas paintings, prints and photographs created by owner Rob Haigh. Able to mock up the art, if sent a photo of the space in which it is to hang.
Address: 178A Batley Rd, Wakefield WF2 0AJ
Phone: 0845 659 0660
Website: lucyart.co.uk

Email: sales@lucyart.co.uk
Twitter.com/lucyart
Facebook.com/LucyArtUK
Instagram.com/robhaighart123

York
The Acorn Gallery

Original art, sculpture and limited edition prints from a huge portfolio of British and international artists.
Address: 5 Market Place, York YO42 2AS
Phone: 01759 307652
Website: theacorngallery.co.uk
Email: info@theacorngallery.co.uk
Twitter.com/theacorngallery
Facebook.com/TheAcornGallery
Instagram.com/theacorngallery
Pinterest.co.uk/theacorngallery

Lotte Inch Gallery

Situated near the Minster in a medieval building, the gallery has regular exhibitions of established and emerging artists complemented by ceramics, design items, small-scale sculpture, jewellery and gifts.
Address: 10 Bootham, York YO30 7BL
Phone: 01904 848660
Website: lotteinch.co.uk
Email: info@lotteinch.co.uk
Twitter.com/lotteinch
Facebook.com/lotteinchyork
Instagram.com/lotteinchyork

The Cat Gallery

A family business entirely devoted to gifts for cat-lovers and their feline friends. Shipping worldwide.
Address: 45 Low Petergate, York YO1 7HT
Phone: 01904 631611
Website: thecatgallery.co.uk
Email: info@thecatgallery.co.uk
Twitter.com/CatGallery
Facebook.com/TheCatGallery
Instagram.com/catgalleryyork

Art of Protest Gallery

Pushing beyond the conversations of social media groups, illuminating the common ground of contemporary art, encouraging conversations on the environment, consumption, identity and the global audience.
Address: 16 Little Stonegate, York YO1 8AX
Phone: 01904 659008
Website: artofprotestgallery.com
Email: info@artofprotestgallery.com
Facebook.com/artofprotestgallery
Instagram.com/artofprotestgallery

Blossom Street Gallery & Framing

Based in the beautiful Micklegate quarter of York, the gallery hosts regular exhibitions of mainly Yorkshire artists, from original work to prints, gifts and cards, with innovative framing. Also stocking art supplies.
Address: 3 Blossom Street, York YO24 1AE
Phone: 01904 623191
Website: blossomstreet.co.uk
Twitter.com/BlossomStYork
Facebook.com/BlossomStYork
Instagram.com/blossomstyork

According to McGee

Contemporary gallery with limited editions and paintings from 20 artists.
Address: 8 Tower Street, York YO1 9SA
Phone: 01904 671709
Website: accordingtomcgee.com
Email: info@accordingtomcgee.com
Twitter.com/according2mcgee
Facebook.com/accordingtomcgee
Instagram.com/accordingtomcgee
Pinterest.co.uk/atmgallery

The New School House Gallery

Over 50 exhibitions since the gallery began in 2009, showing contemporary work from over 450 artists and makers across a wide range of disciplines and media.

Address: Old School House, Peasholme Green, York YO1 7PW
Phone: 07766 656030
Website: schoolhousegallery.co.uk
Email: mail@schoolhousegallery.co.uk
Twitter.com/schoolhousegall
Instagram.com/schoolhousegallery

Pyramid Gallery

Close to the Minster, the gallery shows British made contemporary crafts, jewellery and original prints by 150 makers and artists in regular exhibitions.
Address: 43 Stonegate, York YO1 8AW
Phone: 01904 641187
Website: pyramidgallery.com

York St. Marys

The church dates back to 1020, with the tallest steeple in York. Shows contemporary art exhibitions
Address: Castlegate, York YO1 9RN
Phone: 01904 687687
Website: yorkstmarys.org.uk
Email: enquiries@ymt.org.uk

Centre of Ceramic Art

CoCA exhibits British studio ceramics, with the largest collection in the UK, covering the entire movement in its permanent collection with changing exhibitions and new acquisitions.
Address: Exhibition Square, York YO1 7EW
Phone: 01904 687687
Website: centreofceramicart.org.uk
Email: enquiries@ymt.org.uk

The Japanese Print Shop

Starting in 1976, with the sale of Japanese woodblocks, and later Russian painting, the collection was exhibited at Liberty London from 1984-2012. Specialising in the Meiji, Taisho and Showa periods as well as contemporary work, sourced from over

1,000 studios in St Petersburg with over a million paintings and drawings.
Address: 38 High Petergate, York YO1 7HW
Phone: 01904 651080
Website: russianpaintingsandjapaneseprints.co.uk

The Quilters' Guild Museum Collection

Unique collection of quilts and related artefacts from Britain dating from 1718.
Address: St Anthonys Hall Peasholme Green, York YO1 7PW
Phone: 01904 613242
Website: quiltmuseum.org.uk
Email: Curator@quiltersguild.org.uk
Facebook.com/The-Quilters-Guild-Museum-Collection

NORTHERN IRELAND

Gracehill Gallery

Traditional and Contemporary Irish Art. Gallery.
Address: 3 Mill Street, Ballymena BT43 5AA
Phone: 028 2565 2544
Website: gracehillgallery.com
Email: info@gracehillgallery.com
Facebook.com/gracehillgallery

Gallery One

Family run art gallery, with a range of traditional and contemporary art from around the world, especially emerging and award-winning European, UK and Irish artists. Specialising in Irish Landscape in oils, watercolour, acrylic and mixed media.
Address: 1 Brewery Lane, Cookstown BT80 8LL
Phone: 028 8676 5438
Website: galleryone.co.uk
Email: sales@irishfineart.co.uk

McKenna Gallery

Purpose built gallery on the Strule River.

Solo and group exhibitions over two floors, with lift and curved mezzanine area.
Address: 31 Castle Street, Omagh BT78 1DD
Phone: 028 8224 7105
Website: mckennagallery.com
Email: info@mckennagallery.com
Facebook.com/McKennaGallery

Belfast
Gormleys Fine Art

Founded in 1990, specialising in international and Irish contemporary art, from both established and emerging artists with a gallery also in Dublin. A significant collection of sculpture.
Address: 471 Lisburn Road, Belfast BT9 7EZ
Phone: 028 9066 3313
Address: Gormleys Dublin
27 Frederick St. South, Dublin D02 EP03
Phone: +353 (0)1 6729031
Website: gormleys.ie
Email: info@gormleys.ie

Taylor Gallery

In Belfast's famous Lisburn Road, established in 1998, dealing in the finest Irish art as well as work on paper by internationally renowned artists, such as Andy Warhol, Roy Lichtenstein, Damien Hirst and Francis Bacon. Worldwide client base of institutions, corporate collections and private clients.
Address: 471 Lisburn Road, Belfast BT9 7EZ
Phone: 028 9068 7687
Website: taylorgallery.co.uk
Email: info@taylorgallery.co.uk

Catalyst Arts

At the forefront of the arts scene in Belfast, established 1993. Voluntary and artist-led, their model works by collaboration and community with exhibitions, off-site projects and an outreach program.

Address: 5 College Court, Belfast BT1 6BS
Phone: 028 9031 3303
Website: catalystarts.org.uk
Email: catalystarts@gmail.com
Twitter.com/Catalyst_Arts
Facebook.com/catalystartsgallery
Instagram.com/catalystarts

Ormeau Baths Gallery

Award-winning co-working space in the centre of Belfast, with 15,000 sq. ft. in an historic building, fitted with lift and ramp access, staged area, sound systems and projectors.
Address: 18 Ormeau Avenue, Belfast BT2 8HS
Phone: 028 9076 7266
Website: ormeaubaths.com
Email: members@ormeaubaths.com
Twitter.com/ormeaubaths
Facebook.com/theormeaubaths
Instagram.com/ormeaubaths

ArtisAnn Gallery

Vibrant, contemporary art gallery showing emerging and established artists, many of whom are members of the Royal Ulster Academy of Arts.
Address: 70 Bloomfield Avenue, Belfast BT5 5AE
Phone: 07726 326390
Website: artisann.org
Email: mail@artisann.org
Twitter.com/artisannbelfast
Facebook.com/artisannbelfast
Instagram.com/artisannbelfast

Nicholas Gallery

Established in 1996, dealing in modern and contemporary British and international art including masters such as Bridget Riley, Frank Auerbach and Lucian Freud. European artists are represented by Pablo Picasso, Marc Chagall and Joan Miro among others.
Address: 571 Lisburn Road, Belfast BT9 7GS

Phone: 028 9068 7767
Website: nicholasgallery.co.uk
Email: info@nicholasgallery.co.uk

Golden Thread Gallery

Medium-scale, public funded contemporary art gallery with charitable status, an important role in the provision of art to Belfast and Northern Ireland. Founded in 1998.
Address: 84-94 Great Patrick Street, Belfast BT1 2LU
Phone: 028 9033 0920
Website: gtgallery.co.uk
Email: info@gtgallery.co.uk
Twitter.com/goldenthreadg
Facebook.com/GoldenThreadGallery
Instagram.com/goldenthread_gallery

Eakin Gallery

Situated in the cosmopolitan Lisburn Road, specialising in 20th and 21st century fine Irish art. Belfast's longest standing contemporary art gallery promoting both emerging and established artists with regular solo and group exhibitions.
Address: 237 Lisburn Road, Belfast BT9 7EN
Phone: 028 9066 8522
Website: eakingallery.co.uk
Email: info@eakingallery.co.uk

Art Loves

Creates, commissions, sources and supplies art, prints, sculpture, accessories for hotels and offices across the UK, Ireland and Europe. Also consultants for big brands and large-scale public art projects.
Address: Victoria Lodge 158 Upper Newtownards Road, Belfast BT4 3EQ
Phone: 028 9543 0966
Website: artloves.co.uk
Email: hello@artloves.co.uk
Instagram.com/artlovesltd

Townhouse Gallery

Established in 1996. Framers and gallery exhibiting emerging and established painters, printmakers and photographers with monthly exhibitions.
Address: 125 Great Victoria Street, Belfast, County Antrim BT2 7AH
Phone: 028 9031 1798
Website: townhousestudio.co.uk
Email: George@townhouseart.co.uk
Pinterest.co.uk/pin/248683210656085812

Lisburn
Oakley Art

Established artists, restoration and picture framing
Address: 16 Bridge Street, Lisburn BT28 1XY
Phone: 028 92 673117 / 07841 468585
Website: oakley-art.com

R-Space Gallery

Visual arts and crafts in the Linen Rooms in Lisburn. Aiming to increase access and enjoyment of contemporary art and design. Working with a diverse range of artists in different media, with audiences from a wide range of backgrounds
Address: 32 Castle Street, Lisburn BT27 4XE
Phone: 028 9266 3179
Website: rspacelisburn.com
Email: rspace@linenroomslisburn.com
Twitter.com/rspacelisburn
Facebook.com/rspacelisburn
Instagram.com/rspacegallerylisburn

Londonderry
CCA

Creates ambitious, experimental and engaging art by emerging regional artists collaborating locally, nationally and internationally. There are 5 program streams; research and production, exhibition-making, public programs, publishing and residencies.
Address: 10-12 Artillery Street, Londonderry BT48 6RG
Phone: 028 7137 3538
Website: cca-derry-londonderry.org
Email: info@cca-derry-londonderry.org
Twitter.com/ccadld
Facebook.com/CCADLD
Instagram.com/ccadld

Void

A contemporary art gallery that commissions and produces a visual arts program aimed at challenging the viewers and reaching out to new audiences. National and international artists and organisations collaborate through exhibitions, events, projects and partnerships.
Address: 100 Patrick Street, Londonderry BT48 7EL
Phone: 028 7130 8080
Website: derryvoid.com
Email: admin@derryvoid.com
Twitter.com/DerryVoid
Facebook.com/derryvoid
Instagram.com/derryvoid
Vimeo.com/user25648837/videos

SCOTLAND
Aberdeen
Aberdeen Art Gallery

Founded in 1884 with a sculpture court added in 1905. The main visual arts centre in Aberdeen. Awarded the Art Fund Museum of the Year prize in 2020. Home to one of the finest collections in the country.
Address: Schoolhill, Aberdeen AB10 1FQ
Phone: 01224 523700
Website: aberdeencity.gov.uk/AAGM
Twitter.com/AbdnArtMuseums
Facebook.com/AbdnArtMuseums
Instagram.com/abdnartmuseums
Inspiringartandmusic.Tumblr.com

Aberdeenshire

Milton Art Gallery

20 miles west of Aberdeen, in a renovated farm set in beautiful surroundings, next to the River Dee. Showing Scottish contemporary artists alongside an impressive range of ceramics, jewellery, prints, bronzes and glass work. Near to a brasserie, shops, a children's play area and visitor centre for the Royal Deeside Railway Preservation Society.
Address: Milton Of Crathes, Banchory AB31 5QH
Phone: 01330 844664
Website: miltonart.com
Email: info@miltonart.com
Facebook.com/Milton.Gallery

Tolquhon Gallery

Scottish contemporary art since 1987. Established modern masters and the best emerging artists. Set in the public rooms of a large Victorian farmhouse with a large garden for sculpture. Adjacent to the ruins of Tolquhon Castle, and near the quiet villages of the North Sea coast. Six main exhibitions a year, showing paintings, original prints, sculpture, ceramics, studio glass, wood and jewellery, representing several hundred artists
Address: Tolquhon, Ellon AB41 7LP
Phone: 01651 842343
Website: tolquhon-gallery.co.uk
Email: art@tolquhon-gallery.co.uk
Facebook.com/Tolquhon
Instagram.com/tolquhongallery
Pinterest.co.uk/tolquhon

Lost Gallery

Established in 1994, set in the beguiling Glen Nochty at the side of Moss Hill, the younger sister of the Cairngorms. Showing contemporary art by Scottish artists; paintings, sculpture and photography.
Address: Aldachuie, Strathdon AB36 8UJ
Phone: 01975 651287
Website: lostgallery.co.uk
Facebook.com/lostgallery

Larks Gallery

Contemporary gallery in the beautiful village of Ballater, 8 miles from Balmoral Castle. Local and Scottish-wide artists, both established and emerging, with an exhibition each month.
Address: 10 Braemar Road, Ballater AB35 5RL
Phone: 01339 755888 / 07936 387722
Website: larksgallery.com

Gallery I

The largest collection of traditional and contemporary art in the north of Scotland specialising in Scottish, UK and international art with original paintings, limited edition prints and sculpture.
Address: 2B Garioch Shopping Centre, Inverurie AB51 4UY
Phone: 01467 625780
Website: galleryi.co.uk
Email: info@galleryi.co.uk
Facebook.com/galleryinverurie

Peacock Visual Arts

Since 1974, has supported and promoted the making of prints, videos, photography, performance and site-specific public install-ations, with a digital fabrication studio, screen printing and relief printing studios. The print shop sells a wide range of contemporary art prints by local to international artists. Supported by Aberdeen City Council and Creative Scotland.
Address: 21 Castle Street, Aberdeen AB11 5BQ
Phone: 01453 128393
Website: peacockvisualarts.com
Email: info@peacockvisualarts.co.uk
Twitter.com/PeacockVisArts
Facebook.com/peacockvisualarts

Instagram.com/peacockvisualarts
Flickr.com/photos/peacockvisualarts_
printmaking
Vimeo.com/peacockvisualarts

Ayrshire

Rozelle House Galleries

Gifted to the public in 1968, the estate of Rozelle combines mature woodland, rhododendron walks, parkland and ornamental ponds used throughout the year for sporting events and the Ayr Flower Show. The gallery and museum display objects and art from the collections of South Ayrshire Council as well as regularly changing exhibitions, events and activities.
Address: Rozelle Park, Ayr KA7 4NQ
Phone: 01292 445447
Website: south-ayrshire.gov.uk
Email: rozelle.house@south-ayrshire.gov.uk

Moray

Moray Art Centre

A charity offering exhibitions as well as a full timetable of classes and weekend workshops for all levels. The summer schools attract visitors from all over the world. Situated in an environmentally built and designed centre in Findhorn Bay and next to the internationally acclaimed eco-village, the Findhorn Foundation.
Address: 436 Field Of Dreams, The Park, Findhorn IV36 3TA
Phone: 01309 692426
Website: morayartcentre.org
Email: admin@morayartcentre.org
Twitter.com/MorayArtCentre
Facebook.com/morayartcentre
Instagram.com/morayartcentre

Scottish Borders

Flat Cat Gallery

Showcasing a range of artists in a variety of media. Contemporary and traditional styles. Set in the pretty town of Lauder with a stunning range of ceramics, sculpture, jewellery, gifts and a café.
Address: 2 Market Place, Lauder TD2 6SR
Phone: 01578 722808
Website: flatcatgallery.co.uk
Email: art@flatcatgallery.co.uk

Moy Mackay Gallery

Artwork from Moy Mackay, who draws inspiration from the beautiful Tweed Valley using merino fleece fibres. Also other artists from the Borders and further afield.
Address: 17 Northgate, Peebles EH45 8RX
Phone: 01721 722116
Website: moymackaygallery.com
Twitter.com/moy_mackay
Facebook.com/moymackaygallery
Pinterest.co.uk/moymackay

The Gallery Melrose

In the heart of the Scottish Borders, exhibiting original art, prints, sculpture, jewellery, wood turning and glassware. An on-site bespoke picture framing service.
Address: 23 Market Square, Melrose TD6 9PL
Phone: 01896 208190
Website: thegallerymelrose.co.uk
Email: info@thegallerymelrose.co.uk
Twitter.com/GalleryMelrose
Facebook.com/TheGalleryMelrose
Instagram.com/the_gallery_melrose

Dancing Light Gallery

Exhibits online as well as solo and specialised exhibitions at various venues and art fairs.
Address: Whitmuir By Lamancha, West Linton, Edinburgh EH46 7BB
Phone: 01968 660200
Website: dancinglightgallery.co.uk
Email: info@dancinglightgallery.co.uk
Facebook.com/dancinglightgallery

Hill House Gallery

Run by artists, printmakers and picture framers Owen and Jan Butler. The gallery is run in a former church.
Address: Broughton, Biggar ML12 6HQ
Phone: 07768 690069
Website: hillhousegallery.com
Email: jan@hillhousegallery.com

Coldstream Gallery

Art celebrating the landscape and the natural world through fine art, design and craft from the Scottish Borders and Northumberland, as well as national and international creations.
Address: 51 High Street, Coldstream TD12 4DL
Phone: 01890 882882
Website: whitefoxgallery.co.uk
Facebook.com/whitefoxgallery
Instagram.com/whitefox_gallery

Number Four Gallery

Established and run by artists Jenny Brook Martin. Since 2006, the gallery has been exhibiting and promoting original contemporary artwork
Address: Northfield Farm St Abbs, Eyemouth TD14 5QF
Phone: 01890 771111
Website: numberfourgallery.co.uk
Email: info@numberfourgallery.co.uk
Facebook.com/number4gallery

Dundee
Dundee Contemporary Arts

An internationally renowned centre for contemporary art, with 2 large galleries, 2 cinema screens, a print studio and award-winning learning program, with events, workshops, classes and activities. One of the most successful arts organisations in the UK
Address: 152 Nethergate, Dundee DD1 4DY
Phone: 01382 909900

Website: dca.org.uk
Email: dca@dca.org.uk
Twitter.com/DCAdundee
Facebook.com/DCA.Dundee
Instagram.com/dcadundee

Gallery Q Dundee

Contemporary artists and jewellers exhibiting over 2 floors, with fine art, prints, ceramics, glass and inspired accessories. The gallery supports emerging Scottish artists as well as exhibiting household names.
Address: Queen›s Hotel Buildings, 160, Nethergate, Dundee DD1 4DU
Phone: 01382 220600
Website: galleryq.co.uk
Email: art@galleryq.co.uk.
Facebook.com/gallery.q
Instagram.com/artqdundee

The McManus Galleries

Set in a Gothic Revival-style building in the heart of Dundee encompassing 8 galleries. Showing a 400 million year history, through to decorative art and paintings by present day Royal Academicians
Address: Albert Square, Meadowside, Dundee DD1 1DA
Phone: 01382 307200
Website: mcmanus.co.uk
Email: themcmanus@ leisureandculturedundee.com
Twitter.com/McManusDundee
Facebook.com/McManusDundee
Instagram.com/mcmanusdundee

Argyll and Bute
Tighnabruaich Gallery

Contemporary art and crafts from a range of established and emerging artists, with a series of exhibitions throughout the year. Drawing and painting, as well as design-led jewellery, textiles, glass, ceramics and prints.
Address: Seaside House, Tighnabruaich

PA21 2DR
Phone: 01700 811681
Website: tiggallery.com
Email: info@tiggallery.com
Facebook.com/tiggallery
Instagram.com/tighnabruaichgallery

Fyne Studios

Work expressing the emotional aspect of the wild and rugged west coast of Scotland with the ever changing weather and dramatic light.
Address: Newton Cottage, Newton, Cairndow PA27 8DB
Phone: 01369 860379
Website: fyne-studios.com
Email: info@fyne-studios.com

Argyll Pottery

A pottery blog, with information about makers, events, courses, general news and items for sale.
Address: Dallachullish Farm, Barcaldine PA37 1SQ
Phone: 01631 720503
Website: studiopottery.co.uk
Email: info@studiopottery.co.uk

Juno Design Gallery

Mother and daughter, Maria and Joanne Mackellar have been working since 2001 with designers to showcase design and fine art. Both graduates of Glasgow School of Art, they have travelled far afield to locate interesting and unusual artists and designers.
Address: 142 Argyll St, Dunoon PA23 7NA
Phone: 01369 707767
Website: junogallery.com
Email: jo@junogallery.com

Highlands

Kevin Hunter Scottish Artist

Scottish art and further afield. Takes commissions. Locations across Scotland, including Arran, Glasgow, Glencoe, The Highlands, Hebridean Islands, Orkney, historic and iconic castles, mountains and munros, lochs and the Isle of Sky. Abstract and impressionistic work, as well as cityscapes from around the globe.
Address: St. Andrews Drive, Gourock, Inverclyde. PA19 1HY
Address: 15 East Campbell Street, Glasgow G1 5DT
Phone: 07946 455614
Website: kevinhunterartgallery.com
Email: mail@kevinhunterartgallery.com
Twitter.com/kevinhunterart
Facebook.com/KevinHunterArtist
Instagram.com/kevinhunterartist

Clackmannanshire

The Ruthven Gallery

Quirky and affordable art from paintings to sculpture, drawings, glass, prints, pottery, jewellery and cards. A picture framing service.
Address: 90 High Street, Auchterarder PH3 1BJ
Phone: 01764 664233
Website: theruthvengallery.co.uk
Email: enquiries@theruthvengallery.co.uk
Twitter.com/RuthvenGallery
Facebook.com/TheRuthvenGallery

Grandison Golf Gallery

Original paintings, prints and Giclee canvas prints by William Grandison, a world leading golf landscape artist showing golf courses in the UK and around the world. Private commissions are available.
Address: 5 Sorley's Brae, Dollar FK14 7AS
Phone: 01259 740318
Website: grandisongolfgallery.com
william@grandisongolfgallery.com

Dumfries and Galloway

Tolbooth Art Centre

Set in a former debtor's prison, now home to an award-winning art centre showcasing a permanent display of Kirkcudbright's artist colony and contemporary arts and crafts from across the region and further afield, with a café and gift shop.
Address: Council Offices High Street, Kirkcudbright DG6 4JL
Phone: +44 (1557) 331556
Website: dumgal.gov.uk
Website: dgculture.co.uk/venue/tolbooth-arts-centre-kirkcudbright
Email: stewartry.museum@dumgal.gov.uk
dgculture@dumgal.gov.uk

Kirkcudbright Art Gallery

A national art gallery celebrating and promoting the unique art heritage of Kirkcudbright, South-West Scotland. Operated and managed by D & G Council.
Address: Town Hall St. Mary St, Kirkcudbright DG6 4AA
Phone: 01557 331276
Website: kirkcudbrightgalleries.org.uk
Email: kirkcudbrightgalleries@dumgal.gov.uk
Twitter.com/kbtgalleries
Facebook.com/kirkcudbrightgalleries
Instagram.com/kirkcudbrightgalleries

Gracefield Arts Centre

Program of exhibitions and events, funded by local council.
Address: 28 Edinburgh Road, Dumfries DG1 1JQ
Phone: 01387 262084
Website: dgculture.co.uk/venue/gracefield-arts-centre/
Email: arts@dumgal.gov.uk
Twitter.com/dumfriesmuseum
Facebook.com/DumfriesMuseum

The Gallery at Laurieston

Based in the small village of Laurieston. Images of nature and the landscape in this outstanding region from an award-winning photographer.
Address: Woodbank House, Laurieston DG7 2PW
Phone: 01644 450235
Website: pmcphotography.co.uk
Email: info@pmcphotography.co.uk
Twitter.com/philmcmenemy
Facebook.com/GalleryAtLaurieston

East Lothian

The Found Gallery

Quirky and eclectic fused glass jewellery and photographic glass as well as a rolling program of British arts and crafts from emerging and established makers.
Address: 84 High Street, Dunbar EH42 1JH
Phone: 01368 863030
Website: thefoundgallery.co.uk
Email: info@thefoundgallery.co.uk
Twitter.com/FoundGallery
Facebook.com/TheFoundGallery
Instagram.com/thefoundgallery

Greens & Blues

Located in the beautiful seaside resort of North Berwick, exhibiting a wide variety of original and contemporary art. Emerging and established Scottish artists and those from further afield.
Address: 59 High Street, North Berwick EH39 4HG
Phone: 01620 890666
Website: greensandblues.co.uk
Email: info@greensandblues.co.uk
Facebook.com/greensandbluesgallery
Instagram.com/greensandbluesnb
LinkedIn.com/company/greens-and-blues

Fidra Fine Art

A rolling exhibition of contemporary and Scottish art as well as famous Scottish names from the past hundred years or so.
Address: 7-8 Stanley Road (Main Street), Gullane, East Lothian. EH31 2AD
Phone: +44 (0)1620 249389 / 07981 982464
Website: fidrafineart.co.uk
Email: alan@fidrafineart.co.uk
Twitter.com/FidraFineArt
Facebook.com/FidraFineArt

Christopher Wood

Work from Christopher Wood, graduate from Edinburgh College of Art.
Address: Port Lodge 7 High Street, Dunbar EH42 1EN
Phone: 01368 860232
Website: christopherwood.co.uk
Email: info@christopherwood.co.uk
Facebook.com/christopherwoodartist
Instagram.com/christopherwoodart
Pinterest.co.uk/cwoodrsw

Edinburgh

Paintbox Art Classes

An independent art school by the sea, with a range of courses.
Address: 93/10 Portobello High St, Edinburgh EH15 1AW
Phone: 07852 951592 / 07732 038 063
Website: paintboxartclasses.com
Email: paintboxart@outlook.com
Twitter.com/Paintbox_art

Scottish National Gallery

Collections of art dating from the 16th, 17th, 18th and 19th centuries.
Address: The Mound, Edinburgh EH2 2EL
Phone: 0131 624 6200
Website: nationalgalleries.org
Email: enquiries@nationalgalleries.org
Twitter.com/NatGalleriesSco

Facebook.com/nationalgalleries
Instagram.com/natgalleriessco
YouTube.com/nationalgalleries

Scottish National Portrait Gallery

In a remarkable neo-gothic palace designed by Sir Robert Rowand Anderson, it houses Scotland's heroes and heroines.
Address: 1 Queen Street, Edinburgh EH2 1JD
Phone: 0131 624 6200
Website: nationalgalleries.org
Email: enquiries@nationalgalleries.org
Twitter.com/NatGalleriesSco
Facebook.com/nationalgalleries
Instagram.com/natgalleriessco
YouTube.com/nationalgalleries

Scottish Gallery

One of the oldest commercial galleries in Scotland, with a monthly program of exhibitions highlighting emerging, established and historical artists.
Address: 16 Dundas Street, Edinburgh EH3 6HZ
Phone: 0131 558 1200
Website: scottish-gallery.co.uk
Email; mail@scottish-gallery.co.uk
Twitter.com/ScottishGallery
Facebook.com/scottishgallery
Instagram.com/scottishgallery
LinkedIn.com/company/the-scottish-gallery

Jupiter Artland

Contemporary sculpture garden and gallery just outside Edinburgh.
Address: Bonnington House, Steadings, Wilkieston, Edinburgh EH27 8BB
Phone: 01506 889900
Website: jupiterartland.org
Email: enquiries@jupiterartland.org
Twitter.com/jupiterartland
Facebook.com/JupiterArtland

Instagram.com/jupiterartland
Vimeo.com/jupiterartland
Apps.apple.com/us/app/jupiter-artland

The City Art Centre Café

In the heart of Edinburgh, championing historic and contemporary Scottish visual and applied arts.
Address: 2 Market Street, Edinburgh EH1 1DE
Phone: 0131 529 3993
Website: edinburghmuseums.org.uk
Twitter.com/Edinburgh Museums
Facebook.com/City.Art.Centre.CAC
Instagram.com/museumsgalleriesedinburgh

Arusha Gallery

A contemporary art gallery in the historic New Town part of Edinburgh. An annual program of exhibitions, events and fairs with collaborations with guest artists, curators, festivals and institutions.
Address: 13A Dundas Street, Edinburgh EH3 6QG
Phone: 0131 557 1412
Website: arushagallery.com
Email: info@arushagallery.com
Twitter.com/ArushaGallery
Facebook.com/arushagallery
Instagram.com/arushagallery

The Sutton Gallery

Stimulating exhibitions around the country. Wide variety of work by exciting contemporary artists as well as celebrated British artists from the 20th century.
Address: 17 Dundas Street, Edinburgh EH3 6HZ
Phone: 07854972930
Website: thesuttongallery.com
Email: colinjherd@gmail.com
Twitter.com/SuttonGallery
Facebook.com/TheSuttonGallery

Alpha Art

Family-run gallery showing established and emerging artists from the UK and internationally. Ambitious program of events throughout the year, including several festivals and contemporary art fairs.
Address: 52 Hamilton Place, Edinburgh EH3 5AX
Phone: 0131 226 3066
Website: alpha-art.co.uk
Email: info@alpha-art.co.uk
Twitter.com/alphaartgallery
Facebook.com/alphaart1
Instagram.com/Alpha Art Gallery

Urbane Art Gallery

Contemporary art gallery, allowing in-situ selection of work in your home.
Address: 25-27 Jeffrey Street, Edinburgh EH1 1DH
Phone: 0131 556 8379
Website: urbaneart.co.uk
Email: info@urbaneart.co.uk

Scottish National Gallery of Modern Art

An outstanding collection of modern and contemporary art with world-class sculpture set in beautiful grounds with a pop-up café.
Address: 73 Belford Road, Edinburgh EH4 3DS
Phone: 0131 624 6200
Website: nationalgalleries.org
Email: enquiries@nationalgalleries.org
Twitter.com/NatGalleriesSco
Facebook.com/nationalgalleries
Instagram.com/natgalleriessco
YouTube.com/nationalgalleries

Saorsa Art Gallery

Located in Stockbridge, Edinburgh exhibiting the landscape paintings of gallery owner, Tommy Fitchet and guest artists.
Address: 8 Deanhaugh St, Edinburgh EH4 1LY

Phone: 0131 343 1126
Website: saorsa-art.com
Email: saorsa-art@hotmail.co.uk
Facebook.com/saorsaartgallery
Instagram.com/saorsaartgallery

Gallery Ten

Modern and contemporary art, representing established and emerging artists, master printmakers and artisans. Prints, studio glass and other applied arts from Scottish, national and international makers.
Address: 10 Stafford Street, Edinburgh EH3 7NG
Phone: 07957 855426
Website: galleryten.co.uk
Email: infogalleryten@gmail.com
Twitter.com/TenEdinburgh
Facebook.com/gallerytenedinburgh
Instagram.com/gallerytenart

Open Eye Gallery

Scottish contemporary art, sculpture, crafts, jewellery and ceramics. Established in 1982, and it is one of Scotland's leading contemporary private art galleries. Situated in New Town with an exhibition program throughout the year working closely with private and corporate collectors.
Address: 34 Abercromby Place, Edinburgh EH3 6QE
Phone: 0131 557 1020
Website: openeyegallery.co.uk
Email: mail@openeyegallery.co.uk
Twitter.com/openeyegallerye
Facebook.com/OpenEyeGalleryEdinburgh
Instagram.com/openeyegallerye

Dundas Street Gallery

The gallery is available to rent, . Situated in a prime location in New Town, it can be hired for the week, fortnight, month or evening.
Address: 6 Dundas Street, Edinburgh EH3 6HZ

Phone: 0131 557 4050
Website: dundas-street-gallery.co.uk
Email: art@fasedinburgh.com
Twitter.com/dundasstgallery
Facebook.com/DundasStreetGallery

Union Gallery

Contemporary gallery in the vibrant West End of Edinburgh, showing work from across Scotland and beyond, both established and emerging artists.
Address: 4 Drumsheugh Place, Edinburgh EH3 7PT
Phone: 07828 637217
Website: uniongallery.co.uk
Email: info@uniongallery.co.uk
Twitter.com/UNIONgallery1
Facebook.com/Union.Gallery.Edinburgh
Instagram.com/uniongallery1
Pinterest.co.uk/uniongallery

The Torrance Gallery

Exhibiting contemporary Scottish artists. Founded in 1970 on Dundas Street. Regular, affordable contemporary art exhibitions, and a big mixed exhibition in early spring and Christmas. Exporting highly sought after Scottish contemporary art across the world.
Address: 36 Dundas Street, Edinburgh EH3 6JN
Phone: 0131 556 6366 / 07791 121313
Website: torrancegallery.co.uk
Email: mail@torrancegallery.co.uk
Twitter.com/FionaMcCrindle
Facebook.com/TheTorranceGallery
Instagram.com/torrance_gallery

The Grilli Gallery

Run by Catherine Grilli who has worked in the Edinburgh art scene for 22 years. Exhibiting well known Scottish artists in the gallery, at festivals and London venues.
Address: 20A Dundas Street, Edinburgh EH3 6HZ

Phone: 0131 261 4264 / 07876 013 013
Website: art-grilli.co.uk
Email: catherine@art-grilli.co.uk

&Gallery

An exciting and diverse program of contemporary visual art, showing artists at various stages of their career from Edinburgh as well as the rest of the UK and worldwide.
Address: 3 Dundas Street, Edinburgh, EH3 6QG
Phone: 0131 467 0618 / 07711 285545
Website: andgallery.co.uk
Email: info@andgallery.co.uk
Twitter.com/andgallery
Facebook.com/andgallery.co.uk
Instagram.com/andgallery
Artsy.net/and-gallery-1
Vimeo.com/user110483323
MutualArt.com/Gallery/-Gallery/8342FE6AA1CDDD93

Collective

Established in 1984, Collective supports new work by artists who are at a pivotal stage of their development. In 2018 they moved to Calton Hill which has a purpose-built exhibition space.
Address: 38 Calton Hill, Edinburgh EH7 5AA
Phone: 0131 556 1264
Website: collectivegallery.net
Email: mail@collective-edinburgh.art
Twitter.com/collective_edin
Facebook.com/collectiveedinburgh
Instagram.com/collective_edin
Vimeo.com/collectiveedinburgh
SoundCloud.com/collectiveedinburgh

Fife

Fife Contemporary Art and Craft

An independent visual arts and crafts organisation in St Andrews. Located in various venues through partnerships. Works within Fife, the UK and internationally to bring projects to life.
Address: Fife Contemporary Art & Craft, Town Hall Queen's Gardens, St Andrews KY16 9TA
Phone: 01334 474610
Website: fcac.co.uk
Email: mail@fcac.co.uk
Twitter.com/fifecontemp
Facebook.com/fifecontemp
Instagram.com/fifecontemp
YouTube.com/user/fifecontemporary

Tatha Gallery

Exhibiting the best Scottish art; new and local talent alongside established artists in a beautiful, light-filled gallery with amazing views.
Address: 1 High Street, Newport-On-Tay DD6 8AB
Phone: 01382 690800
Website: tathagallery.com
Email: Helen@tathagallery.com
Email: Lindsay@tathagallery.com
Twitter.com/tathagallery
Facebook.com/TathaGallery
Instagram.com/tathagallery

Fraser Gallery St. Andrews

A family business for over 150 years, exhibiting the very best of contemporary Scottish artists in solo and mixed shows.
Address: 53 South Street, St Andrews KY16 9QR
Phone: 01334 479647
Website: frasergallery.co.uk
Email: enquiries@frasergallery.co.uk

Sproson Contemporary Art Gallery

A bespoke picture framing family business since 1981 with a gallery exhibiting emerging and established local and Scottish artists. Exhibitions throughout the year, also showing ceramics, limited edition prints,

jewellery and cards.
Address: 138 South Street, St Andrews
KY16 9EQ
Phone: 01334 474331
Website: sprosongallery.com
Email: info@sprosongallery.com
Twitter.com/sprosongallery
Facebook.com/sprosongallery
Instagram.com/sprosongallery
Pinterest.co.uk/sprosonartgallery

Glasgow
Scotlandart.com Gallery

The largest fine art gallery in Scotland with more than 1,000 paintings in stock and online. Free worldwide delivery.
Address: 193 Bath Street, Glasgow G2 4HU
Phone: 0141 221 4502
Website: scotlandart.com
Email: sales@scotlandart.com
Twitter.com/scotland_art
Facebook.com/scotlandart
Instagram.com/scotlandartgallery
Pinterest.co.uk/scotlandart

Kelvingrove Art Gallery and Museum

Opened in 1901, with 22 galleries exhibiting art of all kinds. Changing program of temporary exhibitions.
Address: Argyle Street, Glasgow G3 8AG
Phone: 0141 276 9599
Website: glasgowlife.org.uk
Email: info@glasgowlife.org.uk
Twitter.com/kelvingroveart
Facebook.com/Kelvingrove.
GlasgowMuseums
Flickr.com/photos/glasgowmuseums
YouTube.com/user/GlasgowMuseums

Transmission Gallery

The longest standing artist-run space in Glasgow producing contemporary art exhibitions, events, exchanges, residencies

and publications.
Address: 28 King Street, Glasgow G1 5QP
Phone: 0141 552 7141
Website: transmissiongallery.org
Email: info@transmissiongallery.org
Facebook.com/transmissionglasgow

Glasgow Print Studio

Founded in 1972 as an artist-led initiative providing facilities and workshops to artists working in printmaking. Now promotes contemporary and innovative printmaking through exhibitions, learning and conservation. Three floors of studio workshops, galleries, education space and other facilities.
Address: 22 King Street, Trongate, Glasgow G1 5HD
Phone: 0141 552 0704
Website: glasgowprintstudio.co.uk
Email: info@glasgowprintstudio.co.uk
Twitter.com/GlasPrintStudio
Facebook.com/TheGlasgowPrintStudio

Gallery Of Modern Art

GoMa, in the heart of Glasgow has 4 galleries, a café, shop and library. It is a world class art museum, displaying, borrowing and collecting art from around the world.
Address: Royal Exchange Square, Glasgow G1 3AH
Phone: 0141 287 3050
Website: glasgowlife.org.uk
Email: info@glasgowlife.org.uk
Twitter.com/glasgowgoma
Facebook.com/GalleryofModernArt.
GlasgowMuseums
Flickr.com/photos/glasgowmuseums
YouTube.com/user/GlasgowMuseums

The Burrell Collection

Situated in Pollok Country Park to the south side of the city of Glasgow, in a beautiful woodland setting. Work by Rodin, Degas and

Cézanne as well as late Medieval art, Chinese and Islamic Art and Ancient civilizations. With temporary exhibitions and an extensive program of events.
Address: Pollok Country Park, 2060, Pollokshaws Road, Glasgow G43 1AT
Phone: 0141 287 0047
Website: glasgowlife.org.uk
Email: info@glasgowlife.org.uk
Twitter.com/burrellcollect
Facebook.com/TheBurrellCollection.
GlasgowMuseums
Flickr.com/photos/glasgowmuseums
YouTube.com/user/GlasgowMuseums

The Lighthouse

Scotland's centre for design and architecture, with a visitor centre, exhibition space and events venue in the heart of Glasgow. A beacon for creative industries in Scotland with a vibrant program of exhibitions and events. The building was the first public commission completed by Charles Rennie Mackintosh.
Address: 11 Mitchell Lane, Glasgow G1 3NU
Phone: 0141 276 5365
Website: thelighthouse.co.uk
Email: information.theLighthouse@glasgow.gov.uk
Twitter.com/The_Lighthouse
Facebook.com/lighthouseglasgow
Instagram.com/thelighthouseglasgow

St. Mungo Museum Of Religious Life and Art

St Mungo is Glasgow's patron saint, who brought Christianity to Scotland in the 6th century. The museum is built on the site of the medieval bishop's castle. Galleries are full of art and objects that explore the importance of religion in people's lives across time and the world. Aiming to promote respect between different faiths with regular events and talks. The café opens out into the first Zen garden in Britain. Situated near Glasgow Cathedral and opposite Provand's Lordship, which is the oldest house in Glasgow.
Address: 2 Castle Street, Glasgow G4 0RH
Phone: 0141 276 1625
Website: glasgowlife.org.uk
Email: info@glasgowlife.org.uk
Twitter.com/stmungomuseum
Facebook.com/StMungo.GlasgowMuseums
Flickr.com/photos/glasgowmuseums
YouTube.com/user/GlasgowMuseums

The Modern Institute

Founded in 1997, the gallery works with 45 internationally established and emerging artists. Curates projects internationally, and publishes artist books and monographs.
Address: 3 Airds Lane, Glasgow G1 5HU
Phone: 0141 237 1488
Website: themoderninstitute.com
Email: mail@themoderninstitute.com
Twitter.com/TMIGLA
Facebook.com/TheModernInstitute
Instagram.com/TheModernInstitute

Centre for Contemporary Arts

Glasgow's hub for the arts, with a year round program of cutting-edge exhibitions, film, music, literature, spoken word, festivals, Gaelic and performance. Over 334,000 visitors in the past year. Six major exhibitions a year, with national and international artists. The Intermedia Gallery showcases emerging artists.
Address: 350 Sauchiehall Street, Glasgow G2 3JD
Phone: 0141 352 4900
Website: cca-glasgow.com
Email: gen@cca-glasgow.com
Twitter.com/CCA_Glasgow
Facebook.com/CCAGlasgow1
Instagram.com/cca_glasgow
Flickr.com/photos/ccaglasgow
SoundCloud.com/cca-glasgow
YouTube.com/user/ccaglasgow

Glasgow School Of Art

The Exhibitions Department curates a year-round program linking staff research, teaching and learning, student experience, creative networks, contemporary practice and heritage. Talks and events exploring the creative, social and educational nature of contemporary practice. Exhibitions of student work and creative engagement in the wider community.
Address: 167 Renfrew Street, Glasgow G3 6RQ
Phone: 0141 353 4500
Website: gsa.ac.uk
Email: exhibitions@gsa.ac.uk
Twitter.com/gsofa
Facebook.com/glasgowschoolofart
www.gsa.ac.uk/the-hub/
Vimeo.com/glasgowschoolofart
Flickr.com/photos/glasgowschoolart

RGI Kelly Gallery

Founded in 1861, the Royal Glasgow Institute of Fine Arts is an independent organisation, promoting contemporary art and artists in Scotland. Organises the largest and most prestigious annual art exhibition in Scotland, which is open to all artists.
Address: 118 Douglas Street, Glasgow G2 4ET
Phone: 0141 248 6386
Website: theroyalglasgowinstituteofthefinearts.co.uk
Email: theroyalglasgowinstitute@gmail.com

Market Gallery

A charity established in 2000, presenting a varied program of contemporary exhibitions, projects and events, both in the gallery and off-site. Offering a platform for the discussion and experience of contemporary art in Glasgow and internationally.
Address: 334 Duke Street, Glasgow G31 1QZ
Phone: 0141 556 7276
Website: marketgallery.org
Email: market@marketgallery.org
Twitter.com/marketgallery
Facebook.com/MarketGalleryGlasgow
Instagram.com/marketgallery

Glasgow Galleries

A contemporary art gallery in the city centre, exhibiting a range of original work from leading Scottish artists in solo, featured and mixed shows throughout the year. Also selling applied art, such as ceramics, glass, sculpture and jewellery.
Address: 182 Bath Street, Glasgow G2 4HG
Phone: 0141 333 1991
Website: glasgowgalleries.co.uk
Email: info@glasgowgallery.co.uk
Facebook.com/glasgowgalleryltd

Art Prints Gallery

An online store specialising in art prints by new and established artists. The owners have over 20 years' experience selling art prints by local Scottish and international artists.
Address: 14 Clydesmill Grove, Cambuslang Investment Park, Glasgow G32 8NL
Phone: 0141 646 2323
Website: artprintsgallery.co.uk
Email: sales@artprintsgallery.co.uk
Twitter.com/ArtPrintGallery
Facebook.com/ArtPrintsGallery
Instagram.com/artprintsgallery
Pinterest.co.uk/artprintsgall

Patricia Fleming Projects

A contemporary art gallery, showing the work of both emerging and established artists.
Address: 60/64 Osborne Street, Glasgow G1 5QH
Phone: 07968 066708
Website: patriciaflemingprojects.Tumblr.com
Email: studio@patriciaflemingprojects.co.uk
Twitter.com/pfprojects

Facebook.com/pfprojects
Instagram.com/patriciaflemingglasgow

Thistle Gallery

An eclectic mix of paintings, sculpture, ceramics, jewellery and textiles in the West End of Glasgow.
Address: 56 Park Road, Glasgow G4 9JF
Phone: 0141 334 3444
Facebook.com/thistleartgallery

Compass Gallery

Founded in 1969, making it one of the longest established contemporary art gallery in Scotland. Renowned for supporting talented new graduates as well as more established artists. A monthly program of exhibitions, with solo, mixed and the celebrated New Generation Show which is held immediately after the Art School degree shows.
Address: 178 West Regent Street, Glasgow G2 4RL
Phone: 0141 221 6370
Website: compassgallery.co.uk
Email: mail@compassgallery.co.uk

John Green Fine Art

City centre art gallery with oils and watercolours from Scottish, British and Continental artists. Both contemporary and traditional with sculpture, glass, jewellery and ceramics. Solo, featured and mixed exhibitions throughout the year. Picture cleaning and restoration.
Address: 182 Bath Street, Glasgow G2 4HG
Phone: 0141 333 1991
Website: glasgowgallery.com
Email: info@glasgowgallery.co.uk
Facebook.com/glasgowgalleryltd

Inverness-shire

Inverness Museum and Art Gallery

A charity, owned by The Highland Council, promoting culture as well as learning, sport, leisure, health and wellbeing.
Address: Castle Wynd, Inverness IV2 3EB
Phone: 01463 237114
Website: highlifehighland.com
Email: info@highlifehighland.com
Twitter.com/hlhsocial
Facebook.com/HighLifeHighland

Scottish Highland Art

Highland paintings, and lessons with an experienced artist in a beautiful setting.
Address: Artisbs Studio, Edinuanagan, Torness, Inverness IV2 6UG
Phone: 01463 751314
Website: highlandart.com
Email: artist@highlandart.com

Castle Gallery

Situated in the lee of Inverness Castle, with 2 floors of exhibition space. Original contemporary art and applied art from Scotland and Britain, with both emerging and established talent.
Address: 43 Castle Street, Inverness IV2 3DU
Phone: 01463 729512
Website: castlegallery.co.uk
Email: info@castlegallery.co.uk
Facebook.com/castlegalleryinverness
Instagram.com/castleartgallery
Issuu.com/castlegallery
Pinterest.co.uk/castle_gallery

Kilmorack Gallery

One of the foremost commercial art galleries in Scotland. Opened in 1997, in the old parish church outside Beauly. Exhibiting some of the most interesting and collectable artists and sculptors in Scotland.
Address: By Beauly, Inverness IV4 7AL
Phone: 01463 783230
Website: kilmorackgallery.co.uk
Email: art@kilmorackgallery.co.uk

Twitter.com/kilmorackgallry
Facebook.com/Kilmorack-Gallery
Instagram.com/kilmorackart

Alder Arts

Period and modern fine art paintings, with conservation, restoration and framing. 12 miles from Inverness. 2 galleries; specialising in 18th to 19th century oils, etchings, engravings, watercolours and pastels and modern and contemporary art and sculpture.
Address: 4 The Square High Street, Beauly IV4 7BX
Phone: 01463 782247
Website: i31732.wixsite.com/alderarts
Email: info@alder-arts.co.uk
Facebook.com/AlderArts

Perth and Kinross

Galleria Luti

Run by mother and daughter team, Sandie and Marsha Luti. Featuring an impressive company of artists as well as giving a platform for new artists.
Address: 16 Ancaster Square, Callander FK17 8BL
Phone: 01877 339577
Website: gallerialuti.co.uk
Email: info@gallerialuti.co.uk
Twitter.com/gallerialuti
Facebook.com/gallerialuti

Frames Gallery

Started as a picture framers in 1979. Since 1991 have been exhibiting contemporary Scottish artists in a larger exhibition space.
Address: 10 Victoria Street, Perth PH2 8LW
Phone: 01738 631085
Website: framesgallery.co.uk
Email: info@framesgallery.co.uk
Twitter.com/FramesGallery
Facebook.com/framesgalleryperth
LinkedIn.com/in/hugh-goring-28339230

Keltneyburn Smithy Gallery

Designer, who recycles industrial and agricultural scrap metal into sculptures reflecting the natural world.
Address: Nr. Aberfeldy, Keltneyburn PH15 2LF
Phone: 01887 830267
Website: ironfairy.co.uk
Email: scottishironfairy@hotmail.com

Jardine Gallery and Workshop

The gallery exhibits fine art and crafts from the best national and international wildlife artists, alongside the workshop of ceramic sculptor Julian Jardine. Picture framing also available, with regular classes in clay, drawing and painting for adults and children.
Address: 45 New Row, Perth PH1 5QA
Phone: 01738 621836
Website: julianjardine.co.uk
Facebook.com/JardineGallery

The Lemond Gallery

Formed in 2000, originally as an online gallery. It has evolved into a private gallery, now representing over 120 of the best contemporary Scottish artists from all genres with solo and two-person shows.
Address: 4 Thorn Road, Bearsden G61 4PP
Phone: 0141 942 4683
Website: lemondgallery.com
Email: kenlemond@msn.com
Facebook.com/lemondgallery
Instagram.com/thelemondgallery

Perth Museum and Art Gallery

Portraits and photographs to meteorites and Miss Ballantyne's salmon. Always a fascinating array of objects. A regularly changing program of temporary exhibitions.
Address: 78 George St, Perth PH1 5LB
Phone: 01738 632488
Website: www.culturepk.org.uk/museums-and-galleries/perth-museum-and-art-gallery

Email: info@culturepk.org.uk
Twitter.com/CPKMuseums
Facebook.com/PerthMuseum

The Fergusson Gallery

An exciting program of exhibitions and displays with special events and activities.
Address: Marshall Place, Perth PH2 8NS
Phone: 01738 783425
Website: culturepk.org.uk/museums-and-galleries/the-fergusson-gallery
Email: info@culturepk.org.uk
Twitter.com/CPKMuseums
Facebook.com/PerthMuseum

Orkney

Hoxa Tapestry Gallery

Mother and daughter team, Leila and Jo Thomson, both graduates of Edinburgh College of Art, returned home to Orkney. Their work expresses the rhythm of life and landscape of the islands.
Address: South Ronaldsay, Orkney KW17 2TW
Phone: 01856 831395
Website: hoxatapestrygallery.co.uk
Email: enquiries@hoxatapestrygallery.co.uk
Twitter.com/hoxatapestry
Facebook.com/HoxaTapestryGallery
Instagram.com/hoxatapestrygallery
Pinterest.co.uk/hoxatg

Ross and Cromarty

Browns Gallery

Established in 1992 by Scottish artist Gordon Brown, the purpose built exhibition space shows exciting contemporary artwork. Due the success of the gallery, it expanded in 2005, to utilise an old 19th century bake house next to the original gallery, with the architectural design exhibited at the Royal Scottish Academy.
Address: Castle Brae, Tain IV19 1AJ

Phone: 01862 893884
Website: brownsart.com
Email: info@brownsart.com

Shetland

The Shetland Gallery

Located on the island of Yell, this is the most northerly gallery in Britain. Showing the best of Shetland's contemporary art and high-end craft, with work by some of Shetland's most well-known artists exhibited in constantly changing group shows.
Address: Unit 1, Sellafirth Business Park Sellafirth, Sellafirth ZE2 9DG
Phone: 01957 744259
Website: shetlandgallery.com
Email: shona@shetlandgallery.com
Facebook.com/TheShetlandGallery

Stirling

Smith Art Gallery & Museum

Founded in 1874 at the bequest of the artist Thomas Stuart Smith. Mainly focusing on contemporary art, with a museum and library reading room for the "benefit of the inhabitants of Stirling, Dunblane and Kinbuck".
Address: Dumbarton Road, Stirling FK8 2RQ
Phone: 01786 471917
Website: smithartgalleryandmuseum.co.uk

Changing Room Gallery

A stunning art gallery, which is unique in Scotland as it is solely dedicated to contemporary art.
Address: 35 Arcade, Stirling FK8 1AX
Phone: 01786 479361

WALES

Anglesey

Oriel Tegfryn Gallery

Established in 1963 with a respected history as being the premier gallery in north Wales, exhibiting leading artists of the region.
Address: Cadnant Road, Menai Bridge LL59 5EW
Phone: 01248 715128

Brecknockshire

The Lion Street Gallery

Situated in the beautiful Hay-on-Wye, focusing on artists from Wales and the Borders. Rolling group shows throughout the year, with both established and emerging talent. Rated one of the leading art galleries in Wales by Culture Trip. The sister gallery, Erwood Station Gallery, shows applied arts.
Address: 6 Lion Street, Hay-On-Wye HR3 5AA
Phone: 01497 822900
Website: lionstreetgallery.co.uk
Email: thelionstreetgallery@gmail.com
Facebook.com/LionStreetGallery
Instagram.com/thelionstreetgallery

Cardiff

National Museum Cardiff

Part of the seven national museums of Wales.
Address: Cathays Park, Cardiff CF10 3NP
Phone: 0300 111 2333
Website: museum.wales
Twitter.com/AmgueddfaCymru
Facebook.com/amgueddfacymru
Instagram.com/museumwales

Craft In The Bay

Curating, commissioning and selling unique contemporary objects, from jewellery to pottery and fabrics. Local authors are also showcased.

Address: The Flourish, Lloyd George Avenue, Cardiff CF10 4QH
Phone: 01542 810373
Website: makersguildinwales.co.uk
Email: admin@makersguildinwales.org.uk
Twitter.com/MakersWales
Facebook.com/MakersWales
Instagram.com/makerswales

Kooywood Gallery

Address: 8 Museum Place, Cardiff CF10 3BG
Phone: 029 2023 5093
Website: kooywoodgallery.com
Email: enquiries@kooywoodgallery.com

Albany Gallery

Established in 1965 and is one of Wales most successful privately-owned commercial art galleries. Monthly exhibitions of Welsh and British artists with solo and group shows. Exhibitors include Royal Academicians, members of the Royal Cambrian Academy, the New English Art Club and the Society of Women Artists.
Address: 74B Albany Road, Cardiff CF24 3RS
Phone: 029 2048 7158
Website: albanygallery.com
Email: info@albanygallery.com
Twitter.com/albanygallery
Facebook.com/The-Albany-Gallery
Instagram.com/albanygallery

Off the Wall

A gem of a gallery, with a wide range of art from many different artists.
Address: The Old Probate Registry, Cardiff Road, Llandaff, Cardiff CF5 2DQ
Phone: 029 2055 4469

Martin Tinney Gallery

Considered a leading private commercial gallery in Wales, specialising in artists from

Wales, both past and present.
Address: 18 St. Andrew's Crescent. Cardiff. CF10
Phone: 029 2064 1411
Website: artwales.com
Email: mtg@artwales.com
Twitter.com/TheRealArtWales
Facebook.com/MartinTinneyGallery
Instagram.com/therealartwales

Bay Art Gallery

An artist-led creative space in a busy street in Cardiff Bay. There are 16 studios and a flat for research or residency purposes. Gives a platform for emerging artists as well as those at mid-career, from Wales and further afield. There are artist talks, seminars and workshops. Works closely with schools to develop children's understanding of contemporary art.
Address: 54 Bute Street, Cardiff CF10 5AF
Phone: 029 2065 0016
Website: Bayart.org.uk
Email: bayartcardiff@gmail.com
Twitter.com/BayArtCardiff
Facebook.com/BayArtGallery

Ten

Contemporary art gallery.
Address: 143 Donald St, Cardiff CF24 4TP
Phone: 029 2060 0495
Website: gallery-ten.co.uk
Email: info@gallery-ten.co.uk
Twitter.com/gallery__ten

ArcadeCampfa

Artist-led gallery in the Queens Arcade shopping centre. Campfa shows a year-long program of contemporary solo and group exhibitions. Arcade is an experimental project space, which hosts exhibitions, workshops, talks and events. There is a 6-month residency program running twice a year resulting in an exhibition. The organisation is part-funded by Arts Council Wales and Queens Arcade.
Address: Queens Arcade, Queen St, Cardiff CF10 2BY
Phone: 07890 812898
Website: arcade-campfa.org
Email: clare@arcade-campfa.org
Email: george@arcade-camfa.org
Twitter.com/arcadecampfa
Facebook.com/arcadecampfa
Instagram.com/arcadecampfa

G39

An artist-run gallery and creative community for the visual arts. Exhibitions, work placements, peer introductions as well as solo exhibitions, the aim is to encourage and enable those wishing to pursue a career in visual arts.
Address: Curatorial Team, G39 Oxford Street, Cardiff CF24 3DT
Phone: 029 2047 3633
Website: g39.org
Email: post@g39.org

Saltmarshe

Cardiff's only picture maker, with a complete service from printing to presentation.
Address: 352 Caerphilly Rd Heath, Cardiff CF14 4NT
Phone: 029 2065 7585
Website: saltmarshe.com
Email: info@saltmarshe.com

Carmarthenshire

Fountain Fine Art

Founded in 1989, exhibiting some of the finest work from Welsh and British artists. Located in the middle of picturesque Llandeilo, which looks down onto the beautiful Carmarthenshire Towy valley.
Address: 115 Rhosmaen Street, Llandeilo, Carmarthenshire, SA19 6EN
Phone: 01558 824244
Website: fountainfineart.com
Email: contactus@fountainfineart.com

Gwynedd

Oriel Cymru Gallery

Contemporary art from Wales, sold locally, nationally and internationally.
Address: Glanrafon, Pentrefelin, Criccieth LL52 0PT
Phone: 01766 522530
Website: oriel-cymru.com
Email: sales@oriel-cymru.com

Monmouthshire

Iap Fine Art

An established contemporary fine art gallery selling 20th century work from leading artists to private collectors, corporate collections and museums. Starting life in Bethnal Green in the East End of London in 1994, the gallery moved to Chelsea and then St James's. In 2016 the gallery moved to the beautiful Wye Valley, retaining a viewing and events space in Spitalfields, London E1. Working with many museums and public spaces and creating national touring exhibitions such as Chris Gollon's 'Incarnation, Mary and Women from the Bible', which toured English cathedrals.
Address: 15 Church St, Monmouth NP25 3BX
Phone: 0844 561 1833
Website: iapfineart.com
Email: info@iapfineart.com
Twitter.com/IAPFineArt
Facebook.com/IAPFineArt
Instagram.com/iapfineart
YouTube.com/IAP Fine Art - Films & Installations

The Big Sky Gallery

Although exhibiting and selling locally and nationally, the gallery is principally online, shipping worldwide. Works are available to view within the UK. Mainly British art from 1800 to 2000, dealing only in originals from well-known artists. Contemporary art is included but only from those already established in what can be a volatile market.
Address: 17 Twyn Square, Usk NP15 1BH
Phone: 01291 672738
Website: bigskyfineart.com
Email: art@bigskyfineart.com
Twitter.com/bigskyfineart
Facebook.com/bigskyfineart

Montgomeryshire

Art by Osian

Osian is a figurative fine art painter producing expressive work that focuses on the simplicity of shape, colour and texture and the bolder energetic statements of paint. Other work encompasses the hidden, mysterious intensity of the Welsh landscape.
Address: Art by Osian, 3 Short Bridge Street, Llanidloes SY18 6AD
Phone: 07484 763507
Website: osiangwent.com
Email: hello@osiangwent.com
Twitter.com/artbyosian
Facebook.com/artbyosian
Instagram.com/artbyosian

Spectrum Gallery

From 1983 the gallery has shown fine art and studio crafts. Since 2013 the gallery is now an exhibition space for Paul Martinez-Frias and Pamela Taylor, who originally founded the gallery.
Address: 27 Heol Maengwyn, Machynlleth SY20 8EB
Phone: 01654 702877
Website: spectrumgallery.co.uk
Email: art@spectrumgallery.co.uk

Pembrokeshire

Waterfront Gallery

A progressive gallery with regular artists, alongside a dynamic exhibition program. Contemporary work inspired by the

landscape and light found in Pembrokeshire, encompassing fine art, mixed media, sculpture, photography, glass, ceramics, papier-mâche, jewellery, bronze, metal and woodwork.
Address: The Old Sail Loft, Milford Haven SA73 3AF
Phone: 01646 695699
Website: thewaterfrontgallery.co.uk
Email: info@thewaterfrontgallery.co.uk

Llewellyn's Gallery

Photography by Gary Llewellyn, framed and unframed limited edition prints with a bespoke framing service.
Address: Cobourg Shop Upper Frog Street, Tenby SA70 7JD
Phone: 01834 845710 / 07812 996934
Website: garyllewellyn.com
Email: gary@garyllewellyn.com

Powys

Erwood Station Gallery

The largest gallery showing applied art and contemporary craft in Wales with over 60 artists being shown at any one time, using wood, ceramics, metal, glass, paper etc. Set in an eclectic space made of railways carriages, dating from the 1860s, near the banks of the River Wye.
Address: Llandeilo Graban, Builth Wells, Powys. LD2 3SJ
Website: erwoodstation.com
Instagram.com/erwoodstationgallery

Found Gallery

Contemporary art and ceramics with a changing exhibition program showing both emerging and established artists.
Address: 1 Bulwark, Brecon LD3 7LB
Phone: 07736 062849
Website: foundgallery.co.uk
Email: info@foundgallery.co.uk
Twitter.com/found_gallery

Facebook.com/FoundBrecon
Instagram.com/found.gallery
YouTube.com/foundgallery

Reformations.co.uk

Online gallery showing handmade glass clocks and modern glass wall art by Craig Anthony.
Address: Newtown, Powys
Phone: 07498 405569
Website: reformations.co.uk
Email: info@reformations.co.uk

Swansea
Glynn Vivian Art Gallery

This world class gallery in the heart of the city is run by Swansea Council. Historical, modern and contemporary exhibitions, talks, lectures, conferences, live music, performance and events.
Address: Alexandra Road, Swansea SA1 5DZ
Phone: 01792 516900
Website: glynnviviangallery.org
Email: glynn.vivian.gallery@swansea.gov.uk
Twitter.com/GlynnVivian
Facebook.com/GlynnVivian
Instagram.com/glynnvivian
Flickr.com/GlynnVivian
Vimeo.com/user19065755

Attic Gallery

Established in 1962. Showing contemporary work of national importance.
Address: 37 Pocketts Wharf, Swansea SA1 3XL
Phone: 01792 653387
Website: atticgallery.co.uk
Email: sales@atticgallery.co.uk
Facebook.com/atticgallerySwansea

Mission Gallery

Situated in a 19th century converted seaman's chapel. Founded in 1977, nurturing diverse work by emerging artists across

all disciplines from Wales and beyond. A thriving learning and participation program. Cultural partnerships with organisations in New York and Venice building international work through programming, partnerships and residencies.
Address: Gloucester Place, Swansea SA1 1TY
Phone: 01792 652016
Website: missiongallery.co.uk
Email: info@missiongallery.co.uk
Twitter.com/missiongallery
Facebook.com/mission.gallery
Instagram.com/missiongalleryswansea

Galerie Simpson

Artist-run gallery, showing a wide range of artists at every stage of their career. Creative Community initiative with Open Submission Exhibitions.
Address: 217 High St, Swansea SA1 1LN
Phone: 07714 327523
Website: galeriesimpsonswansea.com
Email: info@galeriesimpsonswansea.com

St Davids
Goat Street Gallery

Run by ceramicist, Daniel Wright and textile-maker, Amanda Wright. Situated in a converted 1816 chapel overlooking St David's cathedral. This contemporary art gallery shows international, local and new fine artists and craftmakers with changing exhibitions. You can watch the artists at work in the gallery and participate in workshops.
Address: 28 Goat St., St Davids, Haverfordwest SA62 6RF
Phone: 01437 721119
Website: goatstreetgallery.co.uk
Facebook.com/GoatStreetGallery
Instagram.com/goatstreetgallery

St. Davids Studio Gallery

Located in a Georgian house just off St David's city square. Exhibits the work of 50 or so artists and makers, both established and emerging on permanent display.
Address: 14 Nun St, St. Davids SA62 6NS
Phone: 01437 720648 / 07890 740604

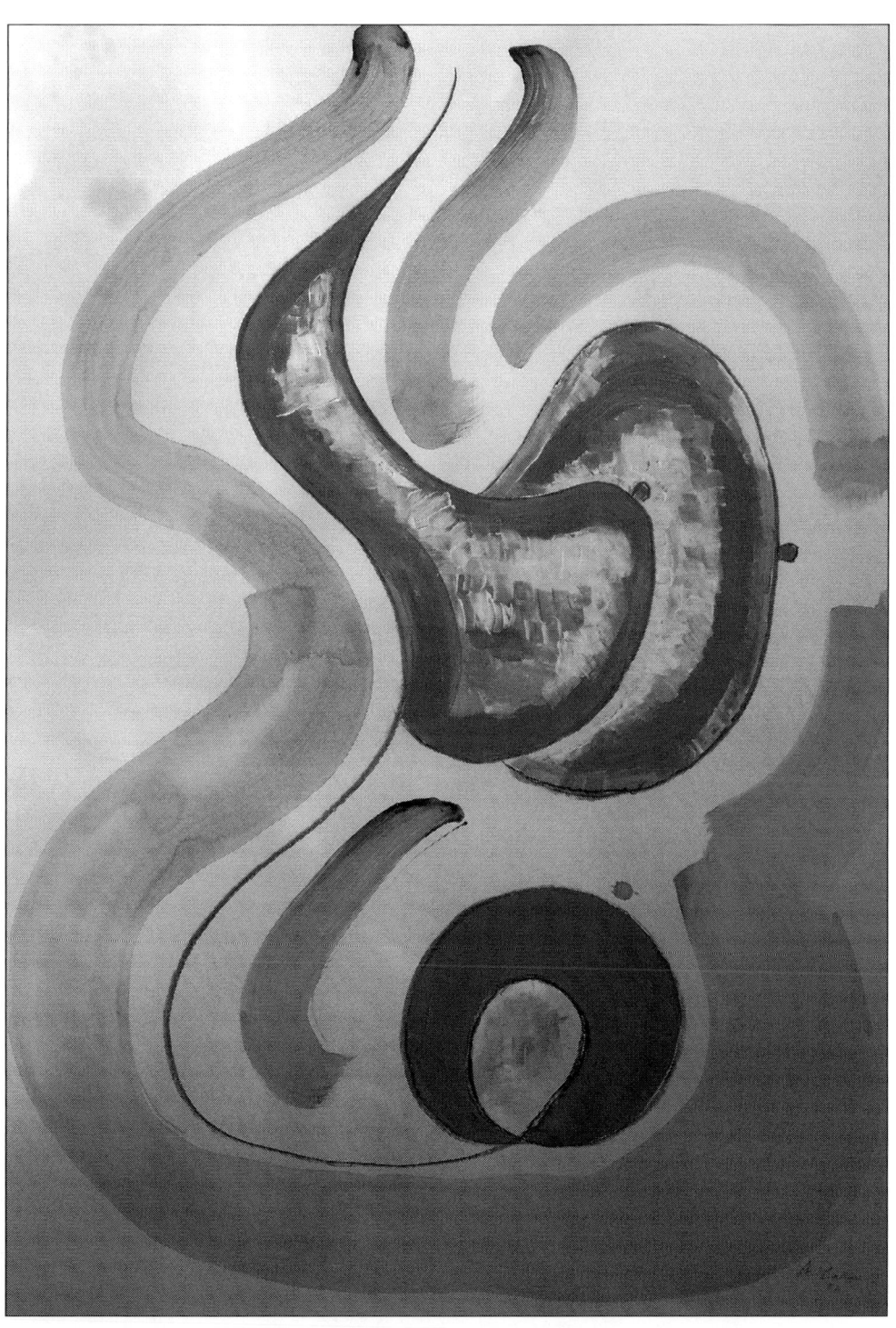

Abstract Nude 7 by Sophie McCallum

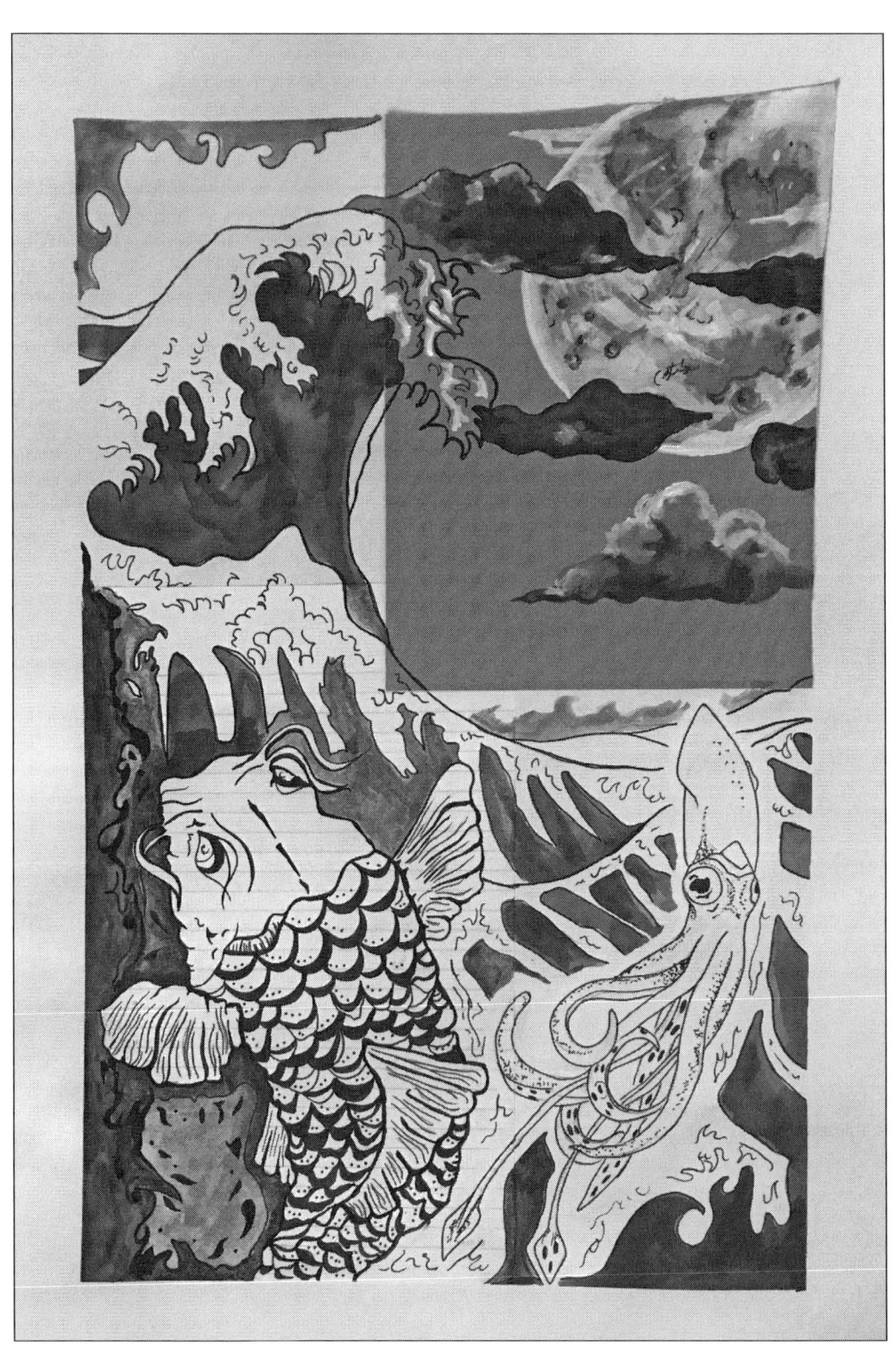

Beneath the Great Wave by Alice Billington

THE REST OF THE WORLD

ALBANIA

Tiranë

Gallery 70 Contemporary Art

Contemporary art in the heart of Tirana. With selected midcareer, established and emerging artists with whom they build long term relationships.
Address: Toptani Shopping Centre, Tirana 1001
Phone: +355 69 204 1859
Website: gallery70.art
Email: info@gallery70.art
Facebook.com/gallery70
Instagram.com/gallery70

AMERICAN SOMOA

The Vanya Taule'alo Gallery

Exhibiting contemporary and traditional Samoan art. Located 4 minutes outside of Apia
Address: Located next to Legends Café
Phone: +685 20011

ANDORRA

Tapiezo

Contemporary art gallery and workshop exhibiting painting and sculpture.
Address: 39 rue Richard Casteau, Roussillon 84220
Phone: +33 6 14 09 46 50
Website: tapiezo.com
Email: tapiezo@tapiezo.com

ARGENTINA

Buenos Aires

Museo de Arte Moderno de Buenos Aires

Public institution run by the Ministry of Culture, created in 1956. A state of the art museum, showing Argentine artists, with a gallery exhibiting the latest in artistic disciplines.
Address: Avenida San Juan 350, Buenos Aires C1147AAO
Phone: +54 11 4300-9139
Website: museomoderno.org
Twitter.com/modernoba
Facebook.com/museodeartemodernodebuenosaires
Instagram.com/modernoba
YouTube.com/user/modernodebuenosaires

Aldo de Souza Gallery

Contemporary art gallery in Buenos Aires showing Argentine and Latin American artists since 1972. Advises international collections and museums, providing a global visibility platform, exporting work to countries such as the USA, Canada, Spain, Brazil, Colombia, Peru, Chile, Venezuela, Puerto Rico and Uruguay.
Address: Arroyo 858, Buenos Aires 1007
Phone: +54 11 4393-0803
Website: aldodesousa.com.ar
Email: arroyo@aldodesousa.com.ar
Facebook.com/AldodeSousaGaleria

Sessa Photo Gallery

Photographs from Aldo Sessa, looking at unexplored lights and shadows which lend narrative, music and journeys to inner reality.
Address: Pasaje Bollini 2241, Ciudad de Buenos Aires 1425
Phone: +54 11 4806-3796
Website: aldosessa.com.ar
Email: sessa.luis@gmail.com

Braga Menendez Contemporary Art (Braga Menendez Arte Contemporaneo)

Contemporary art gallery.
Address: Calle Humboldt 1574, Buenos Aires C1414CTN
Phone: +54 11 4775-5577

Bruggens

Offering a wide range of art from renowned artists to an international market.
Address: Calle Rodriguez Pena 1820, Buenos Aires C1021ABN
Phone: +54 11 4811 4345
Website: bruggens.com
Email: info@bruggens.com
Facebook.com/Bruggens
Instagram.com/bruggensba

Fundación Federico Jorge Klemm

Art gallery, museum and charitable organisation.
Address: Marcelo T de Alvear 626, Buenos Aires 1058
Website: fundacionfjklemm.org
Email: info@fundacionfjklemm.org
Facebook.com/Fundación-Federico-Jorge-Klemm-Oficial
Instagram.com/fundacionklemm
Vimeo.com/user3712852
YouTube.com/ Fundación Klemm

AUSTRALIA
Adelaide, South Australia
Jam Factory

A unique not-for-profit organisation, championing the social, cultural and economic value of craft and design. Inspiring audiences, building careers and extending contemporary craft and design into new markets.
Address: 19 Morphett Street, Adelaide 5000
Phone: +61 8 8231 0005
Website: jamfactory.com.au

Email: contact@jamfactory.com.au
Instagram.com/jamfactoryau
LinkedIn.com/company/jamfactory-contemporary-craft-and-design

Contemporary Art Centre of SA (CACSA)

Address: 14 Porter Street, Parkside 5063
Phone: +61 8 8272 2682
Website: cacsa.org.au

The Light Gallery

A private educational institution promoting the highest level of photographic art. Supporting photographers at all stages of their career .
Address: 138 Richmond Road, Marleston 5033
Phone: +61 8 8354 0839
Website: ccp.sa.edu.au
Email: info@ccp.sa.edu.au
Twitter.com/CCPAdelaide
Facebook.com/ccpadelaide
Instagram.com/ccpadelaide

GAGPROJECTS

Promoting the best local, national and international contemporary artists in a large converted warehouse in Kent Town. Currently representing 26 artists. Collaborates with other artists and institutions.
Address: 39 Rundle Street, Kent Town 5067
Phone: +61 8 8362 6354
Website: gagprojects.com
Email: gag@greenaway.com.au
Twitter.com/gagprojects
Facebook.com/gagprojects
Instagram.com/gagprojects

Artlogic

Combining the creative and the analytical with surprising outcomes. Selling or renting over 1,600 cutting-edge South Australian artworks with promotional videos and live art events.

Address: 62 Amherst Avenue, Trinity Gardens 5068
Phone: +61 432 924 305
Website: artlogic.com.au
Facebook.com/adelaideartlogic
Instagram.com/adelaide_art_logic

Format

With a year-round visual art program, public art and live music as well as the annual Format Festival.
Phone: +61 423 921 656
Address: 15 Peel Street, Adelaide 5000
Website: globalnpo.org/AU/Adelaide

Art Gallery of South Australia

One of the largest art museums in Australia, with nearly 45,000 works spanning 2,000 years. Includes paintings, sculpture, prints, drawings, photographs, videos, textiles, clothing, ceramics, glass, metalwork, jewellery and furniture. Approximately 40% of the collection can be viewed online.
Address: North Terrace, Adelaide 5000
Phone: T +61 8 8207 7000
Website: artgallery.sa.gov.au
Email: info@artgallery.sa.gov.au
Twitter.com/agsa_adelaide
Facebook.com/agsa.adelaide
Instagram.com/agsa.adelaide
Vimeo.com/agsaadelaide

ACE Open

South Australia's flagship gallery, with a year-round program of regional, national and international artists with exhibitions, talks and events.
Address: 55 North Terrace, Adelaide 5000
Phone: +61 8 8211 7505
Website: aceopen.art
Email: admin@aceopen.art
Twitter.com/ACE_Open
Facebook.com/ACEOpenSA
Instagram.com/ACE_Open

Brisbane, Queensland
Queensland Art Gallery

The Gallery of Modern Art is part of the Queensland Cultural Centre. it houses a globally significant collection of contemporary art from Australia, Asia and the Pacific, with ever-changing exhibitions, programs and events. The Children's Art Centre presents interactive art as well as a cinema with films from around the world. Gallery shops and cafés.
Address: Stanley Place, Cultural Precinct, South Bank, Brisbane 4101
Phone: +61 7 3840 7303
Website: qagoma.qld.gov.au
Email: gallery@qagoma.qld.gov.au
Twitter.com/qagoma
Facebook.com/QAGOMA
Instagram.com/qagoma
Open.Spotify.com/user/bnlio4hfskvm52kzicxkkugef

Red Hill Gallery

A comprehensive selection of fine art from mid- and senior career artists with emerging practitioners. Monthly exhibitions of realists, impressionist and contemporary paintings, with works on paper, bronze sculptures, glass, ceramics and many hidden treasures.
Address: 61 Musgrave Road Red Hill, Red Hill 4059
Phone: +61 7 3368 1442
Website: redhillgallery.com.au
Email: art@redhillgallery.com.au
Artchat.com.au

Institute Of Modern Art

Since 1975, the Institute has been the hub of Brisbane's contemporary art scene with an annual program of exhibitions, public programs, publications and offsite programs with Queensland, Australian and international artists. One of Australia's leading independent contemporary art spaces

Address: 420 Brunswick Street Fortitude Valley, Brisbane 4006
Phone: +61 7 3252 5750
Website: ima.org.au
Email: ima@ima.org.au
Facebook.com/InstituteOfModernArt
Instagram.com/ima_brisbane

Suzanne O'Connell Gallery

Championing the most innovative contemporary Aboriginal artists for nearly 2 decades, with a national and international reach. One of the foremost indigenous galleries in Australia with artists working in painting, fibre, sculpture, ceramics, bark and other mediums.
Address: 93 James Street, New Farm 4005
Phone: +61 7 3358 5811
Website: suzanneoconnellgallery.com
Email: admin@suzanneoconnellgallery.com
Facebook.com/suzanneoconnellgallery
Instagram.com/suzanneoconnellgallery

Cairns, Queensland
North Site

A dynamic contemporary art space with original paintings, sculpture, ceramics, jewellery, gifts, books and homewares with fine-art printmaking by leading Aboriginal and Torres Strait Islander artists.
Address: 96 Abbott Street, Cairns City 4870
Phone: +61 7 4050 9496
Website: shop.northsite.org.au
Email: shop@northsite.org.au
Facebook.com/
NorthSiteContemporaryArts
Instagram.com/NorthSite_
ContemporaryArts

Cairns Art Gallery

One of Australia's leading public art galleries with excellent programs and collections relating to the unique heritage and culture of North Queensland and the Asia Pacific.

Address: Corner Abbott & Shields Street, Cairns 4870
Phone: +61 7 4046 4800
Website: cairnsregionalgallery.com.au
Email: info@cairnsregionalgallery.com.au
Twitter.com/cairnsgallery
Facebook.com/Cairns.Art.Gallery
Instagram.com/cairnsartgallery

UnderArt Gallery

One of the most extensive collections of sterling silver jewellery in North Queensland. Also showing quirky sculptures, designer cutlery and Barrier Reef inspired ceramics.
Address: Shop 4, 12 Spence Street, Cairns 4870
Phone: +61 7 4051 3888
Website: underart.com.au
Email: info@underart.com.au

Canberra - Queanbeyan, Australian Capital Territory/New South Wales
National Gallery of Australia

With a collection of nearly 160,000 works of art, including the world's largest collection of Aboriginal and Torres Strait Islander art, as well as Australia's pre-eminent collection of modern international masters.
Address: Parkes Place, Parkes 2600
Phone: +61 2 6240 6411
Website: nga.gov.au
Email: ngawebmanager@nga.gov.au

Bilk Gallery

Gallery for contemporary metal and glass.
Address: Palmerston Lane, Manuka 2603
Phone: +61 2 6162 2761
Website: bilk.com.au
Email: gallery@bilk.com.au
Facebook.com/BilkGallery
Instagram.com/bilkgallery

Canberra Contemporary Art Space

Part of the national network of Contemporary Arts Organisations of Australia (CAOA) which are centres of innovation, testing new ideas for the visual arts. With exhibitions, performances, artists' talks, public programs and publications. Creating an environment for artists to produce high-quality national and international work.
Address: Gorman Arts Centre, 55 Ainslie Avenue, Braddon 2612
Phone: +61 2 6247 0188
Website: ccas.com.au
Email: info@ccas.com.au
Twitter.com/CCAS_Canberra
Facebook.com/canberracontemporary

Darwin, Northern Territory
Northern Centre for Contemporary Art

Open to exhibition proposals from local, national and international emerging and established artists, both for solo and group shows.
Address: Vimy Lane, Parap 0820
Phone: +61 8 8981 5368
Website: nccart.com.au
Email: programmanager@nccart.com.au
Twitter.com/NCC_ART
Facebook.com/
NorthernCentreforContemporaryArt
Instagram.com/nccart_darwin

Museum & Art Gallery Northern Territory

Overlooking the picturesque Fannie Bay, with internationally renowned artistic, cultural and scientific collections and research programs. A dynamic program of exhibitions and the best travelling exhibitions around Australia. Home of the annual Telstra National Aboriginal and Torres Strait Islander Art Awards – the most significant celebration of its kind in the country.
Address: 19 Conacher Street, The Gardens, Darwin 0820

Phone: +61 8 8999 8264
Website: magnt.net.au
Email: info@magnt.net.au
Twitter.com/mag_nt
Facebook.com/magnt.net.au
Instagram.com/mag_nt

Outstation Gallery – Aboriginal Art from Art Centres

Working directly with Aboriginal art centres, presenting and promoting contemporary Indigenous art from both emerging and established artists.
Address: 8 Parap Place, Parap, Darwin 0820
Phone: +61 8 8981 4822
Website: outstation.com.au

Geelong, Victoria
Geelong Art Gallery

A major regional gallery in Victoria, with over 6,000 works of art in its collection. Established in 1896 with a magnificent collection of Australian and European painting, sculpture, printmaking and decorative art that ranges from the 18th century to the present day. Special emphasis on the early images of the Geelong region and the evolution of the city. Strong community engagement.
Address: Little Malop Street, Geelong 3220
Phone: +61 3 5229 3645
Website: geelonggallery.org.au
Email: info@geelonggallery.org.au
Twitter.com/geelonggallery
Facebook.com/geelonggallery
Instagram.com/geelonggallery
YouTube.com/ Geelong Gallery Channel

Gold Coast – Tweed Heads, Queensland/New South Wales
Boomerang Art – Aboriginal Art Gallery

The gallery is a signatory to the Indigenous Art Code and a member of the Aboriginal Art Association of Australia which is committed to fair trade.

Address: 27 Margaret Street, Southport 4215
Phone: 0401 039 931
Website: boomerangart.com.au
Email: werner@boomerangart.com.au
Twitter.com/boomerangart
Facebook.com/boomerangart
Instagram.com/boomerang_art
Pinterest.com.au/BoomerangArt

19 Karen Contemporary Artspace

Exhibitions throughout the year, with both solo and group exhibitions. The gallery has space for two or three solo shows to run concurrently. These tend to have a complimentary or opposing theme. The gallery represents around 80 international and Australian artists with styles and genres from Urban and Street art, to Pop art, Expressionism, Contemporary Figurative, Abstract, Realism, Surrealism, Pop Surrealism and everything in between.
Address: 19 Karen Avenue, Mermaid Beach 4218
Phone: +61 7 5554 5019
Website: 19karen.com.au
Email: info@19karen.com.au
Twitter.com/19KarenGallery
Facebook.com/19KAREN
Instagram.com/19karengallery

Anthea Polson Art

Contemporary Australian art and sculpture, representing the nations' top emerging artists as well as exhibiting major investment works.
Address: Shop 120 Marina Mirage Seaworld Drive, Main Beach 4217
Phone: +61 7 5561 1166
Website: antheapolsonart.com.au
Email: info@antheapolsonart.com.au
Twitter.com/antheapolsonart
Facebook.com/antheapolsonart
Instagram.com/antheapolsonart
Pinterest.co.uk/antheapolsonart

HOTA

The new gallery opens in April 2021, with exclusive celebrations of Queensland artists, a dedicated Children's Gallery, special events, newly-exhibited work from the City Collection and great and surprising art, both indoors and out.
Address: 135 Bundall Road, Surfers Paradise 4217
Phone: +61 7 5588 4000
Website: hota.com.au
Email: hello@hota.com.au
Twitter.com/hotagc
Facebook.com/hotagc
Instagram.com/hotagc
YouTube.com/user/theartscentregc

Ripley's Believe It or Not!

Founded in 1918 by cartoonist and adventurer, Robert Ripley. Showing his collection of unique and incredible artefacts from the 200+ countries he visited.
Address: Cavill Ave, Surfers Paradise 4217
Phone: +61 7 5592 0040
Website: ripleys.com
Email: social@ripleys.com
Twitter.com/ripleys
Facebook.com/RipleysBelieveItorNot
Instagram.com/ripleysbelieveitornot

Tweed Regional Gallery

The gallery has 7 exhibition spaces with a dynamic program of historical to contemporary touring exhibitions. Showing regional, national and international art exclusively. There is the $20,000 Olive Cotton Award for photographic portraiture, with the gallery itself housing a permanent collection of diverse portraiture from Australia. Events and workshops, with an education space, research library, shop and café.
Address: 2 Mistral Road, Cnr Tweed Valley Way, Murwillumbah South 2484
Phone: +61 2 6670 2790

Website: artgallery.tweed.nsw.gov.au
Email: tweedart@tweed.nsw.gov.au
Facebook.com/tweedregionalgallery
Instagram.com/tweedregionalgallery

Maverick Hair & ART Space

Contemporary art with professional hairdressing for men and women showing local emerging artists in an ever-changing space.
Address: First Floor, 1/17 Griffith Street, Coolangatta 4225
Phone: +61 7 5599 3366
Website: maverick.net.au
Facebook.com/beamaverick.coolangatta
Instagram.com/maverick.gc
Pinterest.co.uk/mavericksGC

Hobart and Tasmania

Contemporary Art Tasmania

A member of the Contemporary Art Organisations (Australia), and is assisted by the Australia Council for the Arts, Arts Tasmania and by the Visual Arts and Crafts Strategy.
Address: 27 Tasma Street, North Hobart 7000
Phone: +61 3 6231 0445
Website: contemporaryarttasmania.org
Email: info@contemporaryart.org.au
Facebook.com/contemporaryarttasmania
Instagram.com/contemporaryarttasmania

Brave Art Gallery

20 minutes from Launceston, specialising in Tasmanian contemporary art. Promoting the arts within the broader community, celebrating artistic and cultural creativity by exhibiting, promoting and selling objects of art and culture. Increasing knowledge, enriching the spirit, and stimulating the senses.
Address: 61 Wellington Street, Longford 7301

Phone: +61 3 6397 0000
Website: braveartgallery.com.au
Email: events@braveartgallery.com.au
Facebook.com/BRAVEartGallery

Tasmanian Museum & Art Gallery

TMAG is the leading natural, cultural and heritage organisation in Tasmania.
Address: Dunn Place, Hobart 7000
Phone: +61 3 6165 7000
Website: tmag.tas.gov.au
Email: tmagmail@tmag.tas.gov.au
Facebook.com/tasmuseum
Instagram.com/tasmuseum
YouTube.com/user/tasmanianmuseum

Queen Victoria Museum and Art Gallery

A major destination for art, history and natural sciences in Northern Tasmania, collecting since 1842, with acquisitions and donations from around the world.
Address: 2 Invermay Road, Launceston 7248
Phone: +61 3 6323 3777
Website: qvmag.tas.gov.au
Email: enquiries@qvmag.tas.gov.au
Twitter.com/qvmag
Facebook.com/tasmuseum
Instagram.com/tasmuseum
YouTube.com/user/tasmanianmuseum

146 ArtSpace

Part of Cultural and Tourism Development in the Department of State Growth. Supporting cultural and creative industries in Tasmania.
Address: 4 Salamanca Place, Hobart, 7000 Tasmania
Phone: +61 3 6165 6666
Website: arts.tas.gov.au
Email: info@arts.tas.gov.au
Twitter.com/arts_tasmania
Facebook.com/ArtsTasmania

Melbourne, Victoria
Australian Centre for Contemporary Art

Playing an inspirational and critical role in investing in the artistic and wider communities. Leading the cultural conversation and setting the agenda for contemporary art.
Address: 111 Sturt Street, Southbank 3006
Phone: +61 3 9697 9999
Website: accaonline.org.au
Email: laura.deneefe@acca.melbourne
Twitter.com/ACCA_melbourne
Facebook.com/acca.melbourne
Instagram.com/acca_melbourne
YouTube.com/user/accaonline

Tolarno Galleries

One of Australia's most stimulating exhibitors of contemporary art and design. Established in 1967, with a rich history of presenting innovative and challenging work. Nurtures artists through their careers with early year exhibitions of Bonnard, Dali, Chagall, Matisse, Picasso, Renoir and Vuillard as well as new contemporary masters, both national and international. Work ranges from video, film, photography and installation to painting, sculpture, digital media and cutting edge design with interest from collectors, curators and critics worldwide.
Address: Level 4, 104 Exhibition Street, Melbourne 3000
Phone: +61 3 9654 6000
Website: tolarnogalleries.com
Email: mail@tolarnogalleries.com
Twitter.com/tolarnogallery
Facebook.com/tolarnogalleries
Instagram.com/tolarno
Ocula.com/art-galleries/tolarno-galleries/exhibitions

Edmund Pearce Gallery

Dedicated to the understanding and appreciation of contemporary photography through exhibitions and initiatives.
Address: L 2 37 Swanston Street, Melbourne 3000
Phone: +61 3 9023 5775
Website: edmundpearce.com.au
Email: hello@edmundpearce.com.au
Twitter.com/EdmundPearce
Facebook.com/EdmundPearce
Instagram.com/edmundpearce

Arc One Gallery

Representing some of Australia's most well respected contemporary artists who divulge the diverse culture of the country through a range of media, with exceptional solo and group exhibitions. Artists have been consistently included in major international exhibitions and awards. Supports emerging artists as well as established and mid-career with a vast spectrum of disciplines from painting, installation, video and other electronic media arts.
Address: 45 Flinders Lane, Melbourne 3000
Phone: +61 3 9650 0589
Website: arcone.com.au
Email: mail@arc1gallery.com
Facebook.com/ARCONEGallery
Instagram.com/arconegallery

Flinders Lane Gallery

Contemporary art gallery in the heart of Melbourne. Championing emerging, mid-career and established Australian artists since 1989, with digital media and large scale multi-media installations included. Solo exhibitions throughout the year. Working closely with institutions, businesses, architects and curators to place art in major collections and secure public art commissions.
Address: Level 1, The Nicholas Building, Corner Flinders Lane and 37 Swanston Street, Melbourne 3000
Phone: +61 3 9654 3332
Website: flg.com.au
Email: info@flg.com.au

Facebook.com/flinderslanegallery
Instagram.com/flinderslanegallery
YouTube.com/user/flinderslanegallery

Outre Gallery

Challenges the conventions of an archetypal gallery. Established over 20 years ago. Solo and group exhibitions with Australian and international artists focusing on new contemporary art with a particular emphasis on the figurative.
Address: 249-251 Elizabeth Street, Melbourne 3000
Phone: +61 3 9642 5455
Website: outregallery.com
Email: info@outregallery.com
Facebook.com/outregallerymelb
Instagram.com/outregallery

Bridget McDonnell Gallery

Established in 1983, with regular exhibitions of early Australian painters, artists exhibiting in London from 1880 to 1940, Australian women artists, Australian prints and a Christmas exhibition where everything is priced at under $2,000.
Address: 130 Faraday Street, Carlton 3053
Phone: +61 3 9347 1700
Website: bridgetmcdonnellgallery.com.au
Email: bmcdgallery@bigpond.com

Lorimer Gallery

Melbourne's new cultural centre showing original and contemporary art with private and public events. Waterfront views and 5m ceilings.
Address: 100 Lorimer Street, Docklands 3008
Phone: +61 437 922 686
Website: lorimergallery.com.au
Email: victoria@lorimergallery.com.au
Facebook.com/LorimerGalleryAU

Daine Siinger Gallery

Contemporary art gallery exclusively representing 15 artists from Australia and New Zealand. Also presenting occasional curated exhibitions and solo shows by unrepresented artists.
Address: 325 Flinders Lane, Melbourne 3000
Phone: +61 410 264 036
Website: dainesinger.com
Email: info@dainesinger.com

Kings Artist Run

Contemporary arts organisation supporting a range of artists, writers and performers in the early stages of their careers. Distinct experimental performances, publishing initiatives and exhibitions.
Address: Lvl 1 / 171 King St., Melbourne 3000
Phone: +61 3 9642 0859
Website: kingsartistrun.com.au
Email: info@kingsartistrun.org.au Twitter.com/KINGSartistrun
Facebook.com/kingsartistrunspace
Instagram.com/kingsartistrun

Lindberg Galleries

Contemporary commercial art gallery, concentrating on relationships between artists, collectors, curators, institutions and enthusiasts.
Address: 289 Flinders La, Melbourne 3000
Phone: +61 3 9663 9196
Website: lindbergcontemporary.com.au
Email: david@lindbergcontemporary.com.au
Twitter.com/Lindbergarts
Facebook.com/Lindberg-Galleries

Lesley Kehoe Gallery

Contemporary art suggesting fantasy and romance, creating an environment of beauty, indulging the senses, provoking the intellect and stirring the heart, addressing universal principles that are best expressed by Japanese culture.

Address: 101 Collins Street, Melbourne 3000
Phone: +61 3 9671 4311
Website: kehoe.com.au
Email: gallery@kehoe.com.au

Experimenta Media Arts

Australia's leading organisation dedicated to commissioning, exhibiting and touring contemporary art which is driven by technology, such as bio art, creative coding, robotics, data-driven works, virtual and augmented reality. Working with established and emerging artists, linking them with experts in other fields, including scientists, researchers, engineers, architects and technologists to create ambitious and complex projects.
Address: Level 7/225, Bourke Street, Melbourne 3000
Phone: +61 3 9650 9977
Website: experimenta.org
Email: experimenta@experimenta.org
Twitter.com/experimenta_
Facebook.com/ExperimentaMediaArts

Sarah Scout Gallery

A contemporary art gallery based in Melbourne.
Address: Level 1, 12 Collins Street, Melbourne 3000
Phone: +61 3 9654 4429
Website: sarahscoutpresents.com
Email: info@sarahscoutpresents.com
Instagram.com/sarahscoutpresents

Screen Space

Established in 2010, this gallery focuses on art that uses screen-based technology or engages with screen culture. A rent-free exhibition space to artists and curators.
Address: Ground Floor, 30 Guildford Ln, Melbourne 3000

Phone: +61 3 9012 5351
Website: screenspace.com
Email: info@screenspace.com
Facebook.com/screenspacegallery

Newcastle – Maitland
Newcastle Art Gallery

Owned and run by the City of Newcastle the gallery presents a dynamic range of exhibitions and events.
Address: 1 Laman Street, Newcastle 2300
Phone: +61 2 4974 5100
Website: nag.org.au
Email: artgallery@ncc.nsw.gov.au
Facebook.com/
NewcastleArtGalleryAustralia
Instagram.com/newcastleartgalleryaustralia

CStudios Art Gallery

A contemporary art gallery established in 2013.
Address: Shop 1/738 Hunter Street, Newcastle 2302
Phone: +61 407 107 053
Website: cstudiosartgallery.com.au
Email: info@cstudiosartgallery.com.au
Facebook.com/cstudiosArtGallery

The Lock-Up

Situated in a significant heritage building this is an award-winning, independent, multi-disciplinary contemporary art space and inner city creative hub. Promoting diverse cross-platform and experimental practices with local, national and international artists. This includes exhibitions, events, site-specific installations and performances, residences, creative talks and workshops engaging the arts community and public.
Address: 90 Hunter Street, Newcastle 2300
Phone: +61 2 4925 2265
Website: thelockup.org.au
Facebook.com/TheLockUpArtSpace
Instagram.com/thelockupartspace

Timeless Textiles

The only commercial gallery in Australia dedicated solely to fibre art and artisans. Every year there are 4 local, 4 national and 4 international exhibitions, with artists talks and networking opportunities with artisans, curators, collectors and collaborators.
Address: 90 Hunter Street, Newcastle East 2300
Phone: +61 2 4926 5888
Website: timelesstextiles.com.au
Email: anne@timelesstextiles.com.au
Twitter.com/AnneKempton1
Facebook.com/timelesstextilesgallery
Instagram.com/timelesstextiles
YouTube.com/TimelessTextilesGallery

Seraphine Café

Showing thousands of artworks each year, with hundreds of learning opportunities across the 25 annual exhibitions including the 4,000+ pieces in the collection in an award-winning building.
Address: 228-230 High Street, Maitland 2320
Phone: +61 2 4934 7264
Website: mrag.org.au
Email: linden.pomare@maitland.nsw.gov.au
Facebook.com/Maitland.Regional.Art.Gallery
Instagram.com/maitlandregionalartgallery

M2 Gallery

Established and emerging talent in all fields of art, including painting, performance, photography, illustration and sculpture, with an emphasis on allowing each artists personal style to breathe.
Address: 450 Elizabeth Street, Surry Hills 2010
Phone: +61 416 209 567
Website: m2gallery.com.au
Email: info@m2gallery.com.au
Facebook.com/artbinge

Perth, Western Australia
Art Gallery Of Western Australia

Founded in 1895 in 3 heritage buildings next to Perth Cultural Centre. The gallery is home to the State Art Collection, including the world's best indigenous art and the pre-eminent collection of Western Australian art and design and Australian and International art and design.
Address: Perth Cultural Centre, Perth 6000
Phone: +61 8 9492 6600
Website: artgallery.wa.gov.au
Email: admin@artgallery.wa.gov.au
Twitter.com/ArtGalleryWA
Facebook.com/ArtGalleryWA
Instagram.com/artgallerywa
Vimeo.com/artgallerywa
LinkedIn.com/company/art-gallery-of-western-australia
YouTube.com/user/ArtGalleryWA

Aspects of Kings Park

The best in contemporary Australian and Western Australian craft and design.
Address: 68 Fraser Avenue, Kings Park, West Perth 6005
Phone: +61 8 9480 3900
Website: aspectsofkingspark.com.au
Email: aspects@bgpa.wa.gov.au
Facebook.com/aspectsofkingspark
Instagram.com/aspectsofkingspark
YouTube.com/user/bgpawagovau

Linton & Kay Galleries

A stable of artists from early-, mid-, and late career from Western Australia and the Eastern States. Specialising in 2D and 3D art, including Aboriginal Art with a monthly exhibition.
Address: The Old Perth Technical School, Level 1 / 137 St Georges Terrace, Perth 6008
Phone: +61 8 6465 4314
Website: lintonandkay.com.au

Email: perth@lintonandkay.com.au
Facebook.com/LintonandKayGalleries
Instagram.com/lintonandkay

Windram Art Gallery

A contemporary art gallery.
Address: 256 Mill Point Road, South Perth 6151
Phone: +61 407 957 802
Website: windramart.com.au

Perth Institute Of Contemporary Arts

Year-round program of exhibitions, contemporary dance, theatre and performance with artist residences and interdisciplinary projects. One of the largest exhibition spaces in Australia. Known for its leading role in presenting new work.
Address: 51 James Street, Northbridge 6003
Phone: +61 8 9228 6300
Website: pica.org.au
Email: info@pica.org.au
Twitter.com/PICA_Perth
Facebook.com/PICAARTS
Instagram.com/PICA_Perth

Gallery Central

Original fine art and gifts.
Address: 800 Central Ave, Hot Springs 71913
Phone: +1 501-318-4278
Website: Facebook.com/gallerycentral
Email: gallerycentral@sbcglobal.net

Stala Contemporary

A new art gallery in a refurbished industrial warehouse showing a diverse range of visual arts from WA and beyond.
Address: 12 Cleaver Street, West Perth 6050
Phone: +61 417 184 638
Website: stalacontemporary.com.au
Email: info@stalacontemporary.com.au
Twitter.com/stalacontemp
Facebook.com/stalacontemporary
Instagram.com/stalacontemporary

Form Contemporary Craft & Design

Designing and delivering programs that build and offer skills in creative thinking. Partnering with organisations, schools, businesses and government to bring both local and international practitioners to work in communities, whether they be metropolitan, regional or remote. Developing and managing project spaces combining professional and community use with artistic excellence.
Address: 357 Murray Street, Perth 6000
Phone: +61 8 9226 2161
Website: form.net.au
Email: mail@form.net.au
Twitter.com/formwa
Facebook.com/formwa
Instagram.com/formwa

MOANA Project Space

An artist-run initiative showing contemporary art on a national scale, with an emphasis on young and early career artists, curators and writers from across Australia.
Address: 1F 618 Hay Street, Perth 6000
Phone: +61 432 184 146
Website: moana-ari.com
Email: info@moana-ari.com
Twitter.com/moanaps
Facebook.com/moanaperth
Instagram.com/moana_project_space

PCP – Perth Centre for Photography

Established in 1992, promoting and supporting emerging and established photo-based art from local, national and international backgrounds. Individual and group shows with competitions in different genres.
Address: 100 Aberdeen Street, West Perth 6005
Phone: +61 8 9227 6620
Website: pcp.org.au
Email: info@pcp.org.au
Twitter.com/pcpwa

Facebook.com/pcpwa

Instagram.com/perthcentreforphotography

Gallery 360 Art Gallery Perth WA

The state's largest picture framer, also exhibiting an extensive range of modern and contemporary art from WA artists.
Address: 309 Hay Street, Subiaco 6008
Phone: +61 8 9381 6577
Website: gallery360.com.au
Email: info@gallery360.com.au
Facebook.com/gallery360aus
Instagram.com/gallery.360

Townsville, Queensland
Umbrella Studio Contemporary Arts

Art in the Tropics, a not-for-profit, members based exhibition and studio space driving innovation, experimentation and energising community.
Address: 408 Flinders Street, Townsville 4810
Phone: +61 7 4772 7109
Website: umbrella.org.au
Email: office@umbrella.org.au
Twitter.com/umbrellastudio
Facebook.com/UmbrellaStudio
Instagram.com/umbrellastudiotsv

Sunshine Coast, Queensland
Artisans Gallery Eumundi

Handcrafted designer timber furniture, creative wood art and custom commissions.
Address: 43 Caplick Way, Eumundi 4562
Phone: +61 409 848 098
Website: timbercraftsman.com.au
Email: info@timbercraftsman.com.au
Facebook.com/
DavidSutersTimbercraftsman
Instagram.com/davidsuterstimbercraftsman
YouTube.com/user/UmbrellaStudio86

Red Desert Gallery

One of the leading dealers in Australia for Aboriginal fine art, specialising in central and western desert art with a major focus on the tribal elders from the world's oldest surviving indigenous culture.
Address: 102 Memorial Drive, Eumundi 4562
Phone: +61 7 5442 7172
Website: reddesertgallery.com.au
Email: paulcurtis@reddesertgallery.com.au
Facebook.com/Red-Desert-Gallery-Specialists-in-Aboriginal-Fine-Art

Murra Wolka Creations Aboriginal Artifacts

Third generation family business creating hand painted art, which in Aboriginal means "Murra Wolka". Covering the tribal areas of Gubbi Gubbi, Biri Gubba, Kuku-Yalangi as well as other tribes.
Address: 39 Memorial Drive, Eumundi 4562
Phone: +61 7 5442 8691 / (07) 5442 8572
Website: murrawolka.com
Email: murrawolka@gmail.com

Noosa Regional Gallery

Located on the picturesque Noosa River, established in 1981, this gallery presents a diverse and challenging annual program. Exhibitions from local, national and international artists and curators for private and corporate collections with a shop featuring local artisans.
Address: 9 Pelican Street, Tewantin 4565
Phone: +61 7 5449 5340
Website: noosaregionalgallery.com.au
Email: gallery@noosa.qld.gov.au
Facebook.com/noosaregionalgallery
Instagram.com/noosaregionalgallery

Sydney, New South Wales
Art Gallery of New South Wales

The most important public gallery in Sydney and one of the largest in Australia. Since 1871, the gallery has presented international and Australian art in its beautiful, light-filled spaces with stunning views of Sydney harbour. With colonial and 19th century Australian works and European old masters and galleries full of Asian, Aboriginal and Torres-Strait Islander work. Also regularly changing exhibitions – over 30 a year.
Address: Art Gallery Road, The Domain, Sydney 2000
Phone: +61 1800 679 278
Website: artgallery.nsw.gov.au
Email: artmail@ag.nsw.gov.au
Twitter.com/ArtGalleryofNSW
Facebook.com/ArtGalleryofNSW
Instagram.com/artgalleryofnsw

MCA

Museum of Contemporary Art exhibiting, collecting and interpreting the work of today's artists.
Address: 140 George Street, The Rocks 2000
Phone: +61 2 9245 2400
Website: mca.com.au
Email: reception@mca.com.au
Twitter.com/mca_australia
Facebook.com/mca.australia
Instagram.com/mca_australia

ATTY Gallery

ATTY works with a digital pen and laptop hand drawing animals, taking hundreds of hours over each intricate image. His work is seen in over 60 countries.
Address: 27 Playfair Street, The Rocks, Sydney 2000
Phone: +61 428 305 863
Website: atty.com.au
Email: attydesign@gmail.com
Facebook.com/ATTYDesign
Instagram.com/Attydesign

4A Centre for Contemporary Asian Art

A not-for-profit organisation fostering excellence and innovation in contemporary culture. Its programs are presented throughout Australia and Asia developing the dynamic relationship between both regions.
Address: 181-187 Hay Street, Sydney 2000
Phone: +61 2 9212 0380
Website: 4a.com.au
Email: hello@4a.com.au
Twitter.com/4a_aus
Facebook.com/4ACentreforContemporary AsianArt
Instagram.com/4a_aus

Wollongong, New South Wales
Project Contemporary Artspace

Not-for-profit, artist run artspace.
Address: 255 Keira St, Wollongong 2500
Phone: 0425 857 079
Website: projectgallery.com.au
Email: info@projectgallery.com.au
Facebook.com/ProjectArtSpace
Instagram.com/projectartspace

Wollongong Art Gallery

An impressive collection of Australian, Aboriginal and Asian art showing local, national and international artists along with activities and workshops.
Address: 46 Burelli Street, Wollongong 2500
Phone: +61 2 4227 8500
Website: wollongongartgallery.com
Email: gallery@wollongong.nsw.gov.au
Facebook.com/wollongongartgallery

Impact Art

Paintings for corporations, interior designers, decorators and serviced apartments. Affordable hand painted stretched canvases with a library of over 15,000 images.
Address: U 1 5 Finlayson Street, Wollongong 2500

Phone: +61 2 4229 2350
Website: impactart.com.au
Email: debbie@impactart.com.au
Email: michael@impactart.com.au

AUSTRIA

Vienna

MAM Mario Mauroner Contemporary Art VIENNA

Established in 1972 in Salzburg and subsequently in Vienna, the gallery also has a space for interdisciplinary projects in Vienna.
Address: Weihburggasse 26, Wien 1010
Phone: +43 1 9042004
Website: galerie-mam.com
Email: office@galerie-mam.com
Facebook.com/MarioMauroner
Instagram.com/mariomauroner

Thyssen-Bornemisza Art Contemporary

A foundation of contemporary art since 2002, supporting the production, commissioning and dissemination of unconventional trans-disciplinary projects worldwide.
Address: Himmelpfortgasse 13, Wien
Phone: +43 1 51398560
Website: tba21.org
Email: office@tba21.org
Twitter.com/tba21
Facebook.com/TBA21
Instagram.com/tba_21/
YouTube.com/c/
ThyssenBornemiszaArtContemporary

ArtCore

Contemporary Art Gallery.
Address: Praterstraße 1/3. OG/Shop 33, Wien 1020
Phone: +43 1 8905045

Galerie Senn

Founded in 2000 with selected contemporary art from Austria and internationally. Collaborations with partner galleries, institutions, museums and independent curators as well as between artists.
Address: Schleifmühlgasse 1a, Wien 1040
Phone: +43 1 5852580
Website: galeriesenn.at
Email: office@galeriesenn.at
Facebook.com/gabrielesenngalerie
Instagram.com/gabrielesenngalerie

BAWAG Contemporary

Contemporary art gallery in Vienna.
Address: Franz Josefs Kai 3, Wien 1010
Phone: +43 59 905 919

Kro Art Contemporary

Contemporary art gallery in Vienna
Address: Getreidemarkt 15, Wien 1060
Phone: +43 676 5030532

Graz

Artelier Contemporary

Experimenting and combining materials to create contemporary design. Redesigning classical forms in a new language with an emphasis on visual design as well as utility, sustainability and function.
Address: Griesgasse 3, Graz 8020
Phone: +43 316 834411
Website: artelier-contemporary.at
Email: office@artelier-contemporary.at
Instagram.com/atelier_contemporary
LinkedIn.com/company/atelier-contemporary
behance.net/atelier-contemporary

Linz

Galerie Lehner Inh Dr Frederic Lehner

Founded in 1973, it is one of the oldest existing private galleries Austria. With more than 300 exhibitions by 150 artists with famous names as well as those who have made their debut show. Important representatives of classical

modernity, especially New Objectivity and Expressionism.
Address: Herrenstraße 7, Innenhof, Linz 4020
Phone: +43 1 585462323
Website: galerielehner.at
Email: wien@galerielehner.at

Salzburg
Galerie Frey

An important creative hub since the late 1980s. A vibrant platform for contemporary art for both established and emerging artists.
Address: Erhardplatz 3, Salzburg 5020
Phone: +43 662 840200
Website: galerie-frey.com
Email: andrea.frey@galerie-frey.com
Facebook.com/GalerieFREY

MAM Mario Mauroner Contemporary Art & Sculpture Garden

Address: Prälat-Winkler-Straße 2, Salzburg 5020
Phone: +43 662 623423

Galerie Academia GmbH & Co

Contemporary art gallery in Salzburg.
Address: Residenzplatz 1, Salzburg 5020
Phone: +43 662 845185
Website: kunstnet.at
Email: rodlauer@kunstnet.at

BAHAMAS
The National Art Gallery of The Bahamas

The premier arts institution in the Bahamas. Established by the governement in 1996 as part of an expanded system of museums and nation building, showing the best art in the Bahamas.
Address: Villa Doyle, West and West Hill Streets. Nassau, N.P., The Bahamas
Phone: +1 242-328-5800
Website: nagb.org.bs

Email: info@nagb.org.bs
Twitter.com/NAGBahamas
Facebook.com/TheNAGB
Instagram.com/nagb242
Vimeo.com/thenagb

BAHRAIN
La Fontaine Centre of contemporary art

La Fontaine is an historical monument in the heart of Manama, Bahrain, with an art gallery, international restaurant, conference centre, spa and dance studio. The building has been renovated with spectacular effect – fusing ancient Gulf architecture with contemporary design.
Address: 92 Hoora Avenue, Manama 306
Phone: +973 1723 0123
Website: lafontaineartcentre.net
Email: info@lafontaineartcentre.net
Facebook.com/lafontainebahrain
Instagram.com/lafontainebh

BELARUS
Minsk
Art Belarus Gallery

Contemporary art gallery in Belarus.
Address: Kozlova St., 3, Minsk
Phone: +375 17 284-88-88
Website: artbelarus.by
Email: zimenko@bgpb.by
Email: artbelarus.nci@gmail.com

Gallery U

Art spaces for the exhibition of Belarusian and European contemporary art.
Address: Oktyabrskaya, 19, entrance from Lenina St. yard, Minsk 220030
Phone: +375 29 366-75-16
Website: ygallery.by
Email: info@ygallery.by

BELGIUM

Brussels

Centrale for Contemporary Art

Situated in a former power station in the heart of Brussels, the gallery is the centre of contemporary art in the city. It is committed to a vision of art beyond boundaries, connecting the city and society. Collaborating with both emerging and established artists from Brussels and internationally, exhibiting multidisciplinary work.
Address: Place Ste-Catherine 44, Brussels 1000
Phone: +32 2 279 64 52
Website: centrale-art.be
Email: info@centrale.brussels
Facebook.com/centralebrussels
Instagram.com/centralebrussels
Vimeo.com/centralebrussels

White and Art Gallery

A contemporary art gallery in Elsene.
Address: 46 rue de Stassart, Elsene
Phone: +32 483 25 23 18

118 Contemporary Art Gallery

A contemporary art gallery in Brussells
Address: Rue Blaesstraat 118, Bruxelles 1000
Phone: +32 488 49 32 28

Rossi Contemporary

Exhibiting high-standard emerging and mid-career contemporary artists.
Address: Rivoli Building, Bruxelles 1180
Phone: +32 486 31 00 92
Website: rossicontemporary.be
Email: rossi@rossicontemporary.be
Facebook.com/Rossicontemporary

Galerie Albert 1er

Contemporary art gallery in Brussels.
Address: Rue de la Madeleine 45, Bruxelles 1000
Phone: +32 2 512 19 44
Website: artsite.be
Email: info@galerie-albert1er.be

Map Contemporary Art

Contemporary art gallery in Brussels.
Address: Rue du Marché aux Porcs 4, Bruxelles 1000
Phone: +32 2 217 74 00
Website: dependance.be
Email: info@dependance.be
Facebook.com/idependancel
Instagram.com/dependance_gallery

Galerie vander A

Contemporary art, jewellery and objects, stimulating critical thought and enhancing transversal dialogue.
Address: Av. des Saisons 110-112, Bruxelles 1050
Phone: +32 495 26 42 81
Website: vanderagallery.be
Email: info@vanderagallery.be
Facebook.com/Vander-A-Observatory

Antwerp

Keteleer Gallery

Modern and contemporary art, with important Belgian and international artists both established and emerging.
Address: Pourbusstraat 3 – 5
2000 Antwerp – Belgium
Phone: +32 3 283 04 20
Website: keteleer.com
Email: info@keteleer.com
Facebook.com/keteleer
Instagram.com/keteleer_gallery

Wo-Men Art-Gallery

Wo-men in Fine Art, situated in the historical centre of Antwerp. Represents many national and international artists.
Address: Wolstraat 45, Antwerpen 2000
Phone: +32 475 25 14 02

Website: wmgallery.be
Email: info@wmgallery.be
Facebook.com/WMgalleryAntwerp
Instagram.com/wmgalleryantwerp

International Contemporary Photography and Art Gallery

Address: Pelgrimsstraat 6, Antwerpen 2000
Phone: +32 3 430 49 30

Geukens & De Vil

Contemporary art gallery with strong exhibitions showing a range of Belgian and international artists, both established and emerging.
Address: Pourbusstraat 19, Antwerpen 2000
Phone: +32 50 62 01 04
Website: geukensdevil.com
Email: geukensdevil@geukensdevil.com
Facebook.com/geukensdevil
Instagram.com/geukensdevil

Liege

Musée de l'Art Wallon (Museum of Walloon Art)

Well-known artists from the 16th century to the present day.
Address: Feronstree 86, Liege 4000
Phone: +32 4 221 92 31
Website: museeartwallon.be

Ghent

S.M.A.K.

National and international masterpieces from the Cobra, pop, minimal, conceptual and arte povera genres. Considered the most important collection in Flanders. Often solo and group exhibitions, changing every 4 months showing influential established and emerging international artists side by side.
Address: Familie van Rysselberghedreef, Gent 9000
Phone: +32 9 221 17 03
Website: smak.be

Email: info@smak.be
Twitter.com/smakgent
Facebook.com/SMAK.Gent
Instagram.com/smakgent

Museum voor Schone Kunsten (Fine Arts Museum)

The oldest art museum in Belgium with a vast collection of European painting and sculpture set in an iconic building.
Address: F. Scribedreef 1, Ghent 9000
Phone: +32 9 222 17 03
Website: mskgent.be
Email: museum.msk@stad.gent
Twitter.com/mskgent
Facebook.com/mskgent
Instagram.com/mskgent

Modern Chinese Art Foundation Internat. Org

Chinese contemporary art.
Address: Edward AnseelePlein 6, Gent 9000
Phone: +32 9 233 48 14

Modernpconcepts

Contemporary art gallery in Gent.
Address: Waaistraat 16, Gent 9000
Phone: +32 493 20 78 45

BOLIVIA

National Museum of Art - Museo Nacional de Arte

National museum of art in Bolivia.
Address: Comercio y Socabaya, La Paz 1190

BOSNIA AND HERZEGOVINA

Republika Srpska Art Gallery

Contemporary art gallery.
Address: Trg Srpskikh Junaka 2, Banja Luka 78000
Phone: +387 51 215-364
Website: inyourpocket.com

BOTSWANA

Bernstein Contemporary & Investment Art

Contemporary art in Botswana
Address: 84 Homestead Rd 2090
Phone: +27 72 803 4548
Website: hotfrog.co.za

Warren Siebrits Modern & Contemporary ART

Modern and contemporary art in Botswana
Address: 140 Jan Smuts Ave, Parkwood 2193
Phone: +27 11 327 0000

BRAZIL

A Casa do Parque

Contemporary art in Brazil.
Address: Rua Marechal Severiano de
Queiroz, 455, Cuiaba
Phone: 556533654789

São Paulo

Galeria de Arte Luísa Strina

Contemporary art gallery in São Paulo.
Address: Rua Pe. João Manuel 755, lj. 2, São
Paulo 01411-000
Phone: +55 (11) 3088-2471
Website: galerialuisastrina.com.br
Email: info@galerialuisastrina.com.br

Masp a Baianeira

Private not-for-profit museum founded in
1947, becoming the first modern museum
in the country. Houses the most important
collection of European art in the southern
hemisphere. 11,000 artworks such as paintings,
sculptures, objects, photographs, videos and
clothing from around the world.
Address: AV Paulista, 1578 01310-200 São Paulo
Phone: +55 11 3149 5959
Website: masp.org.br
Twitter.com/maspmuseu
Facebook.com/maspmuseu
Instagram.com/masp

Branche

Contemporary art gallery in São Paulo.
Address: Rua Frei Caneca 1199, São Paulo
01307-003
Phone: +55 (11) 2627-6300
Website: goldentulipbelasartes.com

Baro Galeria de Arte

Opened in 2010 with an international presence
in the Brazilian art circuit. Challenging the
dialogue between artists, curators, collectors
and cultural institutions. Prioritises site-
specific works with a strong emphasis on 70's
and 80's artists with a residency program for
young emerging artists.
Address: Rua Barra Funda 216 (Fr), São
Paulo 01152-000
Phone: +55 (11) 3666-6489
Website: barogaleria.com
Email: gallery@barogaleria.com
Facebook.com/barogaleria
Instagram.com/barogaleria

Rio de Janeiro

Luciana Caravello Arte Contemporanea

The best artists and work to meet the needs
of the client with decades of experience in
the visual arts market. Committed to the
dissemination of art and the formation of
new audiences.
Address: Rua Barão de Jaguaripe 387, Rio de
Janeiro 22421-000
Phone: +55 11 93428-5156
Website: lucianacaravello.com.br
Email:
vendas@lucianacaravello.com.br
Facebook.com/lucianacaravellosp
Instagram.com/lucianacaravellosp
YouTube.com/Luciana Caravello Arte
Contemporânea

CVC

Contemporary art gallery in Rio de Janeiro.
Address: Rua do Rosário 136, Rio de Janeiro

20041-002
Phone: +55 (21) 2126-8200
Website: cvc.com.br

BRITISH VIRGIN ISLANDS

Gallery St Thomas

Contemporary art gallery.
Address: 1 Dronningens Gade, Charlotte
Amalie 00802
Phone: +1 (340) 777-6363

Jonna White Gallery

Contemporary art gallery.
Address: 30 Main St., Charlotte Amalie
00802
Phone: +1 340-774-1201
Website: jonnawhite.com
Email: jonnawhite@earthlink.net

Age Art Gallery

Contemporary art gallery.
Address: 152 Calle Del Santo Cristo, 304
Ponce De Leon Ave. Y/O, San Juan 00901-
1559
Phone: +1 787-771-1100

Donald Schnell Studio

Contemporary art studio and gallery.
Address: 27 Southside Road, Estate Enighed,
Cruz Bay, Saint John 00830
Phone: +1 (800) 253-7107
Website: Facebook.com

BULGARIA

Institute for Contemporary Art

One of the longest running non-
governmental organisations engaged with
visual arts in Bulgaria. In the last decades, the
institute has learnt to open up its work and
position it in the world with manifestations
both locally and internationally.
Address: 134, Vasil Levski Blvd. (entrance

from Ekzarh Yosif St.), 1504, Sofia
Phone: +359 88 751 0585
Website: ica-sofia.org
Email: info@ica-sofia.org

Plovdiv
City Art Gallery

The gallery's collection started in 1881 with
copies of the donors' portraits. The Art
Department was set up in 1911, with 25
works. By 1952, the gallery had a collection
of about 300 works and it continues to grow
to this day.
Address: Ul Knyaz Alexander I 15, Plovdiv
4000
Phone: +359 32 635 322
Website: galleryplovdiv.com
Email: ghgpl1952@gmail.com

Contemporary Space

Founded in 2012 in Varna for contemporary
Bulgarian and foreign authors, with workshops
in visual arts, music and educational
programs related to the formation of a
cultural environment. Exhibitions, lectures,
presentations, training courses and discussions
aiming to focus on the aesthetic and spiritual
aspects of modern life.
Address: Marko Balabanov 23, Varna 9000
Phone: +359 88 825 6797
Website: contemporaryspace.bg
Email: contemp.space@gmail.com
Facebook.com/ContemporarySpace

CAMBODIA

Phu Quoc Gallery of Contemporary Art (GoCA)

Contemporary art in Cambodia.
Address: Group 2, Ong Lang 920000
Phone: +84 899 000 109

CANADA

Alberta

Art Gallery of Alberta

An active resource and research facility, founded in 1924. The AGA has acquired over 6,000 works of art, most of which were produced after 1950. The contemporary collection is mainly Canadian abstract paintings and sculpture and the context they hold in parallel international movements. Also strongly represented are contemporary and historical photography with over 1,500 images.

Address: 2 Sir Winston Churchill Sq., Edmonton T5J 2C1
Phone: +1 780-425-5379
Website: youraga.ca
Email: info@youraga.ca
Twitter.com/yourAGA
Facebook.com/artgalleryofalberta
Instagram.com/youraga

Alberta Craft Council

Developing, promoting and advocating fine art in Alberta, supporting both contemporary and heritage crafts as well as developing the craft sector in studios, businesses and networks. Established in 1980, the Craft Council has 2 galleries and shops in Alberta, Edmonton and Calgary with 15-20 exhibitions each year, showing work by 150+ established and emerging craftspeople.

Address: 10186 106 St, Edmonton T5J 1H4
Phone: +1 780-488-5900
Website: albertacraft.ab.ca
Email: acc@albertacraft.ab.ca
Twitter.com/ABCraftCouncil
Facebook.com/albertacraftcouncil
Instagram.com/albertacraftcouncil

Bugera Matheson Gallery

Some of the best contemporary art from artists across Canada. Appealing to the discerning collector with accessible price ranges. Part of Edmonton's art scene since 1992. Established and emerging artists.

Address: 10345 124 St, Edmonton T5N 1R1
Phone: +1 780-482-2854
Website: bugeramathesongallery.com
Email: angela@bugeramathesongallery.com
Twitter.com/BugeraGallery
Facebook.com/bugeramathesongallery
Pinterest.ca/bugeragallery

Editions Gallery

Paintings from dozens of well-known artists.

Address: 2300-8882 170th St NW, Edmonton T5T 4M2
Phone: +1 780-444-2278
Website: editionsgallery.com
Email: art@editionsgallery.com
Facebook.com/editionsgalleryedmonton
Instagram.com/editions_gallery

Latitude 53

Established in 1973 by a collective of artists, it is one of Canada's oldest artist run centres supporting artists, writers and curators to question, inform and inspire.

Address: 10242 106 St NW, Edmonton T5J 1H7
Phone: +1 780-423-5353
Website: latitude53.org
Email: info@latitude53.org
Facebook.com/Latitude53
Instagram.com/latitude_53

Gallery Walk

An award-winning website giving information on art and artists in communities, both large and small, in British Columbia, Alberta, Saskatchewan, Manitoba and the North

Address: Jasper Ave, Edmonton
Website: gallerieswest.ca
Email: editor@gallerieswest.ca

Harcourt House Arts Centre

One of only 4 public galleries and 1 of the

3 artist-run centres in Edmonton. Delivering a range of services to artists and the community, such as exhibitions, distribution and promotion of contemporary art. Both established and emerging artists from local, regional and national backgrounds as well as collectives and art organisations. A minimum of 10 six-week exhibitions.
Address: 10215 112 St NW, Edmonton T5K 1M7
Phone: +1 780-426-4180
Website: harcourthouse.ab.ca
Email: harcourtinfo@shaw.ca
Twitter.com/harcourthouse
Facebook.com/HarcourtHouse
Instagram.com/harcourt_house
Feeds.feedburner.com/
HarcourtHouseArtistRunCentre

Peter Robertson Gallery

Emerging, mid-career and senior Canadian artists with a wide range of media and subject matter.
Address: 12323 104 Ave NW, Edmonton T5N 0V4
Phone: +1 780-455-7479
Website: probertsongallery.com
Email: info@probertsongallery.com

West End Gallery

Leading established contemporary Canadian painters and inspiring glass artists, many internationally recognised. Photo-realism to abstract, including figurative, landscape and still life in a variety of media.
Address: 10337 124 St NW, Edmonton T5N 1R1
Phone: +1 780-488-4892
Website: westendgalleryltd.com
Email: art@westendgalleryltd.com
Twitter.com/westendgallery
Facebook.com/westendgalleryltd
Instagram.com/westendgallery
Pinterest.ca/westendg/_shop
LinkedIn.com/company/west-end-gallery

Victoria
Madrona Gallery

Contemporary and historical fine art. Canadian masters as well as emerging artists. World-class collection of Inuit carvings, drawings and prints.
Address: 606 View St, Victoria V8W 1J4
Phone: +1 250-380-4660
Website: madronagallery.com
Email: info@madronagallery.com
Twitter.com/MadronaGallery
Facebook.com/madronagallery
Instagram.com/madronagallery

Alcheringa Gallery

A world-leading indigenous art gallery representing artists from Vancouver Island, for more than 35 years with art in private and public collections globally. 4–6 exhibitions annually, with one of the largest fine print collections as well as paintings, carvings and sculpture, jewellery, ceramics and textiles. A long commitment to supporting and promoting artists to preserve indigenous culture.
Address: 665 Fort St, Victoria V8W 1G6
Phone: +1 250-383-8224
Website: alcheringa-gallery.com
Email: info (@) alcheringa-gallery.com
Twitter.com/alcheringa_art

Out Of The Mist Gallery

Carrying on the tradition, started in the 1860s of dealing in classic and contemporary Northwest coast native art. Traditional potlatch masks, basketry, shamanic devices, button blankets, totems, beadwork and artefacts from North American, Oceanic and African tribes.
Address: 740 Douglas St, Victoria V8W 3M6
Phone: +1 250-480-4930
Website: outofthemistgallery.com
Email: oomistg@telus.net

Winchester Galleries

Fine art dealers in Canadian, American and international art. Worldwide client base.
Address: 758 Humboldt St, Victoria V8W 4A1
Phone: +1 250-386-2773
Website: winchestergalleriesltd.com
Email: art@winchestergalleriesltd.com
Twitter.com/WGalleries
Facebook.com/WinchesterGalleriesLtd
Instagram.com/wgalleries

Love's Olde Towne Gallery

Based in Vancouver Island, producing, printing and framing a unique collection of vintage inspired art.
Address: 102-535 Yates St, Victoria V8W 2Z6
Phone: +1 250-385-6722
Website: oldetownegallery.com
Email: skookumbc@gmail.com
Facebook.com/skookumprints
Instagram.com/skookumprints

The Eagle Feather Gallery

First Nations artists, featuring masks, sculptures, panels, paddles, drums, silver, gold, serigraph prints and acrylic paintings.
Address: 633 Courtney St, Victoria V8W 1B9
Phone: +1 250-388-4330
Website: Facebook.com/eaglefeathergallery
Email: info@eaglefeathergallery.com
Facebook.com/eaglefeathergallery

Legacy Art Gallery & Café

University of Victoria's art gallery showing their collection and providing learning opportunities and research into Canadian, Indigenous and international historic and contemporary art.
Address: 630 Yates St, Victoria V8W 1K9
Phone: +1 250-721-6562
Website: legacygallery.ca
Email: legacy@uvic.ca
Twitter.com/uvicgalleries
Facebook.com/UVicLegacyGalleries
Instagram.com/uviclegacygalleries
YouTube.com/University of Victoria Legacy Art Galleries

West End Gallery

Family-run art gallery showing leading Canadian contemporary painters and glass artists, many internationally recognised and collected.
Address: 1994-1203 Broad St, Victoria V8W 2A4
Phone: +1 855-488-4892
Website: westendgalleryltd.com
Email: art@westendgalleryltd.com
Twitter.com/westendgallery
Facebook.com/westendgalleryltd
Instagram.com/westendgallery
Pinterest.ca/westendg/_shop
LinkedIn.com/company/west-end-gallery
YouTube.com/user/westendgallery

Art Gallery of Greater Victoria

Collecting art for nearly 70 years, with significant historic regional art from around the Pacific Rim. One of the finest collections of Asian art in the world. Collaborates widely to create engaging exhibitions and programs.
Address: 1040 Moss St, Victoria V8V 4P1
Phone: +1 250-384-4171
Website: aggv.ca
Email: ahenderson@aggv.ca
Twitter.com/artgalleryvic
Facebook.com/artgalleryvictoria
Instagram.com/artgalleryvic
LinkedIn.com/company/art-gallery-of-greater-victoria

Creations Gallery

The finest Canadian sculpture in a range of mediums from bronze, stone, wood, glass, jade, mastodon and antler. International client base. Located in the famed Empress

Hotel in Victoria, British Colombia.
Address: 721 Government St, Victoria V8W
1W5
Phone: +1 250-380-9397
Website: creationsartgallery.com

The Avenue Gallery

One of the leading boutique art galleries
in the Pacific NW showing contemporary
Canadian fine art. Worldwide client base.
Paintings, sculpture, glass and jewellery.
Address: 2184 Oak Bay Ave, Victoria V8R
1G3
Phone: +1 250-598-2184
Website: theavenuegallery.com
Email: info@theavenuegallery.com
Twitter.com/galleryavenue
Facebook.com/theavenuegallery
Instagram.com/theavenuegallery
Pinterest.ca/avenuegallery
Houzz.com/professionals/artists-and-
artisans/the-avenue-gallery
LinkedIn.com/company/the-avenue-gallery

Eclectic Gallery

Gallery and gift shop featuring local artists,
woodwork and pottery, jewellery and textiles.
Address: 2170 Oak Bay Ave, Victoria V8R
1E9
Phone: +1 250-590-8095
Website: eclecticgallery.ca
Email: chbros@shaw.ca

Manitoba

Winnipeg

Plug In Institute of Contemporary Art

Established in 1972 – the oldest ICA in
Canada. Supporting the arts by presenting,
producing and circulating contemporary
art with research, exhibitions, publications,
education, outreach and advocacy.
Address: 1-460 Portage Ave, Winnipeg R3C
0E8
Phone: +1 204-942-1043
Website: plugin.org

Email: info@plugin.org
Twitter.com/PLUGINICA
Facebook.com/pluginica
Instagram.com/pluginica

Winnipeg Art Gallery

Established in 1912, WAG is the first civic
art gallery in Canada. Situated in an iconic
modernist building. An impressive collection
of over 27,000 artworks with a diverse
program of events and partnerships.
Address: 300 Memorial Blvd, Winnipeg R3C
1V1
Phone: +1 204-786-6641
Website: wag.ca
Email: inquiries@wag.ca
Twitter.com/wag_ca
Facebook.com/wag.ca
Instagram.com/wag_ca
YouTube.com/user/WinnipegArtGallery1

Urban Shaman Gallery

A national leader in Aboriginal art. Working
with emerging, mid-career and established
Aboriginal artists with exhibitions, workshops,
residences and curatorial initiatives.
Address: 203-290 McDermot Ave, Winnipeg
R3B 0T2
Phone: +1 204-942-2674
Website: urbanshaman.org
Email: info@urbanshaman.org

Woodlands Gallery

Established in 1984, representing contem-
porary artists from Canada. Framing and art
consultation.
Address: 535 Academy Rd, Winnipeg R3N
0E2
Phone: +1 204-947-0700
Website: woodlandsgallery.com
Email: info@woodlandsgallery.com
Twitter.com/art4yourwalls
Facebook.com/WoodlandsGallery
Instagram.com/art4yourwalls
Pinterest.ca/art4yourwalls

Fredericton

Beaverbrook Art Gallery

The provincial gallery of New Brunswick, bringing together art and community through exhibitions, programs, education and stewardship.
Address: 703 Queen St, Fredericton E3B 1C4
Phone: +1 506-458-2028
Website: beaverbrookartgallery.org
Email: emailbag@beaverbrookartgallery.org
Twitter.com/BeaverbrookAG
Facebook.com/BeaverbrookArtGallery
YouTube.com/
Galerie d'art Beaverbrook Art Gallery

Newfoundland and Labrador

St John's

Leyton Gallery Of Fine Art

Selling important rising national and international artists living in Eastern Canada. Shipping worldwide.
Address: 6 Clifts-Bairds Cove, St Johns A1C 6M9
Phone: +1 709-722-7177
Website: theleytongallery.com
Email: leytongallery@nf.aibn.com
Twitter.com/leytongallery
Facebook.com/TheLeytonGallery
Instagram.com/leytongallery

Peter Lewis Gallery

A diverse collection from over 12 regionally and internationally inspired artists.
Address: 5 Church Hill, St Johns A1C 3Z7
Phone: +1 709-689-2669
Website: peterlewisgallery.com
Email: tracey@staging.peterlewisgallery.com
Twitter.com/PLewisGallery
Facebook.com/peterlewisgallery
Instagram.com/peterlewisgallery
YouTube.com/Peter Lewis

Newfoundland Canvas Art Gallery & Print Studio

Specialising in giclee reproduction with a wide range of Newfoundland images, in hand-crafted Italian frames.
Address: 20 Cathedral St, St Johns A1C 3Y5
Phone: +1 709-576-7387
Website: newfoundlandcanvas.com
Email: hello@newfoundlandcanvas.com
Facebook.com/newfoundlandcanvas
Instagram.com/newfoundlandcanvas

Northwest Territories

Yellowknife

Northern Images

Sculptures, prints, wall hangings, baskets, jewellery and literature. The retail arm of Arctic Co-operatives Ltd; a community -based organisation working in 32 territories in Nunavut, the Northwest Territories and Yukon, helping to develop services and businesses in the north of Canada.
Address: 935-4801 Franklin Ave, Yellowknife X1A 2N7
Phone: +1 867-873-5944
Website: northernimages.ca
Email: WebSales@ArcticCo-op.com
Email: NI.Yellowknife@ArcticCo-op.com

Nova Scotia

Halifax

Art Gallery of Nova Scotia

The largest museum in Atlantic Canada. Engaging people with art since 1908, with over 18,000 works in their permanent collection.
Address: 1723 Hollis St, Halifax B3J 1V9
Phone: +1 902-424-5280
Website: shop.artgalleryofnovascotia.ca
Email: info.agns@novascotia.ca
Twitter.com/ArtGalleryNS
Facebook.com/ArtGalleryNS
Instagram.com/artgalleryns
YouTube.com/ArtGalleryNovaScotia

Ontario

Toronto

Prefix Institute of Contemporary Art

A public art gallery and arts publishing house fostering the appreciation and understanding of contemporary photographic, media and digital arts through exhibitions, publications and programs.
Address: 124-401 Richmond St W, Toronto M5V 3A8
Phone: +1 416-591-0357
Website: prefix.ca
Email: info@prefix.ca
Facebook.com/PrefixInstituteofContemporaryArt
Instagram.com/prefix_ica

Gallery Arcturus

Not-for-profit contemporary art and education centre funded and run by the Foundation for the Study of Objective Art.
Address: 80 Gerrard St E, Toronto M5B 1G6
Phone: +1 416-977-1077
Website: arcturus.ca
Email: ob-art@arcturus.ca

Bay of Spirits Gallery

Specialising in Indigenous art for over 25 years. One of the leading galleries in Canada featuring hundreds of artists.
Address: 156 Front St W, Toronto M5J 2L6
Phone: +1 416-971-5190
Website: bayofspirits.com
Email: info@bayofspirits.com

Paul Petro Contemporary Art

Exhibiting Canadian and international artists by invitation since 1993.
Address: 980 Queen St W, Toronto M6J 1H1
Phone: +1 416-979-7874
Website: paulpetro.com
Email: info@paulpetro.com
Twitter.com/paulpetrocanada
Facebook.com/paulpetrocontemporaryart
Instagram.com/paulpetrocanada

Beauchamp Art Gallery

Showing more than 300 artists from Quebec and abroad since opening in 1993. A collection of 3,500 contemporary and modern works.
Address: 55 Simcoe St, Toronto M5J 0A4
Phone: +1 416-599-2244
Website: galeriebeauchamp.com
Email: info@galeriebeauchamp.com
Facebook.com/galeriesbeauchamp
Instagram.com/galerie_beauchamp

Liss Gallery

Contemporary fine art and photographs from renowned and upcoming artists.
Address: 140 Yorkville Ave, Toronto M5R 1C2
Phone: +1 416-787-9872
Website: lissgallery.com
Email: brianliss@lissgallery.com
Email: jesse.d.liss@gmail.com
Twitter.com/LissGallery
Facebook.com/LissGallery
Instagram.com/lissgallery

Feheley Fine Arts

Excellence in the field of Inuit art. With over 60 years' experience in traditional and contemporary work from the Canadian Arctic. Instrumental in the development of numerous private, public and corporate collections.
Address: 65 George St, Toronto M5A 4L8
Phone: +1 416-323-1373
Website: feheleyfinearts.com
Email: gallery@feheleyfinearts.com
Twitter.com/FeheleyFineArts
Facebook.com/FeheleyFineArts
Instagram.com/feheleyfinearts
YouTube.com/user/FeheleyFineArts

Museum of Contemporary Art

Aiming to be culturally and socially useful. Promoting exceptional artistic thinking. Empowering the local Toronto art scene,

whilst informing the international.
Address: 158 Sterling Rd, Toronto M6R 2B2
Phone: +1 416-530-2500
Website: museumofcontemporaryart.ca
Email: info@moca.ca

Queen Gallery

Diverse, original and contemporary work both regionally and internationally.
Address: 382 Queen St E, Toronto M5A 1T1
Phone: +1 416-361-6045
Website: queengallery.ca
Email: info@queengallery.ca
Facebook.com/QueenGalleryToronto

Art Gallery of Ontario

A collection of more than 80,000 works from the 1st century to the present. With 45,000 square metres of space, it is one of the largest galleries in N America. Holding the biggest collection of Canadian art. Also a large body of Renaissance, Baroque, European, African, Oceanic, modern and contemporary work, with a huge photography collection as well as drawings and prints and the Henry Moore sculpture centre.
Address: 317 Dundas St W, Toronto M5T 1G4
Phone: +1 416-979-6648
Website: ago.net
Twitter.com/agotoronto
Facebook.com/AGOToronto
Instagram.com/agotoronto
YouTube.com/user/ArtGalleryofOntario

Thompson Landry Gallery

Contemporary Quebecois paintings and sculptures in two galleries.
Address: The Distillery District, The Cooperage, 6 Trinity Street, Toronto, Ontario. M5A 3C4
Address: 32 Distillery Lane, Toronto M5A 3C4
Phone: +1 416-364-4955
Website: thompsonlandry.com
Email: info@thompsonlandry.com

Canadian Art

Award-winning print, digital, educational and programming initiatives. A national not-for-profit foundation supporting art writers. Developing platforms to understand, debate and be inspired by art.
Phone: +1 416 368 8854
Website: canadianart.ca
Email: info@canadianart.ca
Twitter.com/canartca
Facebook.com/canadianart
Instagram.com/canartca

Katharinemulherine Contem

Showcasing the work of emerging and mid-career artists since 1998.
Address: 1086 Queen St W, Toronto M6J 1H8
Phone: +1 416-993-6510
Website: katharinemulherin.com
Email: mulherintorontonewyork@gmail.com

Bau-Xi Gallery

Established in 1965 to showcase Canadian artists on the West Coast. The oldest commercial gallery in Vancouver. Emerging and established artists making exceptional contemporary art with monthly exhibitions.
Address: 350 Dundas St W, Toronto M5T
Phone: +1 416-977-0600
Website: bau-xi.com
Email: info@bau-xi.com
Twitter.com/BauXiGallery
Facebook.com/BauXiGallery
Instagram.com/bauxigallery
Pinterest.ca/bauxiartgallery

Ottawa
Ottawa Art Gallery

Contemporary art gallery.
Address: 2 Daly Ave, Ottawa K1N 6E2
Phone: +1 613-233-8699
Website: oaggao.ca
Email: info@oaggao.ca
Twitter.com/OttawaArtG

Facebook.com/ottawaartgallery
Instagram.com/ottawaartgallery
YouTube.com/Ottawa Art Gallery

Orange Art Gallery

With 12ft ceilings and lots of natural light, the gallery exhibits contemporary art and offers art classes with skilled instructors.
Address: 290 City Centre Ave, Ottawa K1R 7R7
Phone: +1 613-761-1500
Website: orangeartgallery.ca
Email: orangeartgallery@bellnet.ca

Patrick John Mills Contemporary Fine Art Gallery

Expressionist to abstract, Patrick John Mills' work has been collected all over the world, with numerous exhibitions both in Europe and USA.
Address: 286 Hinchey Ave, Ottawa K1Y 1M2
Phone: +1 613-729-0406
Website: patrickjohnmills.com
Email: patrickjohnmills@gmail.com
Instagram.com/patrickjmills
YouTube.com/Patrick John Mills

L.A. Pai Gallery

Exhibiting contemporary Canadian emerging and established artists, and jewellers from Canada and worldwide for 20 years.
Address: 13 Murray St, Ottawa K1N 9M5
Phone: +1 613-241-2767
Website: lapaigallery.com
Email: info@lapaigallery.com
Facebook.com/L.A.PaiGallery
Instagram.com/lapaigallery
Pinterest.ca/lapaigallery

Galerie St-Laurent + Hill

Ottawa's leading contemporary art gallery. Founded in 1977, with a focus on painting, photography and sculpture. Working with private and corporate collectors for more than 40 years.

Address: 293 Dalhousie St, Ottawa K1N 7E5
Phone: +1 613-789-7145
Website: galeriestlaurentplushill.com
Email: info@galeriestlaurentplushill.com
Twitter.com/GSTL_ART
Facebook.com/GalerieStLaurentHill
Instagram.com/GalerieStLaurentHill

Gallery 101

A Non-profit, artist-run charity dedicated to showing visual and media arts. Solo and group exhibitions of Canadian and international contemporary artists each year, using all medium and at all career stages. Also supporting curators, writers and critics.
Address: 280 Catherine Street, Ottawa K1R 5T3
Phone: +1 613-230-2799
Website: gallery101.org
Email: office@g101.ca
Twitter.com/G101Ottawa
Facebook.com/G101Ottawa
Instagram.com/g101ottawa

National Gallery of Canada

Established in 1880 with a single 19th century landscape, the gallery now has 75,000 works of art and an extensive library. It has one of the finest collections of Canadian and Indigenous art in the world as well as masterpieces from many other artistic traditions.
Address: 380 Sussex Dr, Ottawa K1N 9N4
Phone: +1 613-990-1985
Website: gallery.ca
Email: info@gallery.ca
Twitter.com/NatGalleryCan
Facebook.com/nationalgallerycanada
Instagram.com/NatGalleryCan
YouTube.com/user/ngcmedia

Quebec
Beauchamp Art Gallery

Showing the work of more than 300 artists from its inception in 1993. With a collection

of over 3,500 contemporary and modern works from Canada and abroad.
Address: 16 Rue St Jean Baptiste, Baie Saint Paul G3Z 1L9
Phone: +1 418-240-2244
Website: galeriebeauchamp.com
Facebook.com/galeriesbeauchamp
Instagram.com/galerie_beauchamp

Saskatchewan

Regina
Art Gallery of Regina

A dynamic cultural hub focusing on Saskatchewan artists.
Address: 2420 Elphinstone St, Regina S4T 7S7
Phone: +1 306-522-5940
Website: artgalleryofregina.ca
Email: agr@sasktel.net
Twitter.com/agr_regina
Facebook.com/Art-Gallery-of-Regina
Instagram.com/artgalleryofregina

MacKenzie Art Gallery

Saskatchewan's oldest public art gallery with a permanent collection spanning 5,000 years with nearly the same number of works.
Address: 3475 Albert St, Regina S4S 6X6
Phone: +1 306-584-4250
Website: mackenzie.art
Email: info@mackenzie.art
Twitter.com/atthemag
Facebook.com/MacKenzieArtGallery
Instagram.com/mackenzie.art.gallery
YouTube.com/user/atthemag

Slate Fine Art Gallery

Contemporary art from established Canadian artists with a focus on Saskatchewan art. Monthly exhibitions, live performances and special events.
Address: 3424 13th Ave, Regina S4T 1P7
Phone: +1 306-775-0300
Website: slategallery.ca
Email: slate@sasktel.net

Facebook.com/slatefineartgallery
Instagram.com/slategallery

Yukon
Whitehorse

An independent, not-for-profit art gallery and a leading venue for contemporary art in Canada. Works with Canadian and international artists producing exhibitions, off-site projects, residences, learning and community events and publications.
Address: 555 Nelson St, Vancouver V6B 6R5
Phone: +1 604-681-2700
Website: contemporaryartgallery.ca
Email: contact@contemporaryartgallery.ca
Twitter.com/CAGVancouver
Facebook.com/CAGvancouver
Instagram.com/cagvancouver
Vimeo.com/cagvancouver
SoundCloud.com/contemporary-art-gallery

CHINA
Dunhuang Feng Contemporary Art Hall

Address: No.222 Tianshui South Rd, Lanzhou
Phone: +86 18909315811
Website: dhfart.cn

Shanghai
Shanghai Chihan Art Gallery

Address: No.1117, Fuxing East Road, Shanghai
Phone: +86 21 63503828
Website: dianping.com

Shanghai Yihao Art Gallery

Address: No.1, Jianguo Middle Road, Shanghai
Phone: +86 21 54669796
Website: dianping.com

Museum of Contemporary Art Shanghai

The first private contemporary art museum in China, founded in 2005 showing Chinese and international work.
Address: Inner People's Park No.231 Nanjing Rd (W), Shanghai
Phone: +86 21 63279900
Website: mocashanghai.org
Email: info@mocashanghai.org

Shuangcheng Modern Homemade Art Gallery

Address: No.20, Shaoxing Road, Shanghai
Phone: +86 21 52521518
Website: dianping.com

Hushen Gallery

Primarily focused on Asian contemporary art with exhibitions, artists' projects and interdisciplinary programs. Collaborating with major museums, art foundations, curators and critics. Offering long-term strategic planning for collectors and institutions. Established and emerging artists.
Address: F3 Bund 3 No.3 Zhongshan Rd (E-1), Shanghai
Phone: +86 21 63215757
Website: shanghaigalleryofart.com
Email: sga@on-the-bund.com
Instagram.com/shanghaigalleryofart

The Bund Art Gallery

Address: 201 Hankou Rd, Shanghai
Phone: +86 21 63212256
Website: dianping.com

Shanghai Hongqiao Dangdai Art Gallery

Address: No.650 Xianxia Rd, Shanghai
Phone: +86 21 62618834
Website: dianping.com

M97 Gallery

Established in 2006 in Shanghai. Exhibits contemporary and fine art photography from all genres, representing over 30 important emerging and established artists from China and around the world.
Address: No.97 Moganshan Road, Putuo District, Shanghai 200000
Phone: +86 21 62661597
Website: m97gallery.com
Email: info@m97gallery.com
Twitter.com/m97gallery
Facebook.com/M97Gallery
Instagram.com/m97gallery

Beijing

Yijing Space for Contemporary Art

Address: Jiuxianqiao Road No.2 798 Art Zone, Beijing
Website: yishujia.findart.com.cn

Ullens Center for Contemporary Art

Address: No.4, Jiuxianqiao Road, Beijing
Phone: +86 10 84599269
Website: dianping.com

Tang Contemporary Art

Promoting Chinese contemporary art regionally and worldwide, encouraging collaborations between Chinese artists, curators, collectors and institutions and those abroad.
Address: Jiuxianqiao Road No.2 Beijing 798 Art Zone D Qunei, Beijing
Phone: +86 10 84475571
Website: tangcontemporary.com
Email: info@tangcontemporary.com
Facebook.com/tangcontemporary
Instagram.com/tangcontemporaryart
Artsy.net/tang-contemporary-art
Vimeo.com/tangcontemporaryart
Ocula.com/art-galleries/tang-contemporary-art
LinkedIn.com/company/tang-contemporary-art
YouTube.com/Tang Contemporary Art

Chongqing

Huaren Contemporary Art Museum

Address: No.59 Hubin East Rd Huixing

Neighborhood, Chongqing
Phone: +86 23 67451993
Website: huarenart.org

Chengdu
Museum of Contemporary Art Chengdu

Address: C1 W Bldg. Tianfu Software Pk
No.219 Tianhuaer Rd, Chengdu
Phone: +86 28 85980055
Website: chengdumoca.org
Email: Chengdumoca@hotmail.com

Xi'an
Xiangzimiao No.70 Art Gallery

Address: Nanmenli, Xian
Phone: +86 29 87269787
Website: q.Weibo.com

Xi'an Huangcheng Art Museum

Address: S of Rd of 50m to East from
Crossroads of Wulukou, Xi'an
Phone: +86 29 82680185
Website: dianping.com

Cuizimo Art Museum Xi'an

Address: Beilin Museum East Gate No.6
Xianningxue Ln, Xi'an
Website: dianping.com

Hangzhou
Xihu Contemporary Art Gallery

Address: No.182-1, Nanshan Road,
Hangzhou
Phone: 0571-87024609
Website: dianping.com

Harbin
Harbin Pharmaceutical

Contemporary Art Museum
Address: No.2050, Jingjiang West Road,
Harbin
Website: dianping.com

COLOMBIA
San Andres
Artesanias & Accesorios Mara

Located on the island of San Andrés in the
Caribbean Sea. Selling a large variety of
arts and crafts made locally and nationally.
Address: Centro Comercial New Point
Avenida Peatonal Local 133, San Andrés
880001
Phone: +57 315 7704117
Website: marasanandres.com
Email: artesanias@marasanandres.com

COSTA RICA
San José
Museo de Arte y Deseno Contemprorano

An open and multiple space showing the
latest and most dynamic contemporary
art and design from the Central American.
regions, as well as further afield.
Address: Calle 15, San José
Phone: +506 2257 7202
Website: madc.cr
Email: info@madc.cr
Twitter.com/MuseoMADC
Facebook.com/MuseoMADC.CR
Instagram.com/museomadc
YouTube.com/user/madccr

CROATIA
Republika Srpska Art Gallery

Contemporary art gallery.
Address: Trg Srpskikh Junaka 2, Banja Luka
78000
Phone: +387 51 215-364
Website: inyourpocket.com

CUBA

Gildea Contemporary Gallery

Contemporary art from abstract expressionists to sculptors to landscape.
Address: 522 Southard St, Key West 33040
Phone: +1 (305) 797-6485
Website: gildea.gallery
Email: gildeagallerykw@gmail.com
Twitter.com/GildeaGallery
Facebook.com/gildeacontemporarygallery
Instagram.com/gildeagallery
YouTube.com/Gildea Contemporary Art Gallery

Archeo Gallery

Compelling primitive art that is simple and sincere.
Address: 1208 Duval St, Key West 33040
Phone: +1 (305) 294-3771
Website: archeogallery.com
Facebook.com/archeogallery
Instagram.com/archeokeywest
Pinterest.co.uk/archeogallery

CZECH REPUBLIC

Shevchuk Art Gallery

Showing leading contemporary artists in the Czech Republic including paintings by Yuriy Shevchuk – cityscapes, jazz and cars.
Address: Pohorelec 5, Prague 11000
Phone: +420 776 140 519
Website: shevchukart.com
Email: info@shevchukart.com

Art Gallery Sculpio

Contemporary art.
Address: Lipských 2062, Pelhřimov
Phone: +420 602 705 810
Website: sculpio.com
Email: sculpio@sculpio.cz
Facebook.com/sculpio

Joseph Fine Art Gallery

Contemporary art.
Address: Tynska, 1053/21, Stare Mesto, Prague
Phone: +420 222 313 868
Website: josephfineart.com

DOX Centre for Contemporary Art

The largest independent institution focusing on contemporary art in the Czech Republic. Set in a former factory, spanning genres, such as art, literature, theatre and music, to transform everyday experience and create critical public discussion on important issues shaping our world.
Address: Poupětova 793/1, Praha 170 00
Phone: +420 295 568 123
Website: dox.cz
Email: info@dox.cz
Twitter.com/DOXPrague
Facebook.com/DOXPrague
Instagram.com/doxprague
Vimeo.com/doxprague

Art Residence

A creative centre with studios, gallery and café in an historical courtyard with a garden. Gallery exhibits paintings and sculpture, mainly by Czech artists.
Address: Mostecka 14, Prague
Phone: +420 777 713 315
Website: artresidenceprague.com
Email: katerina@artresidenceprague.com

Manoukian Gallery of Modern Art

Paintings by Gagik Manoukian in a range of different styles, from landscape to figurative.
Address: Jilska 9, Prague 110 00
Phone: +420 608 557 679
Website: gagikgallery.com
Email: gagikgallery@yahoo.com
Facebook.com/manokianGalleryofModernArt
Instagram.com/gagik.manoukian

Ostrava
PLATO Ostrava

Contemporary art gallery with 5,000 m² for art.
Address: Janackova 3139/22, Ostrava 70200
Phone: +420 702 206 099
Website: plato-ostrava.cz
Email: magdalena.duskova@plato-ostrava.cz
Email: info@plato-ostrava.cz
Facebook.com/platoostrava
Instagram.com/platoostrava
SoundCloud.com/platoostrava
YouTube.com/PLATO Ostrava

Hradec Králové
Gallery of Modern Art

Founded in 1953 focusing mainly on the development of Czech modern art with a permanent collection from the turn of the 19th and 20th centuries to the work of contemporary artists.
Address: Velke namesti 139/140, Hradec Kralove 500 03
Phone: +420 495 512 538
Website: galeriehk.cz
Email: info@galeriehk.cz
Facebook.com/gmuhk
Instagram.com/gmuhk

DENMARK

Copenhagen
Copenhagen Contemporary

Copenhagen's international art centre, with installations by world renowned artists and new emerging talent. Over 7,000 m² of former industrial space with performance art and huge video works.
Address: Trangravsvej 10-12, København 1436
Phone: +45 29 89 72 88
Website: copenhagencontemporary.org
Email: ida@cphco.org
Email: contact@cphco.org
Facebook.com/cc.copenhagencontemporary
Instagram.com/copenhagen_contemporary

Gallery Christoffer Egelund

Cutting-edge gallery showing high quality Scandinavian and international contemporary work which is experimental and innovative. Large variety of media; works on paper, photos, paintings, sculpture, performance and video, all having unique artistic expression.
Address: Bredgade 75, Copenhagen
Phone: +45 33 93 92 00
Email: info@christofferegelund.dk
Twitter.com/gcenu
Facebook.com/gallerichristofferegelund
Instagram.com/gallerichristofferegelund
Website: christofferegelund.dk.com/in/christoffer-m-egelund

Aarhus
Charlotte Fogh Gallery

Upcoming and established artists working with a range of media and expressions. 7-8 exhibitions a year.
Address: Mejlgade 18 B, Aarhus
Phone: +45 25 69 71 05
Website: charlottefogh.dk
Email: info@charlottefogh.dk
Facebook.com/CharlotteFoghGallery
Instagram.com/charlottefoghgallery
LinkedIn.com/company/charlotte-fogh-contemporary

EGYPT

Cairo
Mashrabia Gallery of Contemporary Art

Contemporary art gallery.
Address: 8th Building, Champollion Street, In Front of QNB bank - Downtown, Cairo 11511

Phone: +20 2 25784494
Website: mashrabiagallery.com

Zamalek Art Gallery

Based in the cosmopolitan area of Cairo, this gallery has been a hub of contemporary Egyptian art for more than 20 years. Exhibiting art pioneers in Egypt and the entire Arab region, both emerging and established artists. Two simultaneous exhibitions on a monthly basis.
Address: 11 Brazil St, Zamalek
Phone: +20 2 27351240
Website: zamalekartgallery.com
Email: admin@zamalekartgallery.com
Twitter.com/zamalekgallery
Facebook.com/zamalekartgallery
Instagram.com/zamalekartgallery

Contemporary Image Collective (CIC)

Art exhibitions, film screenings, knowledge exchange, research projects, publications, a public library and specialised photo production facilities.
Address: 22 Abd El Khalek Tharwat St, Wust El-Balad
Phone: +20 2 23964272
Website: ciccairo.com
Email: info@ciccairo.com
Twitter.com/CairoCIC
Facebook.com/CIC.
ContemporaryImageCollective
Instagram.com/ciccairo

ESTONIA

ArtDepoo Gallery

Estonian modern art and newer foreign art.
Address: Jahu 12, Tallinn 10415
Phone: +372 666 1488
Website: artdepoo.com

HOP Gallery

Developing the field of art and expanding its entry space in Estonia. Protecting the interests of artists, curators, art scientists and art workers and promoting their working and creative conditions.
Address: Hobusepea 2, Tallinn 10133
Phone: +372 646 2887
Website: eaa.ee
Email: ekl@eaa.ee

FINLAND

Helsinki
Museum of Contemporary Art Kiasma

Helsinki's most experimental major museum. Showing either electronic or tangible, musical or performance orientated art. Part of the Finnish National Gallery. Collecting the art of our time, offering art experiences and new perspectives on life.
Address: Mannerheiminaukio 2, Helsinki 00100
Phone: +358 29 4500200
Website: kiasma.fi
Email: info@kiasma.fi

Espoo
EMMA – Espoo Museum of Modern Art

EMMA has the largest exhibition space in Finland. Two collection exhibitions are on permanent display.
Address: Ahertajantie 5, Espoo 02100
Phone: +358 43 8270941
Website: emmamuseum.fi
Email: info@emmamuseum.fi
Twitter.com/emmamuseum
Facebook.com/emmamuseum
Instagram.com/emmamuseum
Vimeo.com/channels/emmamuseum
YouTube.com/user/emmamuseum

FRANCE

Galerie L.J.

Supporting the careers of emerging graphic artists and contemporary painters and sculptors.
Address: 12 Rue Commines, Paris 75003
Phone: +33 1 72 38 44 47
Website: galerielj.com
Email: hello@galerielj.com
Twitter.com/galerielj
Facebook.com/galerielj

Art Jingle

Gallery of contemporary art, urban art and street art, highlighting a new generation of artists and sculptors.
Address: 31 bis, Rue des Tournelles, Paris 75003
Phone: +33 1 40 29 40 03
Website: artjingle.com
Email: info@artjingle.com
Twitter.com/artjingle
Facebook.com/galerieartjingle
Instagram.com/galerieartjingle
Pinterest.fr/artjingle

Galerie Magda Danysz

Continually expanding new territories — rooted in Shanghai and active in London where it has an artist residency program. Exhibiting emerging artists connected with the local and international scenes.
Address: 78 Rue Amelot Paris, Paris 75011
Phone: +33 1 45 83 38 51
Website: magdagallery.com
Email: info@danyszgallery.com
Twitter.com/danyszgallery
Facebook.com/danyszgallery
Instagram.com/danyszgallery
YouTube.com/danyszgallery

Galerie Modus

For 20 years, the gallery has been exhibiting emerging and acclaimed contemporary and street artists.
Address: 23 Place des Vosges, Paris 75003
Phone: +33 1 42 78 10 10
Website: modus-gallery.com
Email: modus@modusgallery.com
Twitter.com/ModusGallery
Facebook.com/ModusArtGallery
Instagram.com/modus.gallery
Pinterest.co.uk/nextstreetgalleryparis

Lebenson Gallery

A platform in the heart of Marais in Paris, for contemporary artists in marginalised areas, from East London to Brooklyn NY.
Address: 56, Rue Chapon, Paris 75003
Phone: +33 9 81 88 75 61
Website: lebensongallery.com
Address: 150 Curtain Road London EC2A 3AR
Email: stephane@lebensongallery.com
Email: director@lebensongallery.com
Email: lebensongallery@icloud.com
Twitter.com/LebensonGallery
Facebook.com/lebensongallery
Instagram.com/lebensongallery

Carre d'artistes Paris

With more than 30 art galleries around the world, from New York to Beijing with more than 600 exhibited artists.
Address: 16 rue Yvonne le Tac, Paris 75018
Phone: +33 1 42 54 97 84
Website: carredartistes.com
Email: bonjour@carredartistes.com
Twitter.com/carredartistes
Facebook.com/Carredartistes.galerie.art.contemporain
Instagram.com/carredartistes
Pinterest.fr/carredartistesofficiel

School Gallery

Championing established artists and young talents for more than ten years.
Address: 81 Rue Temple, Paris 75003
Address: 322 rue Saint Martin, Paris 75003
Phone: +33 1 42 71 78 20
Website: schoolgallery.fr
Email: olivier.schoolgallery@gmail.com

Galerie Popy Arvani

French and international, emerging and established artists.
Address: 7, Rue Jean-Pierre Timbaud, Paris
Phone: +33 1 47 00 87 51
Website: galeriepopyarvani.com
Email: galerie@galeriepopyarvani.com

French Arts Factory

Ceramics, mosaics, sculptors in wood, metal, painters, tapestry-makers. Selecting the most talented in their discipline.
Address: 19 rue de Seine, Paris 75006
Phone: +33 6 60 53 60 54
Website: frenchartsfactory.paris
Email: vemoulin@frenchartsfactory.paris
Facebook.com/Veronique.Moulin.Paris

Nordic Contemporary

Contemporary art gallery.
Address: 13 rue Taylor, Paris 75010
Phone: +33 6 16 12 81 39
Website: nordiccontemporary.com
Email: info@nordiccontemporary.com

Laurence Esnol Gallery

Contemporary art gallery.
Address: Entree 22 7 rue Bonaparte, Paris 75006
Phone: +33 1 46 33 47 01
Website: laurenceesnolgallery.com
Email: laurenceesnolgallery@gmail.com
Email: laurence@laurenceesnolgallery.com
Twitter.com/esnolgallery
Facebook.com/laurence.galerie
Instagram.com/laurenceesnolgallery

Marseille
Carre d'artistes Marseille

With more than 30 art galleries around the world, from New York to Beijing with more than 600 exhibited artists.
Address: 27 cours Honore D Estienne D Orves, Marseille 13001
Phone: +33 4 91 04 09 71
Website: carredartistes.com
Email: bonjour@carredartistes.com
Twitter.com/carredartistes
Facebook.com/Carredartistes.galerie.art.contemporain
Instagram.com/carredartistes
Pinterest.fr/carredartistesofficiel

Lyon
Carre d'artistes Lyon

With more than 30 art galleries around the world, from New York to Beijing with more than 600 exhibited artists
Address: 57 Passage de l Argue, Lyon 69002
Phone: +33 4 78 37 02 14
Website: carredartistes.com
Email: bonjour@carredartistes.com
Twitter.com/carredartistes
Facebook.com/Carredartistes.galerie.art.contemporain
Instagram.com/carredartistes
Pinterest.fr/carredartistesofficiel

Museum of Contemporary Art

With a collection of 1,450 pieces first exhibited from 1984. Created by living artists with a variety of performance art, painting, video installation, sculpture, sound installation, photography, drawing, cinema, computer programming and books with a focus of the immersive world of monumental installations.
Address: 81 Charles de Gaulle dock, Lyon 69006
Phone: +33 4 72 69 17 17
Website: mac-lyon.com

Email: info@mac-lyon.com
Facebook.com/mac.lyon
Instagram.com/maclyon_officiel
YouTube.com/user/mocalyon

Artclub Gallery

Contemporary art gallery.
Address: 22 Place Bellecour, Lyon 69002
Phone: +33 4 78 37 16 37
Website: artclub.fr
Email: artclub-lyon@wanadoo.fr
Twitter.com/ArtclubParis
Facebook.com/artclubgalleryparis

Galerie Ories

Contemporary art gallery.
Address: 33, Rue Auguste Comte, Lyon 69002
Phone: +33 4 78 42 57 07
Website: galerieories.fr
Email: galerieories@hotmail.com

Toulouse
Carre d'artistes Toulouse

With more than 30 art galleries around the world, from New York to Beijing with more than 600 exhibited artists.
Address: 38 rue Alsace-Lorraine, Toulouse 31000
Phone: +33 5 61 12 35 32
Website: carredartistes.com
Email: bonjour@carredartistes.com
Twitter.com/carredartistes
Facebook.com/Carredartistes.galerie.art.contemporain
Instagram.com/carredartistes
Pinterest.fr/carredartistesofficiel

La Fondation Écureuil Pour L'Art Contemporain

Contemporary art.
Address: 3, PL du Capitole, Toulouse 31000
Phone: +33 5 62 30 23 30
Website: caisseepargne-art-contemporain.fr
Email:contact@caisseepargne-art-contemporain.fr

Bam Gallery

Contemporary art.
Address: 52, Rue Raymond 4, Toulouse 31000
Phone: +33 5 61 48 76 08
Website: bam-gallery.com
Email: bam.gallery@wanadoo.fr
Facebook.com/BAM-GALLERY/artsper.com/fr/galeries-d-art/france/1927/bam-gallery

Nice
Carre d'artistes Toulouse

With more than 30 art galleries around the world, from New York to Beijing with more than 600 exhibited artists.
Address: 38 rue Alsace-Lorraine, Toulouse 31000
Phone: +33 5 61 12 35 32
Website: carredartistes.com
Email: bonjour@carredartistes.com
Twitter.com/carredartistes
Facebook.com/Carredartistes.galerie.art.contemporain
Instagram.com/carredartistes

Dijon
FRACB Fonds Régional d'Art Contemporain de Bourgogne

With 700 contemporary works and with the aim of discovering new talents and nurturing artistic practice.
Address: 41, Rue des Ateliers, Dijon 21000
Phone: +33 3 80 67 18 18
Website: frac-bourgogne.org
Email: administration@frac-bourgogne.org

Bordeaux
Carre d'artistes Bordeaux

With more than 30 art galleries around the world, from New York to Beijing with more than 600 exhibited artists.
Address: 66 rue des Remparts, Bordeaux 33000

Phone: +33 5 56 52 88 04
Website: carredartistes.com
Email: bonjour@carredartistes.com
Twitter.com/carredartistes
Facebook.com/Carredartistes.galerie.art.
contemporain
Instagram.com/carredartistes
Pinterest.fr/carredartistesofficiel

NoMuseuM,Contemporary Art Gallery

Contemporary art gallery.
Address: 127, Rue Notre-Dame, Bordeaux
33000
Phone: +33 6 48 09 66 33
Website: Facebook.com
Email: andreric.private@gmail.com
Facebook.com/NoMuseuMcontemporary-
art-gallery

Association Tinbox

Focusing on the idea of a metal box as an
architectonic space in varying scale, that can
be presented in the street, museums, galleries
and schools.
Address: 16, Rue du Portail, Bordeaux
33800
Phone: +33 6 63 27 52 49
Website: galerie-tinbox.com
Email: contact@lagence-creative.com

Galerie DX

Exhibitions reflecting the current artistic
movements from international and young
visual practitioners.
Address: 10, PL des Quinconces, Bordeaux
33000
Phone: +33 5 56 23 35 20
Website: galeriedx.com
Email: galeriedx33@gmail.com
Facebook.com/galeriedx

Strasbourg
Carre d'artistes

With more than 30 art galleries around the
world, from New York to Beijing with more
than 600 exhibited artists.
Address: 11/13 rue des Orfèvres, 67000
Strasbourg
Phone: +33 5 56 52 88 04
Website: carredartistes.com
E-mail: galerie2@carredartistes-stbg.fr
Twitter.com/carredartistes
Facebook.com/Carredartistes.galerie.art.
contemporain
Instagram.com/carredartistes

Eponyme Galeri

Contemporary art gallery.
Address: 3, Rue Cornac, Bordeaux 33000
Phone: +33 5 35 40 07 95
Website: eponymegalerie.com
Twitter.com/EponymeGalerie
Facebook.com/eponyme

GERMANY
Berlin
Daimler Contemporary

Founded in 1977, focusing on the avant-
garde of the 20th century and present.
Address: Alte Potsdamer Str. 5, Berlin 10785
Phone: +49 30 25941420
Website: art.daimler.com
Email: art.collection@daimler.com

Galerie Eigen & Art

Primarily focusing on artists from the
former East Germany and other countries
once located behind the Iron Curtain, with
locations in Leipzig and Berlin. Established
and young artists with film/video,
photography, installation, painting, sculpture
and performance.
Address: 26 Auguststrasse, Berlin
Phone: +49 30 2806605
Website: eigen-art.com
Email: berlin@eigen-art.com

Facebook.com/galerie.eigenart
Instagram.com/galerie_eigenart
Artsy.net/galerie-eigen-plus-art/shows

Berlinische Galerie Museum of Modern Art

Looking at the period 1870 to the present, with modern and contemporary art that originated in Berlin.
Address: Old Jacob Street 124-128, Berlin 10969
Phone: +49 30 78902600
Website: berlinischegalerie.de
Email: bg@berlinischegalerie.de
Twitter.com/bg_museum
Facebook.com/berlinischegalerie
Instagram.com/berlinischegalerie
spotify.com/ berlinischegalerie
YouTube.com/user/BerlinischeGalerie

Galerie of Modern Art Peter Bauer E.K.

Contemporary art gallery.
Address: Kantstr. 47, Berlin 10625
Phone: +49 30 3134564
Website: galerieart.de
Email: mail@galerieart.de

Horton Gallery

The gallery is a member of the New Art Dealers Alliance. No unsolicited submissions.
Address: Alexandrinenstr. 4, Berlin 10969
Website: hortongallery.com
Email: cseanhorton@gmail.com
Instagram.com/sean.horton.presents
Artsy.net/horton-gallery

Egbert Baqué Contemporary

Contemporary art gallery.
Address: Fasanenstr. 37, Berlin 10719
Phone: +49 30 43910880
Website: Facebook.com
Email: eb.contemporary@gmail.com
Facebook.com/ebcontemporary

401 Contemporary

Contemporary art gallery. No unsolicited artist submissions.
Address: Potsdamer Str. 81B, Berlin 10785
Phone: +49 30 47377783
Website: 401contemporary.com
Email: gallery@401contemporary.com

Autocenter

Contemporary art gallery founded in 2001.
Address: Eldenaer Str. 34, Berlin 10247
Website: autocenterart.de
Email: info@autocenter-art.de

Koppe Contemporary

Representing local, national and international artists, both established and emerging.
Address: Knausstr. 19, Berlin 14193
Phone: +49 176 23379278
Website: villa-koeppe.de
Email: galerie@villa-koeppe.de
Facebook.com/GalerieVillaKoeppe
Instagram.com/koeppecontemporary
Pinterest.co.uk/villakoeppe
YouTube.com/user/GalerieVillaKoeppe

Art Laboratory Berlin

Multiple award winning art and research platform founded in 2006 by an international team of art historians and artists presenting the interface of art, science and technology.
Address: Prinzenallee 34, Berlin 13359
Phone: +49 173 6216347
Website: artlaboratory-berlin.org
Email: info@artlaboratory-berlin.org
Twitter.com/ArtLaboratoryB
Facebook.com/ArtLaboratoryBerlin

Hamburg
Xpon-art gallery

Contemporary art gallery.
Address: Repsoldstr. 45, Hamburg 20097

Phone: +49 1511 1507936
Website: xpon-art.de
Email: info@xpon-art.de
Facebook.com/xponart

White Trash Contemporary

Representing emerging artists in an industrial exhibition space of 120 m².
Address: Neue Burg 2, Hamburg 20457
Phone: +49 40 36099935
Website: whitetrashcontemporary.com
Email: infowtc@mac.com
Instagram.com/aartbytes

Glasgalerie Stölting

The glass art gallery was founded in 1988, exhibiting Czech contemporary fine art glass sculpture, with artists who have since gone on to have a worldwide reputation.
Address: Am Sandtorpark 14, Hamburg 20457
Phone: +49 40 32530833
Website: glassart.de
Email: info@glassart.de
Facebook.com/Glasgalerie.Stoelting
Instagram.com/glasgalerie
Pinterest.de/czechglassart

Art Association in Hamburg

Young and international contemporary art, based in Hamburg.
Address: Klosterwall 23, Hamburg 20095
Phone: +49 40 322157
Website: kunstverein.de
Email: hamburg@kunstverein.de
Twitter.com/KunstvereinHH
Facebook.com/KunstvereinHamburg
Instagram.com/kunstvereinhh

Galerie Herold

A family-owned company, founded in 1978, exhibiting leading German and European Impressionism and Expressionism.
Address: Colonnaden 5, Hamburg 20354

Phone: +49 40 478060
Website: galerie-herold.de
Email: herold@galerie-herold.de
Facebook.com/galerieheroldhamburg
Instagram.com/galerieherold

Freiburg
Plexus

Contemporary art gallery.
Address: Route St-Nicolas-de-Flüe 8, Freiburg 1700
Phone: +41 26 321 54 35
Website: galleryplexus.ch
Email: Bernard.chassot@crartrading.ch

Galerie Contraste

Contemporary art gallery.
Address: ruelle des Cordeliers 6, Fribourg 1700
Phone: +41 79 922 71 07
Website: galeriecontraste.ch
Email: info@jphumbert.ch

Au Carmin

Contemporary art gallery.
Address: Planche-Supérieure 29, Freiburg 1700
Phone: +41 26 322 64 05
Website: au-carmin.ch

Musee D'art et D'histoire MAHF

Contemporary art gallery.
Address: rue de Morat 12, Fribourg 1700
Phone: +41 26 305 51 40
Website: fr.ch
Twitter.com/Etat_Fribourg
Facebook.com/Etat.Fribourg
LinkedIn.com/company/etatfr

Cologne
Pop68

Based in Cologne and Paris. Showing

contemporary art including painting, time-based media art, sculpture and installation from different scenes and artistic backgrounds. Emerging and established artists.
Address: Bismarckstr. 68, Köln 50672
Phone: +49 221 16993647
Website: ruttkowski68.com
Email: info@ruttkowski68.com
Facebook.com/Ruttkowski68
Instagram.com/ruttkowski68
Artsy.net/ruttkowski-68

Galerie Seippel

Representing a wide field of contemporary art, such as painting, sculpture, photography, graphics, video, installation and light installation. Exhibitions, workshops and residency programs collaborating with world-wide partners.
Address: Zeughausstr. 26, Köln 50667
Phone: +49 221 255834
Website: galerie-seippel.de
Email: seippelart@t-online.de

Kaune, Posnik, Spohr GMBH

Founded in 2007 with a focus on international photo and video art.
Address: Zeughausstrasse 13, Köln 50667
Phone: +49 221 99203339
Website: gallery-kps.com
Email: info@gallery-kc.com

Galerie Zander S.

6-9 exhibitions annually, with photography, media and conceptual art. Representing international artists from the 20th and 21st century.
Address: Antwerpener Str. 1, Köln 50672
Phone: +49 221 521625
Website: galeriezander.com
Email: mail@galeriezander.com
Facebook.com/galeriezander
Instagram.com/galeriethomaszander

Berthold Pott GmbH

Contemporary art gallery.
Address: Bismarckstr. 60, Köln 50672
Phone: +49 221 17919688
Website: bertholdpott.com
Email: berthold@bertholdpott.com

Temporary Gallery Cologne

Contemporary art gallery with international funding. Solo and group exhibitions, lectures and film.
Address: Mauritiuswall 35, Köln 50676
Phone: +49 221 30234467
Website: temporarygallery.org
Email: info@temporarygallery.org
Facebook.com/Temporary-Gallery
Instagram.com/temporary_gallery

Galerie Christian Lethert

Works with internationally established artists as well as selected emerging artists with solo and group exhibitions, placing work in private and corporate collections and worldwide exhibitions.
Address: Antwerpener Str. 4, Cologne 50672
Phone: +49 4922 13560590
Website: christianlethert.com
Email: info@christianlethert.com
Facebook.com/galeriechristianlethert
Instagram.com/galerie_lethert

Munich
Pinakothek of the Modern Art

One of the largest museums in the world for art, architecture and design of the 20th and 21st centuries.
Address: Barer Street 40, Munich 80333
Phone: +49 89 23805360
Website: pinakothek.de
Email: info@pinakothek.de
Twitter.com/pinakotheken
Facebook.com/pinakotheken
Instagram.com/pinakotheken

MUCA Museum of Urban and Contemporary Art

Creating spaces for young, transient art forms such as street and urban art, linking it with other genres of contemporary art. An emphasis on art education.
Address: Hotterstr. 12, Munich 80331
Phone: +49 89 215524310
Website: muca.eu
Twitter.com/mucamunich
Facebook.com/MUCAmunich
Instagram.com/mucamunich
YouTube.com/MUCA Museum of Urban and Contemporary Art

American Contemporary Art Gallery

Over 170 exhibitions of Abstract Expressionism since 1986.
Address: Maximilianstr. 29, München 80539
Phone: +49 89 29161200
Website: americancontemporaryartgallery.com
Email: info@usa-art-gallery.de

Galerie Flash

Exhibiting established and young artists on an international level, with a focus on painting, photography, graphic art, sculpture, installation and new media. Deliberately varied work creating a bridge between different generations and cultures.
Address: Blumenstr. 21a, München 80331
Phone: +49 89 26019615
Website: galerieflash.de
Email: info@galerieflash.de
Facebook.com/galerieflash
Instagram.com/galerieflash

Art Gallery of the Hypo Cultural Foundation

Over 350,000 visitors each year with 3 large exhibitions annually. Painting, sculpture, graphic art, photography, crafts, fashion and design bringing global art and culture to life.
Address: Theatiner Street 8, Munich 80333

Phone: +49 89 224412
Website: kunsthalle-muc.de
Email: kontakt@kunsthalle-muc.de
Twitter.com/kunsthallemuc
Facebook.com/kunsthallemuc
Instagram.com/kunsthallemuc
YouTube.com/user/MucKunsthalle

Dresden
Art House Dresden

Providing insights in the current world art scene with changing exhibitions and collaborations, educational projects and work in public spaces. Looking at global contemporary art from different origins and generations.
Address: Rahnitz Alley 8, Dresden 01097
Phone: +49 351 8041456
Website: kunsthausdresden.de
Email: kunsthaus@museen-dresden.de
Facebook.com/KunsthausDresden
Instagram.com/kunsthausdresden

Galerie Ines Schulz

Founded in 1998, dedicated to figurative and non-figurative contemporary art. Featuring, amongst others, artists from the former East Germany who have become global names.
Address: Obergraben 21, Dresden 01097
Phone: +49 351 8012243
Website: galerie-ines-schulz.de
Email: info@galerie-ines-schulz.de
Facebook.com/GalerieInesSchulz
Instagram.com/galerie_ines_schulz

Art+Form

Contemporary art gallery.
Address: Bautzner Str. 11, Dresden 01099
Phone: +49 351 8031322
Website: artundform.de
Email: info@artundform.de
Twitter.com/artundform
Facebook.com/artundform
Instagram.com/artundform

GHANA

Accra

Berj Art Gallery

Founded in 1996 championing African and Ghanaian art.
Address: 32 Labone Crescent, opp. Wangara Hotel, Accra
Phone: +233 30 276 4606
Website: berjartgallery.com
Email: info@berjartgallery.com

GIBRALTAR

Libertad Couso Art Gallery

With over 35 years' experience and over 400 works of art by top international artists.
Address: Av. Miguel Cano 6 Local 10, Marbella 29602
Phone: +34 625 321 294
Website: libertadcouso.com

GREECE

Art Space

A unique art centre within pumice rock – the carved chambers of an old winery, dating back to 1861. Exhibiting painting and sculpture from contemporary Greek art as well as continuing the traditional winemaking process.
Address: Exo Gonia, Santorini 847 00
Phone: +30 2286 032774
Website: artspace-santorini.com
Email: info@artspace-santorini.com
Facebook.com/Art-Space-Santorini
Instagram.com/artspace_winery

Tzamia – Krystalla Art Gallery Santorini

Paintings, ceramics, jewellery, objects and gifts on the beautiful Greek island on Santorini.

Address: Marinatou Str. step 570, Fira 847 00
Phone: +30 2286 021226
Website: tzamia-krystallagallery.gr

ALMA Contemporary Art Gallery

Representing and exhibiting some of the most prominent contemporary Greek and international artists. Innovative, pioneering exhibitions across a variety of media and genres. The gallery occupies two locations, in Trikala and in Athens.
Address: 13 Karanasiou, Trikala
Phone: +30 2431 074586
Website: galleryalma.com
Email: almagallery@gmail.com
Twitter.com/alma_artgallery
Facebook.com/almaathens
Instagram.com/alma_athens

National Museum of Contemporary Art

The National Museum of Contemporary Art (EMST) opened in 2000, with over 18,000 m^2 of space. Its collection is composed around an important core of works by Greek and international artists.
Address: Leoforos Kallirois, Amvrosiou Frantzi, Athens 117 43
Website: emst.gr
Twitter.com/EMSTathens
Facebook.com/EMST.
NationalMuseumofContemporaryArt.
Athens
Instagram.com/emstathens
YouTube.com/user/EMSTathens

HOLY SEE (VATICAN CITY)

Vatican Museums

The Vatican Museums are the public art and sculpture museums in the Vatican City.
Address: Viale Vaticano, Rome 00192
Phone: +39 06 6988 4676
Website: museivaticani.va
Email: info.mv@scv.va

Instagram.com/vaticanmuseums
YouTube.com/c/MuseiVaticaniMv

HONG KONG

Koru Contemporary Art

Representing many contemporary artists with a particular emphasis on sculpture in wood, bronze, stone, glass, ceramic and mixed media, painting, prints and photography with a worldwide client base. Offering a lease program to evaluate a piece of art before buying.
Address: Room 4, 16th Floor, Xingwei Centre, 7 HarbourSide Road, Tin Wan, Hong Kong (to Huagui Village)
Phone: +852 2580 5922
Website: koru-hk.com
Email: info@koru-hk.com
Twitter.com/koruhk
Facebook.com/KoruHK

Karin Weber Gallery

One of Hong Kong's oldest galleries with a strong year-round program of exhibitions, talks and collector events. Representing local and international artists since 1999 with directors based in Hong Kong, London and Mumbai.
Address: G/F, 20 Aberdeen Street, Central, Hong Kong.
Phone: +852 2544 5004
Website: karinwebergallery.com
Email: art@karinwebergallery.com
Facebook.com/karinwebergallery
Instagram.com/karinweber_gallery
Artsy.net/karin-weber-gallery

Yan Gallery

Established and emerging Chinese artists.
Address: 22 Pottinger Street, Central, Hong Kong
Phone: +852 2139 2345

Website: yangallery.com
Email: yanart@netvigator.com
Facebook.com/yangallery
Instagram.com/yan_gallery

Galerie du Monde

Founded in 1974, the gallery has been working with modern and contemporary Chinese artists for 46 years. Also promoting emerging talent with a varied program of solo and group exhibitions with a strong focus on works of art on canvas, paper, sculpture, photography and new media.
Address: 108 Ruttonjee Centre, 11 Duddell Street, Central, Hong Kong
Phone: +852 2525 0529
Website: galeriedumonde.com
Email: fineart@galeriedumonde.com
Facebook.com/galeriedumonde
Instagram.com/galeriedumonde
Artsy.net/galerie-du-monde

10 Chancery Lane Gallery

Established and emerging artists from around the world.
Address: 10 Chancery Lane, Soho, Central, Hong Kong.
Phone: +852 2810 0065
Website: 10chancerylanegallery.com
Email: info@10chancerylanegallery.com

Art Statements Gallery

Contemporary art gallery established in 2003, representing renowned international artists. Exhibiting in both Hong Kong and Tokyo.
Address: Unit 2501, 25/F, W50, 50 Wong Chuk Hang Road, Hong Kong
Phone: +852 2122 9657
Website: artstatements.com
Email: hongkong@artstatements.com
Twitter.com/artstatements
Facebook.com/art.statements.7

Galerie Ora-Ora

Exhibiting thought-driven, innovative artists from around the world, bringing new perspectives to modern life and lively dialogue between east and west. Supporting Asian contemporary art and representing artists particularly from Europe and the US in a variety of media.
Address: 105-107, Barrack Block, Tai Kwun, 10 Hollywood Road, Central, Hong Kong
Phone: +852 2851 1171
Website: ora-ora.com
Email: info@ora-ora.com
Facebook.com/GalerieOraOra
Instagram.com/galerieoraora
Artsy.net/galerie-ora-ora
Weibo.com/galerieoraora
LinkedIn.com/company/galerie-ora-ora
YouTube.com/Ora-Ora TV

Contemporary by Angela Li

Promoting contemporary and avant-garde artists from Hong Kong, China and the rest of the world. One of HK's leading contemporary art galleries.
Address: G/F, 248 Hollywood Road, Sheung Wan, Hong Kong
Phone: +852 3571 8200
Website: cbal.com.hk
Email: info@cbal.com.hk
Twitter.com/cbalhk
Facebook.com/cbalhk

HUNGARY

Budapest

Koller Gallery

The oldest Hungarian private art gallery representing Hungarian and international contemporary and modern art with an international client base.
Address: Táncsics Mihály utca 5, Budapest
Phone: +36 1 356 9208
Website: kollergaleria.hu
Email: info@kollergaleria.hu
Facebook.com/KollerGaleria
Instagram.com/kollergallery

Ludwig Museum of Contemporary Art

Research, collection, presentation and promotion of contemporary art with a diverse range of artists with new ideas and perspectives.
Address: Komor Marcell u. 1, Budapest
Phone: +36 1 555 3444
Website: ludwigmuseum.hu
Facebook.com/ludwigmuseum
Instagram.com/ludwigmuseum

Secret Gallery

The mysterious and extraordinary paintings of Ferenc Kő.
Address: O utca 12., Budapest 1066
Phone: +36 1 426 4722
Website: titokgaleria.hu

Trafo House of Contemporary Arts

Embedded in the international contemporary scene, with different genres – theatre, dance, new circus, music and visual arts situated in a post-industrial space. Showing both Hungarian and international artists.
Address: Liliom utca 41, Budapest 1094
Phone: +36 1 456 2040
Website: trafo.hu
Email: sajto@trafo.hu
Facebook.com/trafohouse
Instagram.com/trafohouse
Trafohouse.Tumblr.com
YouTube.com/c/trafohouse

Paloma

With more than 50 emerging talented designers, this is an events venture, art gallery and concept store.
Phone: +36 20 961 9160
Website: palomabudapest.hu

Email: palomabudapest@gmail.com
Facebook.com/PalomaBudapest
Instagram.com/palomabudapest

ICELAND
Reykjavík
National Gallery of Iceland Art Museum

Established in 1884. The main emphasis is on 19th, 20th and 21st century Icelandic art, with the most valuable collection in the country. Also international art. Regular exhibitions.
Address: Fríkirkjuvegur 7, Reykjavik 101
Phone: +354 515 9600
Website: listasafn.is
Email: list@listasafn.is
Facebook.com/listasafn.islands
Instagram.com/listasafnislands
YouTube.com/ Listasafn Íslands / National Gallery of Iceland

Reykjavik Art Museum Kjarvalsstadir

Based in 3 locations. Historic, modern and contemporary Icelandic and international art with a collection of 17,000 pieces. Exhibitions lasting 3-4 months and work on show in public buildings and around the city. Collaborates with numerous festivals. 13,000 school children visit the museum each year.
Address: Flokagata 24, Klambratún Park, Reykjavik 105
Phone: +354 590 1200
Website: artmuseum.is
Email: artmuseum@reykjavik.is
Twitter.com/listasafn
Facebook.com/listasafnreykjavikur
Instagram.com/reykjavikartmuseum
Vimeo.com/listasafnrvk
YouTube.com/user/ListasafnReykjavikur

Berg Contemporary

Providing a diversified forum for contemporary art by representing emerging and established artists. Located in an old glass factory.
Address: Klapparstigur 16, Reykjavik 101
Website: bergcontemporary.is
Email: gallery@bergcontemporary.is
Facebook.com/bergcontemporary
Instagram.com/bergcontemporary
Artsy.net/berg-contemporary

INDIA
Bangalore
Kynkyny Art Gallery

Founded in 2004, to make Indian art more accessible to the world. Supports over 300 emerging and established artists, shipping their work all over the globe.
Address: 104 Embassy Square, 148 Infantry Road, Bengaluru 560001
Phone: +91 6366 559 090
Website: kynkyny.com
Email: art@kynkyny.com
Facebook.com/kynkyny
Instagram.com/kynkynyart

Bhopal
Bharat Bhavan

Opened by the Prime Minister of India in 1982, arts centre with fine art, literature, theatre, cinema, dance and music from Indian artists.
Address: J. Swaminathan Marg, Shamla Hills (Near Upper Lake), Bhopal
Phone: +91-755 2660239
Website: bharatbhawan.org

Chennai
The National Art Gallery

One of the oldest art galleries in India.

10th century painting, religious statues and relics occupy one building, whilst the other contains mostly modern art.

Address: Pantheon Street, Egmore, Chennai 600008

Phone: 044 28193238

Delhi

National Gallery of Modern Art

Collecting work from the 1850s, exhibiting both nationally and internationally, developing an education program and library to hold seminars to encourage arts research.

Address: Jaipur House, India Gate, New Delhi 110003

Phone: +91-11 23386111

Website: ngmaindia.gov.in

Email: ngma.delhi@gmail.com

Gallery Espace

Established in 1989, showing contemporary Indian art.

Address: 16 Community Centre, New Friends Colony, New Delhi 110065

Phone: +91-11 26923287

Website: galleryespace.com

Email: art@galleryespace.com

Facebook.com/GalleryEspace

Instagram.com/galleryespace

Vadehra Art Gallery

Established in 1987 when access to modern art was limited, with the aim of creating a professional platform connecting art with new audiences.

Address: D-178, Okhla Road, Okhla Phase 1, Okhla Industrial Area, New Delhi 110020

Phone: +91-11 65474005

Website: vadehraart.com

Email: art@vadehraart.com

Ojas Art

Encompassing visual and performing arts, music, dance, theatre, fashion and design. Providing a creative space to appreciate art and experience it as a vital expression of the human spirit.

Address: 1A, Qutab Minar, Mehrauli Road, New Delhi

Phone: +91-11 26644145

Website: ojasart.com

Email: art@ojasart.com

Twitter.com/OjasArt

Facebook.com/ojas.art

Instagram.com/ojasart

YouTube.com/user/Ojasartgallery

Kumar Gallery

Modern and Contemporary Indian Art Gallery. Established in 1955.

Address: 11, Sunder Nagar Market, New Delhi 110003

Phone: +91-11 24358875

Website: kumargallery.com

Email: info@kumargallery.com

Facebook.com/kumargallery

Instagram.com/kumarartgallery

Nature Morte Art Gallery

India's premier contemporary art gallery and curatorial experiment. Exhibiting contemporary art in all genres and mediums, made primarily by South Asian artists.

Address: The Dhan Mill, 287-288, 100 Feet Rd, Chhatarpur Hills, Delhi 110074

Phone: +911140687117

Website: naturemorte.com

Email: info@naturemorte.com

Twitter.com/naturemorte

Facebook.com/naturemorteofficial

Instagram.com/naturemorte_delhi

LinkedIn.com/company/nature-morte-delhi

Gallery Freedom

Opened in 1998 with the aim of touching the lives of millions through art. Proceeds from

the gallery are used for health care services in remote and neglected areas of the country.
Address: B-40, Qutab Institutional Area, South of I.I.T. Delhi, New Delhi 110016
Phone: +91-11 47004300
Website: galleryfreedom.in
Email: galleryfreedom@vhai.org
Email: info@galleryfreedom.in

Gallery Threshold

Established in 1997, shows both established and emerging talent, with solo shows, working with traditional materials as well as experimental process-orientated works.
Address: Old Mehrauli Badarpur Road, Lado Sarai, New Delhi 110030
Phone: +91-11 41829181
Website: gallerythreshold.com
Email: thresholdartgallery@gmail.com

Hyderabad
Aalankritha Art Gallery

Established in 2003, the gallery has solo and group shows, working with senior and young artists from all over India.
Address: 41A, Kakateeya Hills, Ext. of Jubilee Road Number # 36, Madhapur, Hyderabad 500081
Phone: +91-40 40207171
Website: aalankritha.com
Email: aalankritha.art@gmail.com

Shrishti Art

One of the leading galleries in South India, with established and emerging contemporary artists working in varied forms and media. With over 100 exhibitions to date, including paintings, sculptures, graphics, etching, drawings, new media and installation.
Address: Plot No.267, Road No15, Jubilee Hills, Hyderabad 500038
Phone: +91-40 23540023
Website: shrishtiart.com
Email: gallery@shrishtiart.com

Iconart Gallery

Established in 2009, with contemporary art exhibitions, workshops and public space art activity, with artists from all over India.
Address: 8-2-681/7/1, Rd No 12, Banjara Hills, Hyderabad 500034
Phone: +91-98499 68797
Website: iconart.in
Email: iconart@gmail.com
Facebook.com/iconartgallery

Jaipur
Gallery Artchil

Established in 2008 in a prestigious space inside Amber Fort, a famous heritage monument. Showing Indian modern and contemporary art.
Address: Amber Fort, West Wing, Jaipur 302028
Phone: +91-141 2530015
Website: artchill.com
Email: sangeetajuneja@hotmail.com
Twitter.com/GArtchill
Facebook.com/artchillgalleries
Instagram.com/artchillgalleries
Pinterest.com/galleryartchill
LinkedIn.com/in/gallery-artchill

Samanvai Art Gallery

Contemporary art from eminent artists from across the country. Located in the heart of the city.
Address: MI Road, 351, 3rd Floor, Ganpati Plaza, Jaipur 302001
Phone: 098290 60588
Website:samanvaiart.com
Email: samanvaiart@hotmail.com
Facebook.com/SamanvaiArtGallery
Instagram.com/samanvaiartgallery

ICA Gallery

Inaugurated in 2008 with a solo show by K. Laxma Goud the gallery has since been doing

exhibitions, camps and art fairs. Partner of the UK company Art 18/21 (www.art1821.com) to work on special projects, international art fairs and multi-site exhibitions.
Address: 73/C, Shankar Nagar Ext, Mount Road, Opp.Ramgarh Mode, Jaipur 302002
Phone: +91-97997 97000
Website: icagallery.com
Email: info@icagallery.com
Twitter.com/Icagallery2
Facebook.com/icagallery
Instagram.com/icagalleryjaipur

Kanpur
Y.S. Multimedia (Photography)

Team of some of the best photographers and cinematographers in the country specialising in contemporary art with a candid shooting style.
Address: 250, 106, Jwala Devi College Road, Gandhi Nagar, Kanpur
Phone: +91-93074 18884
Website: ysmms.weebly.com
Email: akbajpai72@gmail.com

Kolkata
Gallery Kolkata

Founded in 2004 to showcase the best Indian modern and contemporary art. Large viewing area and state of the art facilities, ideal for hosting exhibitions, installations and videos.
Address: 41, 2nd Floor Duckback House, Shakespeare Sarani, Circus Avenue, Kolkata 700017
Phone: +91-33 22873377
Website: gallerykolkata.com
Email: art@gallerykolkata.com
Facebook.com/gallerykolkata
Instagram.com/gallery_kolkata_india

RANGE contemporary art gallery

Established and emerging artists, initiating dialogue between members of the art community.
Address: 54 Lower Range, Beckbagan, Kolkata 700019
Phone: +91-98300 49825
Website: rangegallery.in
Email: abandesai@rangegallery.in
Twitter.com/abie4
Facebook.com/aban.desai
LinkedIn.com/in/abandesai

CIMA Gallery

Established in 1993 by a leading Indian media group. Designed under the guidance of renowned art galleries and museums in London and New York.
Address: Sunny Towers, 43 Ashutosh Chowdhury Avenue, Kolkata 700019
Phone: +91-33 24858717
Website: cimaartindia.com
Email: cima.gallery2011@gmail.com
Twitter.com/cimaartindia
Facebook.com/cimaartindia
Instagram.com/cimaartindia
YouTube.com/Cima Gallery

Experimenter

Considered to be a "pace-setter", making the gallery an active space through its Experimenter Learning Program. Representing some of the most critical contemporary artists worldwide.
Address: 2/1, Hindusthan Rd, Dover Terrace, Ballygunge, Kolkata 700029
Phone: +91-33 40012289
Website: experimenter.in
Email: admin@experimenter.in
Twitter.com/experimenterkol
Facebook.com/ExperimenterGallery
Instagram.com/experimenterkol
Open.Spotify.com/user/ozkz6biseotnclfgo765d2ko7
YouTube.com/Experimenter Learning Program

Aakriti Art Gallery

Showing some of the most unique and finest contemporary work in India, and building up a gateway for Indian art to the world market. Workshops, camps, talks and seminars with 2 galleries – one in Kolkata and the other in New Delhi.
Address: 12/3A, Orbit Enclave, Hungerford St 1st Floor, Kolkata 700017
Phone: +91-33 22893027
Website: aakrititalkart.com
Facebook.com/aakritiartgallery

Masters Collection Art Gallery

Promoting an exclusive range of Indian contemporary art, modern art and paintings by artists across India. The gallery has been recognised internationally. It holds solo and group shows collaborating with well-known corporations. Also supporting emerging artists in different mediums.
Address: G-5, Malayalay Building, 3, Woodburn Park Road, Kolkata 700020
Phone: +91-33 30534053
Website: myindianart.com
Email: info@myindianart.com
Twitter.com/myindianart
Facebook.com/indianart
Picuki.com/profile/myindianart
LinkedIn.com/company/myindianart-com

Chemould
Gallery Chemould

Contemporary art gallery.
Address: Park Street, Near Yamuna Jewellery, Taltala, Kolkata 700071
Phone: +91-33 22298641
Website: gallerychemould.com
Email: sales@gallerychemould.com
Twitter.com/ChemouldPrescot
Facebook.com/ChemouldPrescottRoad
Instagram.com/chemouldprescottroad

Mumbai
Artequest Artgallry

Modern and contemporary art. Recognised for the relentless promotion of emerging artists and providing a platform for interaction between artists and collectors.
Address: Walkeshwar, Mumbai 400006
Phone: +91-96661 31737
Website: artequest.com
Email: artequestartgallery@gmail.com
Twitter.com/ArtequestArt
Facebook.com/artequestartgallery

Art Musings

Founded in 1999, before the area emerged as the 'gallery district'. Trailblazing through its exhibitions in both the gallery and other major venues. Aiming to spread the artist's work across Asia, Europe and North America
Address: Admiralty Building, 1, Colaba Cross Lane, Opposite Dunnen School, Colaba, Mumbai 400005
Phone: +91-22 22163339
Website: artmusings.net
Email: artmusings@gmail.com
Email: art@artmusings.net

Chatterjee & Lal

Emerging and mid-career artists and more recently historical material, building on 20th century histories of art and design. The directors are published authors on art. Exhibiting globally.
Address: 01/18 Kamal Mansion, Floor 1, Arthur Bunder Road, Colaba, Mumbai 400005
Phone: +91-22 22023787
Website: chatterjeeandlal.com
Email: info@chatterjeeandlal.com
Twitter.com/CandLgallery
Facebook.com/chatterjeeandlal
Instagram.com/chatterjeeandlal

Project 88

Located in a renovated century-old metal printing press. International attention, with artists featuring in major collections and museum shows.
Address: Bmp Building, Ground Floor, N A Sawant Marg, Near Fire Station, Narayan Sawant Road, Colaba, Mumbai 400005
Phone: +91-22 22810066
Website: project88.in
Email: contact@project88.in
Facebook.com/project88
Instagram.com/project88mumbai

Galerie Mirchandani Steinruecke

Presenting leading artists and the best of emerging talent. Directors have curated exhibitions at the National Gallery of Modern Art in Mumbai and the Haus der Kulturen der Welt in Berlin. Artwork from the gallery has been acquired by important private collectors and museums.
Address: First Floor, Sunny House, 16/18, Mereweather Road, Behind Taj Mahal Hotel, Colaba, Mumbai 400001
Phone: +91-22 22023030
Website: galeriems.com
Email: info@galeriems.com
Facebook.com/galerie.steinruecke
Instagram.com/galeriemirchandanisteinruecke

Chemould Prescott Road

Contemporary art gallery.
Address: Queens Mans, 3Rd Floor G Talwarkar Marg A K Naik Marg, Fort, Next To Cathedral School, Gpo, Mumbai 400001
Phone: +91-22 22000211
Website: gallerychemould.com
Email: admin@gallerychemould.com
Twitter.com/ChemouldPrescot
Facebook.com/ChemouldPrescottRoad
Instagram.com/chemouldprescottroad

Studio 3 Art Gallery

Indian contemporary and modern art in a wide range of mediums and genres.
Address: Mumbai, Maharashtra
Phone: +91-22 22022873
Website: studio3india.com
Email: info@studio3india.com
Email: studio3@gmail.com (artists)

The Guild Art Gallery

Founded in 1997, discovering and promoting emerging and mid-career artists with work shown at the Tate Modern, as well as galleries in Demark, Rome, Warsaw, Florida, France and Australia.
Address: 28, 3rd Pasta Lane, Next to Tulip Building, end of 3rd Pasta Lane, Shahid Bhagat Singh Road, Colaba, Mumbai 400005
Phone: +91-22 22880195
Website: guildindia.com
Email: theguildart@gmail.com
Twitter.com/The_Guild_Art
Facebook.com/guildindia
YouTube.com/user/theguildart

Tao Art Gallery

Showing painting, photography, sculpture, video, performance and installation arts. Contemporary work by emerging and mid-career artists. The directors have curated international shows in London, Tokyo and Singapore as well as publishing books.
Address: 165, The View, Dr. Annie Besant Road, Worli, Mumbai 400018
Phone: +91-22 24918585
Website: taoartgallery.com
Email: info@taoartgallery.com
Facebook.com/taoartgallery
Instagram.com/taoartgallery
LinkedIn.com/company/tao-art-gallery--india
YouTube.com/Tao Art Gallery

Institute of Contemporary Indian Art

India's biggest and most prestigious art venue.
Address: Icia Building, Next To Rampart
House, K Dubash Marg, Kala Ghoda, Fort,
Opposite Chhatrapati Shivajii Maharaj Vastu
Sangrahalaya Museum Shop, Mumbai 400023
Phone: +91-22 22048138
Website: icia.in
Email: iciagallery@gmail.com
Email: contact@theartstrust.com
Facebook.com/ICIAGallery

India Fine Art

Artists from all over India, with collectors
across the globe.
Address: 3rd Floor, Film Centre Building, 68
Tardeo Road, Mumbai 400034
Phone: +91-22 23520438
Website: indiafineart.com

Gallery Beyond

This gallery was established to focus on
young, contemporary art with fundraisers
for charities such as Save the Children, India.
Address: 130/132, First Floor, Great
Western Building, Shahid Bhagat Singh
Marg, Fort, Mumbai 400023
Phone: +91-22 22837345
Website: gallerybeyond.in

Pune
India House

Dedicated to the exhibition of master artists'
work. Not tied to any specific aesthetic but
of a transformational, international quality.
Autumn, winter and spring exhibitions with
related talks and seminars.
Address: ‹India House›, 53 Sopan Bagh,
Adjoining BJP Office, Opposite Bharati
Vidhyapeeth School, Balewadi, Pune 411045
Phone: +91-20 64108885
Website: ihag.in
Email: contact@ihag.in
Facebook.com/IHAGallery

Surat
Aakar Art Stone Gallery

Pioneering stone sculptures, abstracts and
semi-precious stone slab wash-basins.
Address: 1016, 3rd Floor, Westfield Shopping
Centre, Ghod Dod Road, Surat 395007
Phone: +91-98259 14055
Website: artstonegallery.com
Email: artstonegallery@gmail.com
Email: info@artstonegallery.com

Vadodara
Harmony Arts

A well-established gallery founded by two
engineering brothers, exhibiting Indian and
international art. Collaborating particularly
with Europe and North America.
Address: Gf 12, Trident Shopping Complex
Race Course Circle, Race Course Road,
Vadiwadi, Vadodara 390007
Phone: +91-80877 32360
Website: harmonyarts.com
Email: care@harmonyarts.com
Facebook.com/Harmonyartsindia
Instagram.com/harmonyartsindia
Pinterest.com/HarmonyArtsIND

Varanasi
Modern Art Gallery

4-5 major exhibitions each year mainly with
exemplary work from living artists, with a
wide range of media and subject. Particularly
keen to show the work of emerging or
under-recognised artists, locally, nationally
and internationally.
Address: Ladoni, Varanasi 221001
Phone: +91 9312029825
Website: modernartgallery.co.in
Email: sales@modernartgallery.co.in
Twitter.com/modernartg
Facebook.com/modernartg
Instagram.com/modernartgallerydelhi

IRAN

Tehran

Tehran Museum of Contemporary Art Museum

One of the largest art museums in Iran.
Website: tmoca.com
Email: info@tmoca.com

Soo Contemporary

A multi-function cultural platform, engaging with local art and culture as well as keeping an eye on international trends. Supporting artists through commissions, exhibition and publishing and creating a hub for the exchange of ideas and critical discussions around contemporary art today.
Address: 30 Pourmousa Street, Somayeh Street, Villa Street, Tehran 11369
Phone: +98 21 8880 9808
Website: soocontemporary.com
Email: info@soocontemporary.com
Facebook.com/soocontemporary
Instagram.com/soocontemporary

IRELAND

Burren College Of Art

A small, independent art school situated on the Wild Atlantic Way on the northwest coast of County Clare in Ireland.
Address: Newtown, Galway
Phone: +353 65 707 7200
Website: burrencollege.ie
Email: contact@burrencollege.ie
Twitter.com/burrencollege
Facebook.com/burrencollegeofart
Instagram.com/explore/
locations/10702498/burren-college-of-art
LinkedIn.com/school/burren-college-of-art
YouTube.com/Burren College of Art

Dublin

Gormleys Fine Art

Established in 1990, specialising in international and Irish contemporary art, with a commitment to developing artists. Showing international contemporary artists, such as Warhol, Banksy, Damien Hirst and Keith Haring. Galleries in Belfast and Dublin with a a significant collection of sculpture.
Address: Gormleys Dublin, 27 Frederick St. South, Dublin D02 EP03
+353 (0)1 6729031
Gormleys Belfast
471 Lisburn Road, Belfast BT9 7EZ
Phone:+44 (0)28 9066 3313
Website: gormleys.ie
Email: info@gormleys.ie

Olivier Cornet Gallery

One of Ireland's most dynamic modern and contemporary fine art galleries showing both Irish and international work in a variety of media, including paintings, sculpture, ceramics, photography, fine art prints, digital art and installations.
Address: 3 Great Denmark Street, Off Parnell Square, Dublin D01 H6C0
Phone: +353 87 288 7261
Website: oliviercornetgallery.com
Email: info@oliviercornetgallery.com
Twitter.com/OC_Gallery
Facebook.com/oliviercornet.gallery
Instagram.com/olivier_cornet_gallery
Pinterest.co.uk/OC_Gallery

The Doorway Gallery

Fine art from both Irish and international artists with unique talent. The gallery serves to support artists in achieving international recognition especially through international art fairs and solo shows.
Address: The Doorway Gallery, 24 Frederick Street South, Dublin D02 XP30

Phone: +353 87 991 0650
Website: thedoorwaygallery.com
Email: info@thedoorwaygallery.com
Twitter.com/doorwaygallery
Facebook.com/doorwaygallerydublin
Instagram.com/thedoorwaygallery

Dublin City Gallery The Hugh Lane

Sir Hugh Lane held the first exhibition of Irish art in London in 1904, and continued creating a unique and exceptional collection of modern art, including the first impressionist paintings in any public collection through the UK and Ireland. He presented this collection to what is now Dublin City Council in 1908.
Address: Charlemont House Parnell Square North, Charlemont House Parnell Square North, Dublin D01 F2X9
Phone: +353 1 222 5550
Website: hughlane.ie
Email: info.hughlane@dublincity.ie
Twitter.com/TheHughLane
Facebook.com/thehughlane
Instagram.com/thehughlane

Kerlin Gallery

Kerlin Gallery is a contemporary art gallery in Dublin, Ireland.
Address: 38 Annes Lane, Dublin D02 A028
Phone: +353 1 670 9093
Website: kerlingallery.com
Email: gallery@kerlin.ie
Twitter.com/KerlinGallery
Facebook.com/kerlingallery
Instagram.com/kerlingallery

Gallery Of Photography

Founded in 1978. National centre for contemporary photography, exhibiting and supporting the best international and Irish photographers.
Address: Meeting House Square, Temple Bar, Dublin 2
Phone: +353 1 671 4654

Website: galleryofphotography.ie
Email: info@galleryofphotography.ie
Twitter.com/gop_ireland
Instagram.com/gallery_of_photography_ireland

Oliver Sears Gallery

Irish and international contemporary art, both emerging and established, including applied arts. Also bringing exhibitions to London and New York.
Address: 29 Molesworth St, Dublin
Website: oliversearsgallery.com
Email: info@oliversearsgallery.com
Twitter.com/osearsgallery
Facebook.com/OliverSearsGallery
Instagram.com/oliver.sears
Artsy.net/oliver-sears-gallery

Origin Gallery

Irish and international artists, both emerging and established.
Address: 37 Fitzwilliam St. Upper, Dublin
Phone: +353 1 662 9347
Website: theorigingallery.com
Email: theorigingallery@gmail.com
Twitter.com/Origin_Gallery
Facebook.com/theorigingallery
Instagram.com/origin_gallery

Molesworth Gallery

A leading contemporary art gallery in Ireland representing exciting and accomplished artists. 8 solo and 2 group exhibitions each year with gallery publications. Collaborating with arts centres and museums as well as international art fairs.
Address: 16 Molesworth Street, Dublin 2
Phone: +353 1 679 1548
Website: molesworthgallery.com
Email: info@molesworthgallery.com
Twitter.com/molesworthgall
Facebook.com/MolesworthGallery
Instagram.com/molesworthgallery

ISRAEL

Jerusalem

Gefen Gallery

Contemporary Israeli art representing artists who are pioneering in their field, and have already gained international recognition.
Address: King David Street 6, Mamila Avenue, Jerusalem
Phone: +972 2-624-4506
Website: gefen-gallery.com
Email: daniel@gefen-gallery.com
Facebook.com/GefenGallery
Instagram.com/gefengallery

Eden Fine Art Gallery

A house of successful artists, presented in its own galleries, including a Manhattan flagship on Madison Avenue and through a network of galleries around the world, including in Aspen, London, Mykonos and Dubai
Address: Rehov David HaMelech 2, Jerusalem 94101
Phone: +972 2-624-4831
Website: eden-gallery.com
Email: artists@edengallery.com
Twitter.com/EdenFineArt_
Facebook.com/EdenFineArt
Instagram.com/edenfineart
Pinterest.co.uk/edenfineart
YouTube.com/user/EdenGalleryNYC

Tel Aviv

Tel Aviv Museum of Art

A rich collection of art including European works from the 16th to 19th centuries
Address: 27 Shaul Hamelech Blvd, The Golda Meir Cultural and Art Center, Tel Aviv-Yafo 61332012
Website: tamuseum.com
Email: olgap@tamuseum.com

Magasin III Jaffa

A non-profit exhibition space established by Magasin III Museum for Contemporary Art in Sweden.
Address: Magasin III Jaffa, 34 Olei Zion 6813131 Tel Aviv-Yafo, Israel
Phone: +972 3-9499900
Website: magasin3.com
Email: jaffa@magasin3.com
Facebook.com/magasin3jaffa
Instagram.com/magasiniiijaffa

Noga Gallery of Contemporary Art

A fresh and challenging program of Israeli and international artists, who are included in the finest corporate and private collection and exhibited widely in major museums throughout the world.
Address: Rehov Ehad Haᵓam 60, Tel Aviv 6520219
Phone: +972 3-566-0123
Website: nogagallery.com
Email: info@nogagallery.com
Facebook.com/NogaGalleryofContemporaryArt
Instagram.com/noga_gallery
LinkedIn.com/in/noga-gallery-75563740

Zemack Contemporary Art Gallery

A fresh perspective on contemporary Israeli and international art with 5-6 solo shows a year, collaborating with international galleries and exhibiting a selection of prominent art graduates from the major Israeli art schools.
Address: Rehov Hei Be-Iyar 68, Tel Aviv 6219814
Phone: +972 3-691-5060
Website: zcagallery.com
Email: info@zcagallery.com
Facebook.com/zemackcontemporaryart
Instagram.com/zca_gallery
Artsy.net/zemack-contemporary-art

ITALY

Ufofabrik Contemporary Art Gallery

An independent project for contemporary, open and experimental art. Established and emerging artists with pioneering solo and group shows.
Address: Strada del Marchiò 6, Moena 38035
Phone: +39 0462 573030
Website: ufofabrik.co.uk
Email: ufofabrik@gmail.com
Twitter.com/ufofabrik
Instagram.com/ufofabrik

Rome

Rome Capital Modern Art Gallery

Address: Francesco Crispi Street, 24, Rome 00187
Phone: +39 06 0608
Website: en.galleriaartemodernaroma.it
Email: info@galleriaartemodernaroma.it

MACRO

Contemporary Art Museum Rome
Address: Nizza Street 138, Rome 00198
Phone: +39 06 0608
Website: en.museomacro.org
Email: info@museomacro.it

Galleria Russo

Well-known painters of the 20th century, including Giorgio de Chirico, with whom they had exclusive contact for more than 20 years. Both Italian and international artists.
Address: Via Alibert 20, Rome 00187
Phone: +39 06 678 9949
Website: galleriarusso.com
Email: amministrazione@galleriarusso.com
Twitter.com/galleriarusso
Facebook.com/galleriaarte.russo
Instagram.com/galleriarusso
Pinterest.co.uk/galleriarusso
galleriarusso.Tumblr.com
LinkedIn.com/in/galleria-russo

Spazio Nuovo Contemporary Art

A focus on photography and Latin American work with a commitment to education. Lectures, conferences, tours for school groups, inspiring creativity and a passion for photography and contemporary art.
Address: Via dʾAscanio 20, Rome 00186
Phone: +39 06 8957 2855
Website: spazionuovo.net
Facebook.com/spazionuovoroma
Instagram.com/explore/locations/86620588

Venice

Penny Guggenheim Museum Venice

The personal and remarkable collection of 20th century art owned by the late patron of the arts, Peggy Guggenheim. Located in her former home in Venice, and among the most important museums in Italy for European and American 20th century work.
Address: Palazzo Venier dei Leoni, Dorsoduro 701, I-30123 Venice
Phone: +39 041 2405 411
Website: guggenheim-venice.it
Email: info@guggenheim-venice.it
Twitter.com/GuggenheimPGC
Facebook.com/ThePeggyGuggenheimCollection
Instagram.com/guggenheim_venice
LinkedIn.com/company/guggenheim-venice
YouTube.com/user/VeniceGuggenheim

Art Gallery Bugno

Modern and Contemporary Art and Photography.
Address: Sestiere San Marco 1996/D, Right in Front of La Fenice Theater, Venice 30124
Phone: +39 041 523 1305
Website: bugnoartgallery.com
Email: info@bugnoartgallery.com
Facebook.com/BugnoArtGallery
Instagram.com/bugnoartgallery

Contini Art Gallery

Contini Art Gallery is an established five floor gallery with over 11,000 feet of exhibition space, situated right in the heart of Venice.
Address: San Marco 2288, Calle Larga XXII Marzo, Venice 30124
Phone: +39 041 523 0357
Website: continiarte.com
Email: venezia@continiarte.com
Facebook.com/continigallery
Instagram.com/continiartgallery
Artsy.net/contini-art-gallery
YouTube.com/Contini Art Gallery

Galleria d'Arte L'Occhio

Contemporary art gallery in Venice.
Address: Sestiere Dorsoduro 181-185, 30123, Venice
Phone: +39 041 522 6550
Website: gallerialocchio.net
Email: galleria.locchio@gmail.com
Facebook.com/galleria-darte-locchio-venezia

Giudecca 795 Art Gallery

Emerging artists working in photography, street art and mosaics, painting, sculpture, design and video giving international exposure.
Address: Fondamenta S.Biagio 795, Venice 30133
Phone: +39 340 879 8327
Website: giudecca795.com
Twitter.com/Giudecca795
Facebook.com/Giudecca795ArtGallery

Bonnet /Vander Sluis Gallery

A dynamic mix of young and emerging artists as well as established names in the international art world. Photography, sculpture, painting and mixed media and with private and corporate collections.
Address: Campo Santo Stefano 2950, Venezia 30124
Phone: +39 06 4817 2220
Website: bvdsgallery.com
Email: info@bvdsgallery.com

Juris & Perl SAS di Paolo Juris e C.

Contemporary art gallery.
Address: Sestiere San Marco 2950, Venezia 30124
Phone: +39 041 522 0603
Website: jurisandperl.com
Email: info@jurisandperl.com

Grassi Palace

Sharing knowledge and love for contemporary art with a wide range of events, including exhibitions, conferences, concerts, screenings.
Address: San Samuele Square 3231, Venice 30124
Phone: +39 041 240 1308
Website: palazzograssi.it
Email: ufficiostampa@palazzograssi.it
Twitter.com/Palazzo_Grassi
Facebook.com/palazzograssi
Instagram.com/palazzo_grassi
YouTube.com/user/PalazzoGrassiTV

Florence

Nonfinito Studio & Art Gallery

Studio and art gallery.
Address: Via San Niccolò 75rosso, Firenze 50125
Phone: +39 347 648 7101
Website: nonfinito.it
Email: nonfinitoartgallery@gmail.com
Facebook.com/nonfinitobrogini

Galleria Mentana

In the heart of Florence, collaborating with galleries, cultural centres, public and private exhibition spaces.
Address: R Piazza Mentana 2, Firenze 50122

Phone: +39 055 211985
Website: galleriamentana.it
Email: galleriamentana@galleriamentana.it
Twitter.com/galleriamentana
Facebook.com/galleriamentanafirenze
Instagram.com/galleriamentana
YouTube.com/user/GalleriaMentanaArte

Art Gallery Studio Iguarnieri

Contemporary art in Florence with traditional techniques and a modern approach. All sizes of painting are available and they can be shipped worldwide.
Address: Lungarno Benvenuto Cellini 39, Next to San Niccolò Tower, Florence 50125
Phone: +39 333 834 8277
Website: iguarnieri.it
Email: iguarnieri@iguarnieri.it
Facebook.com/artgallerystudioiguarnieri
Instagram.com/iguarnieri.it

Tornabuoni Arte S.R.L.

Contemporary art gallery.
Address: Lungarno Benvenuto Cellini 3, Firenze 50125
Phone: +39 055 681 2697
Website: tornabuoniarte.it

Galleria Frilli S.R.L.

Named after Antonio Frilli, sculptor and professor of the Fine Arts Academy of Florence. Since 1860, the gallery has worked nationally and internationally with private and institutional clients.
Address: Via Dei Fossi 26 Rosso, Firenze 50123
Phone: +39 055 210212
Website: frilligallery.com
Email: info@frilligallery.com
Facebook.com/FrilliGallery.GalleriaFrilli
Instagram.com/frilligallery
Pinterest.it/galleriafrilli
Weibo.com/FrilliGallery
YouTube.com/Galleria Frilli

Centro di Cultura Contemporanea Strozzina

Contemporary art gallery in Florence.
Address: Palazzo Strozzi, Florence 50123
Phone: +39 055 391 7137
Website: strozzina.org
Email: info@palazzostrozzi.org
Facebook.com/palazzostrozzi
Flickr.com/photos/cccstrozzina
Vimeo.com/cccstrozzina
It.foursquare.com/cccstrozzina

Galleria 360

Contemporary art gallery in Florence.
Address: Via Il Prato 11r, Florence 50123
Phone: +39 055 239 9570
Website: galleria360.it
Email: info@galleria360.it
Twitter.com/Galleria360
Facebook.com/Galleria360
Instagram.com/galleria360

Fabio Fornaciai & C. SAS

Fornaciai Art Gallery, Firenze - Modern and Contemporary since 1956.
Address: Borgo San Jacopo 53/R, Firenze 50125
Phone: +39 055 284720
Website: fornaciaiartgallery.com
Email: galleriafornaciai@gmail.com
Facebook.com/fornaciaiartgallery
Instagram.com/fornaciaiartgallery

Firenzeart Gallery

The Laboratorio Artigiano Cornici, a meeting point for the best Italian and international artists, led to the gallery's foundation. Working with contemporary masters, as well as emerging talent, with 600+ artists online as well as holding important exhibitions.
Address: Piazza Taddeo Gaddi 2/R, close to Ponte alla Vittoria, Florence 50142
Phone: +39 055 224028
Website: firenzeart.com
Email: info@firenzeart.com

Twitter.com/FirenzeArt
YouTube.com/user/firenzeart

Milan
Museo del Novecento

Museum of 20th century art in the city centre.
Address: Marconi Street, 1, Milan 20122
Phone: +39 02 8844 4061
Website: museodelnovecento.org
Email: c.museo900@comune.milano.it
Twitter.com/museodel900
Facebook.com/MuseodelNovecento
Instagram.com/museodel900
Pinterest.it/museodel900

Barbara Frigerio Contemporary Art

Contemporary art gallery in Milan.
Address: Via dell'orso 12, Milano 20121
Phone: +39 02 3659 3924
Website: barbarafrigeriogallery.it
Email: info@barbarafrigeriogallery.it

Antonio Colombo Arte Contemporanea

Contemporary art gallery in Milan, since 1998, focusing mainly on Italian and international new figurative painting.
Address: Via Solferino 44, Milan 20121
Phone: +39 02 2906 0171
Website: colomboarte.com
Email: info@colomboarte.com
Facebook.com/
AntonioColomboArteContemporanea
Instagram.com/antoniocolombogallery

AICA – Andrea Ingenito Contemporary Art

Located near the central Piazza dei Martiri, an important meeting point for international artists. Institutional exhibitions, national and international art fairs, exhibitions and publishing with special focus on the artistic movements of the 1960s and 1970s.
Address: Via Privata Massimiano 25, Milan 20134

Phone: +39 02 3679 8346
Website: ai-ca.com
Email: info@ai-ca.com
Twitter.com/aica_art
Facebook.com/andreaingenito.
contemporaryart
YouTube.com/user/GalleriaAICA

Federico Bianchi Contemporary Gallerie d'Arte

Contemporary art gallery in Milan.
Address: Via Carlo Imbonati 12, Milano 20159
Phone: +39 02 3954 9725
Website: federicobianchigallery.com
Email: info@federicobianchigallery.com
Facebook.com/Federico-Bianchi-Contemporary-Art

Ida Pisani Contemporary Art

Contemporary art gallery established in 2005 with special focus on new artistic research from Eastern Europe (Russia, Romania, Bulgaria and Greece) and South America.
Address: Via Giovanni Ventura 3, Milano 20134
Phone: +39 02 2692 4450
Website: prometeogallery.com
Email: info@prometeogallery.com
Twitter.com/prometeogallery
Facebook.com/PrometeoGallery
Instagram.com/prometeogallery

ProjectB Contemporary Art

Contemporary art in Milan.
Address: Via Borgonuovo 3, Milano 20121
Phone: +39 02 8699 8751
Website: projectb.eu
Email: martina@projectb.eu

FORMAT-Contemporary Culture Gallery

Contemporary art gallery in Milan.
Address: Via Giovanni Enrico Pestalozzi 10 Int.32 ,Milano, Milano 20143

Phone: +39 02 431 2824
Facebook.com/
TheFormatContemporaryCultureGallery

Jerome Zodo Contemporary

Opened in 2010 with the desire to communicate something different and remote that escaped pre-established forms of general knowledge. Also working as an art advisor on Italian post-WWII artists and international masters.
Address: Via Lambro 7, Milano 20100
Phone: +39 02 2024 1935
Website: jerome-zodo.com
Email: info@jerome-zodo.com
Instagram.com/jerome.zodo.gallery
Artnet.com/galleries/jerome-zodo-gallery

Naples
Galleria Alfonso Artiaco4

Contemporary art gallery in Naples.
Address: Piazzetta Nilo n_ 7, Naples 80134
Phone: +39 081 497 6072
Website: alfonsoartiaco.com
Email: info@alfonsoartiaco.com
Twitter.com/GalleriaArtiaco
Facebook.com/galleriaalfonsoartiaco
Instagram.com/galleriaalfonsoartiaco
Artnet.com/galleries/alfonso-artiaco
Artsy.net/alfonso-artiaco

Core Gallery

Contemporary art gallery in Naples.
Address: Piazza San Gaetano 69, Napoli 80138
Phone: +39 333 584 9479
Website: coregallery.it
Email: info@coregallery.it
Facebook.com/www.coregallery.it
Instagram.com/coregallery

AICA - Andrea Ingenito Contemporary Art

Contemporary art gallery in Naples.

Address: Via Cappella Vecchia 8/A, Zona Piazza dei Martiri, Naples 80121
Phone: +39 081 049 0829
Website: ai-ca.com

Museo d'Arte Contemporanea Donnaregina

Museum of contemporary art situated in the historic heart of Naples.
Address: Via Luigi Settembrini, 79, Napoli 80138
Website: madrenapoli.it
Email: info@madrenapoli.it
Twitter.com/museomadre
Facebook.com/museomadre
Instagram.com/museomadre
Open.Spotify.com/user/MuseoMadre

Verona
CAM Casoria Contemporary Art Museum

Founded in 2005, with the aim of becoming a cultural hub, an experimental laboratory and a reference point for global contemporary art.
Address: Duca D›Aosta Street, 63, Casoria 80026
Phone: +39 081 757 6167
Website: casoriacontemporaryartmuseum.com
Email: info@casoriacontemporaryartmuseum.com
Twitter.com/MuseoCAMCasoria
Facebook.com/Cammuseo
It.wikipedia.org/wiki/CAM_Casoria_Contemporary_Art_Museum
YouTube.com/Museo CAM Casoria

Lineadarte

Contemporary art gallery in Naples.
Address: via S.Domenico Soriano 34, Napoli 80135
Phone: +39 081 549 4271
Website: lineadarte-officinacreativa.org
Email: info@lineadarte-officinacreativa.org
Twitter.com/lineadarte

Facebook.com/Lineadarte.OfficinaCreativa
Pinterest.it/lineadarte
YouTube.com/user/lineadarte

Turin

Civic Gallery of Modern and Contemporary Art

One of the most important modern art museums in Italy, with research, conservation and knowledge sharing. Over 40,000 works including painting, sculpture, photographs, decorative arts, works on paper, films and video, targeting a broad audience with permanent and temporary exhibitions, outreach and education.
Address: Magenta Street, 31, Turin 10128
Phone: +39 011 442 9518
Website: gamtorino.it
Email: gam@fondazionetorinomusei.it
Twitter.com/fondtomusei
Facebook.com/torinogam
Instagram.com/gamtorino
Pinterest.it/gamtorino
YouTube.com/Gam Torino

Velan Centro D'arte Contemporanea Gallerie

Non-profit organisation promoting contemporary art, with an exhibition space dedicated to experimentation.
Address: Via Saluzzo 64, Torino 10125
Phone: +39 011 280406
Website: velancenter.com
Email: info@velancenter.com
Twitter.com/velancenter
Facebook.com/velancenter
YouTube.com/user/velancenter

Alberto Peola Galleria d'Arte Contemporanea

Opened in 1989, showing works by contemporary emerging and established artists from Italy and internationally, placing a firm emphasis on new artistic trends exploring personal narrative through different expressive means.
Address: Via della Rocca 29, Turin 10123

Phone: +39 011 812 4460
Website: albertopeola.com
Email: info@albertopeola.com
Twitter.com/PeolaSimondi
Facebook.com/peola.simondi
Instagram.com/galleria.peolasimondi
LinkedIn.com/in/alberto-peola-3656b160

Alessandro Marena Project - Contemporary Art

Contemporary art in Turin.
Address: Via della Rocca 19, Torino
Phone: +39 011 812 9787
Website: alessandromarenaproject.com
Email: press@alessandromarenaproject.com

Franco Soffiantino & C. SAS

International and Italian artists exploring the inter-relationship between art and the surrounding world, with different artistic languages, including video, photography, performance, installation and sculpture. Takes part in major international art fairs, collaborates with museums, institutions and public exhibitions at national and international level.
Address: Via Gioacchino Rossini 23, Torino 10124
Phone: +39 011 1979 4151
Website: francosoffiantino.com
Email: info@francosoffiantino.it

Noire Gallery

Important exhibitions of contemporary art, founded in 1983 as a gallery and publisher of fine art books. Collaborating with emerging artists globally to capture the cultural mutations of a changing world. Interdisciplinary and space-based.
Address: Via Piossasco 29/B, Turin 10152
Phone: +39 011 919 1234
Website: noiregallery.com
Email: info@noiregallery.com
Facebook.com/noiregallery
Instagram.com/noiregallery

Fondazione Sandretto Re Rebaudengo

Since 1995, supporting young Italian and international artists, promoting contemporary work to an ever-wider audience.
Address: Via Modane 16, Turin 10141
Phone: +39 011 379 7600
Website: fsrr.org
Email: exhibition@fsrr.org
Twitter.com/fondsrr
Facebook.com/fondsrr
Instagram.com/fondazionesandretto

Genoa
Guidi & Schoen

Since 2002, representing Italian and international masters of photography. Gallery on 4 floors, allowing for several exhibitions at the same time. Also promoting painting, video, installation and sculpture that is deep in meaning and formally sophisticated. Collaborating internationally and taking part in global art fairs.
Address: Vico della Casana 31, Genova 16123
Phone: +39 010 253 0557
Website: guidieschoen.com
Email: info@guidieschoen.com
Facebook.com/GuidiSchoen
Instagram.com/GuidiSchoen

Pink Summer SNC

Founded in 2005, presenting, usually solo, exhibitions of artists with whom they have a long-term relationship.
Address: Via Lomellini 2, Genova 16124
Phone: +39 010 254 3762
Website: pinksummer.com
Email: info@pinksummer.com
Facebook.com/
PinksummerContemporaryArt
Instagram.com/
pinksummercontemporaryart

Vision Quest Contemporary Photography

Founded in 2008, named after the traditional North American native culture. Contemporary photography, with group and solo exhibitions, art fairs, publications, conferences and meetings, workshops and collaborations with museums and national galleries.
Address: Piazza Invrea 4r, Genova 16123
Phone: +39 010 265629
Website: visionquest.it
Email: info@visionquest.it
Facebook.com/
visionquestcontemporaryphotography
Instagram.com/visionquest_4rosso

Tuscany
Arte Italiana di Cundari Francesca

The first contemporary art gallery featuring only Italian sculptors. 33 artists, with their work shown in a charming, historical setting in bronze, ceramics, alabaster, iron, wood and marble.
Address: VIA BERIGNANO 9, San Gimignano 53037
Phone: +39 0577 940207
Website: isculpture.it
Email: info@isculpture.it
Twitter.com/iSculptureArt

JAMAICA
Jamaica National Gallery

National gallery of Jamaica.
Address: 12 Ocean Blvd., Kingston 14
Phone: +1 876-922-1561
Website: natgalja.org.jm

JAPAN

Fujinoya Contemporary Crafts

Established in 1973. A permanent pottery space of 150 m²
Address: 859 Asanumacho, Sano 327-0831
Phone: +81 283-23-0700
Website: gendaikougeifujinoya.web.fc2.com
Email: fujinoya@sctv.jp

Tokyo

Fuma Contemporary Tokyo Bunkyo-Art

Established in 1982. Contemporary art, concentrating on re-evaluation of post-war art and exhibitions for emerging artists. Regularly takes place at major international art fairs and have collaborated with over 20 museums.
Address: 1-3-9 Irifune, Chuo 104-0042
Phone: +81 3-6280-3717
Website: bunkyo-art.co.jp

The Watarium Museum of Contemporary Art

Contemporary art gallery.
Address: 3-7-6 Jingumae, Shibuya 150-0001
Phone: +81 3-3402-3001
Website: watarium.co.jp
Email: official@watarium.co.jp

Galerie Sho Contemporary Art

Contemporary art gallery.
Address: 3-2-9 Nihombashi Kayabacho, Yaesu 103-0027
Phone: +81 3-3275-1008
Website: g-sho.com

Nichido Contemporary Art

Contemporary art from Japan and internationally.
Address: 4-3-3, Hatchobori 104-0032
Phone: +81 3-3555-2140
Website: nca-g.com
Email: info@nca-g.com

Yoseido Gallery

A complete selection of modern and contemporary Japanese prints, since 1953.
Address: 5-5-15, Ginza 104-0061
Phone: +81 3-3571-1312
Website: yoseido.com

Gallery Seiho

Modern and contemporary sculptures, drawings, prints and other works of art.
Address: 8-10-7, Ginza 104-0061
Phone: +81 3-3573-2468
Website: gallery-seiho.com
Email: seihou@ceres.ocn.ne.jp

Nanzuka

Nanzuka is a contemporary art gallery founded in 2005.
Address: 3-30-10, Jingumae, Shibuya-Ku, Tokyo, Japan
Phone: +81 3-3400-0075
Website: nug.jp
Email: info@nug.jp
Twitter.com/nanzukaung
Facebook.com/nanzuka
Instagram.com/nanzukaunderground

Gallery Koyanagi

Contemporary art gallery.
Address: 1-7-5, Ginza 104-0061
Phone: +81 3-3561-1896
Website: gallerykoyanagi.com
Email: mail@gallerykoyanagi.com

Galerie Nichido

First gallery in Japan to specialise in the Western-style oil painting. Handles work from the French Impressionists to contemporary art, with a large selection of Japanese masters and emerging artists.
Address: 5-3-16 Ginza, Chuo 104-0061
Phone: +81 3-3571-2553
Website: nichido-garo.co.jp
Email: galerie@nichido-garo.co.jp
Facebook.com/gallerynichido
Instagram.com/galerienichido

Snow Contemporary

Contemporary art gallery.
Address: 2-13-12 Nishiazabu, Minato 106-0031
Phone: +81 3-6427-2511
Website: snowcontemporary.com
Email: snow@officekubota.com
Twitter.com/snowcontemp
Facebook.com/snowcontemporary
Instagram.com/snow_contemporary

Takeda Art

Private commercial gallery since 1996 dealing mainly in modern and contemporary masters.
Address: 7-10-11, Ginza 104-0061
Phone: +81 3-6280-6663
Website: takeda-bijyutu.com
Email: info@takeda-bijyutu.com
Twitter.com/takedaart
Facebook.com/TakedaArtCo
Instagram.com/takedaartco

Ando Gallery

Contemporary art gallery.
Address: 3-3-6 Hirano, Koto 135-0023
Phone: +81 3-5620-2165
Website: andogallery.co.jp
Email: office@andogallery.co.jp

Hiroshima

Hiroshima City Museum of Contemporary Art

Established in 1989, the first public art museum in Japan devoted exclusively to contemporary art. Located in Hijiyama Park, famous for its cherry blossoms.
Address: 1-1 Hijiyamakoen, Hiroshima 732-0815
Phone: +81 82-264-1121
Website: hiroshima-moca.jp
Email: hcmca@hcmca.cf.city.hiroshima.jp

Yokohama

Fujimura Contemporary Art

Contemporary art gallery that discovers and nurtures artists, operating nationwide.

Address: 2-91-11 Motomachi, Naka-Ku, Yokohama 231-0861
Phone: +81 45-641-3070
Website: fujimura-art.com
Email: fca@fujimura-art.com
Facebook.com/fujimuraca
Instagram.com/fcajun

Atelier K Art Space

Contemporary art gallery.
Address: 1-6 Ishikawacho, Naka-Ku, Yokohama 231-0868
Phone: +81 45-651-9037
Website: atelier-k.main.jp

JERSEY

The Harbour Gallery Jersey

The largest art and craft gallery in Jersey and the Channel Islands. Managed by the charity Art in the Frame Foundation. Featuring over 70 local artists and crafts workers over 3 floors with a café. Also providing art education for all ages.
Address: Le Boulevard, The Harbour, Jersey JE3 8AB
Phone: +44 1534 743044
Website: theharbourgalleryjersey.com
Email: info@theharbourgalleryjersey.com
Twitter.com/harbourgalleryj
Facebook.com/theharbourgalleryjersey
Instagram.com/theharbourgalleryjersey

Studio 18

Contemporary art gallery.
Address: 23A Beresford Street, Jersey JE2 4WN
Phone: 01534 734920
Website: studio18.co.uk
Email: sales@studio18.co.uk
Facebook.com/artgallery.st.helier

KENYA

Nairobi
Circle Art Gallery

Contemporary art from the East African region.
Phone: +254 790 289991
Website: circleartagency.com
Email: info@circleartagency.com
Facebook.com/circleartagency
Instagram.com/circleartagency

One Off Contemporary Art Gallery

25 years, representing some of the most established artists in Kenya and surrounding countries such as Uganda, Tanzania, Sudan and Rwanda.
Address: 16 Rosslyn Lone Tree Estate Rd, off Limuru Road, Nairobi 00621
Phone: +254 722 521870
Website: oneoffafrica.com
Email: oneoff@africaonline.co.ke
Twitter.com/oneoffgallery
Facebook.com/OneOffContemporary
Instagram.com/oneoff_gallery

SOUTH KOREA

H Contemporary Gallery

Domestic and overseas artists and writers. Actively participating in global art fairs contributing to the development of contemporary art, both locally and internationally.
Address: 3-8 (Unjung-ro 125beon-gil, Bundang-gu, Seongnam-si, Gyeonggi-do, South Korea.
Phone: +82 31-703-7772
Website: hcontemporary.com
Email: info@hcontemporary.com
Instagram.com/h_contemporary_gallery

Ieeyoung Contemporary Museum

A variety of genres of exhibition and culture, from traditional to modernity with a large collection of Korean-American painters. An in-depth study of the achievements of Korean art history. The gallery also shows young artists both at home and abroad.
Address: Yongin 55-1, Yeongdeok-dong, Giheung-gu, Yongin
Phone: +82 31-213-8223
Website: icamkorea.org
Email: ieyoung@icamkorea.org

Seoul
Gallery SUN Contemporary

Contemporary art gallery in Seoul.
Address: Seoul 66, Sogyeok-dong, Jongno-gu, Seoul
Phone: +82 2-720-5789
Website: suncontemporary.com
Email: suncontempo@naver.com
Facebook.com/suncontemporary.korea

Daelim Museum

Contemporary art museum.
Address: Seoul 35-1 Tongui-dong, Jongno-gu, Seoul
Phone: +82 2-720-0665
Website: daelimmuseum.org
Email: Info@daelimmuseum.org
Facebook.com/daelimmuseum
Instagram.com/daelimmuseum
Tv.naver.com/daelimmuseum
YouTube.com/user/DaelimMuseum

Seoul Auction

The leading art auctioneer in the Korean art market. Opened a branch in Hong Kong in 2008. Introducing Korean art to worldwide collectors.
Address: 636-4 Shinsa-dong, Gangnam-gu, Seoul, South Korea
Phone: +82 2-542-2412
Website: seoulauction.com

Hyundai Gallery

With 2 galleries in Seoul and 1 in New York, and 50 years' experience in contemporary Korean art, supporting the quest for beauty.
Address: 14 Samcheong-ro, Jongno-gu, Seoul 03062 South Korea
Phone: +82 2-2287-3500
Website: galleryhyundai.com
Email: mail@galleryhyundai.com
Address: 500 Greenwich St., #202,New York, NY 10013
Phone: +1 216 536 2585
Email: newyork@galleryhyundai.com

Gallery Chosun

Gallery Chosun is a contemporary art gallery.
Address: 64, Buckchon-ro 5-gil, Jongno-gu, Seoul, Korea
Phone: +82 2-723-7133
Website: gallerychosun.com
Email: info@gallerychosun.com
Facebook.com/gallerychosun
Instagram.com/gallerychosun
YouTube.com/gallery chosun

Busan

Goeun Museum

Goeun photography museum.
Address: 16, Haeundae-ro 452beon-gil, Haeundae-gu, Busan, South Korea [48089]
Phone: +82 51-746-0055
Website: goeunmuseum.kr
Instagram.com/goeun_museum_of_photography
YouTube.com/user/goeunmuseum

LATVIA

Riga

Riga Art Space

Contemporary art events of both emerging and established workers as well as hosting other cultural events. 5 exhibitions in the great hall each year, from classics to applied and contemporary art in all genres as well as international art projects. Educational events and workshops for children and adults developing the conversation of cultural synthesis through art and society.
Address: Kungu iela 3, Riga 1050
Phone: +371 67 026 726
Website: makslastelpa.lv
Email: makslastelpa@riga.lv
Twitter.com/makslastelpa
Facebook.com/makslastelpa
Instagram.com/makslastelpa

Art Gallery PUTTI

Gallery of Latvian and international contemporary and conceptual jewellery. 4 themed group or solo exhibitions each year. Silver, gold, precious and semi-precious stones, mammoth ivory and ebony.
Address: Mārstaļu iela 16, Riga
Phone: +371 67 214 229
Website: putti.lv
Email: gallery@putti.lv
Twitter.com/artgalleryputti
Facebook.com/ArtGalleryPutti
Instagram.com/artgalleryputti
Pinterest.co.uk/artgalleryputti
LinkedIn.com/company/art-gallery-putti

LEBANON

Beirut

Beirut Art Center

Contemporary art centre.
Address: Jisr El Wati - Off Corniche an Nahr, Building 13, Street 97, Zone 66 Adlieh., Beirut
Phone: +961 1 397 018
Website: beirutartcenter.org
Email: info@beirutartcenter.org
Facebook.com/BeirutArtCenter
Instagram.com/p/BdpqvKSFUMn/?taken-by=beirutartcenter

LIECHTENSTEIN

Kunstmuseum Liechtenstein

A museum of modern and contemporary art in a black cube building. Sculpture, installations and objects from the state art collection, with particular emphasis on Art Povera and post-minimalist art. Temporary exhibitions of international 20th and 21st century art. The new Hilti Art Foundation exhibition building was added in 2015, showing outstanding works of classical modernism and contemporary art.
Address: Städtle 32, Vaduz
Phone: +423 235 03 29
Website: kunstmuseum.li
Email: mail@kunstmuseum.li
Facebook.com/kunstmuseum
Instagram.com/kunstmuseum_liechtenstein
Vimeo.com/kunstmuseumliechtenstein

LITHUANIA

National Art Gallery

National art gallery of Lithuania.
Address: Konstitucijos pr. 22, Vilnius 08105
Phone: +370 5 212 2997
Website: ndg.lt
Email: egle@ndg.lt
Facebook.com/Nacionaline.Dailes.Galerija

LUXEMBOURG

Contemporary Art Gallery (Kunsthalle Bern)

Institution for contemporary art founded in 1918.
Address: Helvetiaplatz 1, Bern 3005
Phone: +41 31 350 00 40
Website: kunsthalle-bern.ch
Email: info@kunsthalle-bern.ch
Facebook.com/kunsthallebern
Instagram.com/kunsthallebern

Zidoun-Bossuyt Gallery

Contemporary art gallery.
Address: 101, rue Adolphe Fischer, Luxembourg
Phone: +352 26 29 64 49
Website: zidoun-bossuyt.com
Email: contact@zidoun-bossuyt.com
Facebook.com/ZidounBossuytGallery
Instagram.com/Zidoun-Bossuyt Gallery

Forum d'Art Contemporain

The flagship contemporary art institution in Luxembourg and internationally dedicated exclusively to contemporary work. Focused on artistic production rather than collection. Geared towards experimentation and risk-taking that is inherent in the creative process.
Address: 41, rue Notre-Dame, Luxembourg
Phone: +352 22 50 45
Website: casino-luxembourg.lu
Email: info@casino-luxembourg.lu
Twitter.com/CasinoLuxemburg
Facebook.com/casinoluxembourg
Instagram.com/casinoluxembourg
Vimeo.com/casinoluxembourg

NORTH MACEDONIA

Contemporary Art Museum of Macedonia

Museum of the Macedonian struggle for sovereignty and independence. Located between the Museum of Archaeology, the Holocaust Museum of Macedonia, the Stone Bridge and the Vardar River. The Museum of Contemporary Art is the most influential in the Republic of Macedonia, discovering, treasuring and preserving the great value of art and culture of our age.
Address: Samoilova vv, Skopje, 1000
Phone: +389 (0)2 311 77 34
YouTube.com/Muzej Sovremena

MALTA

Valletta Contemporary

An independent exhibition space run by the META Foundation in a 400-year-old former warehouse. Influential local and international contemporary artists, with a dynamic exhibition program. Collaborates with local and international organisations and collectors. Outreach programs and educational initiatives creating a meaningful link between the community and contemporary art.
Address: 15, 16, 17 East Street, Valletta VLT 1253
Phone: +356 7904 1051
Website: vallettacontemporary.com
Email: info@vallettacontemporary.com
Facebook.com/vallettacontemporary
Instagram.com/vallettacontemporary__malta

MEXICO

Museo de Arte Contemporaneo (MARCO)

Promoting international contemporary art, with a particular leaning towards Latin American visual arts. A stage for young artistic talent as well as renowned contemporary artists. Plastic arts, literature, music, film, video and dance – it is a museum to enjoy, experiment and roam.
Address: Zuazua and Jardón S/N, Centro. Monterrey, N.L. Mexico, 64000
Phone: +52 (81) 8262.4500
Website: marco.org.mx
Email: coordinacion@marco.org.mx
Twitter.com/museomarco
Facebook.com/museomarcomty
Instagram.com/museomarco
LinkedIn.com/company/museomarco

Arróniz arte Contemporáneo

Working with the new generation of artists from Mexico and Latin America, developing their careers both locally and internationally by working with other galleries and taking part in international art fairs.
Address: Durango 53, Mexico City 06700
Phone: +52 55 5511 7965
Website: arroniz-arte.com
Email: info@arroniz-arte.com
Twitter.com/GaleriaArroniz
Instagram.com/galeriaarroniz

Garash

Contemporary art gallery.
Address: Av. Álvaro Obregón 49, Mexico City 06700
Phone: +52 55 5207 9858
Website: garashgaleria.com

Celaya Brothers Gallery

Challenging creative limits. Inviting international artists to develop unique concepts and defy the parameters of their time. Supporting creative freedom and exploring innovative expression.
Address: Jalapa 90 Col Roma, México Df
Phone: +52 55 6391 5541
Website: celayabrothersgallery.com
Email: cbg@arto.mx
Twitter.com/celayabrothers
Facebook.com/celayabrothers
Instagram.com/celayabrothers

Museo de Arte Alvar y Carmen T. de Carrillo Gil

Contemporary art gallery.
Museos Y Galerias De Arte
Address: Av. Revolucion No. 1608, Ciudad de Mexico 1000
Phone: +52 55 5550 3983
Website: museodeartecarrillogil.com
Twitter.com/Carrillo_Gil
Facebook.com/museocarrillogil
Instagram.com/museocarrillogil
YouTube.com/ Museo de Arte Carrillo Gil

Fernando Garcia Ponce-Macay Museum

Dedicated to the promotion and dissemination of modern and contemporary

art. Receiving 72,000 visitors each year. Deep educational vocation, with more than 22,000 children each year attending programs, courses, guided tours and workshops. Every 3 months it shows new exhibitions in each of its 15 galleries, moving about 2,000 pieces each time.
Address: 5 De Mayo 409, Puebla 72000
Phone: +52 222 232 4720
Website: macay.org
Twitter.com/museo_macay
Facebook.com/museomacay
YouTube.com/user/tvmacay

MONACO

Le Boudoir de Saint-Paul / Modern & Contemporary Art Gallery

Modern and contemporary art gallery.
Address: 1, PL Général de Gaulle, Saint-Paul-de-Vence 06570
Website: Facebook.com
Email: info@leboudoirdesaintpaul.com
Facebook.com/LeBoudoirDeSaintPaul

MOROCCO

Laredo Art Gallery

Contemporary art gallery.
Address: 67 Rue Taha Houcine, Casablanca 20060
Phone: +212 5222-66027
Website: web.Facebook.com
Email: gjlaredo@gmail.com
Facebook.com/laredoart

MYANMAR

RANGE contemporary art gallery

Emerging and established artists. Initiating dialogue and interaction between artists, art-lovers, students and the public.
Address: 54 Lower Range, Beckbagan, Kolkata 700019

Phone: +91-98300 49825
Website: rangegallery.in
Email: abandesai@rangegallery.in

River Gallery

Artists are now enjoying unprecedented freedoms since Myanmar opened its doors to the world. Representing emerging and established artists in different styles, subjects and media. Exhibiting both nationally and internationally.
Address: 37th Street, Yangon (Rangoon)
Phone: +95 1 378 617
Website: rivergallerymyanmar.com
Email: rivergalleryart@gmail.com
Facebook.com/rivergallerymyanmar
Instagram.com/rivergallerymyanmar

THE NETHERLANDS

Amsterdam
Reflex Modern Art Gallery

Representing over 25 internationally-renowned contemporary artists.
Address: Weteringschans 79 A, Amsterdam 1017 RX
Phone: +31 20 423 5423
Website: reflex-art.com
Email: info@reflexamsterdam.com
Facebook.com/reflexamsterdamgallery
Instagram.com/alexdanielsreflex
Artsy.net/galerie-alex-daniels-reflex
Ocula.com/art-galleries/reflex-amsterdam
Galleriesnow.net/gallery/reflex
Artland.com/galleries/reflex-amsterdam

KochxBos Art Gallery

Committed to new and cutting edge art that adds intellectual and/or aesthetic value to the present time. Astonishing the audience with different and surprising views on who we are as human beings.
Address: Eerste Anjeliersdwarsstraat 36, Amsterdam 1015 NR

Phone: +31 20 681 4567
Website: kochxbos.com

Renssen Art Gallery

Showing the works of Dutch contemporary artist, Erik Renssen sitting side by side with works of the Grand Master, Picasso.
Address: Nieuwe Spiegelstraat 44, Amsterdam 1017 DG
Phone: +31 6 34261770
Website: renssenartgallery.com
Email: info@renssen-art.com
Facebook.com/renssenartgallery
Instagram.com/renssenartgallery

Morren Galleries

Contemporary art gallery in Amsterdam.
Address: Prinsengracht 572, Amsterdam 1017 KR
Phone: +31 20 320 6015
Website: morrengalleries.nl
Email: emorren@morrengalleries.nl
Facebook.com/MorrenGalleries
Instagram.com/morrengalleries
Pinterest.com/morren galleries

ArTicks Gallery

Contemporary art gallery.
Address: Singel 88, Amsterdam 1015 AD
Phone: +31 20 737 1505
Website: articksgallery.com
Flickr.com/photos/articksgallery/albums

Borzogallery

Leading Dutch gallery specialising in NUL/Zero, minimalism and conceptual art. Linking recent modern art with today's contemporary art. One of the oldest Dutch galleries, situated in a 17th century Amsterdam canal house.
Address: Keizersgracht 516, Amsterdam 1017 EJ
Phone: +31 (0)20 626 33 03
Website: borzo.com
Email: info@borzo.com Twitter.com/

BorzoGallery
Facebook.com/borzo.gallery
Instagram.com/borzogallery
Artsy.net/borzo-modern-and-contemporary-art

Red Box Gallery

Contemporary art gallery located in the heart of the historic centre of Amsterdam. Representing talented international artists who work in painting, drawing, sculpture, digital art, photography, video art, installation and performance.
Address: Oudekerksplein 22, Amsterdam 1012 GZ
Website: redstampartgallery.com
Email: info@redstampartgallery.com
Twitter.com/Red_Stamp_Art
Facebook.com/RedStampArtGallery

W139

A presentation and production space for contemporary art. Development-orientated and connective source of art, stimulating artistic and intellectual freedom. An artist-run institution since 1979.
Address: Warmoesstraat 139, Amsterdam 1012 JB
Phone: +31 20 622 9434
Website: w139.nl
Email: info@w139.nl
Twitter.com/w139
Facebook.com/W139Amsterdam
Instagram.com/w139amsterdam

van Zijll Langhout / Contemporary Art

Contemporary art gallery.
Address: Brouwersgracht 161, Amsterdam 1015 GG
Phone: +31 20 770 8990
Website: vzlart.nl
Email: exposities@vanzijlllanghout.nl
Facebook.com/Van-Zijll-Langhout-Contemporary-Art-1383504768555273

Greenbox Museum of Contemporary Art from Saudi Arabia

Contemporary art from Saudi Arabia shown in Amsterdam. Turning attention away from what is en vogue in many White Cube museums in Europe and America, showing an alternative centre of intelligence and creativity in need of space to express itself.
Address: Korte Leidsedwarsstraat 12, Amsterdam 1017 RC
Phone: +31 6 24282884
Website: greenboxmuseum.org
Email: info@greenboxmuseum.org

Keren de Vreede Art Gallery

Contemporary Abstract Expressionism by Dutch artist Keren de Vreede.
Address: Prinsengracht 308a, Amsterdam 1016 HW
Phone: +31 20 717 3485
Website: kerendevreede.com
Email: Lydia@kerendevreede.com

Rotterdam
Witte de With Center for Contemporary Art

Founded in 1990, with exhibitions, commissions, publications, educational and collaborative initiatives. A non-profit organisation who works with artists challenging the present but also looking at how art has been created and experienced in the past – imaging the future forms of art.
Address: Witte de Withstraat 50, Rotterdam 3012 BR
Phone: +31 10 411 0144
Website: wdw.nl
Email: office@wdw.nl
Twitter.com/fkawdw
Facebook.com/fkawdw
Instagram.com/fkawdw
SoundCloud.com/fkawdw
LinkedIn.com/company/witte-de-with-center-for-contemporary-art
YouTube.com/user/wittedewithchannel

Contemporary Art Rotterdam

Contemporary art gallery.
Address: Veerhaven 4, Rotterdam 3016 CJ
Website: artrotterdam.com
Email: info@artrotterdam.com

RAM-Art

Contemporary art gallery working with a limited number of artists over a long time period.
Address: Lloydkade 627, Rotterdam 3024 WX
Phone: +31 10 425 9755
Website: contempo.info
Email: info@contempo.info

The Hague
Baks Modern & Contemporary Art

Contemporary art gallery in the Hague.
Address: Zuidwal 96, ‹s-Gravenhage 2512 XV
Phone: +31 6 34339114
Website: galeriebaks.nl
Email: info@galeriebaks.nl

Arte Fortunata – Modern & Contemporary Interior Art

Art, glass, design and interior objects combined to form one total living concept.
Address: Noordeinde 51, Den Haag 2514 GC
Phone: +31 6 46078103
Facebook.com/artefortunata

Project 2.0

Modern art gallery in the Hague showing work with an intrinsic, timeless quality that is ambitious rather than pretentious.
Address: Noordeinde 102, Den Haag
Phone: +31 70 345 0357
Website: project20.nl
Email: info@project20.nl
Twitter.com/Project2punt0
Facebook.com/project2.0gallery
Instagram.com/project2.0gallery

GEM, Museum voor actuele kunst

Dutch and international contemporary art with 7 exhibitions each year. All media represented, from (video) installations, painting, sculpture, drawing, film and photography. Part of Kunstmuseum Den Hagg and regularly showcases the museum's collection of contemporary art. GEM shares its premises with the Museum of Photography, located next to the Kunstmuseum.
Address: Stadhouderslaan 43, The Hague 2517 HV
Phone: +31 70 338 1111
Website: gem-online.nl
Email: pressoffice@gemeentemuseum.nl
Twitter.com/Gemeentemuseum
Facebook.com/GEMmuseum

Gallery Ramakers

Founded in 1994, housed in a 19th century canal house in the centre of The Hague with a sleekly designed garden for displaying sculpture. 8 exhibitions a year showing established and emerging artists, both national and international with regular exchanges with the Paris Gallery La Ferronnerie.
Address: Toussaintkade 51, The Hague 2513 CL
Phone: +31 70 363 4308
Website: galerieramakers.nl
Email: info@galerieramakers.nl

Quartair

A space for exhibition and artistic debate. Founded in 1992 by art graduates from the Royal Academy of Fine Arts in The Hague at a former bread factory. There are 7 artists' studios and an exhibition space. Showing art both from The Netherlands and abroad, with a focus on co-operation with other cultural institutions.
Address: Bilderdijkstraat 143, 's-Gravenhage 2513 CN
Phone: +31 70 345 8672
Website: quartair.nl
Email: info@quartair.nl
Facebook.com/quartair
Instagram.com/quartair

Utrecht
Morren Galleries

Contemporary Figurative Art.
Address: Burg. Reigerstraat 2a, Utrecht
Phone: +31 30 238 1867
Website: morrengalleries.nl
Email: emorren@morrengalleries.nl
Facebook.com/MorrenGalleries
Instagram.com/morrengalleries

Eindhoven
Cage

Cage presents young, emerging artists from all over the world.
Address: BinnewiertzStraat 27, Eindhoven 5615 HG
Phone: +31 40 243 8852
Website: cage.nl
Email: info@cage.nl

Tilburg
Gallery van Dun - Contemporary Art

Modern contemporary art gallery, with a unique collection of paintings, sculptures and photography.
Address: De Lind 39-41, Oisterwijk 5061 HT
Phone: +31 13 523 4740
Website: galleryvandun.com
Email: info@galleryvandun.com
Facebook.com/galleryvandun
Instagram.com/galleryvandun
LinkedIn.com/company/gallery-van-dun
YouTube.com/Jerome Van Dun

Mr. J.H. De Pont Stichting

Named after the businessman whose estate provided for the establishment of a contemporary art foundation in 1988. Located in a former wool-spinning mill. 3

large exhibitions a year with smaller solo ones.
Address: Wilhelminapark 1, Tilburg 5041 EA
Phone: +31 13 543 8300
Website: depont.nl
Email: info@depont.nl
Twitter.com/De_Pont
Facebook.com/museumdepont
Instagram.com/de_pont_museum

Groningen
Groninger Museum

Founded in 1874. With a large donation in 1987, moved into a purpose built structure opened in 1994 by Queen Beatrix. The design continues to prompt discussions about modern museum architecture.
Address: Museumeiland 1, Groningen 9711 ME
Phone: +31 50 366 6555
Website: groningermuseum.nl
Twitter.com/groningermuseum
Facebook.com/GroningerMuseum
Instagram.com/groningermuseum
YouTube.com/user/HetGroningerMuseum

Nijmegen
Stichting Marzee

A driving force in international, contemporary jewellery and metalwork for more than 40 years. The largest independent gallery for contemporary jewellery in the world. Housed in a former granary on the banks of the river Waal. Representing both established and emerging jewellers. 4 exhibitions each year and the annual Marzee International Graduate Show in the summer.
Address: Lage Markt 3, Nijmegen 6511 VK
Phone: +31 24 322 9670
Website: marzee.nl
Email: mail@marzee.nl

NEW ZEALAND
McAtamney Gallery And Design Store

A diverse collection of modern, contemporary and historical pieces. Landscapes, abstract, figurative and still lives, with a strong focus on portraiture. Leading and emerging artists.
Address: 40 A Talbot Street
Geraldine 7930
(opposite the Village Inn.)
Phone: +64 3 69 37 292
Website: mcatamneygallery.co.nz
Email: carolyn@mcatamneygallery.co.nz
Facebook.com/mcatamneygallery
YouTube.com/user/McAtamneyGallery

Christchurch
Physics Room

Contemporary art and critical discourse. Assisting artists to achieve a higher level of professionalism and creative development. Involving art as a contributing voice in intellectual, social and political debate.
Address: Tuam Street, Christchurch
Phone: +64 3-379 5583
Website: physicsroom.org.nz
Email: physicsroom@physicsroom.org.nz
Facebook.com/ThePhysicsRoom
Instagram.com/physicsroom

Form Gallery

The finest jewellery, glass, ceramics, objects and sculptures from New Zealand's leading contemporary artists.
Address: 468 Colombo Street, Sydenham, Christchurch 8023
Phone: +64 3-377 1211
Website: form.co.nz
Email: info@form.co.nz
Facebook.com/formgallerynz
Instagram.com/formgallerynz

Bryce Art Gallery

A diverse selection of artworks, sculpture and artisan blown glass from New Zealand and international artists.
Address: 21 Paeroa Street, Riccarton, Christchurch 8041
Phone: +64 3-348 0064
Website: brycegallery.co.nz
Email: art2die4@brycegallery.co.nz
Facebook.com/brycegallery

Christchurch Art Gallery (Te Puna o Waiwhetu)

An important public art collection and the largest art institution on the South Island, contributing to the cultural wellbeing of the community.
Address: Montreal St, Christchurch City 8013
Phone: +64 3-941 7300
Website: christchurchartgallery.org.nz
Email: info@christchurchartgallery.org.nz
Twitter.com/chchartgallery
Facebook.com/chchartgallery
Instagram.com/chchartgallery
YouTube.com/user/ChchArtGallery

Coca

Presenting and cultivating contemporary art since 1880, connecting people, artists and the art of our time.
Address: 66 Gloucester Street, Christchurch 8013
Phone: +64 3-366 7261
Website: coca.org.nz
Email: info@coca.org.nz
Twitter.com/cocachch
Facebook.com/CoCAChristchurch
Instagram.com/coca.chch

The National

Specialising in New Zealand contemporary jewellery and solo exhibitions for international jewellery artists. Since relocating and expanding in 2018, now showing sculpture and object-based work.

Exhibiting both established and emerging artists creating links to international practice. 10 exhibitions a year.
Address: 241 Moorhouse Ave, Christchurch City 8011
Website: thenational.co.nz
Email: info@thenational.co.nz
Facebook.com/TheNationalNZ
Instagram.com/thenational_nz

Auckland

Artist Gallery

One of New Zealand's leading sculpture galleries, featuring large-scale works.
Address: 280 Parnell Road, Parnell, Auckland Central 1052
Phone: +64 9-303 1090
Website: artisgallery.co.nz
Email: artis@artisgallery.co.nz

Whitespace Contemporary Art

Contemporary art gallery.
Address: 20 Monmouth St, Grey Lynn, Auckland 1021
Phone: +64 9-361 6331
Website: whitespace.co.nz
Email: dwhite@whitespace.co.nz
Twitter.com/whitespacenz
Facebook.com/whitespacegallerynz
Instagram.com/whitespacegallery
YouTube.com/whitespacegallery

Auckland Art Gallery Toi o Tamaki

Opened in 1888, with the core collection from Sir George Grey. Originally focused on British and European work. Now with 16,000 pieces in the collection and regularly changing exhibitions. Holds historic, modern and contemporary art from New Zealand, beginning with the first contact between Māori and European explorers in the 1600s. Māori and Pacific Island artists are a considerable feature.

Address: Wellesley St E, Corner Kitchener, Auckland Central 1010
Phone: +64 9-307 7700
Website: aucklandartgallery.com
Twitter.com/Auckartgal
Facebook.com/aucklandartgallery
Instagram.com/aucklandartgallery
Weibo.com/aucklandartgallery
YouTube.com/user/aucklandartgallery

Tim Melville Gallery

Contemporary New Zealand, Australian art.
Address: 4 Winchester Street, Auckland
Phone: +64 9-520 5891
Website: timmelville.com
Email: info@timmelville.com
Facebook.com/TimMelvilleGallery
Instagram.com/timmelvillegallery

Kura Gallery

New Zealand art and design with galleries in Auckland and Wellington. Traditional Māori carvings, art and design, jewellery, furniture and genuine pounamu/greenstone.
Address: 188 Quay Street, PWC Tower, Auckland 1010
Phone: +64 9-302 1151
Website: kuragallery.co.nz
Email: auckland@kuragallery.co.nz
Facebook.com/kuragalleryauckland

John Leech Gallery

One of New Zealand's oldest galleries showing significant historical art and indigenous artefacts.
Address: Kitchener St, Auckland 1010
Phone: +64 9-303 9395
Website: johnleechgallery.co.nz
Email: info@johnleechgallery.co.nz

Gow Langsford Gallery

Fostering and promoting the best art from New Zealand and abroad. 2 locations in Auckland.

Address: 26 Lorne Street, Auckland Central 1010
Address: Corner Kitchener and Wellesley Streets, Auckland, 1010, New Zealand
Phone: +64 9-303 4290
Website: gowlangsfordgallery.co.nz
Email: info@gowlangsfordgallery.co.nz
Facebook.com/gowlangsfordgallery
Instagram.com/gowlangsfordgallery
Pinterest.co.uk/gowlangsford

TWO Rooms

Residences and projects by leading international and New Zealand contemporary artists in a converted warehouse in central Auckland.
Address: 16 Putiki St., Auckland
Phone: +64 9-360 5900
Website: tworooms.co.nz
Email: jenny@tworooms.co.nz
Facebook.com/tworoomsgallery
Instagram.com/tworoomsgallery

Seed

An online and events-based commercial art gallery showing innovative New Zealand artists. Promoting the best emerging talent from a new generation of artists.
Address: 23 Crowhurst St, Auckland City 1023
Phone: +64 9-522 5360
Website: seedgallery.co.nz
Email: gallery@seedgallery.co.nz
Twitter.com/seedgallerynz
Facebook.com/seedgallerynz
Instagram.com/seedgallerynz

Haus Of Flox

Working since 2003 as an aerosol and stencil artist with a fine art degree in the inner cityscape of Auckland. Trade mark details include native birds, ferns and flowers with vibrant and confident colour. Also creating prints, publications, murals, graphic design,

live painting, projects and workshops for schools and the wider public. Collaborating widely with charities. Has exhibited in both group and solo shows. One of New Zealand's most recognised contemporary artists.
Address: 13 Great North Rd, Auckland 1021
Phone: +64 9-963 4293
Website: flox.co.nz
Email: showroom@flox.co.nz
Facebook.com/floxnz
Instagram.com/floxnz

Wellington
City Gallery Wellington

Contemporary art gallery with a dynamic program of exhibitions and events, and an international reputation. A hub for local creative life.
Address: 101 Wakefield Street, Te Ngākau Civic Square, Wellington 6011
Phone: +64 4-913 9032
Website: citygallery.org.nz
Email: citygallery@experiencewellington.org.nz
Twitter.com/CityGalleryWgtn
Facebook.com/CityGalleryWellington
Instagram.com/citygallerywellington
YouTube.com/user/citygallerywgtn

Kura Art Gallery

Supporting artists and presenting Maori and New Zealand art and design to the world.
Address: 19 Allen Street, Wellington 6011
Phone: +64 4-802 4934
Website: kuragallery.co.nz
Email: wellington@kuragallery.co.nz
Facebook.com/Kura-Gallery-Wellington

Hamilton
Waikato Society Of Arts

Supporting local artists at every stage of their development with resources, education and exhibition. Several exhibitions each year. Hosts the National Youth Art Award and the New Zealand Painting and Printmaking Award.
Address: Level 1 -120 Victoria Street, Hamilton 3240
Website: wsa.org.nz

ArtsPost Galleries & Shop Waikato Museum

13 galleries featuring 25 new exhibitions and 100 public events annually, inspiring local and international visitors. Telling stories from a regional and global perspective, with visual art, social history tangata whenua (people of the land) and science.
Address: 120 Victoria Street, Hamilton 3204
Phone: +64 7-838 6928
Website: waikatomuseum.co.nz
Email: museum@hcc.govt.nz
Twitter.com/WaikatoMuseum
Facebook.com/waikatomuseum
Instagram.com/waikatomuseum

Tauranga
Tauranga Art Gallery

A constantly changing program of inspiring art from leading, local, national and international artists.
Address: Willow St, Tauranga City 3110
Phone: +64 7-578 7933
Website: artgallery.org.nz
Email: office@artgallery.org.nz
Facebook.com/TaurangaArtGallery
Instagram.com/taurangaartgallery
YouTube.com/TAG Tauranga Art Gallery

The Art Lounge NZ

Fine art gallery and events venue. Showing emerging and established artist from New Zealand. Monthly exhibitions.
Address: 117 Willow Street, Tauranga 3112
Phone: +64 21 202 5061
Website: theartloungenz.com
Email: info@theartloungenz.com
Facebook.com/theartloungenz
Instagram.com/the_art_lounge_nz

Hutt Art Society

An incorporated society, for over 50 years providing a venue for the people of Hutt Valley to meet and practice art.
Address: Myrtle Street, Lower Hutt
Phone: + 64 4 566 0102
Website: huttart.co.nz
Email: huttartsociety@xtra.co.nz
Facebook.com/HuttArt

The Dowse Art Museum

A leading contemporary art museum with regularly changing exhibitions and events.
Address: 45 Laings Rd, Lower Hutt, Wellington 5040
Phone: +64 4-570 6500
Website: dowse.org.nz
Email: enquiries@dowse.org.nz
Twitter.com/thedowse
Facebook.com/thedowse
Instagram.com/thedowse

NIGERIA

Lagos

National Gallery of Modern Art, Lagos

A major art gallery in Lagos, the largest city of Nigeria. It has a permanent exhibition as well as a portrait gallery. The modern sculpture gallery is made up of recent work as well as early forms such as from the Nok culture. There are also sections of contemporary ceramics, glass, painting and textiles.

Red Door Art Gallery

A platform for creativity without societal boundaries. Promoting 'unpredictable' art, believing that art is the ultimate expression of man's inner most thoughts. Collector consulting, valuation, restoration, private and public commissions and exhibitions – the entire art value chain.
Address: 51b Bishop Oluwole St., Victoria Island, Lagos 101241
Phone: +234 701 591 1010
Website: reddoorgallery.co
Email: info@reddoorgallery.com
Twitter.com/RedDoorNG
Facebook.com/RedDoorNG
Instagram.com/reddoorng

CCA, Lagos

An independent visual art organisation focusing on the art and culture of Lagos.
Address: 9 McEwen Street, Yaba, Lagos
Phone: +234 702 836 7106
Website: ccalagos.org
Email: ccalagos@gmail.com
Twitter.com/ccalagos
Facebook.co./ Centre for Contemporary Art, Lagos (CCA,Lagos)

NORWAY

Oslo

Office for Contemporary Art Norway

A foundation created by the Ministry of Foreign Affairs in 2001, serving to develop collaborations in contemporary art between Norway and the international art world.
Address: Nedre Gate 7, Oslo 0551
Phone: +47 23 23 31 50
Website: oca.no
Email: info@oca.no
Twitter.com/oca_norway
Facebook.com/oca.norway
Instagram.com/oca_norway

Khartoum Contemporary Art Center

KCAC is a bar and conceptual art initiative, hosting exhibitions, talks, book launches, debates, performances, screenings, live music and DJs.
Address: Bernt Ankers gate 17, Oslo 0183
Phone: +47 462 63 590
Website: khartoumcontemporary.com

Email: kcac.booking@gmail.com
Facebook.com/khartoumcontemporary
Instagram.com/khartoum_contemporary

International Corporate Art Inc

Art programs that support and communicate your brand images, providing artistic direction and a guideline for selecting art. Art consultants to corporate, maritime and hospitality industries.
Address: 4689 Ponce De Leon Blvd Ste 3, Coral Gables 33146
Phone: +1 (305) 667-4738
Website: icart.net
Email: contact@icartoslo.com
Facebook.com/InternationalCorporateArt
Instagram.com/icart_inc
LinkedIn.com/company/international-corporate-art-limited

Nasjonalgalleriet

The National Museum holds, conserves, exhibits and promotes public knowledge about Norway's largest collections of art, architecture and design.
Address: Universitetsgata 13, Sankt Hanshaugen 0164
Phone: +47 21 98 20 00
Website: nasjonalmuseet.no
Email: info@nasjonalmuseet.no
Twitter.com/nasjonalmuseet
Facebook.com/nasjonalmuseet
Instagram.com/nasjonalmuseet
YouTube.com/nasjonalmuseet

WILLAS contemporary

Promoting internationally acclaimed artists, with a particular focus on contemporary photography.
Address: Tordenskiolds gate 7, Oslo 0160
Phone: +47 913 32 343
Website: willas.com
Email: ellen-k@willas.com
Facebook.com/willascontemporary

Instagram.com/willas_contemporary
Vimeo.com/willascontemporary
Artsy.net/willas-contemporary

Astrup Fearnley Museum of Modern Art

A privately-owned museum with temporary exhibitions of important international art.
Address: Strandpromenaden 2, Oslo 0252
Phone: +47 22 93 60 60
Website: afmuseet.no
Email: s.ovstebo@afmuseet.no
Twitter.com/astrupfearnley
Facebook.com/astrupfearnley
Instagram.com/astrupfearnley
Pinterest.co.uk/astrupfearnley
Vimeo.com/user4068848
LinkedIn.com/company/astrup-fearnley-museet
YouTube.com/user/astrupfearnley

Utopia Retro Modern

20th century design, art and decorative arts, particularly from Scandinavia and Italy.
Address: Kirkeveien 72, Oslo 0364
Phone: +47 21 30 48 85
Website: utopiaretromodern.com
Email: info@utopiaretromodern.com
Facebook.com/utopiaretromodern
Instagram.com/utopiaretromodern

Bergen
Galleri GEO & Ramme Service

Contemporary art gallery.
Address: Olav Kyrres gate 43, Galleri GEO & Ramme Servce, Bergen 5014
Phone: +47 55 32 92 50
Website: gallerigeo.no
Email: post@rammeservice.com

Bergen Kunsthal

Contemporary art exhibitions, concerts and events by international artists, as well as debates and education.
Address: Rasmus Meyers alle 5, Bergen 5015
Phone: +47 55 55 93 19

Website: kunsthall.no
Email: bergen@kunsthall.no
Facebook.com/bergenkunsthall
Instagram.com/bergenkunsthall
Vimeo.com/bergenkunsthall

KODE Art Museums of Bergen

One of Scandinavia's largest museums for art, music, handicraft and design. Spread over 4 museums and 3 composer homes. A wide collection of Norwegian and international contemporary art, with the largest collection of Chinese art in Norway. Art museum for children.
Address: Rasmus Meyers alle 9, Rasmus Meyers allé 3, Bergen 5015
Phone: +47 53 00 97 04
Website: kodebergen.no
Email: post@kodebergen.no
Twitter.com/kodebergen
Facebook.com/kodebergen
Instagram.com/kodebergen

Trondheim
Modern Art Gallery

Central Norway's largest gallery, with renowned national artists. Exhibiting in the region of 70 artists at any one time.
Address: Olav Tryggvasons gate 33, Trondheim 7011
Phone: +47 91 88 10 10.
Website: modernartgallery.no
Email: post@modernartgallery.no
Facebook.com/ModernArtTRD

Lofoten
Tromso Center for Contemporary Art

The oldest art institution in Northern Norway and a premiere gallery for contemporary art in the circumpolar north.
Address: Musegata 2, Tromso 9008
Phone: +47 466 23 586
Website: tromsokunstforening.no
Email: post@tromsokunstforening.no

Facebook.com/TromsoKunstforening
Instagram.com/tromsokunstforening
Vimeo.com/tromsokunstforening

Stavanger
BGE Contemporary Art Projects

Specialises in contemporary art commissions.
Address: Engelsminnegata 17, Stavanger 4008
Phone: +47 918 83 805
Website: bgeart.com
Email: hello@bgeart.com
Facebook.com/bgeart
Instagram.com/bgeart_stavanger

OMAN
Muscat
Bait Muzna Gallery

Established in 2000, promoting modern contemporary art and preserving the essence of Arab art through different mediums. Commissions for large scale projects, locally and internationally.
Address: 8662 Al Saidiya Street, Muscat 113
Phone: +968 22547010
Website: baitmuznagallery.com
Email: art@baitmuznagallery.com
Facebook.com/bait.muzna
Instagram.com/baitmuznaofficial

POLAND
Centre of Contemporary Art

Centre of Contemporary Art in Torun.
Address: ul. Waly Gen. Wladyslawa Sikorskiego 13, Torun 87-100
Phone: +48 56 610 97 00
Website: csw.torun.pl
Email: info@csw.torun.pl
Twitter.com/coca_torun
Facebook.com/csw.torun

Instagram.com/cswtorun
YouTube.com/user/ceeswu

Contemporary Art Gallery

Exhibitions, workshops, courses and performances.
Address: Plac Teatralny 12, Opole 45-056
Phone: +48 77 402 12 35
Website: galeriaopole.pl
Email: lkropiowski@galeriaopole.pl
Facebook.com/gswopole
Instagram.com/gswopole
YouTube.com/G S W OPOLE N O W E

Elektrownia Contemporary Art Gallery

Set in a former power plant, which has been restored. Exhibitions of paining, graphics, sculpture, photography, musical events, dance workshops, theatre etc.
Address: ul. Dehnelow 45, Saturn Mine, Czeladz 41-250
Phone: +48 32 263 00 88
Website: galeria-elektrownia.czeladz.pl
Email: elektrownia-galeria@go2.pl

Warsaw
Galeria Plakatu

Contemporary art gallery.
Address: Rynek Starego Miasta 23, Warszawa 00-272
Website: poster.com.pl
Email: warsaw@poster.com.pl

Centrum Sztuki Wspolczesnej Zamek Ujazdowski

Set in a Baroque castle, presenting exhibitions, performances, cinema and art residences with different fields of art encouraging creativity and exploration.
Address: Jazdow 2, Ujazdow Castle, Warsaw 00-467
Phone: +48 22 628 12 71
Website: u-jazdowski.pl
Email: sekretariat@u-jazdowski. Pl
Twitter.com/u_jazdowski

Facebook.com/centrumsztukiwspolczesne-jzamekujazdowski
Instagram.com/u_jazdowski
Vimeo.com/ujazdowski
SoundCloud.com/user-588930928
Obieg.u-jazdowski.pl
YouTube.com/user/CSWwarszawa

The Museum on the Vistula

Contemporary art museum. Located next to the Copernicus Science Centre and the University of Warsaw Library.
Address: Wybrzeze Kosciuszkowskie 22, Warsaw 00-390
Phone: +48 22 431 07 55
Website: artmuseum.pl
Email: info@artmuseum.pl
Twitter.com/MSN_Warszawa
Facebook.com/MuzeumSztukiNowoczesnej
Instagram.com/msnwarszawa
Vimeo.com/msnwarszawa
YouTube.com/user/museumwarsaw

Kraków
MOCAK Museum of Contemporary Art in Krakow

Investigating the meaning of art by indicating its ethical and cognitive values and links with everyday life. Exhibitions and artistic projects at the museum and beyond. Educational and publishing program.
Address: ul. Lipowa 4, Krakow 30-702
Phone: +48 12 263 40 01
Website: mocak.pl
Email: office@mocak.pl
Twitter.com/mocak_krakow
Facebook.com/mocakkrakow
Instagram.com/mocak_krakow
Snapchat.com/add/mocak_krakow
Vimeo.com/mocak
YouTube.com/c/mocak

Cellar Gallery

Situated in an old cellar with a barrel-vaulted ceiling and uneven floor giving an alternative creative voice to the city, with night-time exhibitions.
Address: Wielopole 12, Kraków 31-000
Phone: +48 604 293 663
Website: cellargallery.art.pl
Email: oxygen3x@gmail.com
Facebook.com/CellarGaleria

Wroclaw

Wroclaw Contemporary Museum

50 years on from the pivotal Wroclaw '70 Visual Arts Symposium which enabled artists to bring forward concepts, designs and interventions for different locations. Showing the work of architects, urban planners, workmen and others who were involved in the project.
Address: plac Strzegomski 2a, Wroclaw 53-681
Phone: +48 71 356 42 57
Website: muzeumwspolczesne.pl
Email: mww@muzeumwspolczesne.pl
Facebook.com/MuzeumWspolczesne
Instagram.com/muzeumwspolczesne
YouTube.com/user/muzeumwspolczesne

Galeria Studio BWA Wroclaw

Contemporary art gallery in Wroclaw.
Address: ul. Ruska 46a/301, Wroclaw 50-079
Phone: +48 660 742 564
Website: bwa.wroc.pl
Email: sekretariat@bwa.wroc.pl
Facebook.com/bwa.wroclaw
Instagram.com/bwawroclaw
YouTube.com/channel/UCbyNVADFBIQwluN5Idech-A

PORTUGAL

Lisbon

Cristina Guerra Contemporary Art

Contemporary art gallery in Lisbon.
Address: Rua Santo António à Estrela, 33, Lisboa 1350-291
Phone: +351 21 395 9559
Website: cristinaguerra.com
Email; info@cristinaguerra.com
Twitter.com/gcristinaguerra
Facebook.com/CristinaGuerraContemporaryArt
Instagram.com/cristinaguerra_gallery

PHILIPPINES

Kulay Diwa Gallery of Philippine Contemporary Art

A privately owned gallery with an independent exhibition area set within a cluster of progressive communities south of Manila. Able to accommodate large-scale works with a spacious garden for sculpture, performance and outdoor programs. Promoting the works of young Filipino artists and fostering cultural interactions between local regions and other countries.
Address: 25 N. Lopez Avenue, Lopez Village, Sucat, Parañaque 1700
Phone: +63 2 826 0574
Website: kulay-diwa.com
Twitter.com/DiwaKulay
Facebook.com/KulayDiwa
Instagram.com/kulay_diwa
YouTube.com/Kulay-Diwa Gallery of Philippine Contemporary Art

PUERTO RICO

Puerto Rico Museum of Contemporary Art

Puerto Rico's leading museum for contemporary art, community engagement

and public commissions.
Phone: +1 787-977-6277
Website: mac-pr.org
Twitter.com/museomacpr
Instagram.com/museomacpr

QATAR

Mathaf Arab Museum of Modern Art

Holding over 9,000 works with major solo and group exhibitions, education programs, dialogue and research exploring and celebrating modern and contemporary art.
Address: Education City off Al-Luqta Street, Al Rayyan
Phone: +974 4402 8855
Website: mathaf.org.qa
Email: mathaf_info@qm.org.qa
Twitter.com/mathafmodern
Facebook.com/MathafModern
Instagram.com/mathafmodern
YouTube.com/user/mathafmodern

ROMANIA

Bucharest
Galateca Contemporary Arts and Design Gallery

Applied art in a beautiful square in Bucharest. A creative space experimenting in a continual and multidisciplinary way.
Address: Str. C.A.Rosetti Nr. 2-4, Bucharest
Phone: +40 376 203 178
Website: galateca.ro
Email: galerie@galateca.ro
Facebook.com/GalerieGalateca
Instagram.com/galateca
YouTube.com/user/GaleriaGalateca

418 Contemporary Art Gallery

Creating a solid and reliable profile of a Bucharest based contemporary art gallery, in the emerging Eastern European art market.

Address: Intrarea Armasului, No.12, Et.2, Bucharest
Website: 418gallery.com
Email: ecaterina.dinulescu@418gallery.com
Facebook.com/418GALLERY
Instagram.com/galateca
YouTube.com/user/GaleriaGalateca

RUSSIA

Arka Gallery of Contemporary Art

A private gallery established in 1995. Exhibitions and international fairs, charitable projects. Cultural international cooperation by holding exhibitions for artists from Korea, China, Japan, the US, Germany and Belgium, some of which have been reciprocated.
Address: Svetlanskaya St., 5, Владивосток 690091
Phone: +7 423 241-05-26
Website: arkagallery.ru
Email: info@arkagallery.ru
Facebook.com/arkagallery.ru
Instagram.com/arka_gallery
Vk.com/arka_gallery

Moscow
Museum of Calligraphy

Situated in the Sokolniki Part in Moscow, with over 5,000 beautiful and transformational calligraphy masterpieces from 70 countries.
Address: Luchevoy 5-y prosek, 2/1, Sokolniki metro station, Sokolniki Park, Москва 107014
Phone: 8 (495) 728-77-58
Website: calligraphy-museum.com
Email: info@calligraphy-museum.com
Facebook.com/calligraphy.museum
Instagram.com/calligraphy.museum

Ruarts Contemporary Art Gallery

Situated in the historical centre of Moscow.

Focusing on contemporary art from video, digital to experimental media from Russian and international artists.
Address: 1st Zachatyevskiy Lane, 10, Москва 119034
Phone: +7 495 637-44-75
Website: ruarts.ru
Facebook.com/ruartsgallery
Instagram.com/ruartsgallery
YouTube.com/Ruarts Gallery

Art4.ru Contemporary Art Museum

Russia's first private museum of contemporary art with 4 exhibitions each month representing established and emerging Russian artists.
Address: Hlinovskiy Tupik St., 4, Metro Arbatskaya, Москва 143350
Phone: +7 499 136-56-56
Website: art4.ru
Email: k@art4.ru
Facebook.com/Art4.ru
Instagram.com/art4museum
YouTube.com/ART4 Museum

The State Central Museum of Contemporary History of Russia

Established in 1917 with the aim of uniting people of different political persuasions, from progressive scholars, cultural figures, writers, publicists and representatives of the Russian revolutionary liberation movement.
Address: Tverskaya St., 21, Москва 125009
Phone: +7 495 699-67-24
Website: sovrhistory.ru
Email: pressa@sovrhistory.ru Facebook.com/sovr.history
Instagram.com/sovr.history
Ok.ru/group/56003914039307

Murtuz Art Gallery

Contemporary art gallery in Moscow.
Address: Bolshaya Nikitskaya St., 22, Москва 125009
Phone: +7 495 690-31-39
Website: murtuz.ru
Email: murtuz@list.ru

FotoLoft Gallery

Contemporary art gallery in Moscow.
Address: Syromyatnichesky 4th pereulok, d. 1/8, building 6, Москва 105120
Phone: +7 (495) 987-38-74
Website: facebook.com/search/top?q=FotoLoft%20Gallery
Email: tkurtanova@gmail.com

Elena Vrublevskaya Gallery

Contemporary art gallery in Moscow.
Address: Rozhdestvensky bulvar, d. 19, Москва 107045
Phone: +7 495 621-35-86
Website: vgallery.ru

Shazina Gallery

Contemporary art from the late 20th century to early 21st century in many styles, genres and forms.
Address: Maly Vlasyevskiy Ln., 5, Москва 119002
Phone: +7 495 509-83-36
Website: shazina.com
Email: info@shazina.com

Center Mars

A private gallery set up by a group of young and daring artists 30 years ago, to introduce the newest and most advanced contemporary art and to provide a platform for these artists to be viewed. Now seeking to restore the public's interest in art and to prevent art being displaced by technologies.
Address: Pushkaryov Lane, 5, Metro: Tsvetnoy Bulvar, Москва 107045
Phone: +7 495 623-66-90
Website: centermars.ru
Email: admin@centermars.ru
Facebook.com/centermars

Instagram.com/center_mars
Vk.com/centermars
YouTube.com/channel/
UCpVx031p1BIryj1I2LWvjvA/videos

Saint Petersburg
Erata Galleries

Russia's largest private collection of contemporary art, with more than 2,800 works from Russian artists. Over 40 exhibitions a year with international recognition.
Address: 199106, Russia, St. Petersburg, Vasilyevsky Island, 29th Line, House 2, Erarta Museum of Contemporary Art
Phone: + 7 (812) 324 08 09
Website: erarta.com
Email: info@erarta.com
Twitter.com/Erarta_Museum
Facebook.com/errata
Instagram.com/erarta_museum/
Vk.com/errata
YouTube.com/user/Erartamuseum

Mokhovaya 18 Gallery of Contemporary Art

Both emerging and international established Russian artists with monthly exhibitions
Address: Mohovaya ul., d. 18, Санкт-Петербург 191028
Phone: +7 812 275-33-83
Website: russianmuseums.info/M124
Email: info@gm18.ru

D-137 Art Club

Well-known masters and young St Petersburg artists with exhibitions, film shows, concerts and publishing.
Address: Rubinshteina St., 15-17, Санкт-Петербург 191002
Phone: +7 981 687-60-51
Website: d137.ru
Email: info@d137.ru
Facebook.com/D137club
Vk.com/club378698

PRO ARTE Foundation

A non-profit non-governmental organisation, established in 1999, promoting contemporary art and culture. Specialising in visual arts, music, architecture, art journalism and design. Supports artistic projects and organisations, holds exhibitions, festivals, concerts, conferences and lectures.
Address: Peter и Paul Fortress 3, 197046, Russia, Санкт-Петербург
Website: proarte.ru
Email: office@proarte.ru
Facebook.com/proarte.foundation
Instagram.com/proarte_foundation
Vimeo.com/proartefoundation/albums
Vk.com/proarte

Samara
Samara Regional Art Museum

The oldest and most prestigious exhibition venue in the Samara region, located in the historical heart of the city. Collaborating with domestic and foreign museums, cultural centres and collectors.
Address: Kuibysheva St., 92, Metro Moskovskaya, Самара 443099
Phone: +7 846 333-46-50
Website: artmus.ru
Email: office@artmus.ru
Facebook.com/artmus.samara
Vk.com/artmus_samara

Chelyabinsk
Picasso

A Picasso art workshop and network teaching excellent craft skills in ceramics, painting, decorative and applied arts.
Address: ул. Свободы, 141, Челябинск
Phone: +7 351 248-79-06
Website: art74.info
Email: picasso-chel@mail.ru

SAINT HELENA

AERENA Galleries & Gardens

Beautiful venues featuring contemporary art and sculpture, as well as furniture, objects and curiosities from the 18th century to the present with over 100 emerging to internationally renowned artists.
Address: 1354 Main St, St. Helena 94574
Phone: +1 707-963-8800
Website: aerenagalleries.bespokecollection.com
Email: info@aerenagalleries.com
Facebook.com/aerenagalleriesandgardens
Instagram.com/AerenaGalleries

SERBIA AND MONTENEGRO

Niš

Nis Art Gallery

A busy hub for artists and collectors, following contemporary art movements and always open to innovations
Address: Teşvikiye Mahallesi Teşvikiye Fırın Sokak no : 11/A
Phone: 0212 258 00 08 / 0538 240 54 79
Website: nisartgallery.com
Email: info@nisartgallery.com

SINGAPORE

NTU Centre for Contemporary Art

A space for critical discourse and new thinking about contemporary art ecosystems in Singapore and Southeast Asia. Showing leading national and international artists; one of the few places in Singapore to do the latter. A dynamic public program of lectures, workshops, open studios and films
Address: Blk 43 Malan Road Gillman Barracks, Singapore 109443
Phone: +65 6339 6503
Website: ntu.ccasingapore.org
Email: ntuccaexhibitions@ntu.edu.sg

Pop And Contemporary Fine Art

Original paintings, limited edition lithographs, screenprints, etching and sculpture in the contemporary and pop art genres.
Address: 350 Orchard Road Shaw House, Tong Building #07-03, Singapore 238862
Phone: +65 6735 0959
Website: popandcontemporaryart.com
Email: contact@popandcontemporaryart.com
Twitter.com/POPSingapore
Facebook.com/PopandContemporaryFineArt
Instagram.com/popartsg

Art-2 Gallery

Contemporary art gallery and art consultants, specialising in sculpture, painting and ceramics with bold exhibitions. Advising on public art, publicity and media relations as well as art collections, exhibitions and other visual art-related events.
Address: 140 Hill Street, Singapore 179369
Phone: +65 6338 8713
Website: art2.com.sg
Email: art@art2.com.sg
Facebook.com/art2gallery
Instagram.com/art2.gallery

Art Season Gallery

Exploring and promoting emerging contemporary Chinese and Asian artists for more than 10 years.
Address: 200 Middle Rd, #01-02, Big Hotel, Singapore 188980
Phone: +65 6741 6366
Website: artseasonsgallery.com
Facebook.com/artseasonsgallery
Instagram.com/artseasonssg

Ipreciation Art Gallery

A fine art company that showcases the best modern and contemporary Asian art, propelling significant and promising artists to the forefront though large-scale exhibitions and installations in public and commercial spaces nationally and globally.

Address: 1 Fullerton Square, Singapore 049178

Phone: +65 6339 0678

Website: ipreciation.com

Email: enquiry@ipreciation.com

Facebook.com/iPRECIATION

Instagram.com/ipreciation

LinkedIn.com/company/ipreciation

YouTube.com/channel/ UC7cdimHs1U8h96Srjzu7vQA/featured

Polar Bear Gallery

Internationally recognised contemporary artists with 10% of profits going to environmentally-related bodies;art reconnects us with nature.

Address: 69a Haji Ln, Singapore 189262

Phone: +65 9169 4880

Website: contemporaryart.com.sg

Email: info@contemporaryart.com.sg

Art Plural Gallery

A unique contemporary art gallery in the heart of the cultural district, with 12,000 square feet of exhibition space across 4 floors. Leading international artists and a significant destination for art collectors worldwide.

Address: 38 Armenian Street, Singapore 179942

Phone: +65 6636 8360

Website: artpluralgallery.com

Email: info@artpluralgallery.com

Instagram.com/artpluralgallery

LinkedIn.com/company/art-plural-gallery

YouTube.com/user/artpluralgallery

Ode To Art

An international array of artists working in paintings, sculptures, photography and installation as well as emerging artists who show international promise. Art consultancy, talks and exhibitions and a love of contemporary art.

Address: Blk 252, North Bridge Rd, #01-36E/F, Raffles City Shopping Centre, Singapore 179109

Phone: +65 6250 1901

Website: odetoart.com

Email: info@odetoart.com

Facebook.com/odetoart.gallery

Instagram.com/odetoartgallery

SLOVAKIA

Bratislava

DOT. Contemporary Art Gallery

Young, emerging artists with authentic content and expression.

Address: Lazaretska 13, DOT. Gallery and Espresso Bar, Bratislava 811 08

Phone: +421 948 663 007

Website: dotgallery.sk

Email: info@dotgallery.sk

Facebook.com/DOT. ContemporaryArtGallery

Instagram.com/dot.gallery

YouTube.com/playlist?list=PLsn4jI3-eM0BcZ_xPthCE5r33qIxPf8hU

SODA gallery - gallery of contemporary art

Contemporary art gallery focusing on a new generation of national, Central and Eastern European emerging artists. Innovative and pioneering exhibitions, with a variety of media and genres.

Address: Skolska 9, Bratislava 81107

Phone: +421 907 853 562

Website: sodagallery.sk

Email: info@sodagallery.sk

Twitter.com/GallerySODA

Facebook.com/SODAgallery

Instagram.com/sodagallery

White & Weiss Contemporary Art Gallery

Exhibiting paintings, sculpture and objects with the most progressive Slovak and Central European artists. 7 exhibitions a year with bilingual publications.
Address: Grosslingova 50, Bratislava 81109
Phone: +421 911 760 651
Website: whiteweiss.com
Email: gallery@whiteweiss.com
Facebook.com/whiteweiss
Instagram.com/whiteweiss_contemporaryart

SLOVENIA

Ljubljana
Museum of Contemporary Art Metelkova (MSUM)

The national institution for modern and contemporary art. Exhibiting 20th Slovene art as well as new contemporary work with a research and educational element.
Address: Tomshicheva ulica 14, Ljubljana 1000
Phone: +386 1 241 68 00
Website: mg-lj.si
Email: info@mg-lj.si
Twitter.com/MGplusMSUM
Facebook.com/MGplusMSUM
Instagram.com/mgplusmsum
YouTube.com/channel/
UCWLuMn0OPNLC1l0YQcxyqDQ

Celje
Gallery of Contemporary Art

Set in the Prince's Mansion this gallery shows major exhibitions of domestic and international art, both contemporary and from recent history.
Address: Trg celjskih knezov 8, Celje 3000
Phone: +386 3 426 51 56
Website: celje.si/en/card/gallery-contemporary-art
Email: centersodobnihumetnosti@celje.si

SOUTH AFRICA

Cape Town
Zeitz Museum Of Contemporary Art Africa (MOCAA)

A public, not-for-profit institution exhibiting, collecting, preserving and researching contemporary African art and its diaspora. Encouraging intercultural understanding and hosting international exhibitions, with educational programs.
Address: South Arm Rd, Cape Town 8001
Phone: +27 87 350 4777
Website: zeitzmocaa.museum
Email: info@zeitzmocaa.museum
Twitter.com/ZeitzMOCAA
Facebook.com/ZeitzMOCAA
Instagram.com/zeitzmocaa

State Of The ART

Selected emerging and mid-career artists from across South Africa. Modern and contemporary art in a variety of mediums. A percentage from each sale goes towards the State of the Art Gallery Award, which promotes emerging artists.
Address: 19 Adderley St, Cape Town 8000
Phone: +27 21 801 4710
Website: stateoftheart-gallery.com
Email: hello@stateoftheart-gallery.com
Twitter.com/JenniferatSOTA
Facebook.com/galleryStateoftheART
Instagram.com/stateofthe_art
Pinterest.co.uk/stateoftheart
LinkedIn.com/company/stateoftheartgalleryYouTube.com/user/JenniferatSOTA

Worldart Gallery

Contemporary art with a leaning towards urban and pop art.
Address: 54 Church St, Cape Town 8001
Phone: +27 21 423 3075
Website: worldart.co.za
Email: charl@worldart.co.za
Twitter.com/worldartsa

Facebook.com/worldartafrica
Instagram.com/worldartgallery
YouTube.com/user/worldartgallerySA

Johannesburg

Johannesburg Art Gallery

The biggest gallery on the sub-continent, located in the business district of Johannesburg. With only 10% of exhibits on display, ranging from artefacts, sculptures, drawings, paintings, prints and lacework. 19th century and contemporary South African art.
Address: Cnr Klein and King George Streets, Joubert Park, Johannesburg, 2044
Phone: +27 11 725 3130
Website: friendsofjag.org
Email: friend@friendsofjag.org
Twitter.com/friendsofjag
Facebook.com/FriendsofJAG
Instagram.com/friendsofjag

Gallery MOMO

Contemporary art with a strong creative and intellectual platform showing South African, continental and international art with a residency program for curators and artists aiming at developing dialogue and cooperation between artists from different parts of the world.
Address: 52 7th Ave., Parktown North 2094
Phone: +27 11 327 3247
Website: gallerymomo.com
Email:odysseus@gallerymomo.com
Twitter.com/gallerymomosa
Facebook.com/GalleryMOMOSA
Instagram.com/gallerymomo

Art on Paper

Contemporary art by young and established South African artists.
Address: 44 Stanley Ave, Milpark 2001
Phone: +27 11 726 2234
Website: artonpaper.co.za
Email: info@artonpaper.co.za

Facebook.com/galleryaop
Instagram.com/galleryaop

Art Eye Gallery

Emerging and mid-career contemporary artists with a global vision and understanding of client's needs and expectations. Specialising in building collection, with pieces that seldom come to market.
Address: Fourways Value Mart Centre, Forest Drive, Lone Hill, Houghton Estate 2062
Phone: +27 71 386 2198
Website: arteye.co.za
Email: submissions@arteye.co.za
Facebook.com/arteyegallery
Instagram.com/arteyegallery
YouTube.com/channel/
UC8m2irXoCTD6TQDuBuYYY7g

Afronova

Exhibitions from artists around Africa, the Indian Ocean and the Caribbean's. Performances, book launches and readings, fashion shows, screenings, gatherings and artist residences, the gallery is a polyphonic platform for African contemporary expression.
Address: Gwigwi Mrwebi St, East London 2001
Phone: +27 83 726 5906
Website: afronova.com
Email: afronova@tiscali.co.za
Facebook.com/afronovagallery
Instagram.com/afronovagallery

Goodman Gallery

Since 1966, an international contemporary art gallery with locations in Johannesburg, Cape Town and London representing artists whose work confronts entrenched power structures and inspires social change.
Address: 163 Jan Smuts Ave, Parkwood, Johannesburg
Phone: +27 72 907 5795

Email: camilla@goodman-gallery.com
Address: 3rd Floor Fairweather House
176 Sir Lowry Rd, Woodstock, Cape Town
Phone: +27 72 018 1293
Email: tony@goodman-gallery.com
Address: 26 Cork Street, London W1S 3ND
Phone: +44 7734 923150
Email: jo@goodman-galleryuk.com
Website: goodman-gallery.com
Twitter.com/Goodman_Gallery
Facebook.com/GoodmanGallery
Instagram.com/goodman_gallery
Artsy.net/goodman-gallery

Berman Contemporary

Representing the growing understanding of
the cultural richness and diversity of South
African contemporary art focusing on a
group of artists living and working in the
country.
Address: 11 Alice Ln, Johannesburg 2196
Phone: +27 11 880 2580
Website: bermancontemporary.com
Email:gallery@ermancontemporary.co.za
Facebook.com/BermanContemporary
Instagram.com/bermancontemporary

Warren Siebrits Modern & Contemporary Art

Modern and contemporary art gallery.
Address: 140 Jan Smuts Ave, Parkwood
2193
Phone: +27 11 327 0000
Website: warrensiebrits.co.za
Email: enquiries@warrensiebrits.co.za

Pretoria
Pretoria Kunskamer Art Gallery and Gift Shop

Specialising in SA masters and contemporary
art. Sources and commissions paintings and
sculpture in various media with a wide price
range.
Address: 63 George Storrar Drive,
Groenkloof, Pretoria 0181
Phone: +27 12 346 0728

Website: pretoriakunskamer.co.za
Email: info@pretoriakunskamer.co.za

Magnolia Dell Open Air Art Exhibition

Promoting young artists and enjoying the
work of more established ones. Regular
exhibitions of classic and contemporary
pieces exhibiting only the finest and often
thought-provoking work.
Address: Magnolia Dell Park, Queen
Wilheliminia St, Pretoria 0002
Phone: +27 71 676 3600
Website: artspta.co.za
Email:artspta@mweb.co.za

Port Elizabeth
Underculture Contemporary

Catering for a culturally aware, discerning
audience, whilst developing powerful, new,
captivating and relevant artists.
Address: 98A Park Dr, Port Elizabeth 6001
Phone: +27 41 373 0074
Website: undercultureconttemporary.co.za

Galerie Noko

Creating an integrated dialogue of cultures
between international, national and local
artists. Also acting as an art advisory and
consultancy. Performance art, installations,
video installations and a dedicated ceramic
exhibition space. Artist residency. Showing
contemporary, modern and abstract art.
Address: 109 Russell Road, Port Elizabeth,
Port Elizabeth 6390
Phone: +27 41 582 2090
Website: galerienoko.com
Email: galerienoko@gmail.com
Twitter.com/galerienoko
Facebook.com/GalerieNOKO
Instagram.com/galerienoko
LinkedIn.com/company/galerie-noko

Bloemfontein

Gallery on Leviseur

Art from contemporary South African artists.
Address: 59 General Dan Pienaar Dr,
Bloemfontein 9301
Phone: +27 82 835 2335
Website: galleryonleviseur.co.za
Email: curator@galleryonleviseur.co.za
Facebook.com/galleryonleviseur

Kotze Kunsgalery / Art Gallery

South African artists including some Old
Masters. Can source work on request.
Address: 44 Genl Dan Pienaar Dr,
Bloemfontein 9301
Phone: +27 82 785 4995
Website: kotzekuns.co.za
Email: info@kotzekuns.co.za

SPAIN

Madrid

Alcion Art Gallery

Reproductions of paintings from the 14th to
middle of 20th century.
Address: Calle Orellana 14, (esquina
Argensola), Madrid 28004
Phone: +34 913 193 037
Website: alcionart.com
Email: info@alcionart.com

Rompar Contemporary Art

Investigating new languages in contemporary
art between the boundaries of conceptual
and minimal art. Representing young and
mid-career artists with 8 exhibitions and
6 international art fairs a year. Since 2013,
the gallery hosts site specific projects in the
heart of rural Ibiza with the aim of creating
a point of encounter and reunion for artists,
curators, museums and friends
Address: Calle Claudio Coello, 14 - BJ,
Madrid 28001
Phone: +34 915 762 813

Website: parra-romero.com
Email: info@parra-romero.com
Twitter.com/parraromerogal
Facebook.com/parraromero
Instagram.com/parraromero

La Fiambrera Art Gallery

Promoting more than 20 national and
international artists with artistic currents
linked to Pop Art, Urban Art, Illustration
and Pop Surrealism.
Address: Calle del Pez # 7, Madrid 28004
Phone: +34 917 046 030
Website: lafiambrera.net
Email: info@lafiambrera.net
Twitter.com/lafiambrerapez7
Facebook.com/lafiambrera
Instagram.com/lafiambrera
Pinterest.es/lafiambrera
YouTube.com/channel/UC_Yb-
hIrtryBOvnPwg_8JzQ

Galería Alegría

Contemporary art gallery in Madrid.
Address: Doctor Fourquet, 35, Madrid
28012
Phone: +34 912 122 526
Website: galeriaalegria.es
Email: sebas@galeriaalegria.es

Sabrina Amrani Gallery

Contemporary art gallery in Madrid.
Address: Calle Madera 23, Madrid 28004
Phone: +34 627 539 884
Website: sabrinaamrani.com
Email: hello@sabrinaamrani.com
Twitter.com/sabrinaamrani
Facebook.com/sabrinaamraniartgallery
Instagram.com/sabrinaamrani
Weibo.com/p/1005057049552338

Madrid Slaughterhouse

A former slaughterhouse converted into
an arts centre reflecting the contemporary
sociocultural environment and support

processes to build the culture of today and tomorrow. A lab for experimentation and promoting new cross-disciplinary formulae.
Address: Legazpi square, 8, Madrid 28045
Phone: +34 915 177 309
Website: en.wikipedia.org

Distrito 4

Contemporary art gallery in Madrid.
Address: Calle conde de aranda 4, Madrid 28001
Phone: +34 913 198 583
Website: distrito4.com

Modern Art Museum of Madrid

Address: Conde Duque st. 9, Madrid 28015
Phone: +34 915 885 928
Website: en.wikipedia.org

Barcelona

Barcelona Museum of Contemporary Art

Provoking enjoyment and interest in contemporary art and culture through the transformative will and impact of people and society.
Address: Plaça dels Àngels, 1, Barcelona 08001
Phone: +34 934 813 368
Website: macba.es/es/inicio
Email: comunicacio@macba.cat
Twitter.com/MACBA_Barcelona
Facebook.com/MACBA.Barcelona
Instagram.com/macba_barcelona
Flickr.com/photos/macba
YouTube.com/user/MACBAwebmaster

Valencia

Valencian Modern Art Institute

Modern and contemporary art museum.
Address: Guillem de Castro, 118, Valencia 46003
Phone: +34 963 176 600
Website: ivam.es
Email: ivam@ivam.es

Twitter.com/gva_IVAM
Facebook.com/gvaIVAM
Instagram.com/gva_ivam
YouTube.com/channel/UCAwyt1_MtPkdCOL427Lsm6w

Sevilla

Andalusian Center for Contemporary Art

Address: Avenida Americo Vespucio, 2, Seville 41092
Phone: +34 955 037 070
Website: caac.es
Email: informacion.caac@juntadeandalucia.es

AJG Contemporary Gallery

Dedicated to promoting the work of leading contemporary artists, encouraging innovation and talent from a new generation of artists from around the world.
Address: c/ Pasaje Francisco Molina, 17 (Pasaje Villasis), Sevilla 41003
Phone: +34 676 460 143
Website: ajggallery.com
Email: info@ajggallery.com

Zaragoza

Museo Pablo Serrano

Contemporary art gallery.
Address: Paseo Maria Agustin 20, Zaragoza 50004
Phone: +34 976 280 659
Website: iaacc.es
Email: difusionmpabloserrano@aragon.es

Malaga

Centro de Arte Contemporáneo de Málaga

A cultural initiative of the City Council of Malaga, promoting and disseminating 20th and 21st century visual art with the aim of becoming an international reference point.
Address: C/ Alemania, s/n, Málaga 29001
Phone: +34 952 208 500
Website: cacmalaga.eu
Email: cacmalaga@cacmalaga.eu
Twitter.com/cacmalaga

Facebook.com/cacmalaga
Instagram.com/cacmalaga
Flickr.com/photos/124836540@N03/sets

Gran Canaria
Atlantic Center of Modern Art

Energising visual arts, critical thinking and artistic culture with a purpose of intercultural dialogue within the framework of Atlantic geostrategy.
Address: Los Balcones, 11, Las Palmas de Gran Canaria 35001
Phone: +34 928 311 800
Website: caam.net
Email: amig@s del caam
Twitter.com/CAAMgrancanaria
Facebook.com/CentroAtlanticoArteModerno
Instagram.com/caamgrancanaria
YouTube.com/user/caamlpa

Galeria De Arte Saro Leon

Formed to serve as a meeting point and platform for artists from the Canary Islands as well as those with Latin America, African, and European origins, taking into account the geographical-cultural reality of the Canary Islands.
Address: Calle Villavicencio16, LAS Palmas DE Gran Canari 35002
Phone: +34 928 384 264
Website: galeriasaroleon.com
Email: info@galeriasaroleon.com
Facebook.com/Galería-de-Arte-Saro-León

Bilbao
Guggenheim Museum Bilbao

Modern and contemporary art.
Address: Abandoibarra Avenue, 2, Bilbao 48009
Phone: +34 944 359 000
Website: guggenheim-bilbao.eus
Email: contacto@guggenheim-bilbao.eus
Twitter.com/MuseoGuggenheim

Facebook.com/guggenheimbilbaomuseo
Instagram.com/museoguggenheim
Flickr.com/photos/34323586@N06
YouTube.com/user/guggenheimbilbao2009

Carreras Mugica

Contemporary art gallery.
Address: 2 Calle de Heros, Bilbao 48009
Phone: +34 944 234 725
Website: carrerasmugica.com
Email: info@carrerasmugica.com
Facebook.com/CarrerasMugica
Instagram.com/carrerasmugica

Bilbao Fine Arts Museum

Contemporary art museum.
Address: Museo Plaza, 2, Bilbao 48009
Phone: +34 944 396 060
Website: museobilbao.com
Twitter.com/museobilbao
Facebook.com/museobilbao
Instagram.com/museobilbao

SRI LANKA
Indika Art Gallery

Living and working in the beautiful fishing village of Tangalla, Indika Pathmananda is Sri Lanka's leading young artists, winning many awards and exhibiting in the National Art Gallery. Painting exquisite wildlife, landscapes and energetic modern abstracts.
Address: Medilla, Tangalle, Sri Lanka, Tangalle 82200
Phone: +94 77 790 3253
Website: dittmer.force9.co.uk
Email: magnetco@sltnet.lk

SWAZILAND
Yebo Contemporary Art Gallery Eswatini

Showcasing the best of contemporary art and design whilst breaking away from stereotypes of African art. Working with talented

professionals and emerging artists giving them domestic and international recognition.
Address: Mpumalanga Crescent, Lobamba H106
Phone: +268 2416 2984
Website: yeboswaziland.com
Email: armstrongaleta@gmail.com
Facebook.com/yebodesigns
Instagram.com/yeboartdesign

SWEDEN

Stockholm

Magasin III Museum for Contemporary Art

One of Europe's leading contemporary art institutions.
Address: Frihamnsgatan 28, Stockholm 115 56
Phone: +46 8 545 680 40
Website: magasin3.com
Email: info@magasin3.com
Twitter.com/magasin3
Facebook.com/magasin3

Wetterling Galleri

A leading contemporary art gallery in Scandinavia with a dynamic program of highly acclaimed international artists and young emerging artists from Sweden. Unable to accept unsolicited approaches.
Address: Kungsträdgården 3, Stockholm 111 47
Phone: +46 8 10 10 09
Website: wetterlinggallery.com
Email: bjorn@wetterlinggallery.com
Facebook.com/wetterlinggallery
Instagram.com/wetterlinggallery
Artsy.net/wetterling-gallery

Young Art

Highlighting the new generation of artists and challenging the boundaries of the traditional art market.
Address: Karlavägen 5, Stockholm 114 24
Phone: +46 73 753 59 99

Website: youngart.se
Email: antonia@youngart.se
Facebook.com/loveyoungart
Instagram.com/loveyoungart

Bonniers Konsthall

Swedish and international contemporary art in central Stockholm.
Address: 19 Torsgatan, Stockholm 113 21
Phone: +46 8 736 42 55
Website: bonnierskonsthall.se
Email: info@bonnierskonsthall.se
Twitter.com/bonnierskonsth
Facebook.com/BonniersKonsthall
Instagram.com/bonnierskonsthall

Gothenburg

Goteborgs Konsthall

Contemporary art and a wide range of programs for all ages.
Address: Gotaplatsen, Gothenburg 412 56
Phone: +46 31 368 34 50
Website: konsthallen.goteborg.se
Email: goteborgs.konsthall@kultur.goteborg.se
Facebook.com/goteborgskonsthall
Instagram.com/goteborgskonsthall

SWITZERLAND

Zurich

Kunsthaus Artes

International exhibitions and one of the largest art collections in Switzerland, from the 13th century to the present. Sponsored by Zurich Art Society, which is one of the biggest art associations in Europe, with around 19,000 members.
Address: Heimplatz 1, 8001 Zurich
Phone: +41 44 253 84 84
Website: kunsthaus.ch
Email: info@kunsthaus-artes.de

Geneva
Centre d'Art Contemporain

Contemporary art gallery in Geneva.
Address: Rue des Vieux-Grenadiers 10,
Genf 1205
Phone: +41 22 329 18 42
Website: centre.ch
Email: marie.debat@centre.ch
Instagram.com/
centredartcontemporaingeneve

Patrick Cramer Galerie

Set in Geneva's art district, specialising
in Chinese contemporary art, whilst
also representing the most exciting and
progressive work from around the world.
Address: Rue de Chantepoulet 13, Genf
1201
Phone: +41 22 732 54 32
Website: cramer.ch
Email: maxime.lassagne@centre.ch

Ribordy Contemporary SARL

Working closely with selected artists,
bringing them to a local and international
audience. Not reviewing unsolicited artist's
submissions.
Address: Rue de Monthoux 12, CH-1201
Geneva
Phone: +41 (0)223217563
Website: ribordythetaz.com
Email: office@ribordythetaz.com
Instagram.com/ribordythetaz

MAMCO – Musée d'Art Moderne et Contemporain, Genève

Mainly working on art from the 1960s in a
3,500m² space – the largest contemporary art
gallery in Switzerland.
Address: Rue des Vieux-Grenadiers 10,
Genf 1205
Phone: +41 22 320 61 22
Website: mamco.ch
Email: info@mamco.ch
Twitter.com/mamco_artmuseum

Facebook.com/mamcogeneve
Instagram.com/mamco_geneve

Jancou Contemporary Art SARL

Residences, solo exhibitions, publications
and collaborations with creative
organisations and institutions - supporting
established and emerging artists
Address: Rue des Bains 63, Genf 1205
Phone: +41 22 321 11 00
Website: marcjancou.com
Email: office@marcjancou.com
Twitter.com/marcjancou
Instagram.com/marcjancoucontemporary

Galerie Daniel Varenne SA

Contemporary art gallery.
Address: Rue Rodolphe-Toepffer 8, Genf
1206
Phone: +41 22 789 16 75
Website: varenne.ch
Email: daniel@varenne.ch

Artvera's

Specialising in master of modern and
contemporary art.
Address: Rue Etienne-Dumont 1, Genf
1204
Phone: +41 22 311 05 53
Website: artveras.com
Email: info@artveras.com
Facebook.com/artverasgallery

Lausanne
Mudac – Museum of Contemporary Design and Applied Arts

Opened in 2000, with an ambitious program
of 5-8 exhibitions each year, bringing together
design with applied and contemporary art
as well as frequent new exhibitions from
the permanent collection. Also showing
performing arts, from dancers to film,
music and performers creating a dialogue
between diverse art forms on a national and
international level.

Address: place de la Cathedrale 6, Lausanne 1005
Phone: +41 21 315 25 30
Website: mudac.ch
Email: info@mudac.ch
Facebook.com/mudac.design.museum
Instagram.com/mudaclausanne

Dubner Moderne

Represents established and emerging contemporary artists who are defining the art scene of today and tomorrow. Solo and group exhibitions. International art fairs. Exhibits work of all mediums, including paintings, photography, sculpture and limited edition prints, with work in private collections and museums throughout the world.
Address: Rue du Grand-Chêne 6, Lausanne 1003
Phone: +41 79 242 78 01
Website: dubnermoderne.ch
Email: art@dubnermoderne.com
Facebook.com/dubnermoderne
Instagram.com/dubnermoderne

Circuit Association d'Art comtemporain

Contemporary art.
Address: Avenue de Montchoisi 9, Lausanne 1006
Phone: +41 21 601 41 70
Website: circuit.li
Email: contact@circuit.li

Galerie Kissthedesign, Design du XXe et Contemporain

A cultural concept store, mixing valuable modern design with contemporary art.
Address: Avenue de Rumine 4, Lausanne 1005
Phone: +41 21 312 14 80
Website: kissthedesign.ch
Email: info@kissthedesign.ch

Bern
Contemporary Art Gallery (Kunsthalle Bern)

Institution for contemporary art founded in 1918.
Address: Helvetiaplatz 1, Bern 3005
Phone: +41 31 350 00 40
Website: kunsthalle-bern.ch
Email: info@kunsthalle-bern.ch
Facebook.com/kunsthallebern
Instagram.com/kunsthallebern

Muster-Meier - Contemporary Fine Art & Projects

Art Gallery based in Bern representing international and Swiss artists.
Address: Brunngasse 14 | Brunngasshalde 31, Bern
Phone: +41 78 849 46 66
Website: muster-meier.gmbh
Facebook.com/mmcontemp
Instagram.com/mmcontemp

Lucerne
Galerie Müller

Contemporary art gallery.
Address: Haldenstrasse 7, Luzern 6006
Phone: +41 41 410 75 74
Website: galeriemueller.ch
Email: galeriemueller@gmx.net

St. Gallen
Kunstmuseum St.Gallen

A broad collection of art from the Middle Ages to the present day.
Address: Museumstrasse 32, St. Gallen 9000
Phone: +41 71 242 06 71
Website: kunstmuseumsg.ch
Email: kunstzone.lokremise@kunstmuseumsg.ch
Twitter.com/KunstmuseumSG
Facebook.com/kunstmuseumsg.ch
Instagram.com/kunstmuseumsg
YouTube.com/channel/UCLVncFqxmqDxk00_XCa-ZyQ?

Galerie Eule-Art

Contemporary art gallery in St Gallen.
Address: Spisergasse 28, Sankt Gallen 9000
Phone: +41 71 222 50 51
Website: eule-art.ch

Macelleria d'Arte

Contemporary art gallery in St Gallen.
Address: Gartenstrasse 11, Sankt Gallen 9000
Phone: +41 71 220 10 35
Website: macelleria-darte.ch
Email: francesco.bonanno@macelleria-darte.ch
Facebook.com/macelleriadartestgallen

Auktionshaus u. Galerie

International art auctions of paintings,
drawing and sculptures by various artists of
different periods.
Address: Löwengasse 3, Sankt Gallen 9000
Phone: +41 71 223 35 81
Website: galeriewidmer.com
Email: info@galeriewidmer.com
Twitter.com/BBWAuktionen
Facebook.comBeurretBaillyWidmerAuktionen
Instagram.com/beurretbaillywidmer

Lugano
Fafa Fine Art Gallery

Specialising in national and international
modern art, as well as exhibiting contemp-
orary work.
Address: Via della Posta 2, Lugano 6900
Phone: +41 79 337 10 81
Website: fafafineart.com
Email: info@fafafineart.com
Twitter.com/FafaGallery
Instagram.com/fafafineartgallery

Five Gallery

Showing masters from the 1970s and 80s as
well as the innovative international creativity
of young talent.
Address: via Canova 7, Lugano 6900
Phone: +41 91 921 11 00
Website: fivegallery.ch

Email: info@fivegallery.ch
Facebook.com/fivegallerylugano
Instagram.com/five_gallery
Pinterest.it/fivegallery

Cortesi Contemporary Lugano

Based in Lugano, London and Milan.
Specialising in European art from the 1950s
to the present. Collaborating widely with
curators, researchers, artists' archives and
foundations.
Address: Via Carlo Frasca 5, Lugano 6900
Phone: +41 91 92 14 000
Email: info@cortesigallery.com
Facebook.com/cortesigallery
Instagram.com/cortesigallery
Artsy.net/cortesi-gallery

De Primi Fine Art

Swiss art gallery dealing in objects d'art,
old masters, modern and contemporary art
offering consultation and advice.
Address: Piazza Cioccaro 2, Lugano 6900
Phone: +41 91 923 48 33
Website: it.deprimi.ch
Email: info@deprimi.ch
Twitter.com/DePrimiFineArt
Facebook.com/deprimifineart
Pinterest.it/deprimifineart

TAIWAN
Modern Art Gallery

Promoting Chinese and international artists
both classic and modern.
Address: online only
Phone: +886 4 9277 3315
Website: smagtw.org
Email: smagtw@yahoo.com.tw
Facebook.com/smagtw
Instagram.com/modernartgallerytw

TAJIKISTAN
Dvael Gallery of Contemporary Art

Contemporary art gallery in Tajikistan.
Address: Dostoevskogo ul., d. 1A, skver
Flora, Омськ 644000
Phone: +7 381 224-61-44

THAILAND
Bangkok

Duke Contemporary Art Space.
Contemporary art in Bangkok.
Address: 999 Phloen Chit Rd, 1st Floor,
Gaysorn Village, Bangkok 10330
Phone: +66 94 647 8888

Museum of Contemporary Art (MOCA)

Museum of Contemporary Art Bangkok.
Address: 499, Kamphaengpet 6th Road, Lad
Yao, Chatuchak, Bangkok 10900
Phone: +66 2 016 5666
Website: mocabangkok.com
Email: info@mocabangkok.com
Instagram.com/mocabangkok
YouTube.com/channel/
UCWkn5Vw97iyB6txWqi0yMPw

TURKEY
Istanbul
Anna Laudel Contemporary

An historic building with 5 floors of
exhibition space, hosting national and
international exhibitions, with workshops
and discussions. Giving emerging young
artists a platform. Taking established artists
to international art fairs. Shop selling prints,
photographs, sculptures, ceramics and
art journals. Opened a second gallery in
Düsseldorf in 2019.
Address: Bankalar Caddesi 10, Karakoy,
Beyoglu, Istanbul

Phone: +90 212 243 32 57
Website: annalaudel.gallery
Email: info@annalaudel.gallery
Twitter.com/laudelgallery
Facebook.com/annalaudel.gallery
Instagram.com/annalaudel.gallery

Elgiz Ça da Sanat Müzesi

Private Contemporary Art Collection.
Address: Sarıyer 34485
Phone: +90 212 290 25 25
Website: elgizmuseum.org
Email: info@elgizmuseumistanbul.org
Twitter.com/ElgizMuseum
Facebook.com/elgizmuseum
Instagram.com/elgizmuseum
Pinterest.co.uk/elgizmuseum

ArtSumer

Contemporary art gallery in Istanbul.
Address: Kemankes Mah. Mumhane Cad.
No: 46, Karaköy, Beyoğlu, Istanbul 34425
Phone: +90 212 251 60 89
Website: artsumer.com
Email: info@artsumer.com
Instagram.com/artsumergallery

PG Art Gallery

One of the first contemporary art galleries
in Turkey, established in 1993. Developing
grassroots artists to gain national recognition.
Now taking work to international art fairs.
Address: Bogazkesen Cad. No:76/B,
Tophane, Beyoglu, Istanbul
Phone: +90 212 263 33 90
Website: pgartgallery.com
Email: info@pgartgallery.com
Twitter.com/pgartgallery
Facebook.com/pgartgallery1
Instagram.com/pgartgallery
YouTube.com/channel/
UCiO8i0w6SA6KlmvxeStHHAg

Gama Gallery

Frequent exhibitions of painting, multimedia

art, conceptual art and performance, with established and emerging European, North American and Turkish artists creating an exchange of cultural ideas and nuances.
Address: TurnacIbasI sok. No: 21, Beyoglu, Istanbul 34433
Phone: +90 212 245 69 22
Website: gamagallery.com
Email: gama@gamagallery.com
Facebook.com/gamaistanbul
Instagram.com/gamagallery
YouTube.com/channel/
UCZTSrtDPTpBSx59drcTGKhA

Borusan Contemporary

Contemporary art gallery in Istanbul.
Address: Baltalimani Hisar Street, Perili Kosk No:5, Sariyer, Istanbul 34470
Phone: +90 212 393 52 00
Website: borusancontemporary.com
Email: info@borusancontemporary.com
Twitter.com/borusancontempo
Facebook.com/BorusanContemporary
Instagram.com/borusancontemporary
YouTube.com/channel/
UCgFq4iyavjq9aOHLGMboshw

Ankara
Cermodern

A contemporary art institution, creating collaborations between the mind and spirit.
Address: Sağlık Mithatpaşa Caddesi, Çankaya 06420
Phone: +90 312 310 00 00
Website: cermodern.org
Email: info@cerrmodern.org
Twitter.com/cermodern
Facebook.com/cermodern06
Instagram.com/cermodern

Izmir
Izmir Museum of Arts & Sculpture

Established in 1952, the museum was later moved from the Kültürpark to its present location on Atatürk Boulevard near the Konak pier. The small museum displays mostly 20th-century paintings and sculptures from Turkish artists, and has a substantial collection of works by Turgut Pura.
Address: Mithat Pasa Cad. No:94 Konak Merkez, Konak, Izmir
Phone: +90 232 482 03 93
Website: guzelsanatlar.gov.tr

UKRAINE
Tsekh Art Gallery

Working with dozens of artists within the international art community, with painting, watercolour, sculpture as well as objects, installations, space decisions, new media etc. Opened a second gallery, Tsekh Vilnius in Vilnius, Lithuania.
Address: Kyrylivska vul. 69, Kiev 04080
Phone: +380 63 131 9481
Website: tsekh.com.ua
Email: zeh.gallery@gmail.com

M17 Contemporary Art Center

Offering art consulting, commissioning, exhibition and participation in art fairs and auctions, promotion in the media and with museums and galleries and a guide to important happening in the local and international art scene.
Address: Gorkogo Street 102 - 104, Kiev
Phone: +380 67 310 6631
Website: m17.kiev.ua
Email: artcenter.m17@gmail.com
Facebook.com/ArtCultFoundation
YouTube.com/user/ArtCultFund

Lviv
Contemporary Sacred Art Gallery Iconart

Sacred icon art from contemporary artists around the Ukraine.
Address: Virmentska St., 26, Lviv 79008
Phone: +380 322 355 295

Website: iconart.com.ua
Email: gallery@iconart.com.ua

UNITED ARAB EMIRATES

Abu Dhabi
Guggenheim Abu Dhabi

A pre-eminent platform for contemporary art, from the 1960s to the present day. A catalyst for scholarship in a variety of fields, particularly the study of history of art in the Middle East in the 20th and 21st centuries. Currently in development.

1x1 Art Gallery

Presenting Indian modern and contemporary art for over 20 years. Collaborating widely with local and international galleries, art fairs and museums. More recently showing Middle East-based artists.
Address: Al Fahad Complex Street 8, Dubai, United Arab Emirates
Phone : +971 (04) 3411287
Website: 1x1artgallery.com
Email: info@1x1gallery.com
Facebook.com/1X1artgalleryuae
Instagram.com/1x1artgallery

Carbon 12

International Contemporary art gallery in Dubai/UAE/Middle-East.
Address: Al Quoz, Dubai
Phone: +971 4 340 6016
Website: carbon12.art
Email: info@carbon12dubai.com
Twitter.com/carbon12gallery
Facebook.com/Carbon12gallery
Instagram.com/carbon12gallery

Alif Art Gallery

A gallery promoting Central Asia's contemporary visual arts, from emerging to mid-market artists across a variety of media with a special focus on Uzbekistan.

Cultivating the dialogue between Central Asia and the Middle East.
Address: Unit 18, P4 Level, Damac Park Towers, DIFC, Dubai 123696
Phone: +971 4 385 9897
Website: andakulova.com
Email: info@andakulova.com

Art Space

Contemporary art gallery in Dubai.
Address: The Gate Village Building 3, Level 2, DIFC, Dubai 506759
Phone: +971 4 323 0820 / +971 50 557 7267
Website: tabariartspace.com
Email: info@tabariartspace.com

The Mojo Gallery

A focal point in a multifunctional artspace, that brings together art, design and new media.
Address: Unit 33 Al Serkal Avenue, Dubai
Phone: +971 (0)4 3477 388
Website: themojogallery.com
Email: gallery@mojo-me.com
Facebook.com/TheMojoGalleryDubai

UNITED STATES OF AMERICA

Akron, Ohio
Akron Art Museum

Modern and contemporary art, showcasing regional, national and international work since 1850, with a strong focus on contemporary painting, sculpture and photography. Nearly 12 exhibitions each year, educational programs and public art projects.
Address: 1 S High St, Akron 44308
Phone: +1 (330) 376-9185
Website: akronartmuseum.org
Email: mail@akronartmuseum.org
Twitter.com/AkronArtMuseum
Facebook.com/AkronArtMuseumOfficial
Instagram.com/akronartmuseum

Pinterest.co.uk/akronartmuseum
LinkedIn.com/company/akron-art-museum
YouTube.com/user/AkronArtMuseum

Albuquerque

Levy Gallery

Contemporary art in all mediums by emerging and established regional, national and international artists. 6 exhibitions a year and selected art fairs.
Address: 514 Central Ave SW, Albuquerque 87102
Phone: +1 (505) 766-9888
Website: levygallery.com
Email: info@levygallery.com
Facebook.com/levygallery
Instagram.com/levygallery
Artsy.net/richard-levy-gallery
YouTube.com/channel/
UCtQ65UTnzhJ6mCW9GjWo0gA

Rio Grande Gallery

Representing the best of southwest art.
Address: 303 Romero St NW Ste S205, Albuquerque 87104
Phone: +1 (505) 610-3156
Website: riograndegallery.com

Arthaus66 Art Gallery

Emerging and established contemporary artists.
Address: 6320 Linn Ave NE, Albuquerque 87108
Phone: +1 (505) 255-0872
Website: arthaus66.com
Email: clarimon@arthaus66.com

Matrix Fine Art

Artist-run gallery with monthly solo or group exhibitions.
Address: 3812 Central Ave SE, Albuquerque 87108
Phone: +1 (505) 595-5197
Website: matrixfineartabq.com
Email: matrixfineartabq@gmail.com

Penfield Gallery of Indian Arts

Zuni fetishes by the best artists from Zuni Pueblo. Pottery by New Mexico Pueblos as well as those of Hopi and Navajo Nation. Hand spun Navajo rugs. Sand painting rugs from the Shiprock area.
Address: 2113 Church St NW, Albuquerque 87104
Phone: +1 (505) 242-9696
Website: penfieldgallery.com
Email: info@penfieldgallery.com

Palette Contemporary Art & Craft

Contemporary art in many different media with international fine art, glass, abstract and contemporary paintings, limited edition signed prints, jewellery, marbles and mid-century modern radios, clocks and watches, all by emerging and established contemporary artists.
Address: 7400 Montgomery Blvd NE, Albuquerque 87109
Phone: +1 (505) 855-7777
Website: palettecontemporary.com
Email: kurt@palettecontemporary.com
Twitter.com/PaletteArtNM
Facebook.com/PaletteContemporary
Instagram.com/palette_contemporary

Amarillo, Texas

Ronnie Layden Fine Art

Photography and painting by Ronnie Layden, a native of Santa Fe.
Address: 901 Canyon Rd, Santa Fe 87501
Phone: +1 (505) 670-6793
Website: ronnielaydenfineart.com
Email: ronnie@ronnielaydenfineart.com
Facebook.com/ronnielayden/wall

Anchorage

International Gallery of Contemporary Art

Exhibition space dedicated to visual and interdisciplinary arts. An art space where experimentation and risk are still possible.

Address: 427 D St, Anchorage 99501
Phone: +1 (907) 279-1116
Website: igcaalaska.org
Email: info@igcaalaska.org
Facebook.com/InternationalGallery
Instagram.com/igca_alaska

Arlington

Arlington Museum Of Art

Exceptional art and shows that are informative and educational.
Address: 201 W Main St, Arlington 76010
Phone: +1 (817) 275-4600
Website: arlingtonmuseum.org
Email: arlingtonmuseum@gmail.com

Atlanta

Atlanta Contemporary

Founded in 1973 as a grassroots artists' cooperative, now one of the Southeast's leading contemporary art centres. Presenting over 200 artists from the local, national and international art scenes. Over 125 annual programs for adults and children with 13 onsite studio spaces.
Address: 535 Means St NW, Atlanta 30318
Phone: +1 (404) 688-1970
Website: atlantacontemporary.org
Email: support@atlantacontemporary.org
Twitter.com/atlcontemporary
Faccbook.com/AtlantaContemporary
Instagram.com/atlantacontemporary

Museum Of Contemporary Art

Collecting significant, contemporary work from Georgia as well as from around the world with 15 exhibitions each year and public programs.
Address: 75 Bennett St NW Ste A2, Atlanta 30309
Phone: +1 (404) 367-8700
Website: mocaga.org
Email: info@mocaga.org
Twitter.com/mocaga
Facebook.com/MOCAGA

Instagram.com/themocaga
YouTube.com/user/TheMOCAGA

Hathaway Contemporary Gallery

Emerging and established artists in a range of media including painting, photography, sculpture, drawing, video, fibre arts and installation.
Address: 887 Howell Mill Rd NW Ste 200, Atlanta 30318
Phone: +1 (470) 428-2061
Website: hathawaygallery.com
Email: info@hathawaygallery.com
Twitter.com/HathawayGallery
Facebook.com/hathawaygallery
Instagram.com/hathaway_gallery

Marcia Wood Gallery

Exceptional young artists and internationally established masters including video, installation, digital media, sculpture and photography. Founded in 1995.
Address: 263 Walker St SW, Atlanta 30313
Phone: +1 (404) 827-0030
Website: marciawoodgallery.com
Email: info@marciawoodgallery.com
Twitter.com/MarciaWoodG
Facebook.com/MarciaWoodGallery
Instagram.com/marciawoodg

Besharat Museum Gallery

Contemporary art gallery.
Address: 175 Peters St SW, Atlanta 30313
Phone: +1 (404) 524-4781
Website: atlanta.besharatgallery.com

Kai Lin Art

Modern and contemporary art dedicated to promoting emerging and established artists in the southeast and beyond. Recognised for being on the cutting edge of art in America by regional, national and international publications.
Address: 999 Brady Ave NW Ste 7, Atlanta 30318

Phone: +1 (404) 408-4248
Website: kailinart.com
Email: info@kailinart.com
Instagram.com/kailinart

pb&j gallery

A contemporary, affordable gallery for the emerging collector, with photography, painting, collage and sculpture.
Address: 35 Howard St SE, Atlanta 30317
Phone: +1 (404) 606-1856
Website: pbj-gallery.com
Email: info@pbj-gallery.com
Facebook.com/pbj.gallery

Pryor Fine Art

Representing more than 60 emerging and established artists from the U.S, Canada, Australia and Berlin. A state and nationwide destination for fine art with commercial clients and private collectors.
Address: 764 Miami Cir NE Ste 132, Atlanta 30324
Phone: +1 (404) 352-8775
Website: pryorfineart.com
Email: ann@pryorfineart.com
Facebook.com/pryorfineart
Instagram.com/pryorfineart
Pinterest.co.uk/pryorfineart

Anaheim

Warehouse Of Contemporary Art

Bringing local artists together to share and exhibit their art.
Address: 1566 W Embassy St, Anaheim 92802
Phone: +1 (714) 991-6465
Website: wocagallery.com
Email: wocaart@gmail.com
Facebook.com/woca.art
Instagram.com/_woca_

Aurora, Illinois

American Design Ltd

Representing since 1967, a diverse group of local, national and international artists in a wide variety of media and styles with exceptional skill and creativity.
Address: 70 S Potomac St, Aurora 80012
Phone: +1 (303) 695-8478
Website: americandesignltd.com
Email: darren@americandesignltd.com

Austin

The Contemporary Austin – Jones Center

Reflecting the spectrum of contemporary art through exhibition, commission, education and the collection with a unique combination of urban and outdoor sites.
Address: 700 Congress Ave, Austin 78701
Phone: +1 (512) 453-5312
Website: thecontemporaryaustin.org
Email: info@thecontemporaryaustin.org
Twitter.com/ContemporaryATX
Facebook.com/TheContemporaryAustin
Instagram.com/contemporaryatx
Vimeo.com/thecontemporaryaustin

Wally Workman Gallery

Established in 1980, specialising in emerging and established artists, with an exhibition space that can hold 50+ artists at one time.
Address: 1202 W 6th St, Austin 78703
Phone: +1 512-472-7428
Website: wallyworkmangallery.com
Email: workman@wallyworkman.com
Twitter.com/WallyWorkman
Facebook.com/wallyworkmangallery
Instagram.com/wallyworkmangallery
Pinterest.co.uk/wallyworkman

Women & Their Work Art Gallery

Supporting local female artists of all disciplines with exhibitions, performances and educational workshops.
Address: 1710 Lavaca St, Austin 78701
Phone: +1 (512) 477-1064
Website: womenandtheirwork.org
Email: info@womenandtheirwork.org
Twitter.com/WTWGallery

Facebook.com/
WomenAndTheirWorkGallery
Instagram.com/womenandtheirwork
YouTube.com/user/wtwgallery

Modern Rocks Gallery

Fine art rock photography from some of the greatest rock photographers.
Address: 916 Springdale Rd, Austin 78702
Phone: +1 (512) 524-1488
Website: modernrocksgallery.com
Email: info@modernrocksgallery.com
Twitter.com/ModernRocks
Facebook.com/ModernRocksGallery
Instagram.com/modernrocksgallery

Lora Reynolds Gallery

Work by emerging, mid-career and established international artists in all media. 6-8 exhibitions annually with 4-6 installations a year. No unsolicited submissions.
Address: 360 Nueces St Ste 50, Austin 78701
Phone: +1 512-215-4965
Website: lorareynolds.com
Email: info@lorareynolds.com

grayDUCK Gallery

A place where art is integral to everyday life, with poetry readings, film, music and performance as well as artwork.
Address: 2213 E Cesar Chavez St, Austin 78702
Phone: +1 (512) 826-5334
Website: grayduckgallery.com
Email: duckduck@grayduckgallery.com
Twitter.com/grayDUCKGallery
Facebook.com/grayDUCKgallery
Artsy.net/gray-duck-gallery

Art Galleries at Black Studies

Contemporary creative expression as well as archives and material culture. Showcasing narratives of Africa and the African Diaspora. Comprised of 2 galleries – the

Christian-Green Gallery and the Idea Lab.
Address: 210 w. 24th St. Austin, TX 78705 | Gordon White Building 2.204 | Phone: +1 (512) 471-1784
Website: galleriesatut.org
Email: kendyllgross@utexas.edu
Twitter.com/galleries_at_ut
Instagram.com/galleriesatut

Bakersfield
Bakersfield Museum of Art

For over 60 years the gallery has been exhibiting and offering unique educational opportunities in the visual arts, inspiring and engaging a diverse audience.
Address: 1930 R St. Bakersfield CA 93301
Phone: +1 (661) 323-7219
Website: bmoa.org
Email: info@bmoa.org
Facebook.com/thebmoa
Instagram.com/thebmoa
YouTube.com/channel/
UCzq5gnJU6fIeb9vOVhyUCjA

Baltimore
Catalyst Contemporary

Contemporary art with dynamic and powerful stories, forging relationships between artists, collectors, creative and civic minded individuals.
Address: 523 N Charles St, Baltimore 21201
Phone: +1 (410) 905-0089
Website: catalystcontemporary.com
Email: gallery@catalystcontemporary.com
Facebook.com/catalystcontemporary
Instagram.com/catalystcontemporary
Artsy.net/catalyst-contemporary
YouTube.com/channel/
UCTzbyXMbK41C5M1c6zyt6Jg

Terrault Contemporary

An artist-run gallery with multidisciplinary exhibitions focusing on innovative techniques on socially relevant themes. A platform for local and regional emerging and mid-career

artists to collaborate and exhibit.
Address: 218 W Saratoga St 3rd Fl,
Baltimore 21201
Phone: +1 (443) 540-1234
Website: terraultcontemporary.com
Email: info@terraultcontemporary.com
Twitter.com/_TERRAULT_
Facebook.com/Terrault-
809931502384840/?fref=ts
Instagram.com/terraultgallery

Winkel Gallery

A contemporary art gallery featuring the
work of self-taught artist Justin Winkel. Also
offering custom framing.
Address: 1715 Aliceanna St, Baltimore
21231
Phone: +1 (443) 873-9441
Website: justinwinkel.com
Email: info@justinwinkel.com
Facebook.com/JustinWinkelFineArt
Instagram.com/justinwinkel

Jordan Faye Contemporary Gallery

Championing the work of early to mid-
career, engaging and thought-provoking
artists, through exhibitions and travelling
shows.
Address: 218 W Saratoga St 5th Fl,
Baltimore 21201
Phone: +1 443-955-1547
Email: jordanfayecontemporary@gmail.com
Facebook.com/curatorJordanFayeBlock
Instagram.com/jordanfayeblock
jordanfayecontemporary.Tumblr.com

Goya Contemporary

Contemporary art gallery, building a
global reputation of the last 20 years for
commitment to artists and their practice and
for hosting visionary exhibitions, publications
and worldwide scholarship. Participating
in the top-tier international and national
art fairs. Collaborating with museums, and
advising on all aspects of private and public
collecting.

Address: 3000 Chestnut Ave, Baltimore
21211
Phone: +1 (410) 366-2001
Website: goyacontemporary.com
Email: gallery@goyacontemporary.com

The Baltimore Museum of Art

Connecting art to Baltimore and Baltimore
to the world. Established in 1914.
Address: 10 Art Museum Dr, Baltimore
21218
Phone: +1 (443) 573-1700
Website: artbma.org
Email: info@artbma.org
Twitter.com/artbma
Facebook.com/artbma
Instagram.com/baltimoremuseumofart
YouTube.com/user/artBMA

Baton Rouge, Louisiana
Baton Rouge Gallery

A multi-media gallery established in 1965.
One of the U.Ss' oldest artist co-ops,
exhibiting local and national artists.
Address: 1515 Dalrymple Dr, Baton Rouge
70808
Phone: +1 (225) 383-1470
Website: batonrougegallery.org
Email: info@batonrougegallery.org
Facebook.com/BRGallery
Instagram.com/brgallery
YouTube.com/user/batonrougegallery

Birmingham, Alabama
Ground Floor Contemporary

A co-operative art gallery promoting visual
arts with exhibitions from established and
emerging artists in a variety of mediums.
Address: 111 Richard Arrington Jr Blvd S,
Birmingham 35233
Phone: +1 (903) 641-6209
Website: groundfloorcontemporary.com
Email: groundfloorcontemporary@gmail.com
Facebook.com/groundfloorcontemporary

Bloomington, Indiana

Pictura Gallery

A non-profit institution celebrating the art of photography contributing to the international dialogue.
Address: 202 S Rogers St, Bloomington 47404
Phone: +1 (812) 336-0000
Website: picturagallery.com
Email: info@picturagallery.com
Facebook.com/gallerypictura
Instagram.com/picturagallery

Boise

Capitol Contemporary Gallery

An exciting and evolving space exhibiting the very best regional artists.
Address: 451 S Capitol Blvd, Boise 83702
Phone: +1 (208) 384-9159
Website: capitolcontemporary.com
Email: capitolcontemporarygallery@gmail.com
Facebook.com/CapitolContemporaryGallery
Instagram.com/capitolcontemporarygallery

Stewart Gallery

Promoting and developing contemporary art since 1987. Representing established and mid-career artists specialising in painting, drawing, sculpture, installation and limited edition prints from non-objective to contemporary realism.
Address: 2230 W Main St, Boise 83702
Phone: +1 (208) 433-0593
Website: stewartgallery.com
Email: seffan@stewartgallery.com

Boston

Robert Klein Gallery

Established in 1980 and one of the most prestigious fine art photography showrooms in the world. Showing an extensive and ever-changing inventory of 19-21st century photographs.

Address: 38 Newbury St Ste #404, Boston 02124
Phone: +1 (617) 267-7997
Website: robertkleingallery.com
Email: inquiry@robertkleingallery.com
Twitter.com/rkgallery
Facebook.com/robertkleingallery
Instagram.com/robertkleingallery

Institute of Contemporary Art

Outstanding contemporary art in all media, including visual art exhibitions, music, film, video and performance. Innovative, experiential learning opportunities for all ages. Programs developing meaning to contemporary art and culture.
Address: 25 Harbor Shore Drive, Boston 02210
Phone: +1 (617) 478-3100
Website: icaboston.org
Email: info@icaboston.org
Twitter.com/ICAinBOSTON
Facebook.com/ICA.Boston
Instagram.com/icaboston

Boston Sculptors Gallery

A co-operative sculpture gallery.
Address: 486 Harrison Ave, Boston 02118
Phone: +1 (617) 482-7781
Website: bostonsculptors.com
Email: bostonsculptors@yahoo.com
Facebook.com/boston.sculptors
Instagram.com/bostonsculptorsgallery
YouTube.com/channel/UCNm849yQLaeuE4bBryQjE-Q

L'Attitude Gallery

Contemporary indoor and outside sculpture for the home, corporate and healthcare environments. With over 90 American and international artists in media such as glass, ceramic, metal, textile, stone and mixed media. Working with clients, architects, interior and landscape designers.
Address: 211 Newbury St, Boston 02116

Phone: +1 (617) 927-4400
Website: lattitudegalleryartnews.blogspot.com
Email: lattitudegallery@yahoo.com
Facebook.com/lattitudegallery

DTR Modern Galleries

Showcasing modern masters, from post-war to 21st century, as well as emerging, mid-career and blue-chip contemporary makers, with a privately-held selection of work by artists such as Banksy, Chagall, Dali, Hockney, Hirst, Lichtenstein, Warhol and others.
Address: 167 Newbury St, Boston 02116
Phone: +1 (617) 424-9700
Website: dtrmodern.com
Email: info@dtrmodern.com
Instagram.com/dtrmodern

Italian Contemporary Art

Contemporary art gallery exhibiting exclusively Italian artists.
Address: 80 Dartmouth St, Boston 02116
Phone: +1 (617) 459-0706
Website: italianvisualart.com
Email: simon@italianvisualart.com
Twitter.com/ArtsItalian
Facebook.com/italiancontemporaryart
Instagram.com/italiancontemporaryartgallery

Bromfield Gallery

One of Boston's premier artist-run galleries, focusing on New England artists in all media including printmaking, sculpture, painting and drawing as well as video, installation and new media.
Address: 450 Harrison Ave, Boston 02118
Phone: +1 (617) 451-3605
Website: bromfieldgallery.com
Email: info@bromfieldgallery.com
Twitter.com/BromfieldArt
Facebook.com/bromfieldgallery
Instagram.com/bromfieldgallery

Gallery NAGA

Established in 1977, focusing primarily on paintings. Representing highly-regarded Boston and New England artists as well as exceptional contemporary photographers, printmakers and sculptors with limited edition furniture from leading makers.
Address: 67 Newbury St, Boston 02116
Phone: +1 (617) 267-9060
Website: gallerynaga.com
Email: mail@gallerynaga.com
Twitter.com/GalleryNAGA
Facebook.com/GalleryNAGA
Instagram.com/gallerynaga
Artsy.net/gallery-naga

Martin Lawrence Art Gallery

World class art in Boston's historic Back Bay.
Address: 77 Newbury St, Boston 02116
Phone: +1 (617) 369-4800
Website: martinlawrence.com
Email: contact@martinlawrencegalleries.com
Twitter.com/TweetMLG
Facebook.com/martinlawrencegalleries
Instagram.com/martinlawrencegalleries
Pinterest.co.uk/MLGfineart

Buffalo
Hallwalls Contemporary Art Center

A contemporary art gallery presenting visual, media, performance and literary arts challenging and extending the traditional boundaries of these art forms, by critically engaging with current issues in the arts and society.
Address: 341 Delaware Ave, Buffalo 14202
Phone: +1 (716) 854-1694
Website: hallwalls.org
Email: ed@hallwalls.org
Facebook.com/Hallwalls
Instagram.com/hallwalls
Vimeo.com/hallwalls
Feeds2.feedburner.com/HallwallsContemporaryArtsCenter
YouTube.com/user/hallwalls

Buen Vivir! Gallery

Art and photography presenting an historical look at change and struggle in everyday life to inspire new generations to participate in the making of a better world.
Address: 148 Elmwood Ave, Buffalo 14201
Phone: +1 (716) 931-5833
Website: buenvivirgallery.org
Email: theresa2@globaljusticeecology.org
Twitter.com/BuenVivirGALL
Facebook.com/BuenVivirGallery

Charlotte, North Carolina
New Gallery of Modern Art

Contemporary art gallery in Charlotte.
Address: 435 S Tryon St, Charlotte 28202
Phone: +1 (704) 373-1464
Website: newgalleryofmodernart.com
Email: info@newgalleryofmodernart.com

Elder Art Gallery

National wide artists bringing communities together through critical thinking and engaging in dialogue to make sense of our world. Representing a variety of artists with a strong emphasis on fine glass art and paintings.
Address: 1520 South Tryon Street, Charlotte 28203
Phone: +1 704-370-6337
Website: eldergalleryclt.com
Email: info@eldergalleryclt.com
Facebook.com/eldergalleryclt
Instagram.com/elder_gallery_clt

Bechtler Museum of Modern Art

The second museum in the country to be designed by Mario Botta, the Swiss architect. Presenting work by the most important and influential artists of the mid-20th century including Miró, Giacometti, Picasso, Calder, Hepworth, Nicholson, Warhol and many others.
Address: 420 S Tryon St, Charlotte 28202
Phone: +1 (704) 353-9200

Website: bechtler.org
Email: daniel.ferrulli@bechtler.org
Email: laura.allison@bechtler.org
Twitter.com/thebechtler
Facebook.com/thebechtler
Instagram.com/thebechtler
Flickr.com/photos/95528799@N05/sets
YouTube.com/c/BechtlerMuseumCLT

Chicago
Museum of Contemporary Art Chicago

An innovative and compelling centre of art from 1945 to the present. One of the largest facilities in the country showing contemporary work, with painting, sculpture, photography, video, film and performance. Also a gift shop, bookshop, 300-seater theatre and a terraced sculpture garden looking onto Lake Michigan.
Address: 220 E Chicago Ave, Chicago 60611
Phone: +1 (312) 280-2660
Website: mcachicago.org
Email: info@mcachicago.org
Twitter.com/mcachicago
Facebook.com/mcachicago
Instagram.com/mcachicago
Pinterest.co.uk/mcachicago
Vimeo.com/mcachicago

Jean Albano Contemporary Art

Emerging and established artists creating unique, cutting edge, creative contemporary art, especially those re-contextualising objects in a non-traditional way. Not accepting unsolicited artist submissions.
Address: 215 W Superior St, Chicago 60654
Phone: +1 (312) 440-0770
Website: jeanalbanogallery.com
Email: jeanalbanogallery@gmail.com

Richard Norton Gallery

Impressionist and modern paintings and sculpture from the late 19th century to the

early 20th century, especially those from Chicago or with scenes of Chicago.
Address: 222 Merchandise Mart Plz Ste 612, Chicago 60654
Phone: +1 (312) 644-8855
Address: Merchandise Mart
Website: richardnortongallery.com
Email: info@richardnortongallery.com
Facebook.com/Richard-Norton-Gallery-LLC-209818916549

The ART Gallery – Contemporary Fine Art

International artists with the mixed flair of contemporary modern, traditional and experimental style; inaugurating eastern/western philosophy.
Address: 211 W 23rd St, Chicago 60616
Phone: +1 (312) 600-8818
Website: artchgo.com
Email: info@theart8.com
Facebook.com/theart8gallery
Instagram.com/theartgallery8

Vertical Gallery

Urban-contemporary art, influenced by urban environments, street art and culture, graffiti, pop culture, illustration and more.
Address: 1016 N Western Ave, Chicago 60622
Phone: +1 (773) 697-3846
Website: verticalgallery.com
Email: info@verticalgallery.com
Twitter.com/verticalgallery
Facebook.com/verticalgallerychicago
Instagram.com/verticalgallery
Pinterest.co.uk/verticalgallery

Melanee Cooper Gallery

Contemporary Art
Address: 740 N Franklin St, Chicago 60654
Phone: +1 (312) 624-9350
Website: melaneecoopergallery.com

33 Contemporary Gallery

Premier contemporary realism and figurative art from emerging and established international artists.
Address: 1029 W 35th St, Chicago 60609
Phone: +1 (708) 837-4534
Website: 33contemporary.com
Email: sergio@33contemporary.com
Facebook.com/artnxtlevelprojects
Instagram.com/33contemporary

Echt Gallery

Providing leadership in the education of studio glass, promoting awareness and excellence in the arts.
Address: 210 W Superior St, Chicago 60654
Phone: +1 (312) 440-0288
Website: echtgallery.com
Email: info@echtgallery.com
Facebook.com/ECHT-Gallery-151466714946740
Instagram.com/echtgallery

Lotton Gallery

American blown glass and lamp work glass and international oil paintings. Located in the historic Bloomingdale's building in Chicago. A family of artists, starting with Charles Lotton, who started in 1970 and is now regarded as the 'Tiffany of the 21st century'. Also incorporating other glass artists.
Paintings by world renowned artists including some of the finest living masters.
Address: 900 N Michigan Ave, Chicago 60611
Phone: +1 (312) 664-6203
Website: lottongallery.com
Email: glass@lottongallery.com
Twitter.com/lottongallery
Facebook.com/lottongallery
Instagram.com/lottongallery
Pinterest.co.uk/lottongallery
lottongallery.Tumblr.com

Schneider Gallery

Contemporary photographic art specialising in Latin American work. Not accepting

unsolicited artist submissions.
Address: 770 N La Salle Dr Ste 401,
Chicago 60654
Phone: +1 (312) 988-4033
Website: schneidergallerychicago.com
Email: schneidergallery@gmail.com
Facebook.com/schneidergallery
Twitter.com/SchneiderCPG
Instagram.com/schneidergallery

Andrew Bae Gallery

Dedicated to introducing contemporary work by Asian artists, primarily from Korea and Japan. 'Asian aesthetics with universal appeal'.
Address: 300 W Superior St Ste 101,
Chicago 60654
Phone: +1 (312) 335-8601
Website: andrewbaegallery.com
Email: andrew@andrewbaegallery.com

Cincinnati

Cincinnati Art Galleries

Established in 1984, specialising in American and European paintings from the 19th and 20th centuries. Exceptional works of art with many styles and schools including western, impressionist, Taos school, Hudson River school, regionalist, tonalist, modernist and abstract. Specialising in the Cincinnatic Golden Age painters. Also representing a select group of highly regarded and prominent contemporary artists.
Address: 225 E 6th St Fl 1, Cincinnati 45202
Phone: +1 (513) 381-2128
Website: cincinnatiartgalleries.com
Email: hausrath@cincyart.com
Email: art@cincyart.com
Facebook.com/cincinnatiartgalleries

Contemporary Arts Center

Since 1939, one of the nation's oldest and most celebrated contemporary art institutions. One of the first venues in the U.S to exhibit Picasso's Guernica as well as other historic exhibitions. Its current home was the first U.S art museum designed by a woman; London-based Zaha Hadid, and it was said to be 'the most important American building to be completed since the end of the cold war'.
Address: 44 E 6th St, Cincinnati 45202
Phone: +1 (513) 345-8400
Website: contemporaryartscenter.org
Twitter.com/cincycac
Facebook.com/cincycac
Instagram.com/cincycac
Vimeo.com/cincycac
YouTube.com/user/CincyCAC

Pendleton Art Center

Nurturing artistic creativity by providing a supportive and inspiration environment for artists with exhibitions, events and educational programs to raise public awareness and appreciation for the arts.
Address: 1310 Pendleton St, Cincinnati 45202
Phone: +1 (513) 421-4339
Website: pendletonartcenter.com

Miller Gallery

Since 1960, the gallery showcases the work of 60 established international, mid-career and emerging artists including 2 and 3 dimensional abstract and representational art in many mediums such as painting, photography, metal, glass and found objects.
Address: 2715 Erie Ave, Cincinnati 45208
Phone: +1 (513) 871-4420
Website: millergallery.com
Email: contact@millergallery.com
Twitter.com/miller_gallery
Facebook.com/MillerGallery
Instagram.com/millergallery

Eiselle gallery

Contemporary art gallery in Cincinnati.
Address: 5729 Dragon Way, Cincinnati 45227

Phone: +1 (513) 791-7717
Website: eiselefineart.com
Email: info@eiselefineart.com

Cleveland

Museum of Contemporary Art Cleveland

Founded in 1968, a leading force in northeast Ohio's cultural scene. Recognised nationally and international for its presentation of contemporary art and ideas.
Address: 11400 Euclid Ave, Cleveland 44106
Phone: +1 (216) 421-8671
Website: mocacleveland.org
Email: info@mocacleveland.org
Twitter.com/mocacleveland
Facebook.com/moCaCleveland
Instagram.com/mocacleveland
YouTube.com/user/MOCACleveland

Shaheen Modern and Contemporary Art

Focusing over the past 6 years on new and recent work by younger contemporary artists in a 4,000 sq. ft. exhibition space, giving them the opportunity to expand their audiences and generate further exhibition opportunities.
Also specialising in the resale of paintings, drawings and sculpture by important modern, post-war and contemporary European and American artists. Prints and multiples by important modern and contemporary artists.
Address: 740 W Superior Ave Ste 101, Cleveland 44113
Phone: +1 (216) 830-8888
Website: shaheengallery.com
Email: info@shaheengallery.com

Bonfoey Gallery

Regional art and framing for over 125 years.
Address: 1710 Euclid Ave, Cleveland 44115
Phone: +1 (216) 621-0178
Website: bonfoey.com
Email: gallery@bonfoey.com
Twitter.com/bonfoeygallery
Facebook.com/BonfoeyGallery
Instagram.com/bonfoeygallery
Pinterest.co.uk/BonfoeyGallery

Colorado

Arts Alive Gallery

Contemporary and classic paintings, photography, jewellery and sculpture, functional ceramics, fibre art and stained glass.
Address: 500 S Main St, Breckenridge 80424
Phone: +1 (970) 453-0450
Website: summitarts.org
Email: gallery@summitarts.org
Facebook.com/summitarts.org

Colarado Springs

Gallery Of Contemporary Art

A recognised leader in the planning and design of arts centres and cultural facilities, providing a multi-dimensional artistic hub for the University of Colorado and the wider community.
Address: 1420 Austin Bluffs Pkwy, Colorado Springs 80918
Phone: +1 (719) 255-3567
Website: uccspresents.org
Email: info@uccspresents.org
Twitter.com/uccspresents
Facebook.com/UCCSPresents
Instagram.com/uccspresents

The Modbo

Rewarded with many awards over the years, including best gallery, best place to see emerging artists, best exhibit, best First Friday and more. A dazzling array of thought-provoking contemporary art.
Address: 17C E Bijou St, Colorado Springs 80903
Phone: +1 (719) 633-4240
Website: themodbo.com
Email: themodbo@gmail.com

Columbus, Georgia

Contemporary Art Matters

Contemporary art with consulting and collection management services.
Address: 243 N 5th St Ste 110, Columbus 43215
Phone: +1 (614) 300-5381
Website: contemporaryartmatters.com
Email: info@contemporaryartmatters.com
Facebook.com/ContemporaryArtMatters
Instagram.com/contemporaryartmatters
Artsy.net/contemporary-art-matters

Keny Galleries

Located in the historic 19th century German Village, sourcing art to fulfil their client's needs. Historic American paintings and works on paper including a range of master watercolours and outstanding paintings from eminent artists. Contemporary regional art, which has national recognition.
Address: 300 E Beck St, Columbus 43206
Phone: +1 (614) 464-1228
Website: kenygalleries.com
Email: info@kenygalleries.com
Facebook.com/KenyGalleries
Instagram.com/kenygalleries

Sherrie Gallerie

Exceptional process-based contemporary art, including glass, ceramics, wood, fibre and art jewellery.
Address: 694 N High St, Columbus 43215
Phone: +1 (614) 221-8580
Website: sherriegallerie.com
Email: sherrie@sherriegallerie.com

Mac

Internationally celebrated, Mac Worthington has been creating abstract art and home décor since the 1970s. Best known for his work in heavy metal, which has found a place in landscapes, homes and business all over the world.
Address: 138 N High St, Columbus 43215
Phone: +1 (614) 582-6788
Website: macworthington.com
Email: macwartist@aol.com

Not Sheep Gallery

Showcasing national and international artists who make a statement about politics, race, ethnicity, environment, women's issues, aging and other cultural and societal issues, giving a voice of dissent.
Address: 17 W Russell St, Columbus 43215
Phone: +1 (614) 565-0314
Website: notsheepgallery.com
Email: caren@notsheepgallery.com

Corpus Christi
K Space Contemporary

A non-profit organisation promoting contemporary art. A forum of creative exchange and experimentation, aspiring to educate and raise awareness of innovative art in South Texas.
Address: 623 N. Chaparral St
Corpus Christi, TX 78401
Phone: +1 (361) 887-6834
Website: kspacecontemporary.org
Email: info@kspacecontemporary.org
Twitter.com/KSpaceContempo
Facebook.com/KSpaceContemporary
Instagram.com/kspacecontemporary

Dallas
Alan Simmons Art & Design

With more than 30 years combined experience with art in public places, they have successfully completed art programs for hundreds of projects around the world. Playing an active role in the Dallas art and philanthropic community. Curating art collections and procuring art from national and international artists for private collectors, foundations, corporations, healthcare institutions, designers, architects and developers including luxury resorts,

multifamily housing, hospital, Fortune 500 corporate offices, numerous residences and 2 presidential libraries.
Address: 1415 Slocum St Ste 105, Dallas 75207
Phone: +1 (214) 745-2526
Website: carnealsimmons.com
Email: info@carnealsimmons.com
Twitter.com/CarnealSimmons
Facebook.com/AlanSimmonsArtDesign
Instagram.com/carnealsimmons

Circuit12 Contemporary

One of Texas' most innovative and unique art spaces, specialising in contemporary and post digital work. Providing a platform for ambitious emerging and mid-career artists, pushing boundaries and bridging gaps. Specialising in works post 2000
Address: 1811 E Levee St, Dallas 75207
Phone: +1 (214) 760-1212
Website: circuit12.com
Email: info@circuit12.com
Twitter.com/circuit12dallas
Facebook.com/Circuit12
Instagram.com/circuit12

McKinney Avenue Contemporary

A non-profit arts organisation advocating creative freedom and presenting all forms of visual art. Supporting local, regional and international artists and providing a forum for critical dialogue.
Address: 1503 S Ervay Street, Dallas TX75215Top of Form
Phone: +1 (214) 953-1212
Website: the-mac.org
Email: info@ the-mac.org
Twitter.com/TheMACdallas
Facebook.com/TheMACdallas
Instagram.com/themacdallas
Pinterest.co.uk/themacdallas

Craighead Green Gallery

The finest in contemporary art from nationally and internationally recognised artists. One of the finest contemporary art galleries throughout Texas and the Southwest representing 40 artists in all mediums, particularly focusing on contemporary paintings, archival pigment prints and sculpture.
Address: 1011 Dragon St, Dallas 75207
Phone: +1 (214) 855-0779
Website: craigheadgreen.com
Email: cg.gallery@craigheadgreen.com
Facebook.com/craigheadgreengallery

Joel Cooner Gallery

Art, antiques and photography from around the world. Specialising in important Tribal, Asian, Oceanic, Pre-Colombian and Ancient artworks.
Address: 1601 Dragon St, Dallas 75207
Phone: +1 (214) 747-3603
Website: joelcooner.com
Email: joel.cooner.gallery@airmail.net

Christopher Martin Gallery

Featuring the work of reverse-glass painter, Christopher Martin and other carefully curated artists.
Address: 1533 Dragon St, Dallas 75207
Phone: +1 (214) 760-1775
Website: christophermartingallery.com
Email: info@christopherhmartin.com
Facebook.com/chmgallery
Instagram.com/christophermartingallery
Artsy.net/christopher-martin-gallery

Barry Whistler Gallery

Contemporary art gallery in Dallas, TX
Address: 2909 Canton St, Dallas 75226
Phone: +1 (214) 939-0242
Website: barrywhistlergallery.com
Email: info@barrywhistlergallery.com
Twitter.com/BarryWhistler
Facebook.com/barrywhistlergallery
Instagram.com/barrywhistlergallery
Artsy.net/barry-whistler-gallery

Denver
Sloane Gallery of Art

Established in 1981, internationally recognised as one of the major dealers in contemporary and modern Russian art.
Address: 1777 Larimer St Ste 1010, Denver 80202
Phone: +1 (303) 595-4230
Website: sloanegalleryofart.com

K Contemporary

Representing mid-career and established national & international artists, with a focus on installation-based and experiential exhibitions.
Address: 1412 Wazee St, Denver 80202
Phone: +1 (303) 590-9800
Website: kcontemporaryart.com
Email: gallery@kcontemporaryart.com
Facebook.com/kcontemporary
Instagram.com/kcontemporaryart
Artsy.net/k-contemporary
Artcld.com/gallery/k-contemporary

Des Moines, Iowa
Olson-Larsen Galleries

Representing over 50 of the finest contemporary artists in the Midwest.
Address: 203 5th St, West Des Moines 50265
Phone: +1 (515) 277-6734
Website: olsonlarsen.com
Email: info@olsonlarsen.com
Twitter.com/olgalleries
Facebook.com/olson.larsengalleries
Instagram.com/olsonlarsengalleries
Artsy.net/olson-larsen-galery

Detroit
Museum of Contemporary Art Detroit

A non-collecting contemporary art museum with visual, literary, music and performing arts pushing us to the edges of contemporary experience.
Address: 4454 Woodward Ave, Detroit 48201
Phone: +1 313-832-6622
Website: mocadetroit.org
Email: info@mocadetroit.org
Twitter.com/mocad
Facebook.com/MOCADetroit
Instagram.com/mocadetroit
YouTube.com/user/mocadvideo

El Paso
Xolo Gallery

A contemporary art gallery in El Paso.
Address: 2812 N Piedras St, El Paso 79930
Phone: +1 (915) 264-2777
Website: xologallery.com

Fontana, California
Fontana Art Association Inc

Local art exhibitions, classes, lectures and performances. Supporting other cultural functions in Fontana. Founded in 1965.
Address: 8536 Sierra Ave, Fontana 92335
Phone: +1 (909) 823-6036
Website: fontanaartassociation.com
Email: inhishandsfineart@outlook.com
Facebook.com/fontanaartassociation

Fort Lauderdale, Florida
The Oliveira Contemporary Art Gallery

Contemporary art gallery in Fort Lauderdale.
Address: 3556 N Ocean Blvd, Fort Lauderdale 33308
Phone: +1 (954) 900-4580
Website: oliveiraart.com
Email: info@oliveiraart.com

Fort Wayne
Artlink

A creative art space and gallery supporting artists through exhibition, education and community engagement.
Address: 300 E Main Street, Fort Wayne, IN 46802
Phone: +1 (260) 424-7195
Website: artlinkfw.com

Email: info@artlinkfw.com
Twitter.com/ArtlinkFtWayne
Facebook.com/artlinkfw
Instagram.com/artlinkfw
YouTube.com/channel/UCDutKZ9yEP-UAQ09yq9qO0g

Fort Wayne Museum of Art

Collecting, preserving and presenting American and related art to engage, educate and enrich wide audiences throughout the region.
Address: 311 E Main St, Fort Wayne 46802
Phone: +1 (260) 422-6467
Website: fwmoa.org
Email: josef.zimmerman@fwmoa.org
Twitter.com/fwmoa
Facebook.com/fwmoa
Instagram.com/fwmoa

Fresno
Fig Tree Gallery

The longest-running artist collective in California, with work ranging from sculpture, painting, drawing, mixed media, performance and illustration.
Address: 644 Van Ness Ave, Fresno 93721
Phone: +1 559-485-0460
Website: figtreegallery.us
Facebook.com/figtreegallery
Instagram.com/figtreegallery644

Garland
Anno Domini Gallery

Representing urban contemporary art and culture since 2000.
Address: 366 S 1st St, San Jose 95113
Phone: +1 (408) 271-5155
Website: galleryad.com
Email: rEvolution@galleryAD.com
Twitter.com/annodomini
Facebook.com/galleryAD

Grand Prairie, Texas
Grant Berg Gallery

Representing around 45 artists at any given time, half of these are local, with the other half from across Canada. Paintings, carving, sculpture and more.
Address: 3-9907 100 Ave, Grande Prairie T8V 0V1
Phone: +1 587-259-6333
Website:grantberggallery.com
Email: grantberggallery@gmail.com
Twitter.com/grantberggallry
Facebook.com/grantberggallery
Instagram.com/grantberggallery

Grand Rapids, Michigan
Urban Institute for Contemporary Arts

Innovative art, movies and educational programs. Sharing perspectives that grow an equitable, thriving culture and community. Contemporary art from the region, nation and international with compelling exhibitions, events, community programs, public art and youth development.
Address: 2 Fulton St W, Grand Rapids 49503
Phone: +1 (616) 454-7000
Website: uica.org
Email: uica@ferris.edu
Twitter.com/UICAgr
Facebook.com/uicagr
Instagram.com/uicagr

Henderson
Elayne LaPorta

Spiritual scenes depicted in oils and prints by Elayne LaPorta. She often travels to research the terrain and history of Bible stories.
Address: 121 S Water St, Henderson 89015
Phone: +1 (702) 568-1168
Website: elaynelaporta.com
Email: fineartinfo@elaynelaporte.com
Twitter.com/ElayneLaPorta

Hialeah
Conde Contemporary

Specialises in representational work, with a concentration on narrative realism, photorealistic portraiture and surrealism.

Address: 204 Miracle Mile, Coral Gables 33134
Phone: +1 (239) 961-0452
Website: condecontemporary.com
Email: info@condecontemporary.com
Facebook.com/condecontemporary
Instagram.com/condecontemporary
YouTube.com/channel/UCYLBM9-ax03-PVVeSdcxPdA?view_as=subscriber

Carol Jazzar Contemporary Art

Contemporary art gallery in Hialeah
Address: 158 NW 91st St, El Portal 33150
Phone: +1 (305) 490-6906
Website: cjazzart.com
Email: carol@cjazzart.com
Facebook.com/caroljazzargallery
Instagram.com/caroljazzar

Honolulu
Aloha Wood Art By The Le Family

Using a woodworking technique called Intarsia, the family create beautifully contoured pieces in a variety of exotic wood types, such as rosewood, narra padauk, jackfruit wood, pheasant wood, redwood and more. Based on the island of O'ahu.
Address: 875 Waimanu St Ste 509A, Honolulu 96813
Phone: +1 (808) 521-1678
Website: alohawoodart.com
Instagram.com/alohawood.art

Fishcake

Home furnishings and a gallery, with art and design for the contemporary home.
Address: 307 Kamani St, Honolulu 96813
Phone: +1 (808) 593-1231
Website: fishcake.us
Email: info@fishcake.us
Facebook.com/fishcake.hawaii
Instagram.com/fishcakehawaii

Houston
Dimmitt Contemporary Art

Contemporary art gallery providing artists and collectors with a platform for new exchanges. Modern and innovative approaches to investing in contemporary art.
Address: 3637 W Alabama St Ste 160, Houston 77027
Phone: +1 (713) 360-6580
Website: dimmittcontemporaryart.com
Email: info@dimmittcontemporaryart.com
Facebook.com/DimmittContemporaryArt
Instagram.com/dimmittart
Artsy.net/dimmitt-contemporary-art
LinkedIn.com/company/dimmitt-contemporary-art-l.l.c.
Pinterest.co.uk/dimmittcontemporaryart

Contemporary Arts Museum Houston

Presenting a thought-provoking arts program and exhibitions that educate and inspire national and international audiences since 1948.
Address: 5216 Montrose Blvd, Houston 77006
Phone: +1 (713) 284-8250
Website: camh.org
Email: info@camh.org
Twitter.com/camhouston
Facebook.com/thecamh
Instagram.com/camhouston
YouTube.com/user/theCAMH

Sarita Ackerman Contemporary Art

A production house and contemporary art gallery, engaging in cutting-edge, experimental work.
Address: 2000 Edwards St, Houston 77007
Phone: +1 (713) 540-6574
Website: saritaackerman.com
Email: saritaackerman@ymail.com
Twitter.com/saritaackerman
Facebook.com/saritaackerman
Instagram.com/saritaackerman

Pinterest.co.uk/saritaackerman
Tumblr.com/saritaackerman

Deborah Colton Gallery

Featuring numerous exhibitions from artists around the world; Asia, the Middle East – the Arab World, Russia, Canada, Latin America and Europe with the goal of encouraging more understanding and cross cultural exchange through the arts. Another strong part of the program is to promote Houston artists and provide a forum to connect Texas, national and international artists to creative active dialogue for positive change.
Address: 2445 North Blvd, Houston 77098
Phone: +1 (713) 869-5151
Website: deborahcoltongallery.com
Email: info@deborahcoltongallery.com

Thornwood Gallery

High quality artwork by international, national and emerging artists for residences, corporate offices and hotels. A wide variety of styles from abstract to impressionism and realism. A complimentary art consulting and advisory service.
Address: 2643 Colquitt St, Houston 77098
Phone: +1 (713) 528-4278
Website: thornwoodgallery.com
Email: info@thornwoodgallery.com
Twitter.com/thornwoodart
Facebook.com/thornwoodart
Instagram.com/thornwoodart

Inman Gallery

Representing contemporary artists from the region, nationally and abroad. Actively supporting emerging artists to gain national and international recognition. Education, community engagement and long-term commitment to artists, with participation in exhibitions at major institutions.
Address: 3901 Main St, Houston 77002
Phone: +1 (713) 526-7800
Website: inmangallery.com

Email: info@inmangallery.com
Facebook.com/inmangallery
Instagram.com/inmangallery
Artsy.net/inman-gallery

Bisong Art Gallery

Contemporary art gallery. Deeply rooted in the community with exhibitions, workshops, painting classes, weddings and corporate receptions. A platform connecting artists with buyers.
Address: 1305 Sterrett St, Houston 77002
Phone: +1 713-498-3015
Website: bisonggallery.com
Email: info@bisonggallery.com

Gray Contemporary

A platform for international artists in a space that exists between the conventions of an artist run gallery and a commercial gallery.
Address: 3508 Lake St, Houston 77098
Phone: +1 (713) 862-4425
Website: graycontemporary.com
Email: info@graycontemporary.com
Facebook.com/graycontemporary
Instagram.com/graycontemporary

18 Hands Gallery

Contemporary art gallery.
Address: 249 W 19thStreet, Houston 77008
Phone: +1 713 869-3099
Website: 18handsgallery.blogspot.com
Email: info@18handsgallery.com

G Gallery

Local, regional and national contemporary artists with a new artist celebrated each month.
Address: 310 E 9th St, Houston 77007
Phone: +1 (713) 869-4770
Website: gspotgallery.com
Email: doria@gspotgallery.com
Twitter.com/RedPublication
Facebook.com/GspotGalleryHouston

Redbud Gallery

Purchasing and selling fine art on a global basis. Contemporary art collection consulting and appraisal.
Address: 303 E 11th St, Houston 77008
Phone: +1 (713) 862-2532
Website: redbudgallery.com
Email: gakopriva@aol.com
Twitter.com/redbudgallery
Facebook.com/RedbudGallery
Instagram.com/redbudgallery
Artsy.net/redbud-gallery

Booker-Lowe Gallery

Aboriginal Fine Art of Australia.
Address: 4623 Feagan St, Houston 77007
Phone: +1 (713) 880-1541
Website: bookerlowegallery.com
Email: info@bookerlowegallery.com
Facebook.com/Booker-Lowe-Gallery-1669499303284647

4411 Montrose

With a building designed by the internationally renowned architect Peter Zweig, it houses the galleries of Barbara Davis, Anya Tish, Geoffrey Koslov and David Shelton. The gallery does not accept unsolicited artist submissions.
Address: 4411 Montrose Blvd, Houston 77006
Phone: +1 (713) 400-5963
Website: 4411montrose.com
Email: 4411montrose@gmail.com

John Palmer Art

Houston artist, founder of the art movement, Escapism.
Address: 1218 Heights Blvd, Houston 77008
Phone: +1 (713) 861-6726
Website: johnpalmerart.com
Email: Ryan@JohnPalmerArt.com
Twitter.com/JohnRossPalmer
Facebook.com/JohnRossPalmerArt
Instagram.com/johnrosspalmerart
Pinterest.co.uk/johnrosspalmerart
YouTube.com/user/JohnPalmerArt

Art Palace

Founded in 2005 to promote emerging talent in Texas. Working closely with artists through exhibition, art fairs, publications, special projects and placement in private and public collection.
Address: 3913 Main St, Houston 77002
Phone: +1 (281) 501-2964
Website: artpalacegallery.com

Rudolph Projects

A fine art gallery showing a vast range of styles, mediums and genres.
Address: 1836 Richmond Ave, Houston 77098
Phone: +1 (713) 807-1836
Website: rudolphprojects.com
Email: antartica@rudolphblume.com
Twitter.com/ArtscanGallery
Facebook.com/rudolphblumegallery

Indianapolis
Long-Sharp Gallery

Prints, works on paper, paintings and sculpture. Specialising in modern and contemporary masters such as Picasso, Warhol, Haring, Myers and Spiller.
Address: 1 N Illinois St, Indianapolis 46204
Phone: +1 (866) 370-1601
Website: longsharpgallery.com
Email: info@longsharpgallery.com
Twitter.com/L_SGallery
Facebook.com/LongSharpGallery
Instagram.com/longsharpgallery

Irvine
Muizz Gallery of Contemporary Art

Contemporary art gallery in Irvine.
Address: Tustin, CA
Phone: +1 (949) 243-0591

Website: muizzgallery.com
Email: sales@muizzgallery.com
Facebook.com/muizzgallery

Orange County Center For Contemporary Art

A space for artists to research and develop their ideas, with exhibitions, publications and projects. Recognising the importance of social engagement, information sharing, critical dialogue and collaborations, weaving contemporary art into the fabric of everyday life. Established in 1980, the gallery is dedicated to freedom of expression.
Address: 117 N Sycamore St, Santa Ana 92701
Phone: +1 (714) 667-1517
Website: occca.org
Email: Info.occca@gmail.com
Twitter.com/Occcart
Facebook.com/groups/OCCCA
Instagram.com/occcart
YouTube.com/channel/
UCKIuV1z2ii7HX8d7j22cOuA

Q Art Salon

Contemporary art gallery in the artist village in downtown Santa Ana with an art walk held every month.
Address: 205 N Sycamore St, Santa Ana 92701
Phone: +1 (714) 835-8833
Website: qartsalon.com
Email: info@qartsalon.com
Twitter.com/qartsalon
Facebook.com/QArtSalon

Ethos Contemporary Art

Contemporary paintings, sculptures and art glass in galleries in Los Angeles and Newport Beach, California. Specialising in Pop Art, Street Art, Lyrical Art, Expressionism and monumental scale art. Representing living masters, and brilliant emerging artists.
Address: 3405 Newport Blvd, Newport Beach 92663

Phone: +1 (949) 791-8917
Website: ethoscontemporaryart.com
Email:ethoscontemporaryart@gmail.com

Ocma Galleries

Modern and contemporary art
Address: 856 San Clemente Dr, Newport Beach 92660
Phone: +1 (949) 759-4848
Website: ocmaexpand.org
Email: info@ocma.net
Twitter.com/OCMA
Facebook.com/OCMuseumofArt
Instagram.com/ocmuseumofart
YouTube.com/channel/
UCKoBDkRUFgDWkBwsbdjwj9g

Jacksonville
MOCA Jacksonville

A non-profit visual arts educational institution serving the community through exhibitions, collections and educational programs focusing on modern and contemporary art, particularly from the 1960s to the present.
Address: 333 N Laura St, Jacksonville 32202
Phone: +1 (904) 366-6911
Website: mocajacksonville.unf.edu
Email: hellomoca@unf.edu
Twitter.com/mocajax
Facebook.com/MOCAjacksonville
Instagram.com/mocajax

Jersey City
Mana Contemporary

An ecosystem of artists, collectors and art enthusiasts.
Address: 888 Newark Ave Ste 6, Jersey City 07306
Phone: +1 (201) 604-2702
Website: manacontemporary.com
Email: hello@manacontemporary.com
Facebook.com/manacontemporary
Instagram.com/manacontemporary

Curious Matter

An exhibition venue for contemporary visual

art in downtown Jersey City.
Address: 272 5th St, Jersey City 07302
Phone: +1 (201) 273-8569
Website: curiousmatter.org
Email: gallery@curiousmatter.org
Facebook.com/CuriousMatter

Kansas City

Blue Gallery

A contemporary fine art gallery.
Address: 118 Southwest Blvd, Kansas City
64108
Phone: +1 (816) 527-0823
Website: bluegalleryonline.com
Email: kellyk@bluegalleryonline.com
Facebook.com/BlueGalleryKC
Instagram.com/bluegallerykc
Issuu.com/bluegallery

Sherry Leedy Contemporary Art

Established in 1985, now one of the oldest
contemporary art galleries in the Midwest.
Representing emerging, mid-career and
internationally established artists making
exciting and technically proficient work in
all mediums. The gallery has placed work in
more than 100 museums worldwide.
Address: 2004 Baltimore Ave, Kansas City
64108
Phone: +1 816-221-2626
Website: sherryleedy.com
Email: sherryleedy@sherryleedy.com

Haw Contemporary

Haw Contemporary shows fine art from
local, national, and international artists.
Address: 1600 Liberty St, Kansas City 64102
Phone: +1 (816) 842-5877
Website: hawcontemporary.com
Email: bill@hawcontemporary.com
Twitter.com/hawcontemporary
Facebook.com/HawContemporary
Instagram.com/hawcontemporary

Kemper Museum of Contemporary Art

A rapidly growing permanent collection of
modern and contemporary art from around
the world. Exhibitions, installations, lectures,
workshops and other creative programs.
Address: 4420 Warwick Blvd, Kansas City
64111
Phone: +1 (816) 753-5784
Website: kemperart.org
Email: communications@kemperart.org
Twitter.com/KemperMuseum
Facebook.com/KemperMuseum
Instagram.com/kempermuseum

Hilliard Gallery

A multi-award winning gallery exhibiting
contemporary art.
Address: 1820 Mcgee St, Kansas City 64108
Phone: +1 (816) 561-2956
Website: hilliardgallery.com
Email: bob@hilliardgallery.com
Twitter.com/hilliardgallery
Facebook.com/hilliardgallery
Instagram.com/hilliard_gallery

Red Star Studios

Representing some of the best in
contemporary art, from the John and Maxine
Belger Family Foundation as well as a rich
variety of local, national and international
artists.
Address: 2100 Walnut St, Kansas City 64108
Phone: +1 (816) 474-7316
Website: redstarstudios.org
Email: shearn@belgerartscenter.org

Leopold Gallery

A fine art gallery providing art consulting
for private collectors and walk-in clients.
Also structures mentoring programs for
teenage artists from the inner city, with art
instruction, field trips and scholarships.
Address: 324 W 63rd St, Kansas City 64113
Phone: +1 (816) 333-3111
Website: leopoldgallery.com
Email: info@leopoldgallery.com
Facebook.com/LeopoldGallery

Instagram.com/leopoldgallery
Pinterest.co.uk/leopoldgallery
YouTube.com/user/leopoldgallery

Kansas City Artists Coalition

A non-profit organisation promoting visual arts awareness in KC and the region supporting the professional growth of artists. Provides a forum through galleries and publications.
Address: 201 Wyandotte St, Kansas City 64105
Phone: +1 (816) 421-5222
Website: kansascityartistscoalition.org
Email: information@kansascityartistscoalition.org
Twitter.com/kansascityarts
Facebook.com/kcartistscoalition
Instagram.com/kcartistscoalition
YouTube.com/channel/UCT2RaudUe3ObK2AY9QgKynA?

Bryon Cohen Gallery

Local, national and international cutting-edge art in all media.
Address: 2020 Baltimore Ave Ste 120, Kansas City 64108
Phone: +1 (816) 421-5665
Website: byroncohengallery.squarespace.com
Email: byroncohengallery.com
Artnet.com/galleries/byron-cohen-gallery

Knoxville, Tennessee

A cooperative of more than 60 artists producing original art and fine crafts.
Address: 422 S Gay St, Knoxville 37902
Phone: +1 865-525-5265
Website: artmarketgallery.net
Email: info@artmarketgallery.net
Facebook.com/Art.Market.Gallery

Art Galleria

Contemporary, modern, abstract and traditional paintings in a range of styles and mediums.
Address: 6703 Kingston Pike, Knoxville 37919
Phone: +1 (865) 583-0044
Website: artgalleriaknoxville.com
Email: info@ArtGalleriaKnoxville.com
Facebook.com/ArtGalleriaKnoxville

Hanson Gallery

Contemporary art gallery in Knoxville.
Address: 5607 Kingston Pike, Knoxville 37919
Phone: +1 (865) 584-6097
Website: hansongalleryfineart.com
Email: info@hansongalleryfineart.com
Facebook.com/Hanson-Gallery-Fine-Art-104597622952169
Instagram.com/hansongalleryfineart

Las Vegas

Amanda Harris Gallery of Contemporary Art

Contemporary art gallery in the arts district.
Address: 900 S Las Vegas Blvd Ste 150, Las Vegas 89101
Phone: +1 (702) 769-6036
Website: Facebook.com/amandaharrisgallery
Email: amanda.nelle@gmail.com

Skye Art Gallery

Up and coming Pop artists from around the world, established American and international artists.
Address: 3500 Las Vegas Blvd S, Las Vegas 89109
Phone: +1 (702) 836-3538
Website: skyeartgallery.com
Email: SKYE@skyeartgallery.com
Twitter.com/skyeartgallery
Facebook.com/skyeartgallery
Instagram.com/skye_artgallery

Centaur Art Galleries

A large selection of fine art from the 16th century to today. One of the largest, most

Los Angeles Center for Digital Art

LACDA is an exhibit space focused art and technology. Dedicated to the propagation of all forms of digital art, new media, digital video art, net art, digital sculpture, interactive multimedia etc. Supporting local and international artists, both emerging and established.
Address: 105 E 4th St, Los Angeles 90013
Phone: +1 (213) 629-1102
Website: lacda.com
Email: rexbruce@lacda.com
Twitter.com/lacda
Facebook.com/LACDA-Los-Angeles-Center-for-Digital-Art-92156698302
Flickr.com/photos/lacda
LinkedIn.com/in/rexbrucelacda

Contemporary Art Gallery

Contemporary art including photography, painting, sculpture and sound/film media projects from mid-career artists, helping them to achieve recognition away from the 'market' ideals, and maybe in doing so changing the 'market' itself.
Address: 5647 Hollywood Blvd, Los Angeles 90028
Phone: +1 (323) 462-1600
Website: c4gallery.com
Email: sales@c4gallery.com

Hive Gallery

Busy contemporary art gallery and arts community hub.
Address: 729 S Spring St, Los Angeles 90014
Phone: +1 213-955-9051
Website: hivegallery.com
Email: info@hivegallery.com
Twitter.com/thehivegallery
Facebook.com/thehivegalleryandstudios
Instagram.com/hivegallery
YouTube.com/channel/UCml5c5pJ7JSGChM81B8eVyQ

The Museum of Contemporary Art

Presenting, collecting and preserving the art of our time. Adapting and questioning the changing definitions of art. Making the work accessible, supporting the multiplicity of perspective and encouraging the urgency of contemporary expression. An artist-founded museum with around 7,000 objects.
Address: 250 S Grand Ave, Los Angeles 90012
Phone: +1 (213) 626-6222
Website: moca.org
Email: info@moca.org
Twitter.com/MOCAlosangeles
Facebook.com/MOCAlosangeles
Instagram.com/moca
Moca.Tumblr.com
YouTube.com/user/MOCATV

Los Angeles Contemporary Exhibitions

Fostering artists who innovate, explore and take risks. Founded in 1978 by a group of artists, exhibiting and advocating for innovations in art-making and public engagement. Has nurtured emerging art forms such as performance art, video art, digital art and installations. Significant exhibitions and public projects, complemented by educational initiatives.
Address: 6522 Hollywood Blvd, Los Angeles 90028
Phone: +1 (323) 957-1777
Website: welcometolace.org
Email: info@welcometolace.org
Twitter.com/welcometolace
Facebook.com/welcometoLACE
Instagram.com/welcometolace
Vimeo.com/lace
YouTube.com/channel/UCKVWGnDf1Vm2tuB1awaj5Qw

Substrate Gallery

Presenting modern and contemporary art associated with various forms of music. Fine art pieces, original prints, limited edition

prints and music related original fine art music photography. Also art lectures and live sound performances.
Address: 709 N Ridgewood Pl, Los Angeles 90038
Phone: +1 (323) 833-6459
Website: substrategallery.com
Email: info@substrategallery.com

Royale Projects

Focusing on the history and continuing advancement of abstraction in painting and sculpture, as well as leading edge conceptual artists, with many high-profile exhibitions.
Address: 432 S Alameda St, Los Angeles 90013
Phone: +1 (213) 595-5182
Website: royaleprojects.com
Email: info@royaleprojects.com
Facebook.com/royaleprojects
Instagram.com/royaleprojects

Louisville
E & S Art Gallery & Framing

Original art by today's bestselling contemporary artists. African American fine art from emerging and established artists. Expert custom framing
Address: 108 S 10th St, Louisville 40202
Phone: +1 (502) 568-2005
Website: eandsgallery.com
Email: staff@eandsgallery.com
Twitter.com/eandsgallery
Facebook.com/EandSGallery
Instagram.com/eandsgallery

Garner Narrative

Contemporary fine art gallery in Louisville.
Address: 642 E Market St, Louisville 40202
Phone: +1 (502) 303-7259
Website: garnernarrative.com
Email: garnernarrative@gmail.com
Facebook.com/garnernarrative
Instagram.com/garnernarrative

Galerie Hertz

Contemporary fine art gallery in Louisville.
Address: 1253 S Preston St, Louisville 40203
Phone: +1 (502) 595-9154
Website: galeriehertz.com
Facebook.com/billy.hertz
YouTube.com/channel/UCfkl4GSn73-cuH2CCYEiMGQ

Madison
Madison Museum of Contemporary Art

Modern and contemporary art which educates and inspires us as individuals and a community. Both established and emerging artists presented in a dynamic space.
Address: 227 State St, Madison 53703
Phone: +1 (608) 257-0158
Website: mmoca.org
Twitter.com/MMoCAMadison
Facebook.com/MMoCAMadison
Instagram.com/mmocamadison

McKinney, Texas
LAST Art Gallery

Art, jewellery and pottery, founded by Gail Delger, an award-winning artist.
Address: 105 W Louisiana St, McKinney 75069
Phone: +1 (469) 534-0902
Website: lastartgallery.com
Email: mckinneyartcompany@gmail.com
Facebook.com/Last-Art-Gallery-832266740137580
Instagram.com/last_art_gallery

Memphis
The Martha and Robert Fogelman Galleries of Contemporary Art

A vastly expanded professional exhibition space for the Department of Art at the University of Memphis bringing together contemporary work from a national and international context.
Address: The University of Memphis

Department of Art Room 230 & 240 Art & Communication Bldg. 3715 Central Avenue, Memphis 38111
Phone: +1 (901) 678-2216
Website: memphis.edu/fogelmangalleries
Facebook.com/fogelmangalleries

L Ross Gallery

Contemporary fine art including paintings, ceramics, kiln-formed glass, bronze sculptures and mixed media pieces.
Address: 5040 Sanderlin Ave Ste 103, Memphis 38117
Phone: +1 (901) 767-2200
Website: lrossgallery.com
Email: art@lrossgallery.com
Facebook.com/LRossGalleryMemphis

Mesa
Mesa Arts Center

The largest and most comprehensive performing, visual and educational arts centre in Arizona, home to theatres, a museum, art studios and more.
Address: 1 E Main St, Mesa 85201
Phone: +1 (480) 644-6500
Website: mesaartscenter.com
Email: ArtsCenterInfo@mesaartscenter.com
Twitter.com/MesaArtsCenter
Facebook.com/MesaArtsCenterAZ
Instagram.com/mesaartscenter

Gebert Contemporary Art Gallery

Contemporary abstract painting and sculpture from an international group of artists, from Belgium, Germany, Mexico, Spain and the U.S. Mainly mid-career and established artists, with a small number of emerging artists.
Address: 7160 E Main St, Scottsdale 85251
Phone: +1 (480) 429-0711
Website: gebertartaz.com
Facebook.com/Gebert-Contemporary-On-Main-125418184185291
Instagram.com/gebertartaz

Miami
Art Rouge Gallery

Contemporary gallery with oil, acrylic and encaustic wax paintings, engraving, intaglio, drawing on paper; bronze, fibreglass sculptures, ceramics and photography from nationally and internationally renowned artists from Latin America and Europe in styles ranging from post impressionism to abstract.
Address: 46 NW 36th St, Miami 33127
Phone: +1 (305) 448-2060
Website: artrouge.blogspot.com
Email: info@artrouge.com

NNamdi Contemporary Miami

Founded by Jumaane N'Namdi, to build private and corporate collections with established, mid-career and emerging artists.
Address: 6505 NE 2nd Ave, Miami 33138
Phone: +1 (786) 332-4736
Website: nnamdicontemporary.com
Email: nncontemporary@gmail.com
Twitter.com/nnamdimiami
Facebook.com/NNamdiContemporary

Harold Golen Gallery

Showing the best in Pop- Surrealist art.
Address: 2294 NW 2nd Ave, Wynwood Miami 33127
Phone: +1 (305) 576-1880
Website: haroldgolengallery.com
Email: info@ haroldgolengallery.com

Robert Fontaine Gallery

A platform for artists at all stages of their career ranging in historical scope from post war to the most current evolutions of digital media, conceptual installation and urban interventionist. National and international exhibitions.
Address: 2111 NW 1st Pl, Miami 33127
Phone: +1 305-397-8530
Website: robertfontainegallery.com
Email: gallery@robertfontainegallery.com
Instagram.com/robertfontainegallery

Cifo Art Gallery

A non-profit organisation to foster cultural exchange by promoting Latin American contemporary art to global audiences. Since 2002, CIFO has granted more than $1.5 million in grants to over 140 artists from Latin America. CIFO is also the guardian of the Ella Fontanals-Cisneros collection, which is one of the most important international collections of modern and contemporary art in the world.
Address: 1018 N Miami Ave, Miami 33136
Phone: +1 (305) 415-6343
Website: cifo.org
Email: info@cifo.org
Twitter.com/cifoart
Facebook.com/CIFOART
Instagram.com/cifoart
Flickr.com/photos/56560327@N06
YouTube.com/user/CIFOArtChannel

Kavachnina Contemporary

An award winning art gallery bringing together highly talented young and long established local and international artists.
Address: 46 NW 36th St, Miami 33127
Phone: +1 (786) 355-4394
Website: kavachnina.com
Email: info@kavachnina.com

Rimonim Art Gallery

Contemporary art and sculptures from national and international artists questioning the purpose, value and role of the creative spirit in our ever-changing world.
Address: 7500 NE 4th Ct, Miami 33138
Phone: +1 (305) 467-6101
Website: rimonimartgallery.com
Twitter.com/rimonimgallery
Facebook.com/rimonimgallery

Milwaukee
Tory Folliard Gallery

Established in 1988, Wisconsin's leading contemporary art gallery. Emerging and established artists predominantly from the Midwest. Monthly exhibitions
Address: 233 N Milwaukee St, Milwaukee 53202
Phone: +1 (414) 273-7311
Website: toryfolliard.com
Email: info@toryfolliard.com
Twitter.com/ToryFolliard
Facebook.com/ToryFolliardGallery
Instagram.com/torygallery
Pinterest.co.uk/tfolliard

Hawthorn Contemporary

Experimental and exploratory contemporary art from artists in national and international areas fostering dialogues that are reflective of the current conditions of our society.
Address: 706 S 5th St, Milwaukee 53204
Phone: +1 (414) 305-2444
Website: hawthorncontemporary.com
Email: info@hawthorncontemporary.com
Facebook.com/hawthorncontemporary
Instagram.com/hawthorncontemporary
YouTube.com/channel/

Delind Fine Art Appraisals

Cleaning and restoration, consulting for private, corporate and museum collections, acquiring and brokering and appraisal.
Address: 751 N Jefferson St, Milwaukee 53202
Phone: +1 (414) 271-8525
Website: delindappraisals.com
Email: wmdelind@execpc.com

Prints.com

Prints available online
Address: 1350 S 108th St, West Allis 53214
Phone: +1 (414) 778-0730
Website: prints.com
Email: customerservice@prints.com

Elaine Erickson Gallery

Contemporary paintings, works on paper

and sculpture. Abstract and representational. Well established and emerging artists. An exquisite selection of African art, including sculpture, masks, textiles, beadwork and utilitarian items.

Address: 207 E Buffalo St, Milwaukee 53202
Phone: +1 (414) 221-0613
Facebook.com/Elaine-Erickson-Gallery-203312293034332

Minneapolis

Midway Contemporary Art

Founded by artists in 2001 as a non-profit, non-collection visual arts organisation with temporary exhibitions, a public research library and regular public programs. Exhibitions primarily focus on commissioning and developing new projects with artists who have typically never shown in the Midwest or US.

Phone: +1 (612) 605-4504
Website: midwayart.org
Email: info@midwayart.org
Twitter.com/midwayart
Facebook.com/midwayart
Instagram.com/midwayart

Groveland Gallery

Founded in 1973, showing the best of Minnesota and regional art, in particular contemporary representational paintings, drawings and prints, with work included in private, corporate, and museum collections throughout the US. Two simultaneous exhibitions, changing every 6 weeks, artist talks and demonstrations.

Address: 25 Groveland Ter, Minneapolis 55403
Phone: +1 (612) 377-7800
Website: grovelandgallery.com
Email: info@grovelandgallery.com
Facebook.com/grovelandgallery
Instagram.com/grovelandgallery

Circa Gallery

Well-crafted, contemporary art. For 30 years the gallery has raised awareness and appreciation for a wide range of contemporary art styles, mediums and expressions.

Address: 210 N 1st St, Minneapolis 55401
Phone: +1 (612) 332-2386
Website: circagallery.org
Email: staff@circagallery.org
Facebook.com/circagallerympls
Instagram.com/circagallery

All My Relations Arts

Contemporary American Indian fine art
Address: 1414 E Franklin Ave, Minneapolis 55404
Phone: +1 (612) 235-4970
Website: allmyrelationsarts.com
Email: arts@nacdi.org
Twitter.com/nacdimn
Facebook.com/allmyrelationsarts

Rosalux Gallery

Founded in 2002, with a roster of 24 contemporary visual Minnesota artists, whose work is in major international collections. Also home to over 80 local artists, building a solid foundation for their careers and a community dedicated to supporting them in meeting their creative goals and reaching new audiences.

Address: 1400 Van Buren St NE Ste 195, Minneapolis 55413
Phone: +1 (612) 747-3942
Website: rosaluxgallery.com
Email: rosalux@rosaluxgallery.com
Facebook.com/rosalux.gallery
Instagram.com/rosalux_gallery

Walker Art Center

Focusing on contemporary visual, performing and media art the gallery takes a global, multidisciplinary and diverse approach to the presentation of art, asking us to examine

the questions that shape and inspire us as individuals, cultures and communities.
Address: 725 Vineland Place, Minneapolis, MN 55403
Phone: +1 (612) 375-7600
Website: walkerart.org
Email: info@walkerart.org

Weinstein Hammons Gallery

Since 1996, the gallery has worked with internationally recognised artists in all media, with a special focus on modern and contemporary photography. Also committed to important photographic retrospectives. Work has been placed in major private collections and museums in the US.
Address: 908 W 46th St, Minneapolis 55419
Phone: +1 (612) 822-1722
Website: weinsteinhammons.com
Email: info@weinsteinhammons.com

Mobile, Alabama
Alabama Contemporary Art Center

A non-profit contemporary art centre founded in 1999 with classes and workshops for children and adults, talks and films serving over 83,500 people in the last 5 years.
Address: 301 Conti St, Mobile 36602
Phone: +1 (251) 208-5671
Website: alabamacontemporary.org
Email: allison @alabamacontemporary.org
Facebook.com/alabamacontemporary
Instagram.com/alabamacontemporary
YouTube.com/channel/
UCGcz1aYRrdJO3DlkCbgUhgw

Nashville
Tinney Contemporary

Working with local, regional, national and internationally established artists.
Address: 237 5th Ave N, Nashville 37219
Phone: +1 (615) 255-7816
Website: tinneycontemporary.com
Email: info@tinneycontemporary.com

The Rymer Gallery

One of the largest contemporary galleries in Nashville's arts district. Showcasing art in a variety of media and experience with a diverse strategy. Part of The Nashville Art Crawl, occurring on the 1st Saturday of each month which draws in 1000's of people.
Address: 233 5th Ave N, Nashville 37219
Phone: +1 (615) 752-6030
Website: therymergallery.com
Email: herb@therymergallery.com
Twitter.com/therymergallery
Facebook.com/therymergallery
Instagram.com/therymergallery

Gallery

One of Nashville's premier art galleries, exhibiting unique paintings by owner, Olga Alexeeva and other local artists.
Address: 1305 Clinton St, Nashville 37203
Phone: +1 (615) 416-2537
Website: ogalleryart.com
Email: ogallery@comcast.net
Twitter.com/OgallerybyOlga
Facebook.com/OGalleryArt
Instagram.com/ogalleryartnashville
Pinterest.co.uk/ogallery0281

New Orleans
Gallery Orange

Emerging and established artists with a high turnover of work at the gallery. Part of the local and international fine art scene in the historic French Quarter of New Orleans.
Address: 819 Royal St, New Orleans 70116
Phone: +1 (504) 701-0857
Website: gallery-orange.com
Email: info@gallery-orange.com
Twitter.com/galleryorange
Facebook.com/galleryorangeNOLA
Instagram.com/galleryorange

Callan Contemporary

Emerging and midcareer American and

international contemporary artists with an emphasis on abstract and figurative painting and sculpture.
Address: 518 Julia St, New Orleans 70130
Phone: +1 (504) 525-0518
Website: callancontemporary.com
Email: stevencallan@callancontemporary.com
Instagram.com/callancontemporary
Artnet.com/galleries/callan-contemporary
Artsy.net/show/callan-contemporary-george-dunbar-meridian

M Contemporary

A roster of regionally and nationally recognised artists, both emerging and established. A small collection of Tribal art.
Address: 906 Royal St, New Orleans 70116
Phone: +1 (504) 523-2022
Website: mcontemporary.com
Email: art@mcontemporary.com

Contemporary Arts Center

Theatre, performance art, dance and concerts. A multidisciplinary arts centre dedicated to the promotion of the art of our time.
Address: 900 Camp St, At St. Joseph's, New Orleans 70130-3971
Phone: +1 (504) 528-3805
Website: cacno.org
Email: info@cacno.org
Twitter.com/cacno
Facebook.com/ContemporaryArtsCenterNewOrleans
Instagram.com/cacnola

Sutton Galleries

A 4th generation family business in the historic French Quarter of New Orleans. Features original oil and acrylic paintings, hand-embellished limited editions and more from American and European artists.
Address: 519 Royal St, New Orleans 70130
Phone: +1 (504) 581-1914
Website: suttonsgalleries.com

Email: admin@suttonsgalleries.com
Twitter.com/suttongalleries
Facebook.com/suttongalleriesnola
Instagram.com/suttongalleriesnola

Jonathan Ferrara Gallery

Monthly exhibition of national and international art, from emerging to established contemporary artists. Featured in many international publications. US and European art fairs. Collaborates with museums and institutions.
Address: 400A Julia St, New Orleans 70130
Phone: +1 (504) 522-5471
Website: jonathanferraragallery.com
Email: info@jonathanferraragallery.com
Twitter.com/JFerraraGallery
Facebook.com/JONATHANFERRARAGALLERY
Instagram.com/jonathanferraragallery
Artsy.net/jonathan-ferrara-gallery
YouTube.com/c/JONATHANFERRARAGALLERY

Ariodante Contemporary Crafts

Fine Art and Craft Gallery.
Address: 535 Julia St, New Orleans 70130
Phone: +1 (504) 524-3233
Website: ariodantegallery.com
Email: deyettedanford@gmail.com
Facebook.com/search/top?q=ariodante%20contemporary%20art%20and%20craft%20gallery
Instagram.com/revlreed

Guthrie Contemporary

Paintings, sculpture and photography
Address: 3815 Magazine St, New Orleans 70115
Phone: +1 (504) 897-2688
Website: guthriecontemporary.com
Email: info@guthriecontemporary.com

RHINO Contemporary Crafts

A non-profit formed in 1984 by artists

Sandra Blair to foster public interest in fine Louisiana crafts and to provide educational opportunity for the community. Exhibiting jewellery, pottery, painting, watercolours, photographs, fibre, glass, mosaics and more.
Address: 2028 Magazine St, New Orleans 70130
Phone: +1 (504) 523-7945
Website: rhinocrafts.com
Email: rhinogallery@gmail.com
Facebook.com/RHINOCrafts
Instagram.com/rhino_contemporary_crafts_co

Cole Pratt Gallery

A contemporary fine art gallery in Uptown New Orleans specialising in the works of Southern artists.
Address: 3800 Magazine St, New Orleans 70115
Phone: +1 504-891-6789
Website: coleprattgallery.com
Email: info@coleprattgallery.com
Twitter.com/coleprattart
Facebook.com/ColePrattGallery
Instagram.com/coleprattgallery

Galerie D'art Francais

Three galleries of contemporary French art
Address: 541 Royal St, New Orleans 70130
Phone: +1 504-581-6925
Website: frenchArtnetwork.com
Email: grtnola@frenchart.net
Galerie Rue Toulouse
Address: Afton Lee, 509 Rue Royale, New Orleans, LA 70130
Phone: +1 (504) 581-5881
Email: grtnola@frenchart.net
Galerie Rue Toulouse
Address: Ocean Avenue between Dolores& San Carlos, Carmel-by-the-Sea, CA 93921
Phone: +1 (831) 625-3456
Email: grtca@frenchart.net

Martin Lawrence Galleries

Contemporary art gallery.
Address: 433 Royal St, New Orleans 70130
Phone: +1 (504) 299-9055
Website: martinlawrence.com
Email: contact@martinlawrencegalleries.com
Twitter.com/TweetMLG
Facebook.com/martinlawrencegalleries
Instagram.com/martinlawrencegalleries
Pinterest.co.uk/MLGfineart

Bee Galleries

Contemporary art gallery in the heart of the French Quarter of New Orleans, owned by Becky Edwards.
Address: 319 Chartres St, New Orleans 70130
Phone: +1 (504) 587-7117
Website: beegalleries.com
Email: beegalleries@aol.com
Facebook.com/BEEGalleries

Boyd Satellite

Representing regional, national and international artists. A contemporary art gallery and alternative art space in the epicentre of the New Orleans Art District.
Address: 440 Julia St, New Orleans 70130
Phone: +1 (504) 581-2440
Website: boydsatellitegallery.com
Email: ginettebone@gmail.com
Facebook.com/boydsatellite

New York
Solomon R. Guggenheim Museum New York

Address: Solomon R. Guggenheim Museum
1071 Fifth Avenue
New York, NY 10128-0173
Phone: 212 423 3500
Website: guggenheim.org
Email: boxoffice@guggenheim.org
Twitter.com/Guggenheim
Facebook.com/guggenheimmuseum
Instagram.com/Guggenheim
YouTube.com/user/Guggenheim

Soho Contemporary Art

A 2,900 sq. ft. gallery in the heart of Manhattan's Lower East Side featuring the work of modern and contemporary masters.
Address: 259 Bowery, New York 10002
Phone: +1 (646) 719-1316
Website: sohocontemporaryart.com
Email: info@sohocontemporaryart.com
Twitter.com/sohocontempart
Facebook.com/SohoContemporaryArt
Instagram.com/sohocontemporaryart

Grey Art Gallery

Postmodern and avant-garde, 19th and 20th century art. Located on the historic Washington Square Park in NY's Greenwich Village.
Address: 100 Washington Sq. E, New York 10003
Phone: +1 (212) 998-6780
Website: greyartgallery.nyu.edu
Twitter.com/NYUGrey
Facebook.com/NYUGrey
Instagram.com/nyugrey
Greyartgallerynyu.Tumblr.com

Agora Gallery

Founded in 1984 by an artist, this gallery is dedicated to the promotion of national and international contemporary artists seeking exposure to the NY market, connecting them with professionals, art collectors and other artists in an ever-growing family dedicated to the world of fine art.
Address: 530 W 25th St, New York 10001
Phone: +1 (212) 226-4151
Website: agora-gallery.com
Email: info@agora-gallery.com
Twitter.com/Agora_Gallery
Facebook.com/AgoraGalleryNY

Alexandre Gertsman Contemporary Art

Group and solo exhibitions showing established Russian-born artists and new, emerging talent. AGCA has the largest collection of paintings, sculptures, photographs, works on paper and objects by contemporary artists from the former Soviet Union in the U.S.
Address: 652 Broadway Fl 2, New York 10012
Phone: +1 (646) 344-1325
Website: agcontemporaryart.com
Email: gertsman@agcontemporaryart.com
Email: reznikova@agcontemporaryart.com
Facebook.com/pages/Alexandre-Gertsman-Contemporary-Art-gallery

Pop International Galleries

Pop Art, Urban Art and Photography influenced by popular culture.
Address: 473 W Broadway, New York 10012
Phone: +1 (212) 533-4262
Website: popinternational.com
Email: art@popinternational.com
Twitter.com/thepopgallery
Facebook.com/popartnyc
Instagram.com/popgallery

Tally Beck Contemporary

Asian contemporary art from East and Southeast Asia. Regular exhibitions and presence at art fairs.
Address: 42 Rivington St, New York 10002
Phone: +1 (646) 678-3433
Website: tallybeckcontemporary.com

Flowers Gallery

Representing over 50 international artists and artist's estates. Over the past 5 decades the gallery has presented over 900 exhibitions in its worldwide locations, as well as in art fairs, public galleries, museums and institutions globally.
Address: 529 W 20th St, New York 10011
Phone: +1 (212) 439-1700
Website: flowersgallery.com
Email: newyork@flowersgallery.com
Twitter.com/flowersgallery

Facebook.com/FlowersGalleries
Instagram.com/flowersgallery
Artsy.net/flowers
www.flowersgallery.com/wechat

DTR Modern Gallery

Additional locations in Boston, Palm Beach and Washington D.C. At the forefront of the modern art marketplace with a significant privately-held selection by modern and contemporary masters.
Address: 458 W Broadway, New York 10012
Phone: +1 (212) 677-2802
Website: dtrmodern.com
Email: info@dtrmodern.com
Instagram.com/dtrmodern

Atlantic Gallery

Owned and managed by a select group of artists, rotating exhibitions feature their work and others, including painting, printmaking, photography and sculpture.
Address: 548 W 28th St, New York 10001
Phone: +1 (212) 219-3183
Website: atlanticgallery.org
Email: info@atlanticgallery.org
Twitter.com/atlanticgal
Facebook.com/Atlantic.Galery
Instagram.com/atlanticgallerynyc

New Museum of Contemporary Art

Founded in 1977, a leading destination for new art and ideas. The only museum in NYC entirely devoted to contemporary art.
Address: 235 Bowery, New York 10002
Phone: +1 (212) 219-1222
Website: newmuseum.org
Email: info@newmuseum.org
Twitter.com/newmuseum
Facebook.com/newmuseum
Instagram.com/newmuseum
YouTube.com/user/newmuseum

Kate Werble Gallery

Contemporary art gallery in New York.

Address: 83 Vandam St, New York 10013
Phone: +1 (212) 352-9700
Website: katewerblegallery.com
Email: info@katewerblegallery.com

Montserrat Gallery

Contemporary art gallery in New York.
Address: 547 W 27th St, New York 10001
Phone: +1 (212) 268-0026
Website: montserrat.us
Email: montserratcontemporaryart@mail.com

AFA Gallery

Since 1984, AFA have represented a stable of unique established and emerging artists, with figurative, contemporary painting and sculpture.
Address: 54 Greene St, New York 10013
Phone: +1 (212) 226-7374
Website: afanyc.com
 Email: info@afanyc.com
Twitter.com/AFANYC
Facebook.com/AFANYC
Instagram.com/afanyc

Eden Fine Arts

Founded in 1997 by Cathia Kimovsky, Eden Fine Arts has evolved into a global network of high-end art galleries in NY, London, Miami and Mykonos. International artists with unique approaches, promoting contemporary optimism and a colourful view of life.
Address: 437 Madison Ave Ste 1, New York 10022
Phone: +1 (212) 888-0177
Website: eden-gallery.com
Email: info@eden-gallery.com
Twitter.com/EdenFineArt_
Instagram.com/edenfineart
Pinterest.co.uk/edenfineart/_created
YouTube.com/user/EdenGalleryNYC

Rehs Galleries

One of the world's leading art galleries specialising in important 19th and 20th century art, especially artists who exhibited at the Paris Salon and London's Royal Academy between 1860 and 1920.
Address: 5 E 57th St, 8Th Floor NY 10022
Phone: +1 (212) 355-5710
Website: rehs.com
Email: info@Rehs.com
Twitter.com/RehsGalleries
Facebook.com/RehsGalleriesInc
LinkedIn.com/in/howardrehs
YouTube.com/channel/
UCCsp3CVcyslmUrq5IsH2bJA

North Las Vegas
Left Of Center Art Gallery

A non-profit organisation, led by Director, Vicki Richardson, building respect for cultural diversity.
Executive Director - Vicki Richardson;
Gallery Director - Marylou Parker
Address: 2207 W Gowan Rd, North Las Vegas 89032
Phone: +1 (702) 647-7378
Website: leftofcenterart.org
Facebook.com/leftofcentergallery

Amanda Harris Gallery of Contemporary Art

Local and visiting contemporary artists.
Address: 900 S Las Vegas Blvd Ste 150, Las Vegas 89101
Phone: +1 (702) 769-6036
Website: Facebook.com
Email: amanda.nelle@gmail.com

Oakland
Sanchez Contemporary

An online contemporary art gallery.
Address: 1951 Telegraph Ave, Oakland 94612
Phone: +1 (510) 350-7871
Website: sanchezcontemporary.com
Email: sanchezcontemporary@gmail.com
Twitter.com/MariaSanchez
Facebook.com/sanchezcontemporary

SLATE contemporary

Slate art operates two companies; Stale contemporary which is a retail gallery and exhibition venue, with 6 shows a year showing 40 artists with a focus on abstract painting and photography, as well as figurative, landscape, nature-based work, mixed media and sculpture. Slate art consulting searches the globe for the best art for the space, partnering with architects, developers and business owners, sourcing and commissioning large-scale paintings, sculptures and public art. Also commissioning murals, build corporate collections and assemble decorative print collections for healthcare, hospitality and work environments.
Address: 473 25th St, Oakland 94612
Phone: +1 (510) 652-4085
Website: slateart.net
Email: info@slateart.net

Chandra Cerrito Contemporary

Providing curatorial expertise, extensive art works and outstanding service to a wide range of clientele, enhancing and enriching environments and our experiences of them.
Address: 480 23rd St, Oakland 94612
Phone: +1 (510) 260-7494
Website: ccartadvisors.com
Email: chandra@chandracerrito.com
Twitter.com/CCC_Art_
Facebook.com/chandracerritoartadvisors

Anthony Holdsworth Studio Gallery

Artwork from Anthony Holdsworth.
Address: 351 Lewis St, Oakland 94607
Phone: +1 510-836-1681
Website: anthonyholdsworth.com
Email: anthony@anthonyholdsworth.com

Oklahoma City
Oklahoma Contemporary

Education, performance and exhibitions, a multidisciplinary contemporary arts organisation.
Address: 1146 N Broadway Dr, Oklahoma City 73103
Phone: +1 (405) 951-0000
Website: oklahomacontemporary.org
Email: pbarrera@okcontemp.org
Twitter.com/okcontemporary
Facebook.com/OklahomaContemporary
Instagram.com/okcontemporary
YouTube.com/channel/
UCnwfRXc8NRLgYLefRD4kpaw

Omaha
Union For Contemporary Art

Strengthening the creative culture of the greater Omaha area, supporting local artists and increasing the visibility of contemporary art within the community. Inspiring positive social change and greater civic engagement, connecting the diverse community in innovative and meaningful ways.
Address: 2423 North 24th Street, Omaha, NE 68110
Phone: +1 (402) 933-3161
Website: u-ca.org
Email: info@u-ca.org
Twitter.com/TheUNIONOmaha
Facebook.com/TheUNIONOmaha
Instagram.com/theunionomaha

Modern Arts Midtown

Contemporary and modern art gallery.
Address: 3615 Dodge St, Omaha 68131
Phone: +1 (402) 502-8737
Website: modernartsmidtown.com
Email: info@modernartsmidtown.com

Bemis Center for The Contemporary Arts

Facilitating the creation, presentation and understanding of contemporary art through an international residency program, exhibitions and educational programs. Giving shape and meaning to the human condition through creativity, trust, courage, diversity, tolerance and the open exchange of ideas and world views.
Address: 2416 Lake St, Omaha 68111
Phone: +1 (402) 933-6622
Website: bemiscenter.org
Email: info@bemiscenter.org

Corporate Art Co.

Art appraisals, procurement and consultancy since 1985.
Address: 1111 N 13th St Ste 201, Omaha 68102
Phone: +1 (402) 558-0376
Website: corporateartco.com
Email: Holly@CorporateArtCo.com

Orlando
Lombard Contemporary Art

Contemporary Art Gallery in Orlando
Address: 1413 E Esther St, Orlando 32806
Phone: +1 (407) 925-9249
Website: lombardcontemporaryart.com
Email: info@lombardcontemporaryart.com

Grand Bohemian Gallery

Monthly exhibitions of local and international art, including paintings, sculpture and jewellery.
Address: 325 S Orange Ave, Orlando 32801
Phone: +1 407-581-4801
Galleries also at Mountain Brook, Charleston, Forsyth Park, Casa Monica and Asheville
Website: grandbohemiangallery.com

HENAO Contemporary Center

One of Orlando's premier alternative art and music venues, collaborating with artists, musicians, poets and makers, marked as a venue to watch as a sign of Orlando's cultural

development.
Address: 5601 Edgewater Dr, Orlando
32810
Phone: +1 (407) 272-0317
Website: henaocenter.com
Email: info@henaocenter.com
Facebook.com/HenaoCenter

Overland Park, Kansas

Nerman Museum of Contemporary Art
A contemporary art museum, named after
its donors Jerry and Margaret Nerman,
opening in 2007. The building was designed
by Korean architect Kyu Sung Woo.
Address: 12345 College Blvd, Overland Park
66210
Phone: +1 913-469-8500
Website: nermanmuseum.org
Twitter.com/NermanMuseum Facebook.
com/NMoCA
Instagram.com/nermanmuseum

Oxnard, California
Studio-Gallery

Showcasing beautiful paintings, prints,
sculpture, jewellery, ceramic art, stained glass,
blown glass, fibre art and more, since 1976.
Address: 2741 S Victoria Ave #H, Oxnard
93035
Phone: +1 (805) 985-1546
Website: mystudiogallery.com
Email: info@mystudiogallery.com

Philadelphia
Larry Becker Contemporary Art

Contemporary art gallery in Philadelphia.
Address: 43 N 2nd St, Philadelphia 19106
Phone: +1 (215) 925-5389
Website: Artnet.com/ Larry Becker
Contemporary Art

Institute Of Contemporary Art

Believing in the power of art and artists
to inform and inspire. Does not accept
unsolicited material.

Address: 118 S 36th St, Philadelphia 19104
Phone: +1 (215) 898-7108
Website: icaphila.org
Email: hello@ica.upenn.edu
Twitter.com/ICAPhiladelphia
Facebook.com/ICAPhiladelphia
Instagram.com/ICAPhiladelphia

Wexler Gallery

Internationally recognised, with the finest in
art and design. Focusing on work that blurs
the line between fine art, decorative art,
sculpture and craft.
Address: 201 N 3rd St, Philadelphia 19106
Phone: +1 (215) 923-7030
Website: wexlergallery.com
Email: mat@wexlergallery.com
Twitter.com/WexlerGallery
Facebook.com/WexlerGallery
Instagram.com/wexlergallery
Pinterest.co.uk/lewiswexler/wexler-gallery

PhilaMOCA

Housed in the historic Finney & Son building,
a former showroom for mausoleums
dating back to 1865. Showing the best in
underground, alternative and DIY culture,
especially in film and performance. Over
300 events a year, from film premiers to art
exhibitions and fashion showcases.
Address: 531 N 12th St, Philadelphia 19123
Phone: +1 (267) 519-9651
Website: philamoca.org
Email: ericbresler@philamoca.org
Twitter.com/philamoca
Facebook.com/philamoca

Philadelphia Art Alliance

Part of the University of the Arts in
Philadelphia, one of the U.S's only universities
dedicated to visual and performing arts,
design and writing. Located on the famous
Avenue of the Arts, with easy access to
world-class theatres, museums and art gallery.
Address: 251 S 18th St Ste 2, Philadelphia
19103

Phone: +1 (215) 545-4302
Website: philartalliance.org
Email: krosenberg@uarts.edu
Twitter.com/uarts
Facebook.com/UArts
Instagram.com/universityofthearts

Twelve Gates Arts

Contemporary Art - South Asian, Middle Eastern, American Asian. Creating projects in the community that cross geographical and cultural boundaries. 12G is a member of the ACAW Consortium, a citywide platform connecting leading NY and Asian based museums and galleries, to present cutting-edge exhibitions, projects and provocative dialogues.
Address: 106 N 2nd St, Philadelphia 19106
Phone: +1 (215) 253-8578
Website: twelvegatesarts.org
Email: info@twelvegatesarts.org

Phoenix

Bentley Gallery

Founded by Bentley Calverley in 1984, building a core of important artists that quickly grew into international regard. Additionally opening in an industrial warehouse in 2004, allowing for large and super-large work to be shown.
Address: 215 E Grant St, Phoenix 85004
Phone: +1 (480) 946-6060
Website: bentleygallery.com
Email: info@bentleygallery.com
Twitter.com/BentleyGallery
Facebook.com/bentleygallery
Instagram.com/bentleygallery
Pinterest.co.uk/bentleygallery
Artsy.net/bentley

9 The Gallery

A contemporary art gallery exhibiting local, national and international artists located in Phoenix's historic Grand Avenue district.
Address: 1229 Grand Ave, Phoenix 85007

Phone: +1 (480) 454-5929
Website: 9thegallery.com
Twitter.com/9TheGallery
Facebook.com/9TheGallery
Instagram.com/9thegallery

6th Avenue Gallery

Art space in downtown Phoenix, with work by Arizona artists and artisans.
Address: 650 N 6th Ave, Phoenix 85003
Phone: +1 (602) 277-9530
Facebook.com/6thavegallery

Lisa Sette Gallery

For over 25 years, the gallery has been showcasing contemporary artists who address the social issues of our time.
Address: 210 E Catalina Dr, Phoenix 85012
Phone: +1 (480) 990-7342
Website: lisasettegallery.com
Email: sette@lisasettegallery.com
Twitter.com/settegallery
Facebook.com/lisasettegallery
Instagram.com/lisasettegallery
Lisasettegallery.Tumblr.com
Artsy.net/lisa-sette-gallery

eye lounge

A collective, artist-run contemporary art space that fosters emerging and established visual artists in downtown Phoenix.
Address: 419 E Roosevelt St, Phoenix 85004
Phone: +1 (602) 430-1490
Website: eyelounge.com
Email: eyelounge@gmail.com
Twitter.com/eyelounge
Facebook.com/eyelounge
Instagram.com/eyeloungephx

Modified Arts

Art gallery, music and performance space in downtown Phoenix.
Address: 407 E Roosevelt St, Phoenix 85004
Phone: +1 (602) 462-5516

Website: modifiedarts.org
Email: info@modifiedarts.org

Pittsburgh
Contemporary Craft

Contemporary art in craft materials. International and national artists with exhibitions, workshops and a unique shop.
Address: 2100 Smallman St Ste 100, Pittsburgh 15222
Phone: +1 (412) 261-7003
Website: contemporarycraft.org
Email: info@contemporarycraft.org
Twitter.com/SCCPgh
Facebook.com/SCCPgh
Instagram.com/SCCpgh
Pinterest.co.uk/sccraft

Portland
PDX Contemporary art

Established in 1996, a forward-thinking gallery representing local and international artists, mixing the conceptual with the personal to create 'intellectually and visually satisfying' pieces. Monthly exhibitions with a more experimental space viewable from the street.
Address: 925 NW Flanders St, Portland 97209
Phone: +1 (503) 222-0063
Website: pdxcontemporaryart.com
Email: info@pdxcontemporaryart.com
Twitter.com/PDXart
Facebook.com/pdxcontemporaryart
Instagram.com/pdxcontemporaryart

Upfor Contemporary Art Gallery

Emerging and established art that examines and challenges cultural and artistic orthodoxies. Exhibitions, international fairs with work placed in important collections and museums globally. Since May 2020, the gallery has gone online, allowing them to focus on advisory and consulting services as well.
Address: 929 NW Flanders St, Portland 97209
Phone: +1 (503) 227-5111
Website: upforgallery.com
Email: welcome@upforgallery.com
Instagram.com/upforgallery
Artsy.net/upfor

Gallery 114

Curated shows, plays, lectures, author readings, live music and film screenings. Founded in 1990 as an artist collective, producing a diverse range of painting, sculpture, video and installation from members and external artists.
Address: 1100 NW Glisan St, Portland 97209
Phone: +1 (503) 243-3356
Website: gallery114pdx.com
Email: contact@gallery114pdx.ocom
Twitter.com/gallery114pdx
Facebook.com/Gallery114PDX
Instagram.com/gallery114
Tumblr/Gallery114
YouTube.com/user/Gallery114PDX

Fourteen30 Contemporary

A contemporary art gallery in Portland.
Address: 1501 SW Market St, Portland 97201
Phone: +1 (503) 236-1430
Website: fourteen30.com
Email: info@fourteen30.com
Facebook.com/Fourteen30-Contemporary-66592887224
Instagram.com/fourteen30
artspace.com/partners/fourteen30

Charles A Hartman Fine Art

Contemporary and modern art with subtle narratives.
Address: 134 NW 8th Ave, Portland 97209
Phone: +1 (503) 287-3886
Website: hartmanfineart.net

Email: charles@hartmanfineart.net
Instagram.com/hartmanfineart

Russo Lee Gallery

Contemporary art by emerging and established Pacific Northwest artists.
Address: 805 NW 21st Ave, Portland 97209
Phone: +1 (503) 226-2754
Website: russoleegallery.com
Email: gallery@russoleegallery.com
Twitter.com/RussoLeeGallery
Facebook.com/RussoLeeGallery
Instagram.com/russoleegallery
Artsy.net/russo-lee-gallery

Augen Gallery

Contemporary art gallery in Portland.
Address: 716 NW Davis St, Portland 97209
Phone: +1 (503) 546-5056
Website: augengallery.com
Email: augendesoto@integra.net
Twitter.com/AugenGallery
Facebook.com/augengallery
Instagram.com/augengallery

Waterstone Gallery

Contemporary art by Northwest artists.
Address: 124 NW 9th Ave, Portland 97209
Phone: +1 (503) 226-6196
Website: waterstonegallery.com
Email: waterstonegallery@yahoo.com
Facebook.com/Waterstone-Gallery-79215292829
Instagram.com/waterstonegallery
YouTube.com/channel/UCENw1rd-qvyq9s3XzMw4GEg

Raleigh
Visual Art Exchange

A hub for a diverse network of artists. Exhibiting the work of over 1,300 artists each year with more than 60 exhibitions. Educational programs culminating in the annual Ignite Creativity Summit.
Address: 309 W Martin St, Raleigh 27601

Phone: +1 (919) 828-7834
Website: vaeraleigh.org
Email: brandon@visualartexchange.org
Facebook.com/visualartexchange
Instagram.com/vaeraleigh
YouTube.com/channel/UCmuAMrDTV6UXkg5BNY3G7Bg

Little Art Gallery

Paintings, pottery, hand-blown glass, jewellery and gifts from regional and national artists.
Address: 432 Daniels St, Raleigh 27605
Phone: +1 (919) 890-4111
Website: Facebook.com/LittleArtGallery
Email: littleartgallery@gmail.com

Reno
Stremmel Gallery

Founded in 1969, specialising in contemporary paintings, drawings and sculpture by mid-career and established American and European artists. Located in a 6,500 sq. ft. architecturally award-winning building. Painting restoration, commercial and residential installation, purchase of single pieces or entire collections of important modern and contemporary work.
Address: 1400 S Virginia St, Reno 89502
Phone: +1 (775) 786-0558
Website: stremmelgallery.com
Email: info@stremmelgallery.com
Twitter.com/stremmelgallery
Facebook.com/stremmel.gallery

Richmond
Institute for Contemporary Art

A non-collecting space dedicated to exploring the art and issues of our time. Does not accept unsolicited work.
Address: 601 West Broad Street, Richmond 23284
Phone: +1 (804) 828-2823
Website: icavcu.org
Email: ica@vcu.edu
Twitter.com/ICAvcu
Facebook.com/ICAVCU

Instagram.com/ICAvcu
YouTube.com/channel/
UCSlFRxf4iZN9tC7z8D1rKkg

Ada Artist Downtown Access

Specializing in emerging and mid-career art since 2003.
Address: 228 W Broad St, Richmond 23220
Phone: +1 804-918-6225
Website: adagallery.com
Email: adagallery@gmail.com
Facebook.com/adagalleryrichmond
Instagram.com/the_ada_gallery

Gallery5

An award-winning, community motivated visual and performing arts centre. Extensive collaborations with cultural, educational, environmental and social organisations, encouraging a more diverse, inclusive and inspired region of art supporters.
Cutting edge contemporary art exhibitions with solo and group shows from emerging to established local to international artists. One of the top venues for unconventional and progressive performance art. A catalyst for new creative initiatives.
Address: 200 W Marshall St, Richmond 23220
Phone: +1 (804) 678-8863
Website: gallery5arts.org
Email: info@gallery5arts.org
Twitter.com/gallery5arts
Facebook.com/gallery5arts
Instagram.com/gallery5arts

Chasen Galleries

Specialising in pairing clients with the perfect artwork for their needs.
Address: 3101 Ellwood Ave, Richmond 23221
Phone: +1 (804) 204-1048
Website: chasengalleries.com
Email: jeff@chasengalleries.com
Twitter.com/chasengalleries

Facebook.com/ChasenGalleries
Instagram.com/chasengalleries
Artcld.com/gallery/chasen-galleries-i

Page Bond Gallery

A wide range of contemporary art, including painting, printmaking, photography, sculpture and ceramics. From emerging, mid-career and established makers, local, national and international artists.
Address: 1625 W Main St, Richmond 23220
Phone: +1 (804) 359-3633
Website: pagebondgallery.com
Email: page@pagebondgallery.com
Twitter.com/PageBondGallery
Facebook.com/pagebondgallery
Instagram.com/pagebondgallery
Pinterest.co.uk/pagebondgallery

Riverside
Riverside Art Museum

Integrating art into peoples' lives in a way that engages, inspires and builds community with high quality exhibits and education programs that instil a lifelong love of the arts.
Address: 3425 Mission Inn Ave, Riverside 92501
Phone: +1 (951) 684-7111
Website: riversideartmuseum.org
Email: info@riversideartmuseum.org
Twitter.com/RAMriverside
Facebook.com/riversideartmuseum
Instagram.com/riversideartmuseum
Pinterest.co.uk/ramarts
YouTube.com/user/RAMriverside

Rochester, New York
Rochester Contemporary Art Center

A non-profit arts centre founded in 1977 hosting numerous curated group exhibitions, collaborations with arts organisations of all kinds and community based projects.
Address: 137 East Ave, Rochester 14604
Phone: +1 (585) 461-2222
Website: rochestercontemporary.org
Email: info@rochestercontemporary.org

Twitter.com/roco137
Facebook.com/rochester.contemporary.art.
center
Instagram.com/roco137
Vimeo.com/user9373114

Sacramento
Verge Center for the Arts

Non-profit arts centre exposing the Sacramento region to internationally recognised contemporary art, as well as providing resources for local emerging and career artists.
Address: 625 S St, Sacramento 95811
Phone: +1 (916) 448-2985
Website: vergeart.com
Email: info@vergeart.com
Twitter.com/vergeart
Facebook.com/VergeArt
Instagram.com/vergeart
YouTube.com/channel/
UCq81tIbzJn0QvQW0HnJW9CQ

Saint Paul

Minnesota Museum-American Art.
Exploring American experiences through art and creativity.
Address: 350 Robert St N Ste 117, Saint Paul 55101
Phone: +1 (651) 797-2571
Website: mmaa.org
Email: info@mmaa.org
Twitter.com/mnmuseum
Facebook.com/mnmuseum
Instagram.com/mnmuseum

Salt Lake City, Utah
Utah Museum of Contemporary Art

An award-winning centre since 1931. Located in downtown Salt Lake City. Encouraging exploration into meaning through art. Stimulating thought and transforming society to shape an engaged and thoughtful global citizenry.

Address: 20 S West Temple, Salt Lake City 84101
Phone: +1 (801) 328-4201
Website: utahmoca.org
Email: communications@utahmoca.org
Twitter.com/utahmoca
Facebook.com/utahmoca
Instagram.com/utahmoca
Pinterest.co.uk/umoca
LinkedIn.com/company/utahmoca

San Antonio
Blue Star Contemporary

Inspiring, innovating and nurturing contemporary art. Developed in 1986, it is one of the first and longest-running non-profit venue for contemporary art in San Antonio. A platform for the work and ideas of local contemporary artists. In 2016, the 11,000 sq. ft. exhibition space was renovated, to provide enhanced presentation for artwork of all media.
Address: 116 Blue Star, San Antonio 78204
Phone: +1 (210) 227-6960
Website: bluestarcontemporary.org
Email: bsc@bluestarcontemporary.org
Twitter.com/bluestartart
Facebook.com/BlueStarArt
Instagram.com/bluestarart

High Wire Arts

Contemporary Art Gallery and event space.
Address: 326 W Josephine St, San Antonio 78212
Phone: +1 (210) 827-7681
Website: highwirearts.com
Twitter.com/HighWireArts
Facebook.com/highwire.arts
Flickr.com/people/119205458@N08
YouTube.com/watch?v=7EsLSfrIThg&feature=youtu.be

Hildebrand Art Gallery

Building a passion for art in San Antonio. Local and national artists.

Address: 735 W Hildebrand Ave, San
Antonio 78212
Phone: +1 (210) 854-0019
Website: hildebrandartgallery.com
Email: randy@hag-sa.com

San Bernardino, California
The Little Gallery of San Bernardino

Contemporary art gallery in San Bernardino.
Address: 459 W 4th St Ste 12, San
Bernardino 92401
Phone: +1 (951) 479-6761
Website: thelittlegallerysb.com
Email: thelittlegallerysb@gmail.com

San Diego
Museum of Contemporary Art

Contemporary art museum in San Diego.
Address: 1001 Kettner Blvd 1100, San
Diego 92101
Phone: +1 (858) 454-3541
Website: mcasd.org
Email: info@mcasd.org

San Francisco
San Francisco Museum of Modern Art

Founded in 1935, this museum for the first
on the West Coast to be dedicated to modern
and contemporary art. Championing the
most innovative and challenging art of its
time, both from modern masters and young
emerging artists.
Address: 151 3rd St, San Francisco 94103
Phone: +1 (415) 357-4000
Website: sfmoma.org
Email: mailto:contemporary_art@sfmoma.org
Visit@sfmoma.org
Twitter.com/sfmoma
Facebook.com/sfmoma
Instagram.com/sfmoma

City Art Gallery

Contemporary art gallery in San Francisco.
Address: 828 Valencia St, San Francisco
94110
Phone: +1 (415) 970-9900
Website: cityartgallery.org
Email: cityartgallery@gmail.com
Facebook.com/cityartgallery.sf
Instagram.com/sfcityartgallery

CK Contemporary

Representing the very best in contemporary
North American and European artists
working across a broad range of styles
and media. Primarily showing realism and
representational art, but does showcase other
genres. Works with new and experienced
collectors.
Address: 357 Geary St, San Francisco 94102
Phone: +1 (415) 397-0114
Website: ckcontemporary.com
Email: lauren@ckcontemporary.com
Email: info@ckcontemporary.com
Facebook.com/ckcontemporary
Instagram.com/ckcontemporary

Tangent Contemporary Art

A distinctive gallery in San Francisco, with
paintings and sculpture by internationally
renowned contemporary artists.
Address: 373 Geary St, San Francisco 94108
Phone: +1 (415) 956-9999
Website: tangentart.com
Email: info@tangentart.com
Facebook.com/tangentcontemporaryart
Pinterest.co.uk/tangentcontemporaryart

Hashimoto Contemporary

With a stable of an eclectic blend of new
contemporary artists.
Address: 804 Sutter St, San Francisco 94109
Phone: +1 (415) 655-9265
Website: hashimotocontemporary.com
Email: info@hashimotocontemporary.com
Twitter.com/Hashimoto_NYCSF
Facebook.com/HashimotoContemporary
Instagram.com/hashimotocontemporary

Modern Eden Gallery

Monthly exhibitions of established and emerging contemporary artists, from realism to surrealism.
Address: 1100 Sutter St, San Francisco 94109
Phone: +1 (415) 956-3303
Website: moderneden.com
Email: info@moderneden.com
Twitter.com/moderneden
Facebook.com/moderneden
Instagram.com/moderneden
Pinterest.co.uk/moderneden

Meyerovich Gallery

For more than 30 years, paintings, works on paper and sculpture by modern and contemporary masters. A strong tradition of working with artists and their estates.
Address: 251 Post St Ste 400, San Francisco 94108
Phone: +1 (415) 421-7171
Website: meyerovich.com
Email: art@meyerovich.com

San Jose
San Jose Institute of Contemporary Art

Founded in 1980 by a group of local artists who wanted to present cutting-edge, innovative art and experimental work in a curated space. Their goal was to get out in front of traditional museum programming and to present the newest work being created in the region.
Address: 560 S 1st St, San Jose 95113
Phone: +1 (408) 283-8155
Website: sjica.org
Email: sarah@sjica.org
Facebook.com/InstituteofContemporaryArtSanJose
Instagram.com/icasanjose

ART ARK Gallery

Presenting exhibitions by artists and curators that engage, educate and inspire the public. Two residences a year, culminating in a solo exhibition.
Address: 1035 S 6th St, San Jose 95112
Phone: +1 (408) 279-0844
Website: artarkgallery.com
Email: genevieve.hastings.artark@gmail.com

Santa Ana
Orange County Center For Contemporary Art

A non-profit, experimental space and art-collective.
Address: 117 N Sycamore St, Santa Ana 92701
Phone: +1 (714) 667-1517
Website: occca.org
Email: Info.occca@gmail.com
Twitter.com/Occcart
Facebook.com/groups/OCCCA
Instagram.com/occcart
YouTube.com/channel/UCKIuV1z2ii7HX8d7j22cOuA

Santa Fe, New Mexico
Centre for Contemporary Arts (CCA)

A centre for contemporary art cinema, visual arts, performances and public programs designed to ignite minds and connect people.
Address: 1050 Old Pecos Trl, Santa Fe 87505
Phone: +1 (505) 982-1338
Website: ccasantafe.org
Email: contact@ccasantafe.org
Facebook.com/ccasantafenm
Instagram.com/ccasantafe

Scottsdale
Scottsdale Museum of Contemporary Art

A museum dedicated to contemporary art, architecture and design with 4 galleries showing work from their growing permanent collection and rotating shows.
Address: 7374 E 2nd St, Scottsdale 85251
Phone: +1 480-874-4666
Website: smoca.org
Email: SMoCA@ScottsdaleArts.org

Gebert Contemporary Art Gallery

Painting, sculpture, video and photography from an international range of artists.
Address: 7160 E Main St, Scottsdale 85251
Phone: +1 (480) 429-0711
Website: gebertartaz.com
Facebook.com/Gebert-Contemporary-On-Main-125418184185291
Instagram.com/gebertartaz

Costello Childs Gallery

Local, national and international from emerging, mid-career and established artists in a broad range of mediums, including painting, drawings, printmaking, sculpture, photography and ceramics.
Address: 2724 N 68th St Ste 1, Scottsdale 85257
Phone: +1 (480) 949-2701
Website: costellogallery.com
Email: info@costellochildsart.com
Facebook.com/Costello.Childs.Contemporary.Gallery
Instagram.com/costellochildsgallery

Bonner David Galleries

Over 30 of the best representational and non-representational artists from around the world in both traditional and contemporary forms.
Address: 7040 E Main St, Scottsdale 85251
Phone: +1 (480) 941-8500
Email: art@bonnerdavid.com
Address: 33E.81st St. #1, New York, NY 10028
Phone: 929.226.7800
Website: bonnerdavid.com
Email: rebecca1@bonnerdavid.com

The Marshall Gallery

A diverse collection of exceptional art, showing work from more than 70 world-class artists. Different genres with diverse styles.
Address: 7106 E Main St, Scottsdale 85251
Phone: +1 (480) 970-3111
Website: themarshallgallery.com
Email: email@themarshallgallery.com
Facebook.com/TheMarshallGallery
Instagram.com/marshallgallery
YouTube.com/user/TheMarshallLeKAE

Legacy Gallery

Representing over 100 national artists, offering the finest in representational and impressionistic art. Since 1988, the gallery has specialised in paintings and sculptures in a wide variety of subject matter, including western, figurative, wildlife, still life and landscape from emerging and established artists. Life-size bronze sculptures.
Address: 7178 E Main St, Scottsdale 85251
Phone: +1 (480) 945-1113
Website: legacygallery.com
Email: janell@legacygallery.com
Twitter.com/Legacy_Gallery
Facebook.com/legacygalleryart

Tilt Gallery

Hand-applied photographic process and mixed media fine art, both contemporary and historical.
Address: 7077 E Main St #14+, Scottsdale 85251
Phone: +1 (602) 716-5667
Website: tiltgallery.com
Email: melanie@tiltgallery.com
Email: info@tiltgallery.com
Twitter.com/TiltGallery
Facebook.com/Tilt-Gallery-145891347586

Xanadu Gallery

Exciting work from some of today's best artists.
Address: 7039 E Main St Ste 101, Scottsdale 85251
Phone: +1 480-368-9929
Website: art.xanadugallery.com
Facebook.com/XanaduGallery
Instagram.com/xanadugallery

Method Art

A gallery with a working studio, to allow visitors to connect and better understand the working process.
Address: 4151 N Marshall Way Ste 3, Scottsdale 85251
Phone: +1 (602) 326-9622
Website: methodart.com
Instagram.com/methodartstudio

Seattle

Frederick Holmes and Company – Gallery of Modern & Contemporary Art

One of Seattle's most vibrant contemporary galleries.
Address: 309 Occidental Ave S, Seattle 98104
Phone: +1 (206) 682-0166
Website: frederickholmesandcompany.com
Email: info@frederickholmesandcompany.com
Facebook.com/Frederick-Holmes-and-Company-Gallery-of-Modern-Contemporary-Art-367110300067336
Instagram.com/frederickholmesandcompany

CoCA

A vital part of the contemporary art scene for 36 years. Presenting contemporary artists from various disciplines with expanded hours for the monthly 1st Thursday art walk between 6-9pm.
Address: 114 3rd Ave S, Seattle 98104
Phone: +1 (206) 728-1980
Website: cocaseattle.org
Email: info@cocaseattle.org
Twitter.com/CoCASeattle
Facebook.com/cocaseattle
Instagram.com/cocaseattle
YouTube.com/channel/UCzXppUgehVjrFvupD5pzsRQ

Davidson Galleries

Since 1973 the gallery has exhibited antique, modern and contemporary works on paper – original fine prints, drawings, paintings and mixed media with an inventory of around 18,000 works spanning five centuries.
Address: 313 Occidental Ave S, Seattle 98104
Phone: +1 (206) 624-7684
Website: davidsongalleries.com
Email: info@davidsongalleries.com
Facebook.com/davidsongalleries
Instagram.com/davidsongalleries
Pinterest.co.uk/davidsongalleries

Stonington Gallery

For over 40 years, the gallery has offered inspiring visual art which embodies the region's history, people, traditions and environment. Included are unparalleled contemporary masterwork, with a special emphasis on carved sculpture – masks, totem poles and panels, as well as fine art glass, prints, jewellery, bronzes and paintings.
Address: 125 S Jackson St, Seattle 98104
Phone: +1 (206) 405-4040
Website: stoningtongallery.com
Email: art@stoningtongallery.com
Facebook.com/StoningtonGallery
Instagram.com/stonington_gallery

Gallery 110

Enriching curated exhibitions, public projects and creative dialogue fostering connection between associated artists and the arts community.
Address: 110 3rd Ave S, Seattle 98104
Phone: +1 (206) 624-9336
Website: gallery110.com
Email: director@gallery110.com
Facebook.com/G110.Seattle
Instagram.com/explore/locations/4182365/gallery-110
YouTube.com/playlist?list=PL8RkAKDZzoTkK-n9Kxz--GOC_A-OodKzG

Core Gallery

Vibrant collective gallery in the heart of the arts district.
Address: 117 Prefontaine Pl S, Seattle 98104
Phone: +1 (206) 467-4444
Website: coregallery.org
Email: info@coregallery.org

Shreveport, Louisiana
Nader's Gallery

Art, framing, accessories and gifts since 1969 with a gallery space of over 10,000 sq. ft.
Address: 524 E Kings Hwy, Shreveport 71105
Phone: +1 (318) 868-3021
Website: nadersgallery.com

St Louis
Soulard Art Gallery

An artist's co-op hosting monthly exhibitions from outside artists and resident artists working in mediums such as ceramics, painting, drawing, photography, light fixtures and jewellery.
Address: 2028 S 12th St, Saint Louis 63104
Phone: +1 (314) 258-4299
Website: soulardartgallery.com
Email: soulardartgallery@gmail.com
Facebook.com/SoulardArtGallery
Instagram.com/soulardartgallery

Art St Louis Gallery Space

Connecting, inspiring and enriching the community with the activity of regional contemporary artists with a gallery/café.
Address: 1223 Pine St, Saint Louis 63103
Phone: +1 (314) 614-4810
Website: artstlouis.org
Email: info@artstlouis.org
Twitter.com/ArtStLouis
Facebook.com/ArtSaintLouis
Instagram.com/art_st_louis
LinkedIn.com/showcase/art-saint-louis-exhibit-services
YouTube.com/user/ArtStLouis

Concrete Ocean Art Gallery

Featuring local Saint Louis art talent
Address: 2257 S Jefferson Ave, Saint Louis 63104
Phone: +1 314-497-0199
Website: Facebook.com/Concrete-Ocean-Art-Gallery-149624395086938
Email: concreteoceanart@gmail.com

Des Lee Gallery

Part of the Sam Fox School of Design and Visual Arts, at Washington University in St Louis.
Address: 1627 Washington Ave, Saint Louis 63103
Phone: +1 (314) 621-8735
Website: desleegallery.com
Email: anschultz@wustl.edu

Houska Gallery

Exhibiting emerging and mid-career artists from the St Louis region.
Address: 4728 Mcpherson Ave, Saint Louis 63108
Phone: +1 (314) 496-1377
Website: houska.com
Email: houskagallerystl@gmail.com
Facebook.com/HouskaGallery
Instagram.com/houskagallery

Duane Reed Gallery

One of the premier galleries in the Midwest, exhibiting internationally recognised contemporary artists working in glass, ceramics, painting, photography and fibre.
Address: 4729 Mcpherson Ave, Saint Louis 63108
Phone: +1 314-361-4100
Website: duanereedgallery.com
Email: info@duanereedgallery.com Twitter.com/dreedgallery
Facebook.com/duanereedgallery
Instagram.com/reedgallery
Artsy.net/duane-reed-gallery
1stdibs.com/dealers/duane-reed-gallery

Philip Slein Gallery

Contemporary and modern painting with a dedication to exhibiting the best abstract paintings by American artists.
Address: 4735 Mcpherson Ave, Saint Louis 63108
Phone: +1 (314) 361-2617
Website: philipsleingallery.com
Email: director@philipsleingallery.com
Twitter.com/PSleinGallery
Facebook.com/philipsleingallery
Instagram.com/philipsleingallery
Pinterest.co.uk/psleingallery

PHD Gallery

An alternative contemporary art space that advances challenging work by ground-breaking local, regional and national artists.
Address: 2300 Cherokee St, Saint Louis 63118
Phone: +1 (314) 664-6644
Website: phdstl.com
Facebook.com/phdgallery

Componere Gallery

Handcrafted art since 1986, featuring local artists in the sunny, 3,600 sq. ft. space.
Address: 6509 Delmar Blvd, Saint Louis 63130
Phone: +1 314-721-1181
Website: componere.com
Email: dmworzel@componere.com
Email: haldeuser@componere.com
Facebook.com/componere

St. Petersburg
Ocean Blue Galleries

Representing established national and international artists.
Address: 284 Beach Dr NE, Saint Petersburg 33701
Phone: +1 (727) 502-2583
Website: oceanblue.gallery
Email: oceanbluegalleries@frontier.com
Twitter.com/OceanBlueArt
Facebook.com/OceanBlueArt

Florida CraftArt

Contemporary ceramics, fibre, glass, jewellery, metal, mixed media and wood handcrafted by 250 Florida artists. The only non-profit gallery exclusively dedicated to fine craft. With 20 artists' studios.
Address: 501 Central Ave, St Petersburg 33701
Phone: +1 (727) 821-7391
Website: floridacraftart.org
Email: info@floridacraftart.org
Twitter.com/FloridaCraftArt
Facebook.com/FloridaCraftArt.org
Instagram.com/florida_craftart_gallery
YouTube.com/channel/UC_GHgnuhssWn1qhCTZinT8Q

Articles

With 30 years of experience representing regional and national artists. A monthly exhibition and custom framing.
Address: 1445 Central Ave, Saint Petersburg 33705
Phone: +1 (727) 898-6061
Website: articlesstpete.com
Email: articlesstpete@gmail.com
Facebook.com/articlesstpete/lesliecurrangallery
Instagram.com/articlesstpete
lesliecurrangallery
collectors.exchange

Duncan McClellan Gallery

Contemporary glass art gallery and working hot-shop (glass blowing facility). With over 100 internationally acclaimed artists shown in monthly rotating exhibits.
Project.Phone: +1 (813) 760-6600
Website: dmglass.com

Nuance Galleries

Cuban and other fine art for over 35 years, now online. Owner, Rob Rowen, is showcasing unique Cuban art at galleries and museums whilst also working for the Global Action Network which improves conditions

in Nepal and Africa.
Address: 2924 Central Ave, Saint Petersburg 33712
Phone: +1 (813) 875-0511
Website: nuancegalleries.com
Email: nuancegalleries@earthlink.net

Myers Antiques Auction Gallery

Florida's only speciality antiques auction house, established in 1970, offering fresh-to-the-market fine art and antiques from estates in Florida, New England, and New York.
Address: 1600 4th St N, Saint Petersburg 33704
Phone: +1 (727) 823-3249
Website: myersfineart.com
Email: auctions@myersfineart.com
Twitter.com/MyersFineArt
Facebook.com/myersauctiongallery
Instagram.com/myersfineart
Pinterest.co.uk/myersauctions
Myersauctiongallery.Tumblr.com
LinkedIn.com/company/myers-fine-art-and-antiques-auction-gallery

Red Cloud Indian Arts

Native American arts. Jewellery by the Yellowhorse family and other artists. Pottery and storytelling dolls, glass and paintings from young new artists.
Address: 214 Beach Dr NE, Saint Petersburg 33701
Phone: +1 (727) 821-5824
Website: redcloudindianarts.com
Email: redcloud1@tampabay.rr.com
Facebook.com/Red-Cloud-Indian-Arts-166656520011223
Instagram.com/hrambeaux

Shapiro's

Handmade American crafts from local artists, including jewellery, glasswork, clay, pottery, wooden boxes, jewellery boxes, clocks, Judaica, metal sculpture and home accessories.

Address: 300 Beach Dr NE, Saint Petersburg 33701
Phone: +1 (727) 894-2111
Website: shapirosgallery.com
Email: info@shapirogallery.com
Facebook.com/shapirogallery

Soft Water Studios

Contemporary art gallery in St Petersburg.
Address: 515 22nd St S, Saint Petersburg 33712
Website: softwaterstudios.com
Email: softwaterstudiosfl@gmail.com

Zen Glass Studio

The Tampa Bay area's premier lampworking and glass art studio offering corporate workshops and private instruction as well as hand blown glass jewellery, glassware, marbles, sculpture, figurines, wall art, multimedia, installations and more.
Address: 600 27th St S, Saint Petersburg 33712
Phone: +1 (727) 323-3141
Website: zenglass.com
Email: info@zenglass.com
Twitter.com/zenglass
Facebook.com/ZenGlassStudio

The Gallery

Emerging local and internationally recognised contemporary artists, with paintings, sculptures, lithographs and photographic prints, exhibitions and events.
Address: 200 Central Ave Ste 111, Saint Petersburg 33701
Phone: +1 (727) 324-6730
Website: libertinefineart.com
Email: info@LibertineFineArt.com
Twitter.com/libertineart
Facebook.com/libertinecontemporary
Instagram.com/libertinecontemporary

Stockton

Stockton Art League

Supporting artists, education and the development of the visual arts within the region. Founded in 1936 as a critique sessions, followed by a sketching group. Made up of professional, semi-professional and amateur artists. Providing programs, workshops and activities , promoting mutual cultural exchange with other organisations and the community and opportunities for exhibitions, both solo and group.
Address: 1902 Pacific Ave, Stockton CA 95204
Phone: +1 (209) 466-6604
Website: stocktonartleague.org
Email: gallery@stocktonartleague.org
Twitter.com/stocktonart
Facebook.com/stocktonartleague
Instagram.com/thestocktonartleague

Tacoma, Washington

Mavi Contemporary Art

Exhibiting fine art, focusing primarily on sculpture, photography and painting supporting the work of both local and international artists.
Address: 502 6th Ave, Tacoma 98402
Phone: +1 (253) 759-6233
Website: mavigallery.com
Email: director@mavicontemporary.com
Email: info@mavicontemporary.com

Proctor Art Gallery

Some of the best local art in the region in a wide range of styles and medium.
Address: 3811 N 26th St, Tacoma 98407
Phone: +1 (253) 759-4238
Website: proctorart.com
Email: pamelaphelps@proctorart.com
Facebook.com/proctorartgallery
Instagram.com/proctor.art.gallery

Tallahassee, Florida

621 Gallery

Non-profit arts exhibition and programs space, showing progressive and innovative contemporary art, events and programs. Representing 150-200 local and national artists with 2-4 solo and group exhibits a month from Sep-June. Student to established artists.
Address: 621 Industrial Dr, Tallahassee 32310
Phone: +1 (850) 222-6210
Website: 621gallery.org
Email: 621galleryinc@gmail.com
Twitter.com/621Gallery1
Facebook.com/the621gallery
Facebook.com/621Annex
Instagram.com/621_gallery

Venvi Art Gallery

Exclusive, original fine art work for collectors from acclaimed artists.
Address: 2901 E Park Ave Ste 2800, Tallahassee 32301
Phone: +1 (850) 322-0965
Website: venviartgallery.com
Email: Brinda@VenviArtGallery.com
Facebook.com/Venviartgallery
Instagram.com/venviartgallery
LinkedIn.com/company/venvi-art-gallery
YouTube.com/channel/UC-VQDLLKHbtXG3LE-7Z0k6Q

Signature Art Gallery

A dynamic and exciting contemporary art gallery with a broad selection of work, including landscape, abstract, figurative, still life and photography.
Address: 2782 Capital Cir NE, Tallahassee 32308
Phone: +1 850-297-2422
Website: signatureartgallery.com
Facebook.com/Signature-Art-Gallery-94288957456

Tampa
Usf Contemporary Art Museum

University of South Florida, Institute for Research in Art. A contemporary art museum, with a graphic studio, working on public art and art in health.
Address: 3821 Usf Holly Dr, Tampa 33620
Phone: +1 (813) 974-4133
Website: ira.usf.edu

Cass Contemporary

Contemporary art space and studio, focusing on art from all levels; local to international, with exhibitions, lectures and workshops from emerging and established artists. Also art consulting to private and corporate collectors, such as hospitals, banks and restaurants. A space for individuals to view and engage with the art community.
Address: 2722 S Macdill Ave, Tampa 33629
Phone: +1 (813) 839-7135
Website: casscontemporary.com
Email: info@casscontemporary.com
Twitter.com/CASStampa
Facebook.com/casscontemporary
Instagram.com/casscontemporary

Tempe, Arizona
Art In Metal

Work by Lyle London inspired by the natural work, especially spiral geometry and helical topology, which features strongly in his work, including most of his suspended sculptures and all of his 3D prints.
Address: 219 S Siesta Ln Ste 101, Tempe 85281
Phone: +1 (480) 894-9369
Website: artinmetalusa.com
Twitter.com/london_lyle
Facebook.com/lyle.london.52
Instagram.com/explore/tags/lylelondon
YouTube.com/user/n828dv/featured

Collier Gallery

Custom picture and art framing, including original hand carved, gilded frames. The gallery includes the fine art estate of Lon Megargee, 20th century Western, WPA and contemporary Southwestern fine art with vintage rodeo photography reproduced in a very large format.
Address: 1733 E Mckellips Rd Ste 110, Tempe 85281
Phone: +1 (480) 947-2787
Website: colliergallery.com
Email:collier@colliergallery.com
Facebook.com/CollierGallery

Toledo
Toledo Museum of Art

Founded in 1901, the museum has earned a global reputation for innovative and extensive education programs on an architecturally significant campus. Art from all over the world, and from every time period.
Address: 2445 Monroe St, Toledo 43620
Phone: +1 (419) 255-8000
Website: toledomuseum.org

Tucson
Museum of Contemporary Art

Tucson's only museum devoted exclusively to contemporary art from around the globe. Applying creative solutions to the problems of today and tomorrow through the vehicle of contemporary art, with an ambitious, innovative program responsive to the wants and needs of our community. Rotating exhibitions from local to internationally renowned contemporary artists, spurring dialogue and fostering empathy. MOCA Tucson resides on the ancestral lands of the Tohono O'odham people.
Address: 265 S Church Ave, Tucson 85701
Phone: +1 (520) 624-5019
Website: moca-tucson.org
Email: info@moca-tucson.org
Twitter.com/mocatucson
Facebook.com/MOCATucson
Instagram.com/mocatucson

Desert Artisans' Gallery

Run by local Southern Arizona artists, representing over 60 of the best artists in the area, working in a variety of media, including clay, glass, jewellery, paintings, photography and wood.
Address: 6536 E Tanque Verde Rd, Tucson 85715
Phone: +1 520-722-4412
Website: desertartisansgallery.com
Email: info@desertartisansgallery.com
Facebook.com/DesertArtisansGallery
Instagram.com/desertartisansgallery

Dinnerware Contemporary Arts Gallery

In Tucson, Arizona, "Dinnerware" means contemporary arts. A non-profit art gallery in its 32nd year. Partially supported by the Southern Arizona Arts and Culture Alliance and a number of commercial businesses friendly to Dinnerware's mission of revitalisation of the arts, through exploration of innovative business models.
Address: 210 N 4th Ave, Tucson 85705
Phone: +1 (520) 792-4503
Website: Facebook.com/ DinnerwareArtspace
Email: dinnerwareartspace@gmail.com

Tulsa

108 Contemporary

Fine contemporary art in traditional craft materials, such as glass, paper, ceramics, fibre, metals, mixed media and wood as well as a wider range of contemporary art forms, such as installation, performance and video components.
Address: 108 E Brady St, Tulsa 74103
Phone: +1 (918) 895-6302
Website: 108contemporary.org
Email: info@108contemporary.org
Facebook.com/108contemporary
Instagram.com/108contemporary
YouTube.com/channel/ UCCeyGEQQJ67o3hthu4ln7GQ

M A Doran Gallery Inc

Celebrating 38 years in Tulsa as a premier art gallery showcasing contemporary work by local, regional and national artists.
Address: 3509 S Peoria Ave Ste 180, Tulsa 74105
Phone: +1 (918) 748-8700
Website: madorangallery.com
Email: maryann@madorangallery.com
Twitter.com/MADorangallery
Facebook.com/MADoranGallery
Instagram.com/madorangallery3509

The Art Market

Specializing in classic & contemporary Native American Art, picture framing, and art appraisal.
Address: 5014 S Sheridan Rd, Tulsa 74145
Phone: +1 (918) 664-0626
Website: indianarttulsa.com
Email: sales@indianarttulsa.com

Virginia Beach

MOCA – Virginia Museum of Contemporary Art

Exhibitions feature painting, sculpture, photography, glass, video and other visual media from internationally acclaimed artists as well as artists of national and regional renown. Studio art classes, educational outreach programs and outdoor art shows, involving a diverse regional public in the rich and active language of contemporary visual art.
Address: 2200 Parks Ave, Virginia Beach 23451
Phone: +1 (757) 425-0000
Website: virginiamoca.org
Email: info@virginiamoca.org
Twitter.com/VirginiaMOCA
Facebook.com/VirginiaMOCA
Instagram.com/virginiamoca
Artsy.net/virginia-moca
YouTube.com/user/VirginiaMOCA

Stravitz Sculpture & Fine Art Gallery

Featuring the bronze sculptures of Richard Stravitz and fine art by local and international artists.

Address: 1217 Laskin Rd, Virginia Beach 23451

Phone: +1 (757) 305-9411

Website: sculpture-bronze.com

Email: richardstravitzsculpture@cox.net

Twitter.com/stravitzgallery

Facebook.com/stravitzgallery

Instagram.com/richardstravitz

Pinterest.co.uk/stravitzart

Washington

If Art Gallery

Showing contemporary art by artists from South Carolina, the rest of the United States and Europe.

Address: 1223 Lincoln St, Colombia 29201

Phone: +1 (803) 238-2351

Website: ifartgallery.blogspot.com

Email: wroefs@sc.rr.com

701 Center For Contemporary Art

Non-profit visual arts centre promoting the understanding and enjoyment of contemporary art, the creative process and the role of art and artists in the community, via the gallery and its Artist-in-residence program.

Address: 701 Whaley St, Second Floor, Colombia 29201-5900

Phone: +1 (803) 779-4571

Website: 701cca.org

Email: info@701cca.org

Twitter.com/701CCA

Facebook.com/701CCA

Instagram.com/701cca

Winston-Salem

South-eastern Center for Contemporary Art (SECCA)

Educating and involving audiences in the art of our time. Diverse programs exploring the dynamic relationship between art and society; supporting the creation of significant new art; illuminating trends and issues in contemporary art. A public forum for the promotion of diverse ideas and scholarship for areas unrecognised by the mainstream.

Address: 750 Marguerite Dr, Winston-Salem 27106

Phone: +1 (336) 725-1904

Website: secca.org

Email: info@secca.org

Twitter.com/seccacontempart

Facebook.com/SECCAContempArt

Instagram.com/seccacontempart

LinkedIn.com/company/southeastern-center-for-contemporary-art-secca-

YouTube.com/user/SECCAWS

Yonkers, New York

Elisa Contemporary Art

Representing artists from around the world since 2007, focusing on the power of art to heal and transform lives. Emerging to late career artists with residential and corporate art consulting.

Address: 5622 Mosholu Ave, Riverdale 10471

Phone: +1 (212) 729-4974

Website: elisacontemporaryart.com

Email: Lisa@ElisaArt.com

Twitter.com/LCooperArt

Facebook.com/ElisaContemporaryArt

Instagram.com/elisacontemporaryart

Pinterest.co.uk/lisacooper1

LinkedIn.com/in/lisacooper

Lehman College Art Gallery

Serving the interests of the diverse audience from the Bronx and greater New York City since 1984, specialising in thematic group exhibitions that bring together famous artists with emerging talents. With a strong education component, with community outreach programs, from young students to

senior citizens.
Address: 250 Bedford Park Blvd W, Bronx 10468
Phone: +1 (718) 960-8731
At: Lehman College
Website: lehmangallery.org
Email: lehmancollegeartgallery@gmail.com
Facebook.com/lehmancollege.artgallery
Instagram.com/lc_art_gallery

UZBEKISTAN

Dvael Gallery of Contemporary Art

Contemporary art gallery in Uzbekistan.
Address: Dostoevskogo ul., d. 1A, skver Flora, Омськ 644000
Phone: +7 381 224-61-44

VIETNAM

Hanoi

Vincom Center for Contemporary Art (VCCA)

A non-profit art centre, sponsored by Vingroup JSC with a mission to connect artists with the community and the global arts scene. With international infrastructure and facilities, VCCA works with both domestic and international artists.
Address: 72A Nguyen Trai, R3-B1 Royal City, Thanh Xuan, Hanoi 10000
Phone: +84 24 6666 0606
Website: vccavietnam.com
Email: info-vcca@vingroup.net
Facebook.com/VCCAVIETNAM

Nguyen Art Gallery in Hanoi

Promoting art from Vietnamese artists, mainly oil on canvas and lacquer paintings. Focusing on emerging artists which communicate the imaginative aspects of culture, reflecting spiritual, social and political concerns. Also showing established artists, shipping worldwide.
Address: 31 a, Van Mieu Street, Dong Da District, Dong Da, Hanoi 10000
Website: nguyenartgallery.com
Email: order@nguyenartgallery.com
Facebook.com/NguyenArtGalleryVietnam

CUC Gallery

A leading contemporary art gallery showing paintings, drawings, photographs, sculpture, installation, video and prints. Emerging, mid-career and established Vietnamese artists collaborating internationally.
Address: A4703, Keangnam Hanoi Landmark Tower a E6, Pham Hung Rd, A4703, Keangnam Hanoi Landmark Tower a E6, Pham Hung Rd, Hanoi, Vietnam, Hanoi 10000
Website: cucgallery.vn
Email: contact@cucgallery.vn
Facebook.com/cucgalleryvietnam
Instagram.com/cucgalleryhanoi

Art Vietnam Gallery

An international gallery showing contemporary Vietnamese art in painting, sculpture, lacquer, photography, video and prints.
Address: 24 Ly Quoc Su, Hanoi
Phone: 84 24 3862 3184 / 84 9 0475 1001
Website: artvietnamgallery.com
Email: info@artvietnamgallery.com

Hanoi Art Gallery

Exhibiting the latest paintings by Vietnamese contemporary artists, both emerging and internationally recognised.
Address: 36 Trang Tien, Hanoi
Phone: +84-39347192
Website: hanoi-artgallery.com
Email: hanoiart36@gmail.com
Facebook.com/hanoiart36

Ho Chi Minh City
Galerie Quynh

Contemporary art gallery in Ho Chi Minh City.
Address: 118 Nguyen Van Thu, Dakao Ward, District 1, Ho Chi Minh City 700000
Phone: +84 838 227 218
Website: galeriequynh.com
Email: info@galeriequynh.com

Blue Space Art Gallery

Contemporary art from Vietnam. Consultancy for collectors.
Address: 97A Pho Duc Chinh St., Dist 1, Ho Chi Minh City Fine Arts Museum, Ho Chi Minh City 70000
Phone: 0838 213 695
Website: vietnamartist.com/blue-space-art-gallery
Email: info@vietnamartist.com
Twitter.com/VietnamArtist
Facebook.com/VNArtist
Pinterest.co.uk/Vietnamart

VietnamArtist.com

The oldest and most trusted online art gallery for two leading galleries in Vietnam; Particular Art Gallery and Blue Space Art Gallery, both based in Ho Chi Minh City.
Address: 97A Pho Duc Chinh St., D.1, Ho Chi Minh City
Website: vietnamartist.com
Email: info@vietnamartist.com
Twitter.com/VietnamArtist
Facebook.com/VNArtist
Pinterest.co.uk/Vietnamart

Vietnam ART Gallery

With long experience collecting, exhibiting, identifying and developing new talent. A destination for international cultural institutions, private collectors and diplomatic visits.
Address: 80 Nguyen Hue St., Ben Nghe Ward, Dist.1, Ho Chi Minh City 70000
Phone: +84 838 242 058
Website: vietnampainting.vn
Email: info@vietnampainting.vn

Hoi An
ASIAN Gallery and Bookstore

A unique combination of fine art photography and documentary styles from the French-born photographer Réhahn, with portraits of Vietnam, Cuba and India.
Address: 13, Nguyen Phuc Chu, Hoi An 51000
Phone: +84 93 526 01 76
Website: rehahnphotographer.com
Email: Assistant.rehahn@gmail.com

VIRGIN ISLANDS
Art at Top Hat

Local and international fine art, handcrafted jewellery, local pottery, antiques and collectables.
Address: 52 Company St, Christiansted 00820
Phone: +1 (340) 513-3558
Website: Facebook.com/artattophatvi
Email: tophat0055@gmail.com

ZAMBIA
Bernstein Contemporary & Investment Art

Worldwide art promotion.
Address: 84 Homestead Rd 2090
Phone: +27 72 803 4548
Website: the-art-world.com/galleries/sa-bernstein.htm
Email: bernstein@telkomsa.net Twitter.com/theartworld
Facebook.com/theartworldpage
Pinterest.co.uk/theartworld

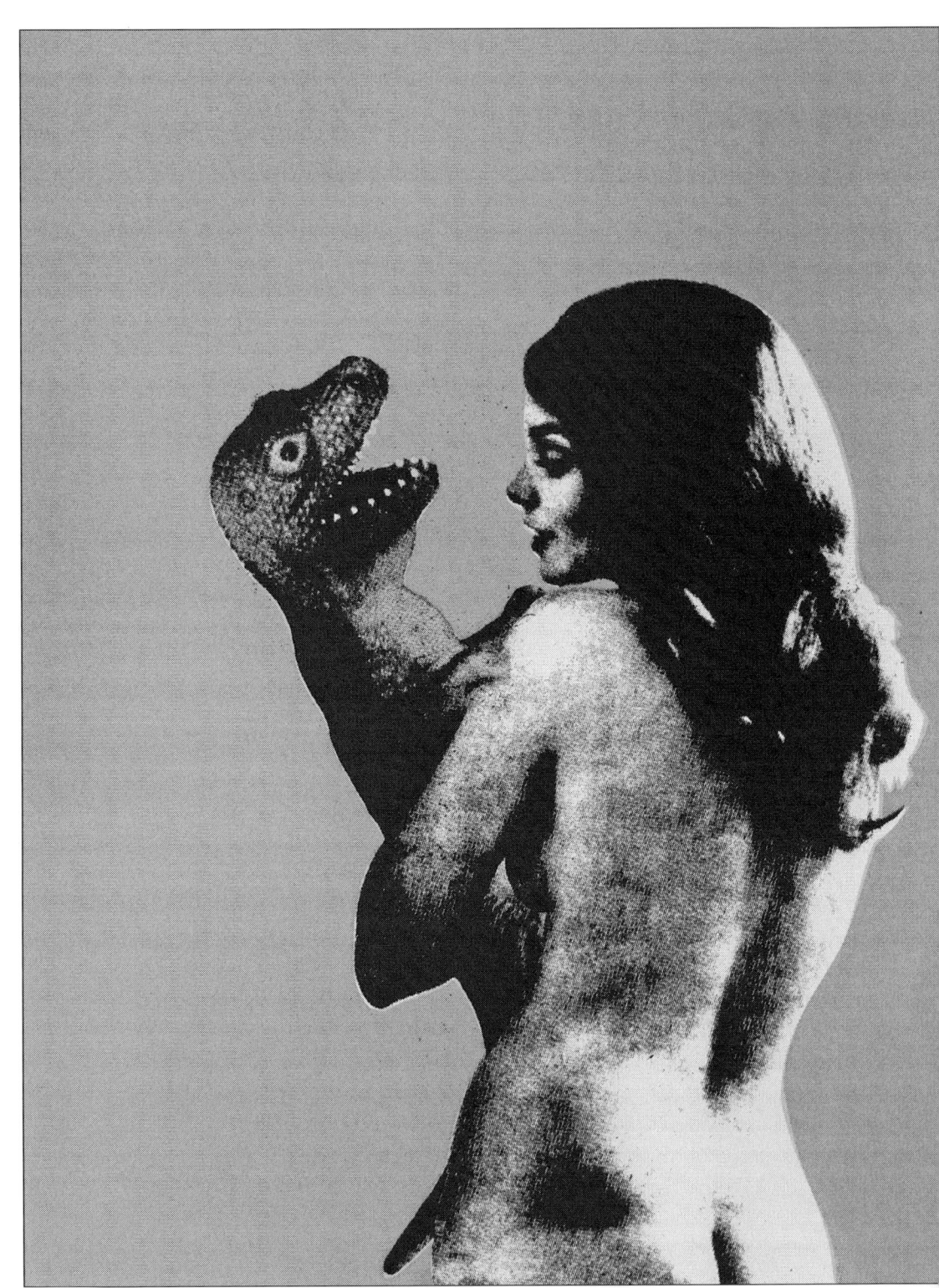

Bundle of Joy in Black by Cameron Twins

ART FAIRS

January

Este Arte, Punta del Este, Uruguay,

A cultural landmark, where South American art systems meet, exchange ideas and thrives, empowering both private and institutional collections and creating a space for dialogue between artists, collectors and curators.
Website: estearte.com
Email: info@estearte.com
Facebook.com/ESTEARTEfair
Instagram.com/esteartefair/?hl=es-la
Open.spotify.com/
show/6spM0rnao6LG6QXPkYlX8b
YouTube.com/channel/
UCzVHOmPketfQwU40xLG2DYQ

Original Miami Beach Antique Show, Florida, US

More than 700 dealers from over 30 countries in the 5-day show. From jewellery, watches and handbags to artwork, furniture and home décor.
Website: originalmiamibeachantiqueshow.com
Email: info@usantiqueshows.com
Twitter.com/USAntiqueShows
Facebook.com/OfficialPage.
USAntiqueShows
Instagram.com/usantiqueshows

Mayfair Antiques & Fine Art Fair, London, UK

Collectors, interior designers and discerning individuals from around the world, with 40 exhibitors showing period, art deco and mid-century furniture, as well as 20th century jewellery, traditional and contemporary paintings and sculpture and many other interesting and desirable objects d'art spanning the centuries.
Website: mayfair-london.co.uk/the-mayfair-antiques-fine-art-fair
Email: info@mayfair-london.co.uk
Twitter.com/MayfairLondon1
Facebook.com/mayfairlondondirectory
Pinterest.co.uk/mayfairlondondir/_created

Palm Beach Modern and Contemporary, Florida, US

Blue chip contemporary, post-war works from international galleries.
Website: artpbfair.com
Email: info@artmiami.com
Twitter.com/artmiamifairs
Facebook.com/
PalmBeachModernandContemporary
Instagram.com/artmiamifairs

Art Innsbruck, Austria

Contemporary art, classic modernism, pop art and other currents of the 19th – 21st centuries including paintings, works on paper, print editions, original prints, sculpture, objects/installations, artists books, photographs, new media and other treasures.
Website: art-innsbruck.com/index.php/de
Email: office@art-innsbruck.com
Facebook.com/art.innsbruck
Instagram.com/artinnsbruck

Fog Design + Art, San Francisco, California, US

Contemporary art that shifts, morphs and reveals itself through multiple forms and dimensions.
Website: fogfair.com
Email: fog@fogfair.com
Twitter.com/fogfair
Instagram.com/fogfair/?hl=en

Outsider Art Fair, New York, US

Self-taught artists created outside the mainstream from both legendary and newly discovered artists.
Website: outsiderartfair.com
Email: info@outsiderartfair.com

Twitter.com/OutsiderArtFair
Facebook.com/outsiderartfair
Instagram.com/OutsiderArtFair

SEA Focus, Singapore

Showcasing contemporary art from Southeast Asia, providing a platform to propel diverse cultural exchanges.
Website: seafocus.sg
Email: info@seafocus.sg
Facebook.com/SEAFocusSG
Instagram.com/seafocus
YouTube.com/channel/
UCAoGjheqDcGrsLABpQ3ZroQ

First Art Fair, Amsterdam, Netherlands

Contemporary art including painting and sculpture, glass, photography and jewellery from renowned and young artists represented by 30 galleries from The Netherlands.
Website: expohour.com
Email: sales@expohour.com
Twitter.com/expohour
Facebook.com/expohour
Linkedin.com/company/expohourevents

Taipei Dangdai, Taiwan

99 leading galleries with over 40,000 visitors in 2020, celebrating the city's unique and dynamic art scene and global creativity in the wider art market in Asia.
Website: taipeidangdai.com
Email: info@taipeidangdai.com
Facebook.com/taipeidangdaiartfair
Instagram.com/taipeidangdai

Untitled, San Francisco, California, US

With a selected curatorial team identifying and curating a selection of galleries, artist-run exhibition spaces and non-profit institutions in dialogue with an architecturally designed venue.
Website: Artsy.net/fair/untitled-art-san-francisco-2020

Miami Antiques + Art + Design Show, Miami, Florida, US

With over 100 premier exhibitors from the U.S., Canada, Europe and South America showing antiques and decorative arts from the 17th – 20th centuries.
Website: miamiantiquesartdesign.com
Email: info@dolphinfairs.com
Twitter.com/miamiantiques
Facebook.com/Miamiantiquesartdesign

Decorative Antiques & Textiles Fair (Winter), London, UK

A family owned event launched in 1985, uniting the antiques and interior design trades, with 3 fairs a year – late January, mid-May and late Sep/early Oct.
Website: decorativefair.com
Email: fairs@decorativefair.com
Twitter.com/decorativefair
Facebook.com/decorativefair
Instagram.com/decorativefair
Pinterest.co.uk/decorativefair

Bruneaf (Brussels Non-European Art Fair) Winter, Brussels, Belgium

Occurring twice a year, in Jan and June, dedicated to old and selected tribal arts.
Website: bruneaf.com
Email: info@bruneaf.com
Twitter.com/bruneaf
Facebook.com/Bruneaf
Instagram.com/bruneaf

London Art Fair, London, UK

Showcasing the most outstanding modern and contemporary art of our time, with 129 galleries from 14 countries and over 23,000 visitors in 2020.
Website: londonartfair.co.uk
Email: laf@upperstreetevents.co.uk
Twitter.com/londonartfair
Facebook.com/Londonartfair
Instagram.com/londonartfair

AADLA Fine Art & Antiques Show, New York, US

25 galleries and dealers showing Old Master drawing, Indian bronzes, English furniture and rare books.
Website: aadlafair.com
Email: mwhitepr@gmail.com

Arte Fiera Bologna, Italy

International exhibition of contemporary art.
Website: artefiera.it
Email: socialartefiera@bolognafiere.it
Facebook.com/artefiera

The Winter Show, New York, US

A leading art, antiques and design fair in America, showing work from ancient times to the present day.
Website: thewintershow.org
Email: office@thewintershow.org
Twitter.com/thewintershowny
Facebook.com/thewintershownyc
Instagram.com/thewintershownyc

Master Drawings New York, US

1,000 years of art, shown in one week.
Website: masterdrawingsnewyork.com
Email: enquiries@masterdrawingsnewyork.com
Email: press@masterdrawingsnewyork.com
Twitter.com/MasterDrawingNY
Facebook.com/MasterDrawingsNY
Instagram.com/masterdrawingsny

Brafa (Brussels Antiques & Fine Arts Fair), Belgium

Created in 1956, it is one of the world's oldest and most prestigious art fairs, showing modern and contemporary art and antiques.
Website: brafa.art
Email: info@brafa.be
Twitter.com/brafaartfair
Facebook.com/brafaartfair
Instagram.com/brafaartfair
Linkedin.com/company/brafaartfair
YouTube.com/c/BRAFAArtFair

Art Geneve, Geneva, Switzerland

Contemporary and modern art from international galleries.
Website: artgeneve.ch
Email: presse@palexpo.ch
Instagram.com/artgeneve

India Art Fair, New Delhi, India

Modern and contemporary art from South Asia.
Website: indiaartfair.in
Email: info@indiaartfair.in
Twitter.com/India_ArtFair
Facebook.com/IndiaArtFairDelhi
Instagram.com/indiaartfair

Photo LA, Santa Monica, California, US

International Los Angeles photographic art exhibition.
Email: info@photola.com
Twitter.com/photolafair
Facebook.com/photolafair
Instagram.com/photolafair
Artsy.net/fair/photo-la-2019

Art 3f Paris, France

European artists and makers showing to an international audience.
Website: art3f.fr
Email: info@art3f.com
Twitter.com/art3fsalon
Facebook.com/art3f

Art Palm Beach, Florida, US

Emerging and masterworks of contemporary art with 85 international galleries presenting work in every medium.
Website: nextlevelfairs.com/artpalmbeach

February

LA Art Show, Los Angeles, California, US

More than 120 galleries from over 20 countries exhibiting paintings, sculpture, works on paper, installation, photography, fashion, design, video and performance in more than 200,000 sq ft of exhibition space.
Website: laartshow.com
Email: info@laartshow.com
Twitter.com/LAArtShow
Facebook.com/LAartshow
Instagram.com/laartshow

Zona Maco, Mexico City

Bringing together leading and emerging national and international art galleries, exhibiting jewellery, textiles, limited editions and decorative objects as well as contemporary and vintage photography.
Website: zsonamaco.com
Email: info@zonamaco.com
Twitter.com/ZonaMaco
Facebook.com/zonamaco
Instagram.com/zonamaco
Artsy.net/zonamaco-2020

Art Rotterdam, Netherlands

Young art from The Netherlands.
Website: artrotterdam.com
Email: info@artrotterdam.com
Twitter.com/artrotterdam
Facebook.com/ArtRotterdam
Instagram.com/art_rotterdam

Nomad St Moritz, St Moritz, Switzerland

Outstanding work for discerning collectors.
Website: nomad-circle.com
Email: info@nomad-circle.com

Rotterdam Photo, Netherlands

An annual photography fair with talks, workshops and a fringe program throughout the city.
Website: rotterdamphotofestival.com
Email: communicatie.rotterdamphoto@gmail.com
Facebook.com/rotterdamphotofestival
Instagram.com/rotterdamphoto

Material, Mexico City

Contemporary art fair offering an experimental platform for artists in Latin America.
Website: material-fair.com
Artsy.net/material-art-fair

Art Karlsruhe, Germany

Classic modern and contemporary art.
Website: art-karlsruhe.de
Email: info@messe-karlsruhe.de
Twitter.com/artKARLSRUHE
Facebook.com/artkarlsruhe
Instagram.com/art_karlsruhe

Felix LA, Los Angeles, California, US

Prioritising connoisseurship, collaboration and community between galleries from Europe, North America, China, South Africa and Australia.
Website: felixfair.com
Facebook.com/FelixArtFair
Instagram.com/felixartfair

Stockholm International, Sweden

Founded in 1978 with the Swedish Art and Antique Dealers Association (SKAF), with antiques, vintage, modern design, art and curiosities for sale.
Website: antikmassan.se
Email: antikmassan@stockholmsmassan.se
Facebook.com/antikmassan?ref=ts&fref=ts
Instagram.com/antikmassan
YouTube.com/user/antikmassan

Art Palm Springs, California, US

The desert's largest selection of post-war and contemporary art.
Website: art-palmsprings.com
Twitter.com/artpalmsprings?lang=en
Facebook.com/ArtPalmSprings
Instagram.com/artpalmsprings

Art Wynwood, Miami, Florida, US

An international art fair showing leading works of contemporary art from around the world.
Website: artwynwood.com
Email: info@artmiami.com
Twitter.com/artmiamifairs
Facebook.com/ArtWynwood
Instagram.com/artmiamifairs

Palm Beach Show, Florida, US

International exhibitors showing.
Website: palmbeachshow.com
Email: Info@palmbeachshow.com
Twitter.com/PalmBeachShow
Facebook.com/PalmBeachShow?ref=nf
Instagram.com/palmbeachshowgroup
Pinterest.co.uk/pbshowgroup
Vimeo.com/palmbeachshowgroup
YouTube.com/channel/
UCHeVLCnL3epI8HeOGiD7ZAw

Art Los Angeles Contemporary, California, US

The international contemporary art fair of the West Coast.
Website: artlosangelesfair.com
Email: info@artlosangelesfair.com
Twitter.com/ALAContemporary
Facebook.com/ALAContemporary
Instagram.com/alacontemporary

Frieze Los Angeles, California, US

Frieze is the leading magazine of contemporary art and culture.
Website: frieze.com/fairs
Email: info@frieze.com
Twitter.com/frieze_magazine
Facebook.com/friezemagazine
Instagram.com/frieze_magazine

Investec Cape Town Art Fair, South Africa

Contemporary art from Africa and the world.
Website: investeccapetownartfair.co.za
Email: marketing@fieramilano.co.za
Facebook.com/ICTArtFair

Instagram.com/investeccapetownartfair
Artsy.net/investec-cape-town-art-fair
YouTube.com/channel/
UC3r_8crq7sLR2gHd6LruL6g

Arte Genova, Genoa, Italy

In its 16th edition, showing work from more than 150 galleries, from timeless masterpieces to unprecedented experiments of contemporary artists.
Website: artegenova.com
Email: giulia@fierenef.com
Facebook.com/artegenova
Instagram.com/artegenova
YouTube.com/channel/
UCp8LCAWmEIGHJvsDoNgRrsA

Palm Springs Modernism Show & Sale (Spring), California, US

85 leading national and international dealers offering furniture, decorative and fine arts from the 20th century.
Website: palmspringsmodernism.com
Email: info@dolphinfairs.com
Facebook.com/PalmSpringsMOD

The Artist Project, Toronto, Canada

Contemporary art fair.
Website: theartistproject.com
Email: info@theartistproject.com

American Indian Art Show San Francisco, San Rafael, California, US

American Indian and tribal art showcasing the best in indigenous art from around the world.

Art Fair Philippines, Manila, Philippines

The best in modern and contemporary Philippine visual art.
Website: artfairphilippines.com
Twitter.com/artfairph
Facebook.com/artfairph
Instagram.com/artfairph

Naples Art, Antique and Jewellery Show, Florida, US

Stunning collections of internationally acclaimed exhibitors showing the most beautiful treasures of the last several thousand years with major works of art, antique and estate jewellery, furniture, porcelain, Asian antiquities, American and European silver, glass, textiles, sculpture, contemporary art and more
Website: naplesshow.com
Email: Info@palmbeachshow.com
Twitter.com/PalmBeachShow
Instagram.com/palmbeachshowgroup
Vimeo.com/palmbeachshowgroup

1–54 Contemporary African Art Fair, Marrakech, Morocco

Contemporary art from Africa and its diaspora, providing a platform for contemporary dialogue and exchange including lectures, film screenings and panel debates from leading international curators, artists and experts. The title '1-54' is a reference to the fair's ethos of the 54 countries that make up the African continent.
Website: 1-54.com
Email: info@1-54.com
Twitter.com/154artfair
Facebook.com/154ContemporaryAfricanArtFair
Instagram.com/154artfair
Artsy.net/1-54?m-id=ca13&utm_medium=referral&utm_source=fair-1-54&utm_campaign=widget
YouTube.com/channel/UCsWKpfSB3mtX6eiq8Ip_zxw

Arco Madrid, Spain

An international contemporary art fair which celebrates its 40th anniversary in 2021, making it an essential component in the international circuit for the promotion and dissemination of art.
Website: ifema.es
Email: feriaarcomadrid@gmail.com
Twitter.com/feriaarco
Facebook.com/FeriaARCO
Instagram.com/feriaarco
Artsy.net/arco-madrid
YouTube.com/user/feriaARCOmadrid

Art Madrid, Madrid, Spain

Contemporary art fair, in its 16th year, showcasing around 50 national and international galleries and artists of all disciplines.
Website: art-madrid.com
Email: art-madrid@art-madrid.com
Twitter.com/artmadridferia
Facebook.com/artmadridferia
Instagram.com/artmadridferia

Collect Fair for Modern Craft and Design, London, UK

Established by the Crafts Council in 2004, the fair brings together international galleries showing work by living contemporary craft artists.
Website: craftscouncil.org.uk/collect-art-fair
Email: collect@craftscouncil.org.uk
Twitter.com/CraftsCouncilUK
Facebook.com/CraftsCouncilUK
Instagram.com/craftscouncil
Pinterest.co.uk/CraftsCouncilUK/_created
YouTube.com/channel/UCYYL-qgMdl3adnB_BkoNi9g

Just Mad, Madrid, Spain

International contemporary art fair.
Website: justmad.es
Email: info@artfairs.es
Twitter.com/justfairs
Facebook.com/JUSTARTFAIRS
Instagram.com/justfairs

The Art Show (ADAA), New York, US

Organised by the Art Dealers Association of America with a variety of genres and practices from national and international origins.

Website: artdealers.org/the-art-show
Email: gboyd@artdealers.org
Twitter.com/The_ADAA
Facebook.com/
ArtDealersAssociationofAmerica
Instagram.com/the_adaa
Pinterest.co.uk/The_ADAA/_created

Art3f Toulouse, France

European artists and makers showing to an international audience.
Website: art3f.fr/index.php
Email: info@art3f.com
Twitter.com/art3fsalon
Facebook.com/art3f

Hybrid Contemporary, Madrid, Spain

Held in the bedrooms of a hotel, the fair shows exhibition projects from art galleries, project spaces and artist-run initiatives.
Website: hybridart.es/fair
Email: fair@hybridart.es
Twitter.com/hybrid_arte
Facebook.com/hybridarte
Instagram.com/hybrid_arte

Mercanteinfiera Spring, Parma, Italy

Dedicated to antiques, modernism and collectables.
Website: mercanteinfiera.it
Email: info@fiereparma.it
Twitter.com/mercantefiera
Facebook.com/mercantefiera
Instagram.com/mercanteinfiera_parma
Pinterest.it/Mercanteinfiera/_created

March

Art Bahrain Across Borders (ArtBAB), Sanabis, Bahrain

Exploring Bahraini contemporary art and its foundation in the Kingdom's rich art heritage, including VR and AI art, with a diverse speakers program and work with Bahraini craftspeople.
Website: artrabbit.com/events/artbab-2019-art-bahrain-across-borders

Collective Design Fair, New York, US

Created in 2013 by a group of designers, gallerists, collectors and creators to present a current vision of collectible design, bringing together the work of 20th century masters, established and emerging studios.
Website: collectivedesignfair.com
Email: info@collectivedesignfair.com
Instagram.com/collectivedf

Volta New York, New York, US

A platform for international galleries with ambitious solo and group presentations.
Website: voltaartfairs.com/new-york/2020-galleries
Email: info@voltashow.com
Twitter.com/VOLTAartfairs
Facebook.com/VOLTAartfairs
Instagram.com/voltaartfairs

Art on Paper, New York, US

100 galleries featuring top modern and contemporary paper-based art.
Website: thepaperfair.com/ny
Email: hello@amp.events
Twitter.com/artMRKT
Facebook.com/
artmarketproductions?ref=hl
Instagram.com/artmarketproductions

Collectible, Brussels, Belgium

A fresh selection of international galleries.
Website: collectible.design
Email: info@collectible.design
Facebook.com/collectiblefair
Instagram.com/collectiblefair

NY International Antiquarian Book Fair, New York, US

American and international dealers presenting rare books, maps, manuscripts, illuminated manuscripts and ephemera, with specialities in art, medicine, literature, photography, autographs and first editions

which have all been examined carefully for completeness and bibliographic accuracy.
Website: nyantiquarianbookfair.com
Email: info@sanfordsmith.com
Facebook.com/nybookfair/?ref=hl
Instagram.com/nybookfair

Scope New York, US

Ground-breaking contemporary art with over 60 exhibitors forging the way for emerging artists and galleries.
Website: scope-art.com
Email: info@scope-art.com
Twitter.com/SCOPEArtShow
Facebook.com/SCOPEARTSHOW
Instagram.com/SCOPEArtShow
Artsy.net/fair/scope-miami-beach-2019

The Armory Show, New York, US

Leading international galleries showing both modern masters and cutting-edge contemporary work.
Website: thearmoryshow.com
Email: info@thearmoryshow.com
Twitter.com/thearmoryshow
Facebook.com/ArmoryShow
Instagram.com/thearmoryshow
Linkedin.com/company/the-armory-show/about/?viewAsMember=true
YouTube.com/channel/UCuKzOhtx5B4UmHqfCncLTow/featured?view_as=subscriber

Contemporary Art Ruhr, Essen, Germany

Innovative, avant-garde and inspiring.
Website: contemporaryartruhr.de
Email: mail@contemporaryartruhr.de
Facebook.com/contemporaryartruhr
Instagram.com/contemporaryartruhr.de

Independent, New York, US

Breaking down hierarchies in the art world by bringing in more emerging galleries as well as the blue chip ones.
 Website: independenthq.com

Email: contact@independenthq.com
Twitter.com/independent_hq?lang=en
Facebook.com/independentny
Instagram.com/independent_hq/?hl=en

Object & Thing at Independent, New York, US

Contemporary art and design from international contemporary art galleries.
Website: object-thing.com
Email: info@object-thing.com
Instagram.com/object_thing

Tefaf Maastricht, Maastricht, Netherlands

The world's premier art fair for fine art, antiques and design, with over 275 dealers from 20 countries. Half the fair is dedicated to old master paintings and antiques, with the other half focusing on modern and contemporary art, photography, jewellery, 20th century design and works on paper.
Website: tefaf.com/fairs/tefaf-maastricht
Email: info@tefaf.com
Twitter.com/tefaf
Facebook.com/TEFAF
Instagram.com/tefaf
Artsy.net/tefaf

Affordable Art Fair, London, UK

Contemporary art from £50-£6,000, both at the fair and online.
Website: affordableartfair.com
Email: enquiries@affordableartfair.com
Twitter.com/aaflondon?lang=en
Facebook.com/AffordableArtFair
Instagram.com/affordableartfairuk
Pinterest.co.uk/affordableart/_shop

Art Central, Hong Kong, China

In partnership with the United Overseas Bank for its 6th edition in 2021.
Website: artcentralhongkong.com
Email: info@artcentralhongkong.com
Facebook.com/artcentralhk
Instagram.com/artcentralhk

Chelsea Antiques Fair, London, UK

International art, antique and glass product exhibition with estate jewellery, vintage clothing, collectables and vintage home and decor.
Website: penman-fairs.co.uk
Email: info@penman-fairs.co.uk

The Open Art Fair (BADA), London, UK

BADA (The British Antique Dealers' Association) is the leading trade association for the fine art, design & antique community.
Website: bada.org
Twitter.com/bada1918
Facebook.com/BADA1918
Instagram.com/bada1918
Pinterest.co.uk/BADA1918

Art Basel in Hong Kong, China

Established in 1970, Art Basel is the leading global platform for the art world, with world class fairs in Basel, Miami Beach and Hong Kong and more recently online, showing 20th and 21st century art.
Website: artbasel.com/hong-kong
Twitter.com/ArtBasel
Facebook.com/artbasel
Instagram.com/artbasel
Weibo.com/artbasel
Linkedin.com/company/art-basel
YouTube.com/user/artbasel

MIA Photo Fair, Milan, Italy

The most important photographic art fair in Italy, founded in 2011.
Website: miafair.it/Milano
Email: sofia.boffardi@miafair.it

Affordable Art Fair, Brussels, Belgium

Contemporary art for €60 – €7,500, with more than half the work priced under €5,000. The Affordable Art Fair is a global phenomenon with fairs in London, New York, Amsterdam, Brussels, Hamburg, Hong Kong, Milan, Stockholm, Singapore, Melbourne, which welcome 1000s of art lovers to each fair. The works of young and emerging artists are exhibited alongside established names, in a relaxed and friendly atmosphere.
Website: affordableartfair.com/fairs/brussels
Email: brussels@affordableartfair.com
Facebook.com/AffordableArtFairBrussels
Instagram.com/affordableartfairbrussels
Pinterest.co.uk/affordableart/brussels

Art Fair Tokyo, Japan

The largest art fair in Japan and the oldest in Asia, featuring a wide range of art from antiques and crafts to nihonga painting, modern art and contemporary art.
Website: artfairtokyo.com
Twitter.com/artfairtokyo_
Instagram.com/artfairtokyo

Ceramic Art London, UK

The foremost contemporary ceramic event in the UK, with first time and international exhibitors.
Website: ceramicartlondon.com
Twitter.com/CeramicArtLDN
Facebook.com/ceramicartlondon
Instagram.com/ceramicartlondon

Art Dubai, UAE

The Middle East's leading international art fair putting the Middle East and the surrounding areas of North Africa and South Asia on the global map.
Website: artdubai.ae
Email: info@artdubai.ae
Twitter.com/artdubai
Facebook.com/artdubai.artfair
Instagram.com/artdubai
Linkedin.com/company/art-dubai
YouTube.com/user/artdubai

Chaco (Chile Arte Contemporáneo), Santiago, Chile

The international platform for contemporary arts in Chile.
Website: chaco.cl
Email: media@feriachaco.cl
Facebook.com/FeriaCh.ACO
Instagram.com/feriachaco/?hl=es-la
YouTube.com/user/FeriaCHACO

Drawing Now, Paris, France

Hosting 74 international galleries showing more than 300 artists and 2,000 works.
Website: drawingnowartfair.com
Email: info@drawingnowartfair.com
Twitter.com/DRAWINGNOWPARIS
Facebook.com/Drawingnowartfair
Instagram.com/drawingnowartfair

Eurantica, Brussels, Belgium

International fine art fair specialising in fine art; vintage, design, contemporary art, modern art and classic paintings.
Website: eurantica.be
Email: eurantica@fairtime.be
Facebook.com/euranticabrussels
Instagram.com/eurantica

Art Nordic, Copenhagen, Denmark

Up to 250 artists from 30 nations. The biggest art fair in Scandinavia creating a unique forum for dialogue and the exchange of ideas.
Website: art-nordic.dk
Email: kontakt@art-nordic.dk
Facebook.com/artnordic
Instagram.com/art_nordic

April

Art Beijing, Beijing, China

Website: expohour.com/art-beijing

Paris Tribal, France

Tribal art from Africa, America, the Himalayas, Indonesia and Oceania.

Website: paristribal.com
Email: contact@colonnes.com
Facebook.com/paristribal
Instagram.com/paristribal

PAD (Paris Art + Design), Paris, France

Website: padesignart.com/paris
Twitter.com/padesignart
Facebook.com/padesignartonline
Instagram.com/padesignart

SP-Arte (São Paulo International Art Festival), São Paulo, Brazil

International contemporary art fair
Website: sp-arte.com
Twitter.com/sp_arte
Facebook.com/feira.sparte
Instagram.com/sp_arte
Flickr.com/photos/sp-arte/albums
Artsy.net/sp-arte
YouTube.com/user/FeiraSPArte

Art Paris, France

Paris's major spring fair for modern and contemporary art, which in its 23rd edition brought together 140 galleries from over 20 countries with a special emphasis on Europe, but also exploring the creative hubs of Asia, Africa, the Middle East and Latin America.
Website: artparis.com
Email: contact@artparis.com
Twitter.com/ArtParisArtFair
Facebook.com/ArtParisArtFair
Instagram.com/artparisartfair
Artsy.net/art-paris

Paris Photo – New York, US

The largest photographic international art fair for over 20 years.
Website: parisphoto-newyork.com
Email: info@parisphoto.com
Twitter.com/parisphotofair
Facebook.com/parisphotofair
Instagram.com/parisphotofair
Linkedin.com/company/paris-photo-fair

Arte BA (Art Fair Buenos Aires), Argentina

Contemporary art fair.
Website: arteba.org
Email: info@arteba.org
Twitter.com/arteba
Facebook.com/arteBA
Instagram.com/artebafundacion
Flickr.com/photos/arteba
Vimeo.com/arteba
YouTube.com/channel/
UC6PmSxXYKnzSRw0Um3EjReA

Art Vancouver, Vancouver, Canada

Western Canada's largest contemporary art fair, with over 10,000 visitors annually.
Email: info@artvancouver.net
Facebook.com/artvancouverexhibition
Instagram.com/artvancouver
Linkedin.com/in/art-vancouver-29298522
YouTube.com/channel/
UCt0z42bs1UoqDkRNmdqDFhA

Dallas Art Fair, Texas, US

Modern and contemporary art by leading national and international galleries.
Website: dallasartfair.com
Email: dafinfo@dallasartfair.com
Twitter.com/DallasArtFair
Facebook.com/DallasArtFair
Instagram.com/dallasartfair

MiArt, Milan, Italy

International modern and contemporary art fair in Milan.
Website: miart.it/en/home-en
Email: miart@fieramilano.it
Twitter.com/MiArtMilano
Facebook.com/miart.milano
Instagram.com/miartmilano
Artsy.net/miart
Linkedin.com/showcase/miart

Almoneda Antik Passion Spring, Antiques and Art Fair, Madrid, Spain

30 years of bringing antiques and collectables together, from the 18th century to the present day.
Website: ifema.es/en/almoneda
Email: almoneda@ifema.es
Twitter.com/antikpassion
Facebook.com/Almoneda.AntikPassion
Instagram.com/almoneda.
antikpassion/?hl=es
YouTube.com/channel/
UCwtULEFbZqQmoQh-qb7KM7w

Salone Internazionale del Mobile, Milan, Italy

A global benchmark event for the furnishing and design sector.
Website: salonemilano.it
Twitter.com/isaloniofficial
Facebook.com/salonedelmobileofficial
Instagram.com/isaloniofficial
Pinterest.co.uk/isaloni/_created
Flickr.com/photos/isaloni
Linkedin.com/company/isaloni
YouTube.com/user/isaloni

The Decorative Antiques & Textiles Fair (Spring), London, UK

A family-owned event launched in 1985, uniting the antiques and interior design trades, with 3 fairs a year – late January, mid-May and late Sep/early Oct.
Website: decorativefair.com
Email: fairs@decorativefair.com
Twitter.com/decorativefair
Facebook.com/decorativefair/?ref=hl
Instagram.com/decorativefair

PArC (Peru Arte Contemporaneo), Lima, Peru

The most important international art fair in Peru, now in its 8th year.
Website: en.parc.com.pe
Email: info@parc.com.pe
Twitter.com/parcoficial
Facebook.com/parc.oficial
Instagram.com/parc.oficial

Art Brussels, Belgium

Contemporary art fair in Brussels.
Website: artbrussels.com/en
Email: artbrussels@easyfairs.com
Twitter.com/artbrussels
Facebook.com/artbrusselsfair
Instagram.com/artbrussels
YouTube.com/channel/UCtJL5Hy1o8D7_
t3xZS9LA-w

Art Cologne, Cologne, Germany

Contemporary, modern and post-war art
fair with leading, established and emerging
international galleries.
Website: artcologne.com
Email: artcologne@koelnmesse.de
Facebook.com/artcolognefair
Instagram.com/artcolognefair
Artsy.net/art-cologne

Artexpo New York, US

The world's largest fine art trade show.
Website: redwoodartgroup.com/artexpo-
new-york
Email: info@artexponewyork.com

Art Market San Francisco, California, US

Contemporary art fair in San Francisco.
Website: artmarketsf.com
Email: hello@amp.events
Twitter.com/artMRKT
Facebook.com/
artmarketproductions?ref=hl
Instagram.com/artmarketproductions

Supermarket (Stockholm Independent Art Fair), Sweden

An annual artist-run art fair in Stockholm,
Sweden.
Website: supermarketartfair.com
Email: info@supermarketartfair.com
Twitter.com/supermarketart
Facebook.com/supermarketartfair
Instagram.com/supermarketart

Urban Art Fair, Paris, France

The first international fair dedicated to urban
art.
Website: urbanartfair.com
Email: info@urbanartfair.fr
Twitter.com/urbanartfair?lang=fr
Facebook.com/urbanartfair
Instagram.com/urbanartfair

Art3f Luxembourg, Luxembourg

Contemporary art fair in Luxembourg.
Website: art3f.fr/index.php/en/home-
luxembourg
Email: info@art3f.com
Twitter.com/art3fsalon
Facebook.com/art3f

Discovery Art Fair, Cologne, Germany

Contemporary art and exchange with 100
international exhibitors and around 10,000
art lovers.
Website: discoveryartfair.com
Email: info@discoveryartfair.com
Twitter.com/lookforart
Facebook.com/discoveryartfair
Instagram.com/discoveryartfair
Vimeo.com/discoveryartfair
Linkedin.com/company/discovery-art-fair

Luxembourg Art Fair, Luxembourg

Contemporary art fair in Luxembourg.
Website: luxartfair.com
Email: info@galleryartfair.com
Facebook.com/luxartfair

Market Art Fair, Stockholm, Sweden

The leading art fair in the Nordic region,
founded in 2006 by galleries from Denmark,
Finland, Iceland, Norway and Sweden.
Website: marketartfair.com
Email: info@marketartfair.com
Facebook.com/marketartfair
Instagram.com/marketartfair

Salon International du Livre Rare et de'l Objet d'Art, Paris, France

International salon of rare books and objects d'art.
Website: salondulivrerare.paris
Facebook.com/salondulivrerare

Contemporary Art Fair, Paris, France

Contemporary art fair in Paris.
Website: contemporary-art-fair-paris.com
Email: info@art3f.com

Auckland Art Fair, New Zealand

Contemporary art fair in Auckland.
Website: artfair.co.nz
Email: hello@artfair.co.nz
Twitter.com/aucklandartfair
Facebook.com/AucklandArtFair
Instagram.com/aucklandartfair

Kunst RAI, Amsterdam, Netherlands

A national art fair for contemporary and visual arts and design with 60 leading galleries reflecting the diversity and quality of Dutch work, including painting and sculpture, photography and graphic art, contemporary glass, ceramics and jewellery.
Website: kunstrai.nl
Email: info@kunstrai.nl
Facebook.com/kunstrai
Instagram.com/kunstrai

Lausanne Art Fair, France

European artists and makers showing to an international audience.
Website: lausanneartfair.com
Email: info@art3f.com

London Original Print Fair, UK

Original prints spanning 5 centuries with 50 exhibitors with a wealth of specialist knowledge.
Website: londonoriginalprintfair.com
Email: info@londonoriginalprintfair.com
Twitter.com/londonprintfair

Facebook.com/LondonPrintFair
Instagram.com/londonoriginalprintfair

May
Art Monte Carlo, Monaco

Contemporary art fair in Monte Carlo.
Website: artmontecarlo.ch

Frieze New York, US

Frieze is the leading magazine of contemporary art and culture.
Website: frieze.com/fairs/frieze-new-york
Email: info@frieze.com
Twitter.com/frieze_magazine
Facebook.com/friezemagazine
Instagram.com/frieze_magazine

Superfine New York, US

Contemporary art fair in New York.
Website: superfine.world

Future Fair, New York, US

An art fair working for a collaborative art market.
Website: futurefairs.com
Email: hello@futurefairs.com
Instagram.com/futurefairs

Art New York, US

The best in global contemporary art, and an opportunity to buy important, never-before seen works from both the primary and secondary markets.
Website: artnyfair.com
Facebook.com/artnewyorkfair

Object & Thing, New York, US

Reimagining the art and design fair concept with object-based 20th and 21st century works from leading international art and design galleries.
Website: object-thing.com
Email: info@object-thing.com
Instagram.com/object_thing

1–54 Contemporary African Art Fair, New York, New York, US

Contemporary art from Africa and its diaspora, providing a platform for contemporary dialogue and exchange including lectures, film screenings and panel debates from leading international curators, artists and experts. The title '1-54' is a reference to the fair's ethos of the 54 countries that make up the African continent.
Website: 1-54.com/new-york
Email: info@1-54.com
Twitter.com/154artfair
Facebook.com/154ContemporaryAfricanArtFair
Instagram.com/154artfair
Artsy.net/1-54?m-id=ca13&utm_
medium=referral&utm_source=fair-1-
54&utm_campaign=widget
YouTube.com/channel/
UCsWKpfSB3mtX6eiq8Ip_zxw

Tefaf New York Spring, US

The world's most prestigious art market focusing on modern and contemporary art and design.
Website: tefaf.com/fairs/tefaf-new-york-spring
Email: info@tefaf.com
Twitter.com/tefaf
Facebook.com/TEFAF
Instagram.com/tefaf
Artsy.net/tefaf

Museums + Heritage Show, London, UK

The sector's largest event with more than 2,500 heritage professionals taking part, looking at the latest technology, products and services from over 150 leading suppliers.
Website: show.museumsandheritage.com
Email: info@museumsandheritage.com
Twitter.com/MandHShow
Facebook.com/MandHShow
YouTube.com/channel/
UCVaLUqbeSgDuq-CPlkssoCA?view_
as=subscriber

Eye of the Collector, London, UK

Leading galleries, dealers and artists on a creative journey from ancient to contemporary.
Website: eyeofthecollector.com
Instagram.com/eyeofthecollectorlondon

Arco Lisboa, Portugal

Over 70 national and international galleries with interesting portfolios.
Website: ifema.es/en/arco-lisboa
Email: feriaarcomadrid@gmail.com
Twitter.com/feriaarco
Facebook.com/FeriaARCO
Instagram.com/feriaarco

Draw Art Fair London, UK

Housed in the Saatchi Gallery, showing work from old masters to contemporary drawing. The first art fair dedicated to modern and contemporary drawing with an international reach, showing work from 16 countries, as far afield as Japan and Russia.
Website: drawartfair.com
Email: info@drawartfair.com
Twitter.com/drawartfairldn
Facebook.com/DRAWARTLONDON
Instagram.com/drawartfairlondon
Artsy.net/draw-art-fair-london

Chicago Antiques, Art + Design Show, Illinois, US

60 leading national and international exhibitors showing antiques, decorative and fine arts from antiquity to 20th century.
Website: chicagoantiquesartdesign.com
Email: info@dolphinfairs.com
Twitter.com/ChicagoAADS
Facebook.com/ChicagoAADS

Just LX, Lisbon, Portugal

Contemporary emerging art, with newly discovered galleries and artists.
Website: justlx.pt
Email: info@justlx.pt
Twitter.com/justfairs

Facebook.com/JUSTARTFAIRS
Instagram.com/justfairs

Photo London, UK

Based in Somerset House, the fair brings together many of the world's leading galleries and dealers, as well as providing a platform for emerging artists and galleries who are pushing the boundaries of the medium.
Website: photolondon.org
Email: info@photolondon.org
Twitter.com/photolondonfair
Facebook.com/photolondonfair
Instagram.com/photolondonfair
Artsy.net/photo-london

Tbilisi Art Fair, Georgia

An international contemporary art fair focused on emerging and mid-career artists, especially those on the eastern and southern frontiers of Europe.
Website: tbilisiartfair.art
Email: info@tbilisiartfair.art
Facebook.com/tbilisiartfair
Instagram.com/tbilisiartfair/?hl=en

Glasgow Contemporary Art Fair, Scotland

A contemporary art fair taking place at the iconic Kelvingrove Art Gallery and Museum.
Website: gcaf.co.uk
Email: glasgowcaf@btinternet.com
Instagram.com/glasgow contemporary_art_fair

ART (Art Revolution Taipei), Taipei, Taiwan

Contemporary art fair in Taiwan.
Website: arts.org.tw
Email: artrevolution@arts.org.tw

Prague Photo, Czech Republic

Contemporary and classic photography from the Czech Republic, Italy, Slovakia, France and Saudi Arabia.
Website: praguefoto.cz
Email: info@praguefoto.cz
Facebook.com/PraguePhotoFestival
Instagram.com/praguephotocz

Umschlagplatz Coburg, Germany

Contemporary art fair in Coburg, Germany.
Website: umschlagplatz-coburg.de
Email: info@umschlagplatz-coburg.de
Facebook.com/artcoburg

June

GZ–Basel, Switzerland

Contemporary art with the theme 'Beyond' inspiring art with meaning such as discovery, hope and creation, promoting emerging and more recognised artists internationally.
Website: gz-basel.com
Email: mail@galeriazero.info
Twitter.com/galeriazero
Facebook.com/GZART2012
Instagram.com/galeriaz

Arch Moscow, Russia

The best platform for networking in the field of architecture, design, development and construction.
Website: archmoscow.ru
Email: info@expopark.ru

Art Vilnius, Lithuania

The largest event of visual arts in Eastern Europe, in its 11th year, hosting 40 galleries and 150 artists from 9 countries.
Website: artvilnius.com
Email: info@artvilnius.com
Facebook.com/artvilnius
Instagram.com/artvilnius

Tokyo International Art Fair, Japan

Paintings, sculpture, photography, illustration and multimedia by award-winning and the best emerging talent.
Website: tokyoartfair.com
Email: office@globalartagency.com
Twitter.com/GlobalArtAgency
Facebook.com/tokyoartfair?ref=hl
Linkedin.com/company/global-art-agency
YouTube.com/channel/UCO_
izBDNYqhmOGNdLBPDFPg

Bruneaf Summer, Brussels, Belgium

An art fair that occurs twice a year, in January and June, dedicated to old and selected tribal arts.
Website: bruneaf.com
Email: info@bruneaf.com
Twitter.com/bruneaf
Facebook.com/Bruneaf
Instagram.com/bruneaf

Scope Basel, Switzerland

In its 12th year, showing contemporary art with 70 international exhibitors and 10 breeder program galleries.
Website: scope-art.com/show/basel-2018
Email: info@scope-art.com
Twitter.com/SCOPEArtShow
Facebook.com/SCOPEARTSHOW
Instagram.com/SCOPEArtShow

Volta Basel, Switzerland

Website: voltaartfairs.com/basel
Email: info@voltashow.com
Twitter.com/VOLTAartfairs
Facebook.com/VOLTAartfairs
Instagram.com/voltaartfairs

Liste: the Young Art Fair, Basel, Switzerland

The international fair for new discoveries in contemporary art.
Email: info@liste.ch
Facebook.com/listeartfairbasel
Instagram.com/liste_art_fair_basel
YouTube.com/channel/UCFTYXVYY_a6Q-duQwSQ_JwA

Design Miami/Basel, Switzerland

The global forum for design, with a sister show in Miami, USA. Incorporating the world's top galleries with 20th and 21st century furniture, lighting and objets d'art.
Website: basel2020.designmiami.com
Email: info@designmiami.com
Twitter.com/designmiami
Facebook.com/DesignMiami

Instagram.com/designmiami
Pinterest.com.au/designmiamifair
YouTube.com/channel/UCPXRu0ZO7Bcvx-lQ0tqBhGw

Photo Basel, Switzerland

Switzerland's first international art fair dedicated solely to photography, hosted during the Art Basel week.
Website: photo-basel.com
Email: info@photo-basel.com
Facebook.com/photobasel
Instagram.com/photobasel
Linkedin.com/company/photo-basel

I Never Read, Basel, Switzerland

An art book fair in Basel with over 120 publishers from around the world, exploring the relationship between contemporary art production, art presentation and the book, with interactive installations, film, music, panel discussions, a radio station, and sport activities.
Website: ineverread.com
Email: info@ineverread.com
Facebook.com/ineverreadartbookfairbasel
Instagram.com/ineverreadartbookfairbasel

The Art & Antiques Fair Olympia, London, UK

London's longest running art and antiques fair of nearly 50 years, showing pieces from antiquity to the present day.
Website: olympia-art-antiques.com
Email: ed.maccurrach@clarionevents.com
Twitter.com/OlympiaAntiques
Facebook.com/olympiaartandantiques
Instagram.com/olympiaartantiques

Art BaselSwitzerland

Our Basel fair brings the international art world together. It features over 250 leading galleries and more than 4,000 artists from five continents. Many high-quality exhibitions take place concurrently in and around Basel, creating a region-wide art week.

Website: artbasel.com/basel
Twitter.com/ArtBasel
Facebook.com/artbasel
Instagram.com/artbasel
Weibo.com/artbasel
Linkedin.com/company/art-basel
YouTube.com/user/artbasel

Melbourne Art Fair, Australia

Providing a world class platform for contemporary art for over 30 years, with iconic and new work.
Website: melbourneartfair.com.au
Email: maf@melbourneartfoundation.com
Twitter.com/MelbArtFair
Facebook.com/melbourneartfair
Instagram.com/melbourneartfair

Rhy Basel: the Young Art Fair, Switzerland

Contemporary art from photography to digital art, graphics, painting, sculpture and installations from both young and established artists.
Website: rhy-art.com
Email: basel@rhy-art.com
Twitter.com/rhyartfairbasel
YouTube.com/user/swissartfairs

Masterpiece London, UK

Hosted at the Royal Hospital Chelsea, with art, design, furniture and jewellery from antiquity to the present day from 150 international exhibitors, spanning every major market discipline.
Website: masterpiecefair.com
Twitter.com/MasterpieceFair
Facebook.com/MasterpieceFair
Instagram.com/masterpiecefair
Artsy.net/fair/masterpiece-online-2020

July

Market Art + Design, Bridgehampton, NY, US

Modern and contemporary art and design.
Website: artmarkethamptons.com
Email: hello@amp.events
Twitter.com/artMRKT
Facebook.com/artmarketproductions?ref=hl
Instagram.com/artmarketproductions

Art Bodensee, Dornbirn, Austria

Contemporary art fair in Dornbirn, Austria.
Website: artbodensee.messedornbirn.at

Art Santa Fe, New Mexico, US

With over 40 art shows spanning 11 years, located in New York, Miami, Santa Fe and San Diego attracting more than 100,000 visitors each year, this fair shows the best in contemporary and modern art and design.
Website: redwoodartgroup.com/art-santa-fe
Email: info@redwoodartgroup.com
Twitter.com/redwoodartgroup
Facebook.com/redwoodartgroup
Instagram.com/redwoodartgroup
Linkedin.com/company/redwood-art-group
YouTube.com/c/RedwoodArtGroup

Art Aspen, Colorado, US

Aspen's first and only fair dedicated to presenting the best in modern and contemporary art.
Website: art-aspen.com
Email: info@art-aspen.com
Facebook.com/ArtAspen
Twitter.com/artaspenfair?lang=en
Instagram.com/artaspen

Seattle Art Fair, Washington, US

Modern and contemporary art, showcasing work from the vibrant arts community of the Pacific Northwest.
Website: seattleartfair.com
Email: info@seattleartfair.com
Twitter.com/seattleartfair
Facebook.com/seattleartfair
Instagram.com/seattleartfair

New York Antique Jewellery & Watch Show, US

Antique and estate jewellery with more than 100 elite dealers.
Website: newyorkantiquejewelryandwatchshow.com
Email: info@usantiqueshows.com
Twitter.com/USAntiqueShows
Facebook.com/OfficialPage.
USAntiqueShows
Instagram.com/usantiqueshows

August

100% Design, Johannesburg, South Africa

Africa's leading exhibition for contemporary design.
Website: 100percentdesign.co.za
Email: 100percent@reedexpoafrica.co.za
Twitter.com/100designsa
Facebook.
com/100PercentDesignSouthAfrica
Instagram.com/100percentdesignsa
Linkedin.com/showcase/100percent-design-sa
YouTube.com/channel/
GSfOoGwmL9iwbXGQE3A?view_
as=subscriber

SP-Arte/Foto, São Paulo, Brazil

The most important photographic event in Brazil. A platform for cultural and artistic exchange.
Website: sp-arte.com
Twitter.com/sp_arte
Facebook.com/feira.sparte
Instagram.com/sp_arte
Flickr.com/photos/sp-arte/albums
Artsy.net/sp-arte
YouTube.com/user/FeiraSPArte

Art-O-Rama, Marseilles, France

Contemporary art fair.
Website: art-o-rama.fr/archive/2020-en/
Email: contact@art-o-rama.fr

Chart Art/Design Fair, Copenhagen, Denmark

The leading contemporary art fair in the Nordic region.
Website: chartartfair.com
Email: info@chartartfair.com
Facebook.com/chartartfaircph
Instagram.com/chart_artfair
Artsy.net/chart-art-fair

Art Jakarta, Indonesia

Contemporary art fair in Indonesia.
Website: artjakarta.com/2021
Email: info@artjakarta.com
Facebook.com/Artjakarta.ID
Instagram.com/artjakarta

September

100% Design, London, UK

Combining the world's most sought after brands with a wealth of emerging talent. Demonstrating the breadth of the best in high-quality design, detail and craftsmanship..
Website: designlondon.co.uk/news/
introducing-design-london
Email: info@designlondon.co.uk
Twitter.com/designlondon
Facebook.com/designlondonshow
Instagram.com/design.london

ArtRio, Rio de Janiero, Brazil

One of the main art events in Latin America, showing works by the great masters side by side with emerging artists.
Website: artrio.com
Email: contato@artrio.com
Facebook.com/feiraartrio
Instagram.com/artrio_art
Vimeo.com/artrio
YouTube.com/user/ArtRio2011

Cosmoscow, Moscow, Russia

Showing works by more than 200 contemporary artists.
Website: cosmoscow.com
Email: info@cosmoscow.com

Facebook.com/cosmoscowfair
Instagram.com/cosmoscowfair
YouTube.com/channel/
UCFKq0DWGwXylp6G_X3I_pLQ/
videos?view_as=subscriber

FNB Art Joburg, South Africa

The leading art fair in Johannesburg, the cultural and economic capital of Africa.
Website: artjoburg.com
Email: info@artjoburg.com
Twitter.com/fnbartjoburg
Facebook.com/FNBArtJoburg
Instagram.com/fnbartjoburg
Artsy.net/fnb-art-joburg?m-id=ca13&utm_medium=referral&utm_source=fair-1-54&utm_campaign=website-text

Tribal Art London, UK

Internationally recognised after its start in 2007 in a small gallery space off the Portobello Road. Now over 10 years old, it is held in the Mall Galleries in the prestigious art heartland of St James's.
Website: tribalartlondon.com
Facebook.com/tribalartlondon
Instagram.com/tribalartlondon

Contemporary Istanbul, Turkey

The leading annual art fair in Turkey, where Europe and Asia meet, showing contemporary art from the wider region.
Website: contemporaryistanbul.com
Email: info@ci.com.tr
Twitter.com/Contemporaryist
Facebook.com/contemporaryistanbul
Instagram.com/contemporaryistanbul

Positions Berlin Art Fair, Germany

Contemporary and modern art from an international city.
Website: positions.de
Email: info@positions.de
Twitter.com/positionsberlin
Facebook.com/positionsberlin

Instagram.com/positions.artfair
Open.spotify.com/
how/7tJxOgdGTHaGDZhaVsWVOa
Artsy.net/positions-berlin

Sydney Contemporary, Australia

The country's largest and most diverse gathering of local and international galleries with over 90 galleries showing the work of 400 leading and emerging artists from more than 12 countries.
Website: sydneycontemporary.com.au
Email: info@artfairsaustralia.com.au
Twitter.com/sydcontemporary
Facebook.com/SydneyContemporary
Instagram.com/sydneycontemporary

Lapada Art & Antiques Fair, London, UK

A foremost international showcase for art and antiques, held in Berkeley Square. 100 exhibitors showing art, antiques, design and decorative arts.
Website: lapadalondon.com
Email: fair@lapada.org
Twitter.com/LAPADAorg
Facebook.com/lapada
Instagram.com/lapada_association

Restauro, Ferrara, Italy

International restoration exhibition – the most important international event dealing with economy, conservation, industry, technology and promotion of cultural and environmental heritage.
Website: salonedelrestauro.com
Email: info@salonedelrestauro.com
Twitter.com/salonerestauro
Facebook.com/salonedelrestauro
Instagram.com/salonedelrestauro
Linkedin.com/company/salonedelrestauro
YouTube.com/user/FieraRestauro

ArtBo (Bogota Art Fair), Colombia

National and international galleries at one of the most significant cultural showcases of

the visual arts in Columbia.
Website: artbo.co
Email: adriana.alba@ccb.org.co
Twitter.com/feriaartbo
Facebook.com/feriaartbo
Instagram.com/feriaartbo
Flickr.com/photos/camaracomerbog/
collections/72157676779628267
YouTube.com/channel/
UCC1dS7SRo1n3YcrqRiQmQow

Beirut Art Fair, Lebanon

Modern and contemporary art with a focus on the Middle East and Mediterranean basin.
Website: beirut-art-fair.com
Email: info@beirut-art-fair.com
Twitter.com/BEIRUTARTFAIR
Facebook.com/BeirutArtFair?ref_
type=bookmark
Instagram.com/beirutartfair

Photofairs Shanghai, China

Fine art photography and moving image from leading international galleries with an international audience.
Website: photofairs.org/shanghai

La Biennale Paris, France

One of the world's leading art events bringing together internationally renowned art spanning 6,000 years of art from all continents and disciplines.
Website: labiennaleparis.com
Email: camille@sna-france.com
Twitter.com/LaBiennaleParis
Facebook.com/LaBiennaleParis
Instagram.com/labiennaleparis
YouTube.com/user/SNABiennale

Goldsmiths' Fair, London, UK

The premier UK showcase for contemporary jewellery and silver; a treasure trove of creativity, design innovation and outstanding craftsmanship.
Website: thegoldsmiths.co.uk

Email: info@thegoldsmiths.co.uk
Twitter.com/GoldsmithsCo
Facebook.com/TheGoldsmithsCompany
Instagram.com/TheGoldsmithsCompany
Pinterest.co.uk/goldsmithsco
Linkedin.com/company/the-
goldsmiths%27%E2%80%8B-company
YouTube.com/channel/
UCoUPc2TwvcBcxlDzMHeOigA

Expo Chicago, Illinois, US

Contemporary and modern art with leading international galleries from the US, Europe, Asia and Latin America.
Website: expochicago.com
Email: info@expochicago.com
Twitter.com/expochicago
Facebook.com/expochicago
Instagram.com/expochicago
Artsy.net/expo-chicago

KIAF Art Seoul, South Korea

20th Korea international art fair.
Website: kiaf.org
Facebook.com/kiafArtSeoul
Instagram.com/kiafartseoul
Blog.naver.com/kiafstory

Lima Photo, Peru

International exhibition of photographic galleries.
Website: limaphoto – feria internacional de galerías de fotografía
Email: informes@limaphoto.com.pe
Twitter.com/artealdia
Facebook.com/LimaPhotoOK

SWAB Barcelona, Spain

Showcasing emerging talent in contemporary art.
Website: swab.es
Email: info@swab.es
Twitter.com/SwabArtFair
Facebook.com/swabartfair
Instagram.com/swabartfair

Artsy.net/swab-barcelona
Vimeo.com/swabartfair

Vienna Contemporary, Austria

Austria's leading international contemporary art fair with attention to emerging markets connecting east and west.
Website: viennacontemporary.at
email: info@viennacontemporary.at
Facebook.com/viennacontemporary
Instagram.com/viennacontemporary
Viennacontemporarymagazine.wordpress.com

British Art Fair, London, UK

Founded in 1988 and the only fair dedicated to modern British art, showing key 20th and 21st century artists from the early modernists to Young British Artists and contemporary street art.
Website: britishartfair.co.uk
Email: robert@britishartfair.co.uk
Twitter.com/BritishArtFair
Facebook.com/britishartfair
Instagram.com/britishartfair

Art Athina, Athens, Greece

Athen's biggest annual art celebration'
Website: art-athina.gr

Decorative Antiques & Textiles Fair, London, UK

A family-owned event launched in 1985, uniting the antiques and interior design trades, with 3 fairs a year – late January, mid-May and late Sep/early Oct.
Website: decorativefair.com
Email: fairs@decorativefair.com
Twitter.com/decorativefair
Facebook.com/decorativefair
Instagram.com/decorativefair

October

Fine Art Print Fair, New York, US

The biggest art fair dedicated to fine prints, celebrating 500 years of printmaking. More than 160 international galleries showing old masters to contemporary work.
Website: ifpdafoundation.org/printfair
Email: info@ifpda.org
Twitter.com/ifpda
Facebook.com/IFPDAdotORG
Instagram.com/IFPDA
Artsy.net/ifpda-print-fair

Outsider Art Fair Paris, France

Contemporary art fair in its 8th year.
Website: outsiderartfair.com/paris
Email: info@outsiderartfair.com
Twitter.com/OutsiderArtFair
Facebook.com/outsiderartfair
Instagram.com/OutsiderArtFair

Palm Springs Modernism Show & Sale, California, US

85 premier national and international dealers offering furniture, decorative and fine arts representing all design movements of the 20th century. Now in its 20th year.
Website: palmspringsmodernism.com
Email: info@dolphinfairs.com
Facebook.com/PalmSpringsMOD

Texas Contemporary, Houston, Texas, US

Modern and contemporary fine art and design in its 9th year.
Website: txcontemporary.com
Email: hello@amp.events
Twitter.com/artMRKT
Facebook.com/artmarketproductions?ref=hl
Instagram.com/artmarketproductions

YIA (Young International Art Fair), Paris, France

Contemporary art by young international artists.

Website: en.parisinfo.com/paris-show-exhibition/137439/yia-art-fair
Email: contact@loulikids.com

Art International Zurich, Switzerland

One of the most important and well-established art markets in Switzerland, with paintings, graphics sculpture and photography since 1999.
Website: art-zurich.com
Email: info@art-zurich.com
Twitter.com/artfairzurich
Facebook.com/artzurich
YouTube.com/user/artzurich

Kunst Zürich, Switzerland

For 27 years, this fair showcases painting, sculpture, photography and multimedia art, from figurative to abstract, small and large scale, with wide-ranging, high-quality choice.
Website: kunstzuerich.ch
Email: welcome@kunstzuerich.ch
Twitter.com/Kunstzuerich
Facebook.com/kunstzurich

Art3f Lyon, France

European artists and makers showing to an international audience.
Website: art3f.fr/index.php
Email: info@art3f.com
Twitter.com/art3fsalon
Facebook.com/art3f

Fine Art Asia, Hong Kong, China

Asia's leading art fair, showing antiquities spanning 5,000 year, from ancient Chinese bronzes to contemporary art, as well as art from both Asia and the West.
Website: Fine Art Asia
Email: info@aaifair.com

PAD London, UK

London's leading fair for 20th Century design and decorative arts set in the vibrant heart of Mayfair.

Website: padesignart.com/London
Twitter.com/padesignart
Facebook.com/padesignartonline
Instagram.com/padesignart

1–54 Contemporary African Art Fair, London, UK

Contemporary art from Africa and its diaspora, providing a platform for contemporary dialogue and exchange including lectures, film screenings and panel debates from leading international curators, artists and experts. The title '1-54' is a reference to the fair's ethos of the 54 countries that make up the African continent
Website: 1-54.com/London
Email: info@1-54.com
Twitter.com/154artfair
Facebook.com/154ContemporaryAfricanArtFair
Instagram.com/154artfair
Artsy.net/1-54?m-id=ca13&utm_medium=referral&utm_source=fair-1-54&utm_campaign=widget
YouTube.com/channel/UCsWKpfSB3mtX6eiq8Ip_zxw

Art Market Budapest, Hungary

Central and Eastern Europe's leading international art fair with exhibitors from over 40 countries and an annual audience of over 30,000 international visitors.
Website: artmarketbudapest.hu
Email: info@artmarketbudapest.hu
Facebook.com/ArtMarketBudapest
Instagram.com/ArtMarketBudapest

Frieze London and Frieze Masters, London, UK

Frieze is the leading magazine of contemporary art and culture.
Website: frieze.com/fairs/frieze-london
Email: info@frieze.com
Twitter.com/frieze_magazine
Facebook.com/friezemagazine
Instagram.com/frieze_magazine

Sunday Art Fair, London, UK

An annual art fair in London which supports the young, emerging and most exciting artists and galleries from around the world.
Website: sundayartfair.com
Email: info@sundayartfair.com
Twitter.com/sundayartfair
Facebook.com/sundayartfairsundayartfair?fref=ts
Instagram.com/sundayartfair

Manchester Art Fair, UK

One of the UK's most ambitious fairs, selling modern and contemporary paintings, sculpture, photography and editioned prints from UK and international galleries.
Website: manchesterartfair.co.uk
Email: liam.whitehead@holdenmedia.co.uk
Twitter.com/McrArtFair
Facebook.com/McrArtFair
Instagram.com/McrArtFair
YouTube.com/channel/UCxpZF1a7fuO3A2ZX6RJnFlg

Art Verona, Italy

Contemporary art fair in Verona.
Website: artverona.it
Email: staff@artverona.it
Twitter.com/artverona
Facebook.com/artveronafieradarte
Instagram.com/artverona
YouTube.com/user/ArtVerona

Paris Internationale, France

Promoting emerging artists and rediscovering more established figures. Founded in 2015 as a disruptive alternative to the traditional art fair.
Website: parisinternationale.com
Email: contact@parisinternationale.com

Asia Now, Paris, France

Showing the diversity of contemporary art from Asia.
Website: asianowparis.com
Email: contact@asianowparis.com
Facebook.com/AsiaNowParis
Instagram.com/asianow

FIAC International Contemporary Art Fair, Paris, France

Founded in 1973, showing some of the most influential masters worldwide in modern and contemporary art and design.
Website: fiac.com/en-gb.html
Email: info@fiac.com
Twitter.com/fiac
Facebook.com/fiacparis
Instagram.com/fiacparis
Linkedin.com/showcase/fiac-
YouTube.com/channel/UCtNxjRsywo-bzXBU-8k3atw/featured

Art Toronto (TIAF), Canada

Showing national and international art including work from First Nations, Inuit and Métis people.
Website: arttoronto.ca/en/home.html
Email: info@arttoronto.ca
Twitter.com/ArtToronto
Facebook.com/ArtToronto
Instagram.com/art_toronto
YouTube.com/channel/UCqrWT0hnEDA1JCw0qqEZzRQ

AADLA Fine Art & Antiques Show, New York, US

Representing 25 galleries showing old master drawings, Indian bronzes, English furniture and rare books.
Website: aadlafair.com
Email: info@aadlafair.com
Facebook.com/AADLAMERICA

Winter Art & Antiques, London, UK

Representing 70 of the top UK dealers, showing over 20,000 works of art, antiques, furniture, sculpture, jewellery, textiles and collectors' pieces.
Website: olympia-antiques.com
Email: ed.maccurrach@clarionevents.com
Twitter.com/OlympiaAntiques

Facebook.com/olympiaartandantiques
Instagram.com/olympiaartantiques

SOFA Chicago, Illinois, US

Sculpture objects, functional art and design.
Website: sofaexpo.com
Email: info@sofaexpo.com
Twitter.com/sofaexpo?lang=en
Facebook.com/sofaexpo
Instagram.com/sofaexpo

Asian Art in London, UK

Showing work from leading international
dealers focusing on art from Asia.
Website: asianartinlondon.com
Email: info@asianartinlondon.com
Twitter.com/asianartlondon
Facebook.com/asianartinlondon
Instagram.com/asianartinlondon

ART SG, Singapore

The leading art fair in Southeast Asia,
showing the most visionary and exciting
contemporary art from the region and
around the world.
Website: artsg.com
Email: info@artsg.com
Facebook.com/artsgfair
Instagram.com/art.sg
YouTube.com/channel/UC_
T1da4JAEJhIHMV6pFnjfA

November

Abu Dhabi Art, UAE

Diverse public engagement, art installations
and exhibitions, talks and events, throughout
the year, leading up to the contemporary art
fair in November.
Website: abudhabiart.ae
Email: info@abudhabiart.ae
Twitter.com/AbuDhabiArt
Facebook.com/AbuDhabiArt
Instagram.com/abudhabiart
Artsy.net/abu-dhabi-art
YouTube.com/c/AbuDhabiArt

Art021 Shanghai, China

A part of the Shanghai International Arts
Festival, bringing together the top galleries
and institutions.
Website: art021.org
Email: info@art021.org
Facebook.com/ART021-Shanghai-
Contemporary-Art-Fair-451115545062917
Instagram.com/art021_sh
Weibo.com/p/1002063873240492

Art Thessaloniki, Greece

International contemporary art fair.
Website: art-thessaloniki.helexpo.gr
Email: infotif@tif.gr
Facebook.com/Tif.Helexpo
YouTube.com/
playlist?list=PLkGbBOEm_M-
r6wDM6wkm2wqC8ek_3QIko

Exponatec Cologne, Germany

International Trade Fair for museums,
conservation and heritage at Koelnmesse.
Website: exponatec.com
Email: exponatec@visitor.koelnmesse.de
Facebook.com/Exponatec?fref=ts
Instagram.com/exponatec

Loop Barcelona, Spain

LOOP is a platform for video art, artists'
films and moving image.
Website: loop-barcelona.com
Email: communication@screen-barcelona.
com
Twitter.com/LOOPBarcelona
Facebook.com/loopbarcelona
Instagram.com/loopbarcelona
YouTube.com/channel/
UCStM53MFVoslCZ3LbLBwS0A

Tefaf New York Fall,, US

The world's leading art fair since 1988, with
over 300 dealers internationally.
Website: tefaf.com/fairs/tefaf-new-york-fall
Email: info@tefaf.com

Twitter.com/tefaf
Facebook.com/TEFAF
Instagram.com/tefaf
Artsy.net/tefaf
Linkedin.com/company/tefaf

Artissima, Turin, Italy

Italy's most important contemporary art fair, with an international presence and focusing on experimentation and research.
Website: artissima.art
Email: info@artissima.it
Twitter.com/ArtissimaFair
Facebook.com/ArtissimaFair
Instagram.com/ArtissimaFair
YouTube.com/channel/
UCriukvcfrg57G375dep3Y7g

Art X Lagos, Nigeria

West Africa's premier international art fair, showcasing the best contemporary and modern art from Africa and its Diaspora.
Website: artxlagos.com
Email: media@artxlagos.com
Twitter.com/artxlagos
Facebook.com/artxlagos
Instagram.com/artxlagos
Linkedin.com/company/artxcollective
YouTube.com/channel/
UCz17HjrEmwAFEwejdF7yEsw

Discovery Art Fair, Frankfurt, Germany

International artists in a communicative atmosphere.
Website: discoveryartfair.com/fairs/
Frankfurt
Email: info@discoveryartfair.com
Twitter.com/lookforart
Facebook.com/discoveryartfair
Instagram.com/discoveryartfair
Vimeo.com/discoveryartfair
Linkedin.com/company/discovery-art-fair

Downtown Design Dubai, UAE

The Middle East's leading design fair for trade professionals to discover high-quality design from around the world.
Website: downtowndesign.com
Email: info@downtowndesign.com
Twitter.com/DowntownDesignD
Facebook.com/
downtowndesigndubai?fref=ts
Instagram.com/downtowndesignd
Linkedin.com/company/downtown-design/?trk=biz-companies-cym

West Bund Art & Design, Shanghai, China

Leading galleries from China and across the world showcasing the best of modern and contemporary art.
Website: westbundshanghai.com
Instagram.com/westbundartfair
Weibo.com/p/1002063984324238
Artsy.net/west-bund-art-and-design
YouTube.com/West Bund Art & Design

Paris Photo, France

The largest photographic international art fair for over 20 years.
Website: parisphoto.com
Email: info@parisphoto.com
Twitter.com/ParisPhotoFair
Facebook.com/parisphotofair
Instagram.com/parisphotofair
Linkedin.com/company/paris-photo-fair

Art Dusseldorf, Germany

Contemporary art fair in Dusseldorf.
Website: art-dus.de
Email: pr@art-dus.de
Facebook.com/artdusseldorf
Instagram.com/artduesseldorf

Feriarte, Madrid, Spain

Exclusive art and antiquities with more than 90 antique dealers and art galleries, including paintings and contemporary sculpture by artists of note.
Website: ifema.es/feriarte
Email: visit.registro@ifema.es

Twitter.com/feriaferiarte
Facebook.com/FERIARTE
Instagram.com/feriaferiarte
YouTube.com/user/feriaFeriarte

Fine Arts Paris, France

International art fair showcasing 55 galleries.
Website: finearts-paris.com
Email: contact@finearts-paris.com
Twitter.com/fineartsparis
Facebook.com/fineartsparis
Instagram.com/fineartsparis

PAN Amsterdam, Netherlands

Over 110 galleries, antique dealers and art dealers showcasing paintings, antiques, modern and contemporary art, jewellery, photography, designer furniture and objects from ancient and exotic cultures.
Website: pan.nl
Email: info@pan.nl
Twitter.com/pan_amsterdam
Facebook.com/PANAmsterdam
Instagram.com/pan_amsterdam
YouTube.com/user/PANAmsterdambeurs

London Photograph Fair, UK

Based in Somerset House, the fair brings together many of the world's leading galleries and dealers, as well as providing a platform for emerging artists and galleries who are pushing the boundaries of the medium.
Website: photolondon.org
Email: info@photolondon.org
Twitter.com/photolondonfair
Facebook.com/photolondonfair
Instagram.com/photolondonfair
Artsy.net/photo-london
Linkedin.com/company/photo-london-fair
YouTube.com/channel/UCq4xUecWjD7J-2ZSUsteckQ

Cologne Fine Art & Design, Cologne, Germany

Modern art, applied art, old masters, works on paper and design, with this international fair for more than 50 years.
Website: colognefineart.com
Email: colognefineart@visitor.koelnmesse.de
Facebook.com/CologneFineArt
Instagram.com/colognefineart
Artsy.net/cologne-fine-art-and-design

Salon: Art+Design, New York, US

Running for over a decade, presenting the world's best design – vintage, modern and contemporary, with blue chip 20th century and contemporary art.
Website: thesalonny.com
Email: info@thesalonny.com
Twitter.com/thesalonny
Facebook.com/theSalonNY
Instagram.com/thesalonny

Design Miami, Miami Beach, Florida, US

The global forum for design, with a sister show in Basel, Switzerland. Incorporating the world's top galleries with 20th and 21st century furniture, lighting and objects d'art.
Website: shop.designmiami.com
Email: info@designmiami.com
Twitter.com/designmiami
Facebook.com/DesignMiami
Instagram.com/designmiami
Pinterest.co.uk/designmiamifair
YouTube.com/channel/UCPXRu0ZO7Bcvx-lQ0tqBhGw

December
Miami Project, Florida, US

Working with a focused selection of modern and contemporary galleries from around the globe, Miami Project presents a diverse selection of work by leading artists to a high level audience in a custom built, museum quality environment in the heart of Miami Beach.
Website: miami-project.com
Email: hello@amp.events
Twitter.com/artMRKT

Facebook.com/
artmarketproductions?ref=hl
Instagram.com/artmarketproductions

Scope Miami Beach, Florida, US

140 international exhibitors, with 60,000 visitors over the 6 day fair, leading the charge for the emerging contemporary art market.
Website: scope-art.com/show/miami-beach-2021
Email: info@scope-art.com
Twitter.com/SCOPEArtShow
Facebook.com/SCOPEARTSHOW
Instagram.com/SCOPEArtShow
Artsy.net/fair/scope-miami-beach-2019

Aqua Art Miami, Miami Beach, Florida, US

A contemporary art fair at Miami Beach, during Miami Art Week.
Website: aquaartmiami.com
Email: nkorniloff@artmiami.com
Twitter.com/artmiamifairs
Facebook.com/aquaartmiami
Instagram.com/artmiamifairs

Art Miami, Florida, US

The finest investment quality modern and contemporary art, from the world's leading international art galleries.
Website: artmiami.com
Email: info@art-miami.com
Twitter.com/artmiamifairs
Facebook.com/artmiamifair
Instagram.com/artmiamifairs
Artsy.net/art-miami

Context Art Miami, Florida, US

Developing and reinforcing emerging and mid-career artists, shown by 80 international galleries
Website: contextartmiami.com
Email: info@contextartmiami.com
Twitter.com/artmiamifairs
Facebook.com/ContextArtMiami
Instagram.com/artmiamifairs
Artsy.net/context

Ink Miami, Florida, US

Modern and contemporary works on paper.
Website: inkartfair.com
Email: info@ifpda.org
Twitter.com/inkmiamiartfair?lang=en
Facebook.com/inkartfair
Instagram.com/inkmiamiartfair

Pinta Miami, Florida, US

Modern and contemporary Latin American Art Show, including Spain and Portugal.
Website: pinta.art
Email: info@pintamiami.com
Twitter.com/PINTAMiami
Facebook.com/PintaArtFair
Instagram.com/pintamiami
YouTube.com/channel/
UCPG8zCZ_8L_6CQWQcQC6-AA

Art Basel in Miami Beach, Florida,

Established in 1970, Art Basel is the leading global platform for the artworld, with world class fairs in Basel, Miami Beach and Hong Kong and more recently online, showing 20th and 21st century art.
Website: artbasel.com/miami-beach
Twitter.com/ArtBasel
Facebook.com/artbasel
Instagram.com/artbasel
Weibo.com/artbasel
Linkedin.com/company/art-basel
YouTube.com/user/artbasel

Nada Miami (New Art Dealers Alliance), Miami Beach, Florida

The New Art Dealers Alliance (NADA) is the definitive non-profit arts organization dedicated to the cultivation, support, and advancement of new voices in contemporary art.
Website: newartdealers.org
Email: info@newartdealers.org
Twitter.com/newartdealers
Facebook.com/newartdealersalliance
Instagram.com/newartdealers

Pulse Art Fair, Miami, Florida, US

15 years in Miami. Has since begun trading
as Volta Miami.
Website: pulseartfair.com
Email: info@pulseartfair.com
Facebook.com/PULSEArtFair
Instagram.com/pulseartfair

Untitled, Miami Beach, Florida, US

An international, curated art fair focusing on
all disciplines of contemporary art.
Website: untitledartfairs.com/miami-beach
Email: info@untitledartfairs.com
Twitter.com/UNTITLEDFAIRS
Facebook.com/UNTITLEDartfair
Instagram.com/untitledartfair

INTERVIEWS WITH ARTISTS

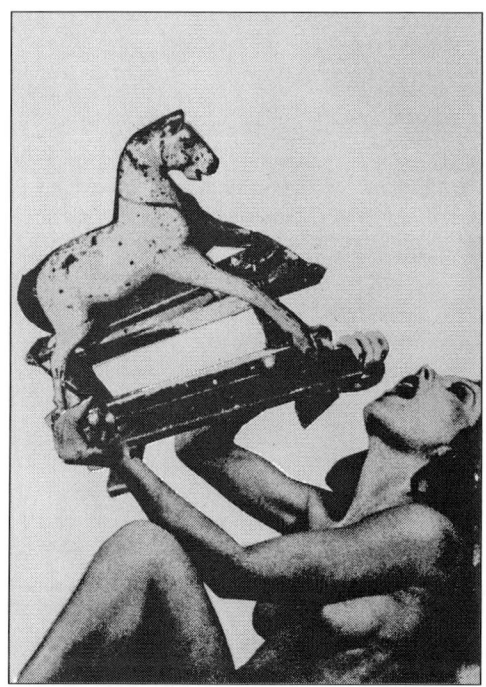

Rockin' n Rollin' in Black by Cameron Twins

The Cameron Twins-
Abigail and Phebe Cameron

1. Did you do any formal training as an artist?

After studying art throughout school, we did a one year Art Foundation course and both went on to complete a BA in Fine Art. We both graduated with first class degrees, and were then accepted onto a one-year post-graduate artist programme.

2. When did you start marketing your artwork?

As the prize winners of the 2021 Leicester Print Workshop Award Student Prize, we were invited to put on a solo exhibition in September 2021.

This was the first small step we took towards marketing our work, as Covid had prevented any previous opportunities. After the positive feedback we received from this, we decided to take the plunge and set up a formal business as a collaborative artists' duo.

We also make sure to keep our website and instagram page updated and current as a form of marketing and networking with other artists.

3 How did you find and approach art galleries?

We find it useful to use instagram and social media to find artists and galleries who display work with a similar aesthetic and feel to our own, and follow steps and advice given on their social media accounts and sometimes even contacting them directly about their experiences. We are always dropping into galleries, visiting exhibitions, attending artist talks and collecting leaflets. If possible, we have found it really helpful to chat to gallery staff and other established or exhibiting artists in person if we can.

4 What response did you get?

Responses can be very mixed, we have found it is always better to try and contact a named person within a gallery, rather than just contacting the gallery's general contact details. You are less likely to be overlooked, with your details lost in a sea of emails, if you have a name to refer to.

We feel, realistically if you can get a gallery to follow you on instagram that's a huge positive step, from which you might get opportunities offered to you.

5 Has your work been included in any exhibitions?

Yes we have had many: Loughborough University 2021 Degree Show Exhibition (18th - 27th June 2021) Solo Show: 'Reimagined Recollections' at Leicester Print Workshop Gallery, Leicester City Centre (24 September - 3rd October 2021); 'Colour: Impulse+Sensation' (GA Group Show) at Martin Hall Gallery, Loughborough (7th March - 3rd April 2022); Wooden Box Gallery, Ramsgate: Joint Show with Tim Jarzabek (26 April -7th May 2022); Exhibition - Brick Lane Gallery: Contemporary Painting Exhibition (16 - 29th August 2022)

6 Which platforms do you use to market your art?

We use instagram and our website primarily, with Tiktok, Pinterest and Facebook linked to these.

We also reach out to creative community groups such as interior designers.

7 Any other tips?

Keep talking to people about your art, keep looking for new inspiration so get yourself outside of your studio into the real world every now and again!

Don't be discouraged by knock-backs, just keep pushing on, remember to keep thinking of new and creative ways to expand your network and get yourself noticed.

Artists' Bio

The Cameron Twins are a collaborative artists' duo of identical twins who work together in a range of different media including screen print, digital montage, photography, casting, sculpture and installation. Their work uses an oversaturated bright colour palette to create a surreal quality. The vivid colours and child-like naïve aesthetic of images allow them to work playfully, exploring the ideas surrounding childhood imagination and dreams within their art practice.

Website: www.camerontwins.art
Instagram: @cameron.twins_art

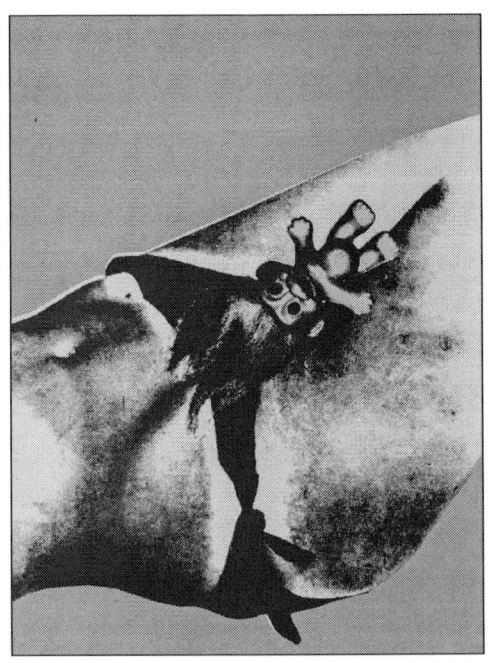

Bikini Bottoms in Black by Cameron Twins

Bang by Joe Webb

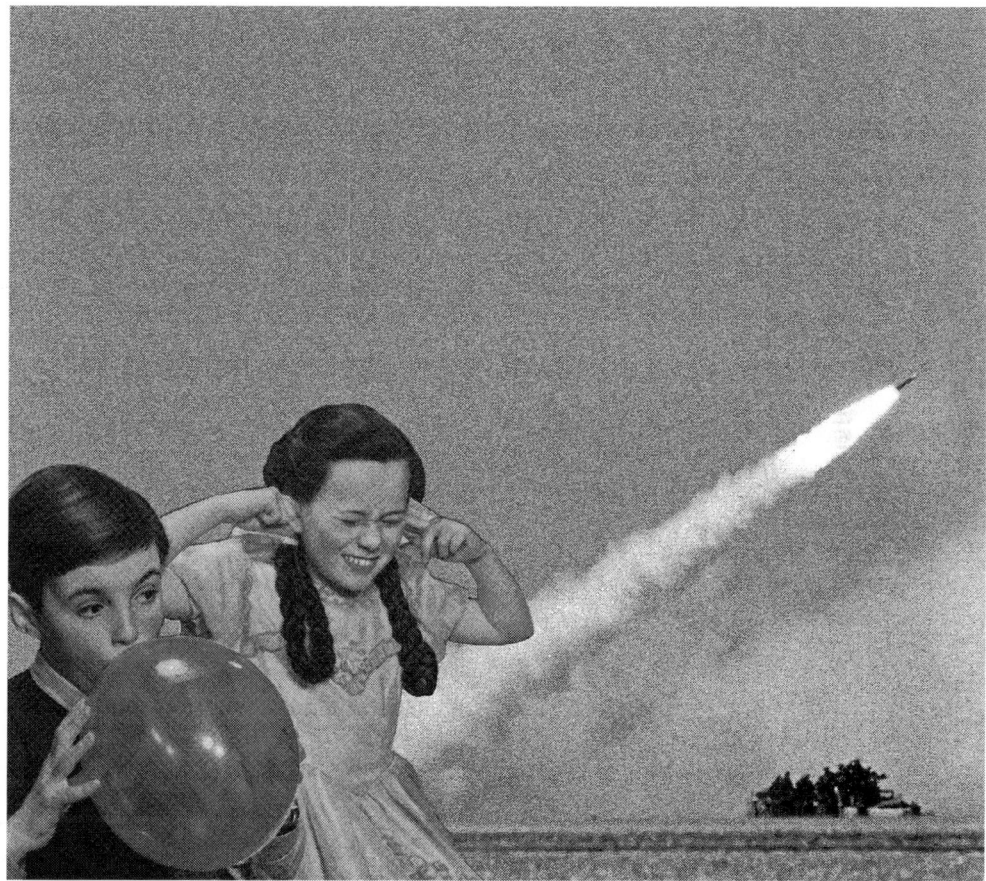

Joe Webb

1. Did you do any formal training as an artist?

Yes I studied at art college, way back in the 90's. I have a BA in Fine Art.

2. When did you start marketing your artwork?

I always made artwork as a child. I obsessively drew and painted even though no-one else in my family was particularly artistic. After art college I took a ten-year break from making art, and worked as a website and graphic designer, before deciding to return to art. I started making the collages and artwork that are in my recognisable style in 2010. At first I just made the hand-made collages for fun and, and to take a break from working on the computer. But then somehow it turned into my full-time job!

3. How did you find and approach art galleries?

I entered a collage of mine into a competition with the Saatchi Gallery, and amazingly it won! The prize was to exhibit the piece in the gallery. After that, I was approached by some galleries, as well as me contacting a few that I wanted to work with.

4. What response did you get?

Sometimes you don't hear back at all, but I found by speaking to the galleries that suit your work, it wasn't too difficult to get a positive response. They were usually open to trying a new printed edition out to see how it would be received.

5. Has your work been included in any exhibitions?

Yes, I've had a couple of solo shows at the Saatchi Gallery, Hang Up Gallery, Jealous Gallery and this year at Red Eight Gallery in central London. My latest show featured new larger-scale canvas works. We sold nearly all of the pieces and the exhibition seemed to be well received. The timing worked out well with coming out of the Covid lockdowns too...everyone seemed happy to be out and around people again doing normal everyday things.

6. Which platforms do you use to market your art?

I found Facebook really helpful at first, and now instagram has taken over as my main platform. I don't use social media for any personal stuff, holiday photos or anything like that. Instagram works great for me as an online gallery to communicate and share my artwork with the whole world.

7. Any other tips?

Don't give up on your passions and make the art that interests you, don't just follow trends or fashion as that won't be fulfilling in the long run.

Artist's Bio

Joe Webb creates hand-made collages with a message. Webb reimagines found imagery using simple and concise edits to make thought-provoking artworks. He looks at issues such as the environment, war, inequality and questions our place in the universe asking us to become more aware, conscious and content.

Joe has exhibited and sold work internationally.

He supports, with artwork donations, charities such as The Eden Project, Heart Research UK and the The Big Issue. He lives and works in the UK

Website: www.joewebbart.com
Instagram: www.instagram.com/joewebbart/

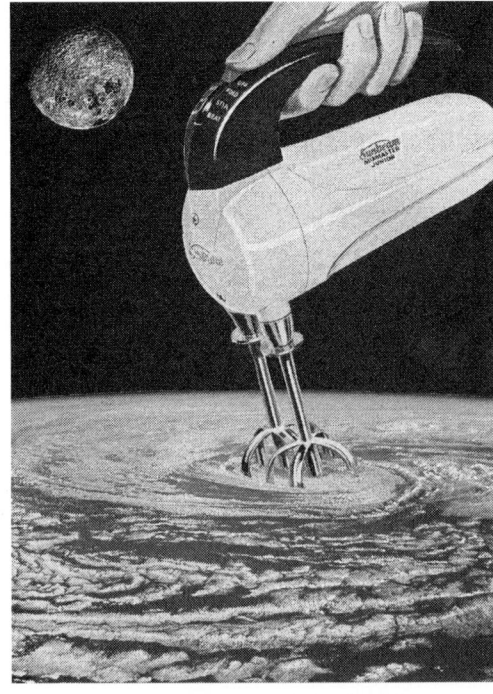

Stirring up a Storm by Joe Webb

The March for Our Lives—Security Blankets by Ayelet Lindenstrauss Larsen

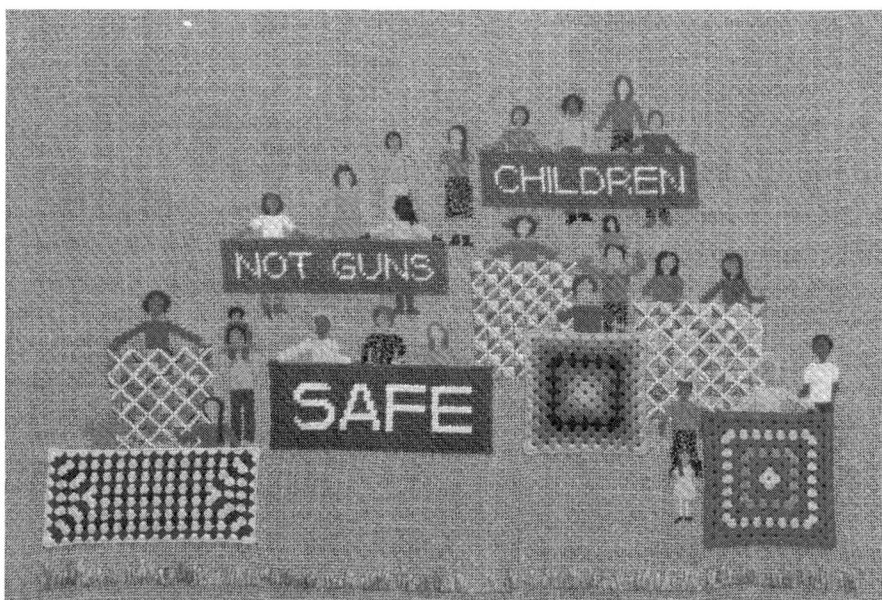

Ayelet Lindenstrauss Larsen

1. Did you do any formal training as an artist?

Not much. I was in a class studying ethnic embroidery traditions for several years and took a couple of drawing classes, but other than that, no.

2. When did you start marketing your artwork?

In the 1990s, when I thought I was ready: I was making the kind of work I wanted to be making.

3. How did you find and approach art galleries?

Since I worked in fiber art, it was pretty clear which galleries showed it. I sent out slides, and I brought slides to one gallery in person.

4. What response did you get?

The packets I sent with images were not so successful. When I brought my images to the gallery in person, they invited me to participate in several of their shows and sold most of the pieces I showed there.

5. Has your work been included in any exhibitions?

This has been the main way of showing my work. I have exhibited in many juried and some invitational fiber art exhibitions over the years, in the US and internationally, and particularly in miniature textile exhibitions since I often work on a small scale. I have also participated in all-media art exhibitions when the theme interests me. In one of these, I won the first prize which was a one-person show in that gallery. That was a wonderful experience, even though it was during the pandemic.

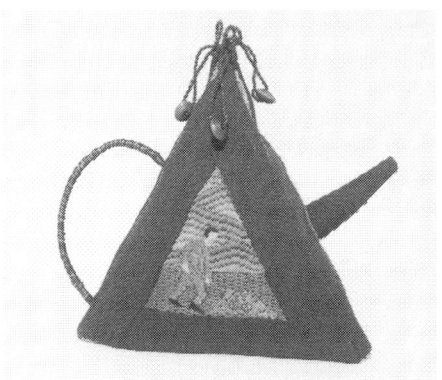

Workman's Lunch and Tea
by Ayelet Lindenstrauss Larsen

Artist's Bio

Ayelet Lindenstrauss Larsen is a fiber artist and and also a mathematician. Her work is inspired by historical textiles but deals with contemporary subjects, including mathematical objects that she finds visually interesting.

Website: www.surfacedesign.org/author/alindens/

6. Which platforms do you use to market your art?

All but one of the pieces I have sold were sold in exhibitions. One of the organizations I belong to – the Surface Design Association, allows members to have a page with images of several artworks, so I rotate images on that website. And I have had images of my work in books and magazines.

7. Any other tips?

When I was a teenager I was already committed to making fiber art, but at one point, I very consciously decided not to try to do it for a living. This meant I have much less time in which to make art, but I have complete freedom: to use the labor-intensive techniques that I love even if they don't make sense commercially, to explore what interests me at any time, to experiment with unpopular styles. You always wonder what might have been, but I don't regret that choice.

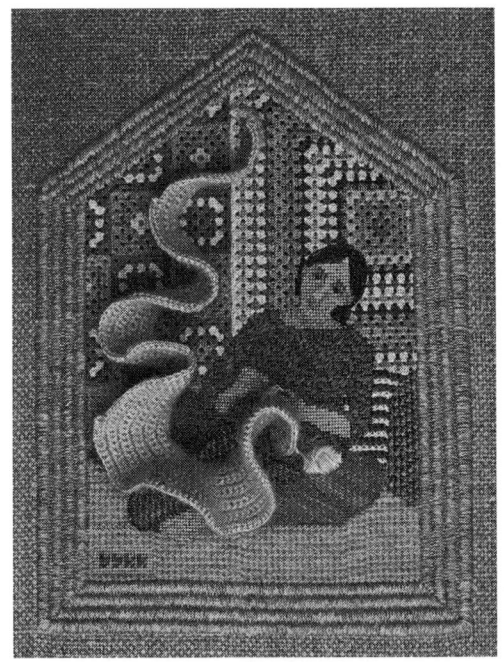

Crocheting the Coronavirus away
by Ayelet Lindenstrauss Larsen

Borrowed Time by Alice Billington

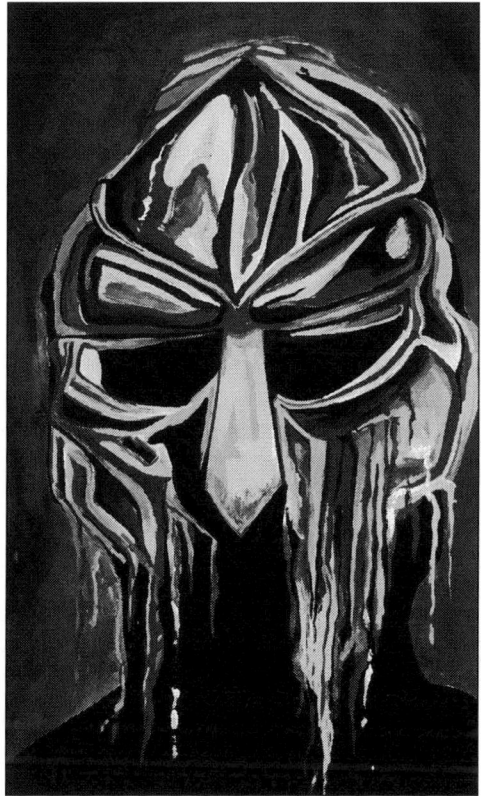

Alice Billington

Did you do any formal training as an artist?

Despite a keen interest in art since early childhood, I chose to follow the academic path after finishing school as opposed to the creative one. After completing a one-week long taster in Kingston School of Art for their foundation course, I knew that the structured approach to an art education was not for me and that I felt most artistically free exploring my own style. At university I found opportunities to continue being creative and pursuing my craft alongside my studies, so I never had any regrets.

When did you start marketing your artwork?

When I was 16, my aunt commissioned me to create two pieces to be part of a play about the life of an artist. After the play, people from the audience inquired about the art and where to buy it. When my aunt came back to me with this news, and substantially more money on top of my commission, I knew that there was potential to sell my artwork. I started with friends and family, including designing and creating a logo for a friend's dog walking business, and eventually I was doing commissions for strangers.

How did you find and approach art galleries?

I am yet to approach art galleries with my work but, when I move on to this stage, I will use this book to begin contacting galleries.

What response did you get?

Once I have reached out, I look forward to seeing what opportunities come next.

Has your work been included in any exhibitions?

Outside of art exhibitions in school for A-Level and the Gifted and Talented Programme, I have not had my work included in any exhibitions. Hopefully, this book will allow me to find galleries which fit with my style.

Which platforms do you use to market your art?

My online portfolio is on WordPress and I use Instagram to share my art. I believe Instagram to be the most effective platform as it is widely used, allows easy sharing, and can be linked to a personal account.

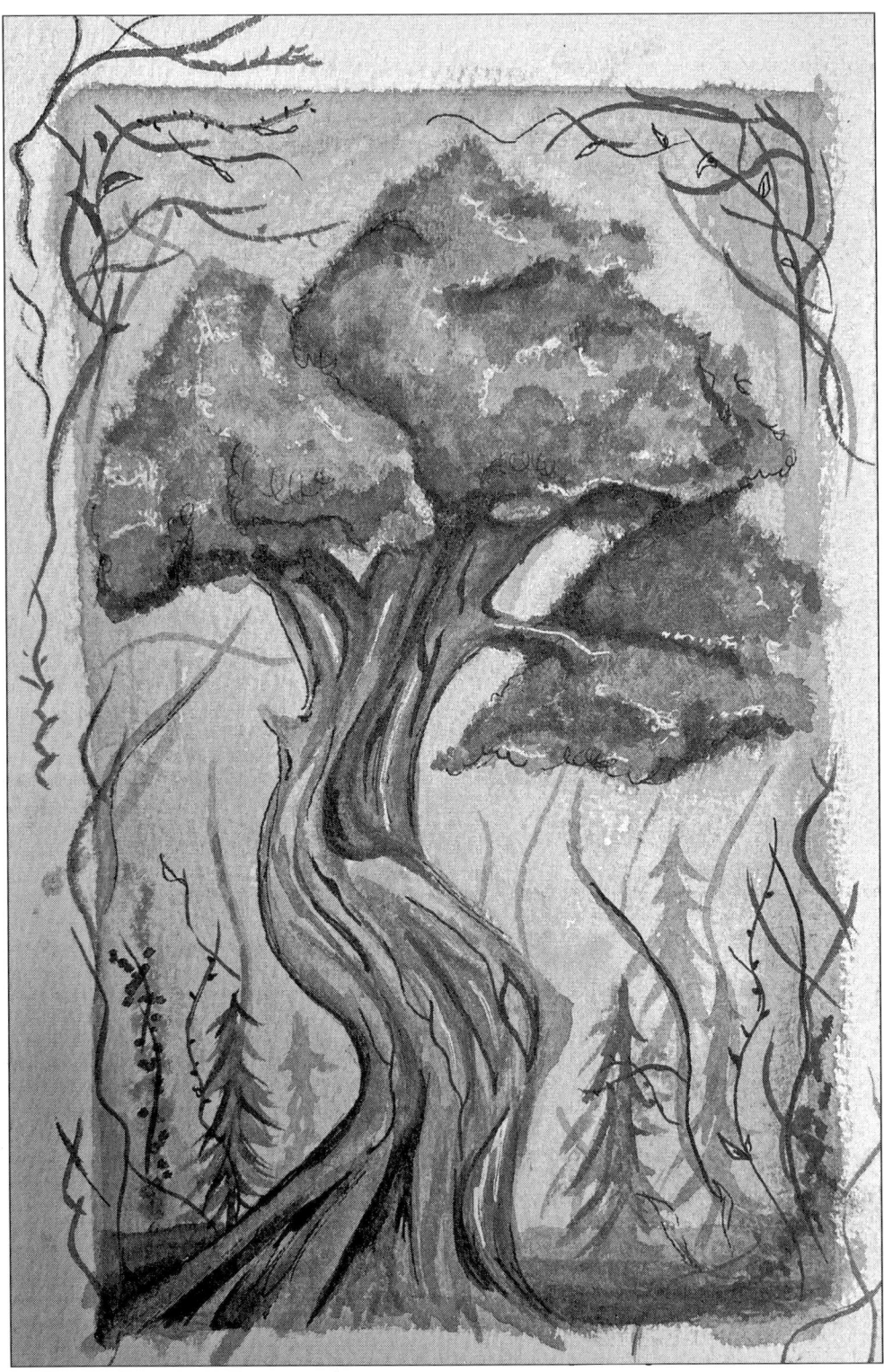

Mycorrhiza by Alice Billington

Any other tips?

In regard to developing an artist style, I think it is important to push yourself outside of your comfort zone as this is where the greatest growth lies. It is tempting when you know something works, artistically, to continue doing that but trying a new style, medium or approach can be highly rewarding. I also believe it is important to study other artists; classical, modern and contemporary, to expose yourself to new styles, discover what has been done before and consider where your work fits. You can see how these styles are echoed in culture, such as in film and fashion, which I think is one of the most inspiring parts about being an artist.

Artist's Bio

Alice is an artist with a focus on illustration and mixed media, often of natural subject matter. She recently graduated from the University of Bristol where she studied Geography and specialised in topics on the urban environment and human-nature relations. Currently she works as an arts and media assistant for a charity and publishing company in London. Her interests include cycling, yoga and walking her dog.

Website:alicebillingtonart.wordpress.com
Instagram @alicebillingtonart.

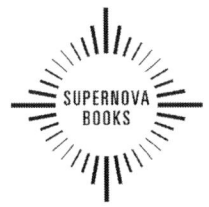

SUPERNOVA
BOOKS

For more great books on art go to:

www.supernovabooks.co.uk

www.aurorametro.com

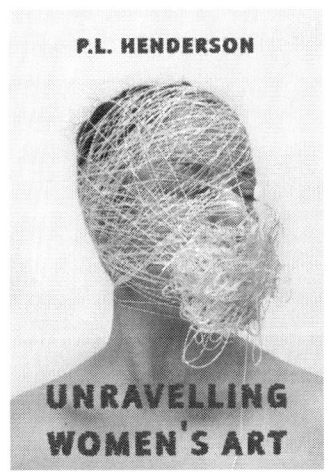

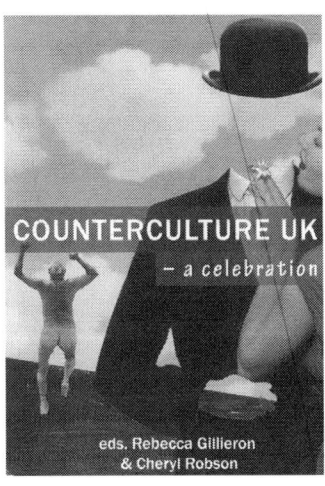

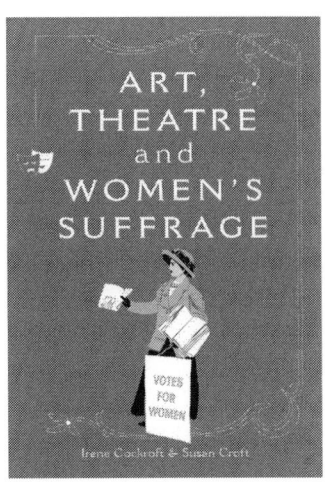

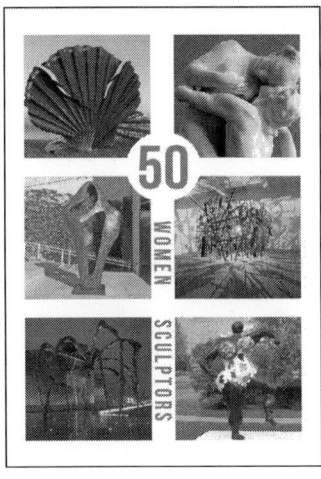